STEVE EARLE

Fearless Heart, Outlaw Poet

By David McGee

Backbeat
Books

San Francisco

Published by Backbeat Books
600 Harrison Street, San Francisco, CA 94107
www.backbeatbooks.com
email: books@musicplayer.com

An imprint of the Music Player Network
Publishers of *Guitar Player, Bass Player, Keyboard, EQ,*
   and other magazines
United Entertainment Media. Inc.
A CMP Information company

CMP
United Business Media

Distributed to the book trade in the US and Canada by
Publishers Group West, 1700 Fourth Street, Berkeley, CA 94710

Distributed to the music trade in the US and Canada by
Hal Leonard Publishing, P.O. Box 13819, Milwaukee, WI 53213

Cover design by Richard Leeds—BigWigDesign.com
Text design and composition by Leigh McLellan
Front cover photo © David Corio/Michael Ochs Archives.com

Library of Congress Cataloging-in-Publication Data

McGee, David, 1948–
   Steve Earle : fearless heart, outlaw poet / By David McGee.
      p. cm.
ISBN-13: 978-0-87930-842-1
ISBN-10: 0-87930-842-7 (pbk. : alk. paper)
   1. Earle, Steve. 2. Rock musicians--United States--Biography.
I. Title.
   ML420.E176M34 2005
   782.421642092--dc22   2005028889

Printed in the United States of America

05 06 07 08 09   5 4 3 2 1

contents

Elijah's Church

"Earle's Chapel is a special
place in all of our lives."
—Barbara Earle

"This is where I want to be buried."

Tall, sturdy, strong, his determined countenance weathered by the elements of his native Alabama, Elijah Earle stood at the foot of an imposing elm tree, a long-blade knife gripped firmly in his right hand. Newly transplanted to Cherokee County, a tiny east Texas community formed around Prairie Branch Creek, Elijah began carving his initials in the tree trunk. At his side stood second wife Mary Elizabeth (Tatum) Jarrett, a faint smile crossing the gentle features of her plain face. She knew that when Elijah set his mind to something, he usually made it happen.

Elijah had come west from Scottsboro, Alabama, in 1840, with his first wife, Maxcey Blanchett; a baby boy, Albert Franklin; and a yoke of oxen in tow. His brother, Allan, had joined him on the trip, then went on further west before returning to Elijah's fold, where he spent the remainder of his years.

"They had heard that this land was similar to what they had. And they were evidently pretty adventurous, so they packed up everything and came to east Texas," his great-grandson, Jack Earle, says. "Bought quite a bit of land around there."[1]

In 1840 Elijah Earle traced the circle that would embrace all succeeding generations of Earles. More than a century later, in 1958 his great-great-grandson, Stephen Fain Earle, was baptized in Earle's Chapel, and at 19 said, "This is where

I want to be married." And so he was. Stephen, with a gift for music, memorialized the sacred place in a song he wrote and titled "Elijah's Church": "In Elijah's Church is where I was baptized / And where I took me a wife."

Through good times and bad—and for the Earles struggle is commonplace—Elijah's circle grew, constant, steadfast. As much as anyone in the Earle family tree, Stephen Fain—he of the restless heart, the folk poet's temperament, and the taste for the edge—tested its love and found it bountiful, and forgiving. He will test it again; it's in the blood. And if he should fall, he will find the circle unbroken, and in his family's hearts, a place he can run to.

By and by, Lord, by and by.

chapter 1

The Hard Way: A Template

Elijah Earle did more than settle down on four acres of land near Prairie Branch Mill: he built a little community, named after its central gathering place, Earle's Chapel, which today would be referred to as a multipurpose venue. Built by Elijah, the one-room wood-frame building served not only as a Methodist Episcopal Church (although, as Jack Earle points out, "he specified that anybody of any faith, any minister that wanted to have a service, could hold services there, with preference being given to the Methodist Church"[1]), but also as a school and community meeting house. Elijah owned a gristmill and a sawmill, and he worked the land on a farm he built about a mile down the road from Earle's Chapel. There he raised tomatoes (a crop so abundant in that part of east Texas that less than a century later the area would be dubbed the "tomato capital"), corn, and probably peanuts. Eventually Earle's Chapel grew large enough to warrant having its own post office.

In 1880 Elijah was buried, according to his wishes, in what is now called the Earle's Chapel Cemetery, in its first grave. His son Albert Franklin, who had come west with his father as a baby, died in 1932 and was also buried in Earle's Chapel Cemetery. The younger Earle's tombstone inscription reads, "He fought the fight; the victory won."[2]

Of Albert Franklin's eight children, the youngest, Albert Milton—nick-named Booster—took after his granddad the most. Booster continued working

Elijah Earle (1804–1880), Steve's great-great grandfather, founder of Earle's Chapel.

the land on the family farm after all his siblings had moved away. By all accounts, even as a youth, Booster never lacked for ambition or imagination, and when both coalesced, the results were always interesting, to say the least. Once he and a friend caught an alligator, charged the curious ten cents to view it, and then took their reptilian headliner on the road, transporting it by truck westward, getting only so far as Colorado before the hapless creature perished. Undaunted, Booster and his buddy got another few days of shows out of their dead prey—which, when alive, pretty much lay there dumbfounded and inert anyway—before the inevitable decay made their venture untenable.[3]

Booster got down to more serious business after marrying Jewell Wall, a lovely, forthright young lady from Indian Gap, Texas. He farmed, later hired on with the Railway Express, and, ever the entrepreneur, took what savings he had and opened a service station and country store in nearby Jacksonville, Texas, where the family moved.

When the Great Depression undermined his livelihood, Booster went back to what had never betrayed him—the land—and made a living raising tomatoes, peanuts, peaches (the Earle family farm once boasted 6,000 trees), and Christmas trees.[4] The family made do and grew to six members with the four children Booster and Jewell produced: a daughter, Bettye, was the first, followed by sons Arlon, Jack, and Neil.

Born December 22, 1933, Jack spent his first eight years of public education at a country school in Ironton, Texas, but attended high school in Jacksonville.

Outgoing, smart, and athletic, he possessed both brawn and sensitivity—he was both a star football player and a member of an all-state barbershop quartet. Singing wasn't his only musical talent; he was fluent, by ear, on piano and ukulele (and brother Arlon had a genuine gift as a musician, being a piano pounder of some note in the Earle family's circle of friends). *The Grand Ole Opry* radio show had long been a regular Saturday night presence in the Earle household, and so to a lesser extent was *The Louisiana Hayride*. WSM—the 50,000-watt Nashville-based radio station from whence the Opry broadcast emanated—"really boomed in [in Jacksonville],"[5] says Jack, but by high school his interests had moved away from country music.

"I kinda was into the pop music. Nat 'King' Cole, the Mills Brothers, and this sort of music. My brothers, though, were solid country fans."[6]

But sports, music, even girls, it could fairly be said (and surprisingly so for a hunky, handsome teenage lad) all took a backseat to Jack's overriding ambition to light out for the wild blue yonder. Flying had been the primary passion of his young life: "There was nothing I wanted more to be than a commercial pilot."[7] He hung around the airfield in Jacksonville, doing whatever chores he could muster up in return for flying lessons. At age 16 he had taken his first solo flight; a year later he had earned a passenger license. The grizzled barnstormer who owned the airfield was big into trading planes, and when he found one he wanted, he would send Jack and another eager young whippersnapper to close the deal and bring back the new aircraft. Their jaunts took them as far north as Ann Arbor, Michigan, and west to California and various burghs in between, to hand off one weatherbeaten bird for another that they would have to spruce up to render it flightworthy.

"We got real good at changing oil and unsticking valves," Jack told the author Lauren St. John in her unauthorized biography, *Hardcore Troubadour: The Life and Near Death of Steve Earle*. "Those little airplanes, you'd have ones that had been sitting out in the field for two or three years without even starting. You'd throw in the oil, change it by hand about a jillion times, crank it up, and clear all the birds' nests and cobwebs out of it and depart. And it was great. We thought nothing of it. Now I kinda shudder when I think."[8]

Between flying, sports, and his girlfriend, Jack had a full plate. So he didn't take much notice when, while playing ping-pong at his girlfriend's house one evening, a skinny 13-year-old girl new to the neighborhood wandered into the room. "He thought I was the scrawniest, pitiful little thing when he met me," Barbara Earle—then Barbara Thomas—recalls.[9]

Barbara Thomas had taken a wrenching route to Jacksonville, coming by way of Memphis and Nashville, Tennessee (where she was born). Divorce split up her parents, Helen and James Walter Groover, when she was still in the cradle; as a toddler she shuttled between her grandparents' house in Nashville, various relatives' places, and Memphis's swanky Peabody Hotel, which was managed by her stepfather Emmett Thomas, whom her mother had married when Barbara was five years old.

When Barbara was eight, Helen divorced Thomas. As an escape from her troubles, Helen took to the bottle, whiling away long hours in solitary drinking binges in her room with the door closed. Alone again, Helen uprooted her daughter once more and this time moved to Longview, Texas, where she began straightening out her life, first by joining Alcoholics Anonymous. In the program she met Sam Fain, a bachelor, recovering alcoholic, and businessman with his own hardware store in Jacksonville, Texas. Fain, a close friend of AA co-founder Bill Wilkinson (popularly known as "Bill W."), fell hard for Helen, and she for him. A good man with solid values and an easygoing temperament, Fain was a godsend. Soon the couple was married and Helen and Barbara were relocating to Jacksonville. When Barbara was 13, her mother gave birth to the only child she would have by Sam Fain, a baby boy named Nick.

Although Barbara had spent much of her youth as caretaker to her mother, Helen remained the woman she admired most, and still does. "My mother was actually a really, really brilliant woman," Barbara says. "When she worked at the Millington Naval Air Station in Memphis she was the manager of the ship service department, which was a lot of responsibility in those days, and she was the first civil service employee there. All together, her drinking years weren't many but they were just devastating for her. She was a very tiny person and very ladylike, so it was just a real departure. But we were real lucky—when mother met Sam her life got straightened out real quick. I admire my mother more than any woman I've ever known. She was a complete lady."[10]

Helen did more than kick her addiction—she helped others with similar problems in the community and was in all respects a pillar of the community.

Seeing her mother's struggle and ultimate triumph taught Barbara a valuable lesson early in life, namely that more than one person can reside in a single body. "There really are two people," Barbara explains. "There's the brilliant, talented person, and that's the real person, and then there's the person who's affected by the disease, and that's another person altogether. So I understood for a time that what I had wasn't really my mother. I don't think of her being her at all in her bad years, because it really wasn't, and that's the thing that's sometimes hard to understand."[11]

"Barbara's mother," Jack says emphatically, "was just the greatest lady in the world."[12]

Jack's path crossed Helen Thomas's in the summer before his senior year in high school, when he got a job at the department store where Helen worked as bookkeeper and office manager. Always one to make a good impression on others, Jack soon was being invited to lunch at Helen's house, and there he saw Barbara with new eyes.

No longer the "scrawniest, pitiful little thing" of her early adolescence, Barbara, about to enter her junior year in high school, was developing into a fetching, well-mannered young lady with striking features and curves in all the right places. Jack more than took note—he asked her out. They dated all through the school year. After graduation Jack matriculated to Texas A&M in College Station to study architectural engineering, then a year later, strapped for money, transferred to Sam Houston College in Huntsville, where he majored in agriculture.

Their romance bloomed, with only one hitch. At one point during his college years, Jack opined that he and Barbara ought to date other people while he was away. This worked out fine until Jack came home from school one weekend to find Barbara out on a date; incensed, he ran off her would-be paramour—only to have Barbara find out that *he* was in town to rent a tuxedo to wear on a date to a college dance. She gave him what-for in a missive etched in acid, and he walked the line thereafter.

Jack proposed to seventeen-year-old Barbara, and they were married shortly after she graduated from high school, in July 1953. Their original plan to be wed at Earle's Chapel was altered by Jack's volunteering for the U.S. Army draft in order to take a year off what would otherwise have been a three-year commitment. At the time the United States was engaged in a bloody, fruitless war with North Korea, and the draft was first devouring those at the lowest end of the economic spectrum, a bit of insight that led Jack to enlist before his number was called.

In February 1954, Jack got word that he was being sent to Korea by way of Fort Monroe, Virginia, where he was transferred to join an anti-artillery unit awaiting its marching orders. Still stateside in May, he learned that Barbara was pregnant at about the same time he got news that he was Korea-bound to serve as a radar technician. A guardian angel arrived in the form of an army chaplain, who arranged for Jack, fleet of fingers on the typewriter to the tune of ninety words per minute, to be reassigned instead to a company clerk's position at Fort Monroe for the duration of his service.

Barbara's pregnancy was a troubled one. During the Christmas holidays in 1954, she developed pre-eclampsia, or toxemia, a condition potentially fatal to both mother and baby. Then on Saturday, January 17, 1955, she went into labor with a breech birth. For two days she endured labor pains, Jack always at her side. "It looked like it was going to be a long thing," Jack recalls.[13] He was due to report for KP duty at 4:00 A.M. on Monday, January 19.

"When four o'clock came I called my unit and told them I couldn't come to KP, my wife's in labor," Jack says. "And they said, 'Oh, yeah, you will. We'll let you know when the baby's born.' So I went on down and did my KP. About noon they came and told me, and I dropped everything and ran full tilt to the hospital. I think if I'd had to do it again and they told me I had to come to work, I'd just hang up! [Laughs.] But back in those days, man, it would have been tough."[14]

At the end of his two-mile run, Jack held, for the first time, his new baby boy, whom he and Barbara named Stephen Fain Earle, after Barbara's stepfather Sam Fain, "because Sam was a great influence in our lives," says Barbara.[15] Stephen's grandfather, Booster Earle, was there in spirit too. He had sent along a Prince Albert tobacco can filled with soil from the Earle farm to ensure that the first earth to touch his grandson's feet would be Texas soil. The unspoken purpose of this unofficial "baptism" was to inspire in young Stephen a sense of independence, single-mindedness, and the straight-shooting attitude common to all natives of the Lone Star State.

Funny thing about the baby Stephen Fain: he was talking in near-complete sentences in no time, it seemed, but he waited 16 months before he walked (or at least walked within sight of anyone who might have documented him doing so earlier). And when he did rise up on his chubby legs, he scampered the full length of his grandparents' house as if he had been doing so since emerging from the womb.

But talk, yes, early on; words came pouring out, and in Jack's recollection, by the time Stephen's brother Mark Neil was born on February 15, 1957, his first-born was talking up a storm. "When he was like two or something he was sitting there carrying on a pretty good conversation—and he never has quit yet," Jack says, laughing.[16]

"I didn't realize he was that unusual at that point because he was the first child, and I was only 18 when he was born, and I thought they all came like that," says Barbara. "He was a real easy-to-have-around child, as long as you were willing to talk to him. Now, if you didn't want to hear anybody talk, and wanted somebody to be quiet, it would be a different story."[17]

"Fighting It All the Way"

Shortly after his son Mark's birth, Jack was discharged from the army and moved the family down the road from Jacksonville about 15 miles, to Palestine. During his army years Jack had joined his unit's flying club and gained more experience as a pilot. Now he put the GI Bill to use taking flying lessons to earn his commercial license, hoping this would be the entrée to an airline pilot's job. His timing couldn't have been worse. Following the end of the Korean War, the workplace was flooded with hundreds of experienced military pilots returning home with résumés and, as Jack puts it, "thousands of hours in big airplanes,"[1] qualifications that dwarfed anything Jack could offer. They were getting the plum jobs Jack had longed for since his youth.

His training on the GI Bill had sent him 55 miles northeast of Palestine, to Tyler, Texas (which holds the distinction of being the site of the largest Confederate ordnance plant in the Civil War). There he befriended the fellows who worked in the control tower, and they took such a liking to him that they urged him to put in an employment application and join them. It wasn't flying, but it would get him close enough to airplanes so that maybe one day, when a pilot's job opened up, he might realize his ultimate ambition. It was then that fate intervened to create an opportunity for Jack Earle that changed his life.

It's hard to imagine a time now, with the skies so crowded with planes, that pilots once were essentially on their own, flying by visual flight rules, or

VFR. The pilot's only obligation was to tell the flight controller in the tower the altitude at which he planned to fly. Unlike today, the controller was not charged with watching the skies to track and notify aircraft when one might fly too close to another. Unbound from any restrictions regarding their altitude or course, pilots of the day routinely entertained passengers by flying low enough to ensure breathtaking views of sights of interest on the ground below.

"So it was a standard practice when an air carrier wasn't running way behind, to get to the Grand Canyon and make two or three turns, turn right first and then left, so everybody gets a look," Jack explains. "It was real common."

Common, that is, until June 30, 1956, when a TWA Super Constellation (flying from Los Angeles to Chicago with 70 passengers on board) and a United Airlines DC-7 (also en route to Chicago from Los Angeles, with 58 passengers aboard) collided over the Grand Canyon, killing 128 passengers and crew from both aircraft. It was the first air accident in history to kill more than 100 people.

When an investigation revealed the flaws in the Civil Aeronautics Administration's (CAA, which in 1958 became the Federal Aviation Agency with oversight responsibility for both civilian and military aircraft) air traffic control system, Congress—which had previously cut the CAA's budget—took action by appropriating $250 million to the CAA to upgrade the air traffic control system with new radar surveillance gear, new control towers, more air traffic controllers, and more rules to govern the increasingly busy skies.

Jack was hired as an air traffic controller and stayed on the job for another 30 years. He was assigned to a field in El Paso, then a woebegone border town, dry, dusty, flat and home to a wild and woolly populace that knew its fair share of hard partying across the bridge in Juarez, Mexico, and the violence—domestic and otherwise—so common in towns where cultures clash daily. But for two years the Earle family enjoyed a fairly placid life in El Paso, living hand to mouth on Jack's meager salary, pretty much embodying the title sentiment of the Oklahoma-born populist country singer-songwriter James Talley's *Got No Bread, No Milk, No Money, but We Sure Got a Lot of Love*. It was in El Paso where a fascinated three-year-old Steve first saw Elvis Presley in a televised performance on "The Ed Sullivan Show." And it was in El Paso where Barbara gave birth to her third child on October 11, 1958, a daughter named Katherine Kelly Earle.

Two years into their stay in El Paso, Jack was transferred to a Strategic Air Command (SAC) base in Lake Charles, Louisiana, and Barbara was pregnant with their fourth child. Eventually the family settled into a house across the river in Sulphur, Louisiana, first on the bayou (to the delight of Steve and Mark, who made the swamps their personal playground), then in a well-tended suburb where they bought a ranch house. The second Earle

Jack and Barbara Earle at Earle's Chapel in 1968, after renewing their wedding vows on their 25th anniversary: "We started out young with kids right away and not much sense, didn't make that much, and we were fighting it all the way," Jack says.

daughter, Stacey Carole, was born there on September 25, 1960. Petite and blond, she was diagnosed with epilepsy, which went into remission when she was five but returned again in her adult years.

The culture in the Earle household was centered on literature, music, and the oral tradition. Barbara and Jack were, and are, big readers—so much so that they maintain a storage room now simply to hold all their books. They read pretty much everything, but especially, in Jack's case, the classics (of contemporary writers, John Grisham is a favorite), and in Barbara's both popular fiction and nonfiction.[2]

"My mom likes to read schlock too, just because she's got to be reading at all times," Stacey relates. "That's where we knew and appreciated great readings and writings. We're very much Jack and Barbara Earle—all of us."[3] But Barbara also loves poetry, and it was poetry she was reading to Steve before and after Mark was born, because she got tired of reading children's stories.

Music filled the house, Jack still devoted to classic American pop, Barbara to country music as well as popular operettas that her stepfather Sam Fain had introduced her to and taken her to see in Dallas. Two long-standing family favorites were *The Chocolate Soldier* (which, tellingly, was based on a George Bernard Shaw play with a strong pacifist theme) and the Sigmund Romberg–Dorothy Donnelly evergreen *The Student Prince*.

Add to this heady mix the storytelling gamesmanship among the Earle men, to which Steve was exposed right out of the crib, courtesy his granddaddy Booster Earle, who knew how to spin a yarn and saw in his first grandchild a malleable pupil. Steve and Booster were close from day one of Steve's life, and Booster made sure Jack's son knew everything he knew about the world. Steve was fairly grafted onto his hip, following him around everywhere he went, Booster obliging with a tall tale at the drop of a hat, or some candy, or a train ride to the next town and back.

Then there was the annual deer-hunting expedition that brought the Earle men together for some male bonding, young Steve among them in the company of his father and granddaddy. According to Barbara, male bonding is about all it was, because the bounty from these trips was scarce indeed. If nothing else, Steve came home with a motherlode of grist for his burgeoning literary mill.

"[Steve] kind of grew up in a storytelling situation, because I read to him, his granddaddy Earle told stories all the time, and all the men in the Earle family went deer hunting every year," says Barbara. "Camped out in the big thicket in Texas. I never did think they did a lot of deer hunting, because they didn't bring home any meat, but they spent a lot of time telling tall tales. Steve started out going to those things with Jack. The stories that come from there are the grown-up versions of things he told as a little boy.

"From the time he went to first grade, he told stories, and then when he learned to write, he wrote them. Now, nobody could read what he wrote; he still can't write legibly. It's horrible. But he wrote stories about everything he saw, and told stories before he wrote them."[4]

Faith, too, was an abiding presence in the Earles' life. Not a Bible-thumping, intolerant, my-way-or-the-highway Pentecostalism, but a faith tempered by the family's struggles, both economic and emotional. At one of their stops, both Jack and Barbara sang in their Methodist church's choir, and all the children were regular churchgoers too. And when they're visiting Jacksonville, they never miss a service at Earle's Chapel. "Earle's Chapel is a special place in all of our lives," says Barbara.[5] "We've not always been as faithful about getting to church as we should have been," she adds, "but we've always had a lot of faith."[6]

Stacey Earle: "We were raised with praying hands and a sobriety prayer on our walls at home. It goes way back; it's very thick."

In an environment rich in art, music, and literature, Steve not only came by a gift of gab easily, but also gained an early recognition of words and pronunciations, and taught himself to read well ahead of starting his formal education at age six and a half in Louisiana. Elementary school was a breeze for him, though it offered few intellectual challenges for a boy who read well above his grade level before he was even enrolled, and read on a wide variety of subjects—and talked incessantly about them all and peppered Barbara and Jack with question after question about what he'd been reading.

"He was the absolute opposite of his image through the years," Barbara says. "He was a sweet child, real bookish and real interested in everything. Didn't like to fight, wasn't aggressive in any respect. His brother, 13 months

The Earle children with various cousins in 1969. Steve is at the top, holding a guitar; Stacey is front and center, mugging for the camera; Kelly is far left, with arms folded; Mark is third from right, holding the youngest Earle child, Patrick.

younger, was aggressive and athletic and so forth. Steve wasn't. He was never in trouble in school, his teachers loved him because he was smart. It was just when he got to about seventh grade, and they absolutely didn't have what he needed in school anymore. Now they might; there are schools for people like him, but there weren't then. When he was in first grade in Louisiana, his teacher, who had been teaching many, many years, called us to school and said, 'I'm not gonna have enough for him to do. He knows so much about so many things.'"[7]

The stability Barbara and Jack thought they had found in Lake Charles–Sulphur was short lived. The family that had once moved five times in five years was about to do it again. In April 1963 Jack was reassigned to San Antonio upon the closing of Chenault Air Force Base in Lake Charles. The debts starting piling up as he and Barbara struggled to pay both the mortgage on their Louisiana home while it was up for sale and the $75 a month rent they were being charged for a battered, weatherbeaten house on a quarter horse ranch in Converse, Texas.

However much Jack and Barbara bemoaned their circumstances, their children romped through a sort of earthly paradise on the ranch, surrounded by horses, fishing in the lakes on the property, and sneaking into the weekend races at the nearby San Antonio Drag Raceway. Summer meant trips with Booster to pick peaches on the farm in Jacksonville, and for Mark and Steve, days spent barefoot and shirtless in cutoff jeans around Cibolo Creek, exploring the caves that had been exposed from rock falling out of the bluffs.

And whenever the entertainment, or the money, or both threatened to flag, there were always the family drives. The kids jammed into the car, Barbara riding shotgun, Jack behind the wheel, he'd head out in one direction, then let each of his children tell him where to turn next. He'd keep on going until he got to someplace else. Animated discussions about everything under the sun—music, politics, sports, school, the current issues of the day—made time fly, and Jack and Barbara often entertained the troops with their impeccable duet singing. Years later, in a song titled "The Other Kind," Steve would sing of seeking refuge "in aluminum and steel" and how the open road made the years fall away. There could be no better capsule description of what these family drives meant to the Earles—back out on that road again, they could escape, however fleetingly, their precarious financial state and let their imaginations carry them to new, exotic places.

Sometimes there were beautiful accidents. Once when Barbara was having trouble with her bridgework, a friend suggested she go visit one of the cheap dentists in Mexico where, she was assured, the work would be done just as good as in the States and for a fraction of the price it would cost in Texas. Plus they worked on Sunday!

Down to Piedras Negras they went one Sunday, laughing and singing and talking all the way. They got to the dentist before noon, he examined Barbara and said that for $15 he could have a new bridge ready for her at around two o'clock that afternoon. To pass the time Jack decided to drive south out of Piedras Negras and see the countryside.

"And we drove about four or five miles, and there was a real pretty park and a creek ran through it, they had a playground," Jack recalls. "It was still morning, so we just drove in there and let the kids out to play. About noon, here comes all these people—mariachis, dancers; people hung up decorations, and they had all these shaved-ice vendors and lemonade vendors, and they were making fajitas and what have you. It was really fun."[8]

"It's like a carnival," Kelly told Lauren St. John in *Hardcore Troubadour*. "There had to be a hundred people there … And it was probably one of the best days of our lives. We were covered with different-colored stuff from all these ices, stuffed with all kinds of Mexican food and cotton candy, coming down from a horrible sugar high, all in the back of the station wagon. It was one of the few times were totally silent on the way home."[9]

And according to Jack, Barbara's $15 bridge lasted another 20 years.

A little more than a year into their stay in Converse, the Earles moved again, a few miles east, to the town of Schertz, a once-bustling farming community that had come on hard times. An acquaintance of Steve's named Jack Watson, son of an Air Force lifer, grew up on Randolph Air Force Base and had friends in Schertz. At the time the Earles moved there, Watson remembers the town as being "real rural, right on a two-lane road. Lots of fields. Old houses. Long way to the store. It wasn't even really a town. It was kind of a poor place.

I've seen pictures of it on TV since, and it ain't that way anymore. It was real beautiful and quiet, but it was poor. Those guys didn't have much."[10]

Years later Steve would reminisce about his time in Schertz between songs during his concerts. He boiled his experience there down to a simple, striking anecdote: "It was a place with a lot of large, square-headed guys named Otto who beat the shit outta me on a regular basis."[11]

There probably were a fair share of Ottos in Schertz back then, despite its small population (it is no longer the lonely outpost Jack Watson described, with a population of more than 26,000). In addition to the Schertz family, the original settlers numbered more than a few families of German extraction, including the Schneiders, the Seilers, the Boettigers, and the Mergeles. And as he went through junior high and into high school, Steve did run afoul of some contemporaries who didn't appreciate the cut of his jib and made their displeasure known in a physical way. How many of these ruffians were named Otto, though, remains an open question, but the point is made.

Shertz represented yet another new beginning for Jack and Barbara, a chance to regain their financial footing. Being moved because of Jack's job was one thing; sometimes, though, when the debts were getting out of control, they had to move simply to find cheaper housing. "It was tough," Jack says. "We started out young with kids right away and not much sense, didn't make that much, and we were fighting it all the way. I must admit that there's, I guess, two moves that came as a result of some money problems."[12]

It was in this most unlikely of spots that Steve Earle began to find himself. School was less challenging with each new year, but he had immersed himself in literature of all kinds. In addition to the likes of Mark Twain, he was especially drawn to the work of Beat authors and poets—William S. Burroughs, Jack Kerouac, Allen Ginsberg, and Gregory Corso—who called to him with their words, their images, their rhythms, their outrage, their intellect, and their embrace of their otherness.

Steve had tried to fit in all along. He had been the dutiful son and the model student. But he found there was not much in the classroom to engage his curious mind. Traditionally, boys made their mark in Texas by being good at sports, especially football, but Steve wasn't. He tried, tried hard, and he had a passion for both football and baseball, but he lacked the skills and coordination. Unlike brother Mark, who excelled on the field.

"Steve was real stiff, and clumsy, really," Jack says. "He didn't do well in any kind of sports, so he was glad when he wasn't pushed into Little League. Mark was darn good. Steve came out for Pop Warner the first year there was a Pop Warner football team at Randolph Air Force Base. Went out and started practicing, and he was really having trouble. He was so stiff. Mark was still playing baseball and wasn't allowed to try out for football until baseball season was over. So when baseball was over, Mark worked out two or three days with the football team, and when they made their cuts Steve went and Mark stayed. That was a hard day for the family."[13]

From late 1963 through 1964 America and world witnessed momentous change. First came the November 1963 assassination of President John F. Kennedy in Dallas (Jack had taken Steve and Mark to see the president's motorcade in San Antonio the day before the assassination).[14]

On the much smaller stage of Schertz, Texas, the same period would prove pivotal for a young man looking for something, though he could not yet speak its name.

chapter 3

Outcast Ascending

Jack Earle had little use for Ralph Carl Powers, a young black man from San Antonio. He was a "thug really; pretty worthless kid," in Jack's estimation, who had wandered over to the upscale area known as Alamo Heights and got into a scuffle. Dicky Renfro, from a wealthy family, produced a gun during the argument, but Powers, undeterred, attacked him anyway. Powers wrested the gun from Renfro's control and shot him dead.

At this time in Texas, families of murder victims were allowed to hire their own prosecutors to assist the district attorney in prosecuting the case. The Renfro family did so, and Powers, represented by a public defender, was convicted. "He didn't stand a chance," Jack says of Powers. "His trial didn't last long at all and he was sent right on to death row."[1]

Outraged over what he believed was a rigged case, Jack wrote a letter to Texas governor John Connolly, urging he issue a stay of execution. That became a moot point on June 29, 1972, when, in the landmark *Furman v. Georgia* case, the United States Supreme Court voided 40 death penalty statutes. The sentences of 629 death row inmates around the country—including Ralph Carl Powers's—were voided and the death penalty suspended when the court found existing statutes to be invalid. (Four years later, however, in *Gregg v. Georgia*, the court reinstated the death penalty in Texas, Florida, and Georgia, states that had rewritten their death penalty statutes to address the flaws the court had cited in *Furman*.)

Powers's sentence was commuted to life.

"It was just sort of accepted that that's the way it was; they didn't make a big deal out of it in Texas," Barbara says of the Lone Star State's famously liberal application of the death penalty. "This was a particular case that we got interested in, and it caused us to stop and really think about [the death penalty] for the first time. And we decided that that's not something that ought to be happening. I don't think two wrongs make a right, for one thing. If it's wrong to kill, it's wrong to kill. Those people have to be punished, but they can sit there forever. . . . It's a premeditated murder, no matter what somebody does. When you pick a time that you're going to actually take a human life and sit there and watch it . . ."[2] Her voice trails off.

Steve took note of both his father's moral outrage and his activism. "That was the first time I ever saw anybody take any sort of individual political action," he says.[3]

* * *

When his firstborn had finally tapped out of sports for good, by fifth grade, Jack bought him a trumpet, and Steve joined the school band. He was a quick study on the instrument and, according to Jack, "was doing pretty good on it."[4] But his run in the band was a scant two years, because in seventh grade the band director kicked him out of class.[5]

That hardly mattered to Steve by then, because he had found a new and enduring muse in the Beatles. He had learned about the quartet from his mother's stepbrother, his uncle Nick Fain, who was only five years older than Steve but way ahead of the curve in terms of his hipness quotient. Nick knew about the Beatles and owned their first album before they came to America. Nick was what Steve wanted to be—not merely a hipster, but a guy through whom music surged naturally and beautifully. Lean, blond, and driven, Nick Fain had a life force about him that mesmerized Steve. He had overcome daunting physical obstacles. A case of polio at age five left him totally paralyzed temporarily. Therapy gave him mobility and use of everything but his left shoulder and arm, which remained paralyzed; his left arm eventually withered.

Nick was a natural at music. He started out playing the trombone, mastered it, and then moved on to guitar, learning from recordings and stringing his guitar backward so that he could fret with his right hand; he also became an accomplished blues piano player. Once Nick taught Steve his first basic chords and how to get music out of them, his young nephew was hooked—hooked on the guitar and hooked on Nick as a role model, an arbiter of hip, and his guide into the otherness he found in the Beats' literature and felt himself a part of.

"Nick was a tremendous influence on Steve in a lot of ways," Jack says. "Music-wise that's where he really got into it and really got into his guitar. It was amazing that when he got that guitar, a week after he had it you were hearing some pretty fancy chords. Wasn't long at all until he was really playing it well."

Then came February 9, 1964, when he saw and heard the Beatles making their U.S. television debut on *The Ed Sullivan Show*.

"Everything changed," he said.[6]

A devoted Elvis fan up to that point, Steve did more than admire the Beatles. After seeing their dynamic performance, he started mimicking their movements in front of a mirror, a tennis racket standing in for the guitar he wished he owned. He was fired up by the joy animating each Liverpudlian's face as he sang; by the authority and energy of their physical presence: how John Lennon would slightly rock at the knees as he performed; how Paul would tilt his head and arch his eyebrows and drive the girls in the audience into hysterics; how George locked into his instrument and played with such fluid grace; how Ringo bobbed his head in time with the rhythm, his Beatle-cut hair flopping all over the place. Steve responded to the power of their music: "All My Loving," the irresistible "She Loves You," and even the show tune from *The Music Man* that Paul had introduced as being by "our favorite American group, Sophie Tucker," "Til There Was You."

As Steve admitted in the February 2004 issue of *Tracks* magazine, though, what most caught his attention was the Beatles' garb—he loved their clothes.

"In the beginning, the whole Beatles thing, even for me, was as much about fashion—the suits, the haircuts—as music. I even remember looking for the guys in the audience because I was a guy and there weren't as many of them. But there were some, and because it was New York, it was the first time I saw guys besides the Beatles who combed their hair and wore clothes like that."[7]

Musically, it was the group's third appearance on the Sullivan show that sealed the deal for Steve. Broadcast from Miami, it featured the group in two segments, as Sullivan always did, and the music they made that night cut through to Steve's marrow.

"They did an unbelievable version of 'This Boy' that was the best singing I ever heard John Lennon do, on record or anywhere—period. That said, at first I was most drawn to Paul McCartney. I ended up playing bass for a while—I played bass for Guy Clark's band when I first moved to Nashville—and that probably was part of the reason I was interested in McCartney. But I also liked his melodies. In the Beatles' early period, Lennon's stuff was based a lot on

Chuck Berry and Little Richard—rock 'n' roll that I had heard before. What McCartney was doing had been done before too, but I didn't recognize it, so to me it was new. He was more rooted in English music hall music and musicals, and I found that aspect interesting. But as time wore on, it was Lennon for me, and I'm a Lennon guy to this day."[8]

And it was his enthusiasm for the Beatles that begat one of the major themes of Steve's life: sex, girls, and sex with girls. "The Beatles were also part of my discovery that the way to get through high school is to get yourself declared an honorary girl. I promise you, I got laid before any of my friends did, and the Beatles were part of it. The people I talked to about Beatles records and who knew every song, just as I did, were all girls."[9]

The Beatles in specific and the British Invasion in general led Steve deeper into rock 'n' roll and deeper into a private world centered on the music he was absorbing as if by osmosis. For nearly three years he was only a fan, albeit a dedicated one. Having no outlet for his energy on the field of play, lacking the identity that came with being an athlete, he retreated socially, keeping his own counsel and growing markedly less voluble. Others in his family considered his near-hermetic turn as a typical phase of adolescence. Steve, according to Lauren St. John, saw it differently: "I talked a lot, but what I discovered is it bothered people when I talked."[10]

In late 1963 Steve's grandfather, Booster Earle, began complaining of a "weird feeling" in his head. Admitted to the hospital in Jacksonville, he was diagnosed with colon cancer that had metastasized to his brain. Jack and Barbara had him transferred to a hospital in San Antonio, where doctors determined that his condition was inoperable and terminal. He died in April 1964 and was buried in Earle's Chapel Cemetery.

In 1967 tragedy visited again when his other grandfather, Sam Fain, died. A year earlier he had suffered a severe stroke, and the physical aftershock—his speech and memory were affected—spurred gossip in the Fains' social circle that Sam was back on the bottle. Helen was so unnerved by the rumormongering that she holed up in the house with Sam, not even bothering to go to work anymore. At Barbara and Jack's urging, the Fains moved to Schertz, where Sam could be closer to the VA hospital when he needed help and Helen would be in a more supportive environment. Things were fine for a while, but Sam suffered another serious stroke and died without ever leaving the hospital again. Helen, who had been working in San Antonio and rebuilding her life, "just kind of came apart," Barbara says, "and Nick did too."[11]

Her main mooring in life now lost, Helen began drinking with a vengeance. Barbara and Jack endured the increasing bouts of inebriation as best they could while trying to shield their children from their grandmother's dark side, when the booze would transform her from a classy, sophisticated lady into an angry, bitter, backbiting terror. Finally, knowing she needed help, and at the

Steve (with guitar) in a student production at the start of his ninth-grade year at Oliver Wendell Holmes High School. Shortly before this photo was taken, he had performed "Mr. Bojangles"; shortly after, he left school for good.

urging of her daughter and son-in-law, Helen checked into a rehab center in San Antonio. At the Alpha Home she became a model patient, and ultimately wound up with a management position there, lending her experienced hand in helping others recover.

Nick, in the meantime, moved in with the Earles, sharing a bedroom with Steve and Mark. Now approaching his senior year in high school, Nick was way out there, by the standards of the time, playing in a band that practiced in the Earles's carport and rattled the house's foundation, raising hell in school and out, associating with shady characters and generally cutting a wide swath as a rambunctious ne'er-do-well. And fully embracing all the accoutrements of a rock 'n' roll lifestyle, including drugs.

To Steve, though, Nick "was my hero."[12]

From Nick Steve received the Holy Grail: a guitar. And with it, an identity. "It was clear he had found something," Mark remembers. "He played the guitar constantly. Everywhere he went, he carried it."[13]

He carried it, he studied its personality, he developed a hard focus with one aim: to make his instrument talk to, through and for him. He was trying to work out his favorite Beatles and Elvis songs on guitar, trying to master Bob Dylan's folk style and Johnny Cash's eclectic mix of folk, country, and gospel. School became entirely secondary to his mission. His real education was coming from Nick and would include, in a couple of years, his first toke on a marijuana joint.

With Steve's grades plummeting, his behavior becoming more aloof, and his appearance increasingly disheveled, Jack put his foot down: he seized Steve's guitar and locked it in a cupboard, telling his son to get his act together in the classroom. Only then could he have his guitar back.

Jack awoke the next morning to find the cupboard wrenched off its hinges, and the guitar and Steve long gone, but not far away. He was wandering aimlessly around Schertz, seeing what was out there and hearing all the music he could imagine. To the Houston *Chronicle*'s Marty Racine (who made a point of checking in with Steve with each new album release, and filed reports in his "Pop Music" column that are the most insightful accounts of the artist's early years), Steve explained his wandering ways as the product of craving "unstructured days.

"When I was growing up I'd go to this creek and I'd wander along this creek for miles and miles and miles. It was an oasis of wilderness, and I'd wander for hours—until I got to be a teenager where I'd be tellin' my parents that I'd be spending the night at somebody's house when actually I'd be walking around the streets at night. When a car came I'd hide in the bushes. It was sort of a game. I'd stay up all night and try not to be seen, just getting away with it.

"But mainly it was a chance just to be by myself, a chance to hear myself think."[14]

But there was more going on in Steve's life than music and antisocial behavior. In that Summer of Love, with the counterculture seeping into mainstream America; with the Beatles startling the rock 'n' roll world with the revolutionary *Sgt. Pepper's Lonely Hearts Club Band*; with the Monterey Pop Festival bringing together a vibrant rainbow of towering artists—from soul giant Otis Redding, to the psychedelic, blues-drenched pyrotechnics of Jimi Hendrix; from the hardcore blues rock of Janis Joplin with Big Brother and the Holding Company to the ear-splitting thunder and power of the Who. Protest, political activism, and a new social consciousness were everywhere. Steve, all of 13, experienced a defining moment in his young life when he saw the film version of Truman Capote's best-selling "nonfiction novel" *In Cold Blood*, a searing, explicit account of the brutal murder of the Clutter family in rural Kansas by drifters Perry Smith and Dick Hickock, and the killers' subsequent execution by hanging. If the music, the Vietnam War, the charged political atmosphere, the drugs, the free love made their mark on his outlook, so did this story. It's as if everything that had shaped Steve Earle to that point and would come to define him in the future coalesced in this one fateful year.

"That was a mind-blower," he told salon.com interviewer Andrew O'Hehir in November 2002. "Later I read [the book]. What I always remember is the scene when Perry Smith is getting ready to be executed, and he's worried about soiling himself because he's heard that happens. He wanted them to let him go to the bathroom one more time, and they told him there wasn't time. Then the chaplain intervenes on his behalf. There's an illustration of the inhumanity of the death penalty—in other words, what it does to us.

"It took me years to be able to hang words on that. And it took talking to many murder victims' family members for me to get to the point that, you know what? My objection to the death penalty isn't that I'm trying to get to save anybody on death row. I'm trying to keep me from going to hell. In a democracy, if the government kills somebody, then I kill somebody, and I object to the damage that does to my spirit. Period."[15]

It wasn't yet fully formed, but the template for an outlaw poet with a fearless—and tender—heart was nearing completion; its basic architecture was in place, but there were more metaphysical, and chemical, inquiries into his sense of otherness to come. Even at this stage, his brother Mark saw in his older sibling a young man apart from the society around him, consciously so, and on the road to God only knows where.

"Steve very early on … started going a different route altogether. He was treated as an outcast, he kind of saw himself as not succeeding in some ways that were considered normal, I guess … and that probably was something that pushed him out seeking something else."[16]

The Other Kind

Steve began his performing career almost as an act of self-preservation—not in the sense of music being his only toehold in the world, but rather as a way to keep himself together in the face of his mother's devastating illness and the toll it took on his family.

In the Earle household the blessed event of April 4, 1967—the birth of the fifth Earle child, Patrick Collins Earle—came with an unsettling shadow. Barbara began experiencing the symptoms of postpartum depression, and the little-understood illness followed its typical course, ultimately disabling her psychologically. She spent most of her time on the couch, oblivious to noise from the television that was always turned on. The transformation in her personality was dramatic. Once a fount of energy, she now had none, nor did she have any enthusiasm for books, music, the issues of the day, her own family, or any of the animating passions that had defined her life. No mere "baby blues" this; Barbara was disintegrating right before her family's frightened, confused eyes.

For the next two years she was in and out of hospitals in San Antonio, ultimately submitting to three series of electroconvulsive therapy. Fortunately, the treatments did slowly bring her back and without any ill effects. But things weren't the same with the family. For one thing, like most mental health expenses, Barbara's psychiatric care wasn't covered by insurance. Jack, already struggling to cover her bills and those of the household, was working double shifts but still being hounded mercilessly by creditors.

During this time Steve was making significant strides as a musician. Under Nick's tutelage, he had become a fluent guitarist with a good sense of rhythm and dynamics. He noticed from reading album liner notes that many of the artists he admired wrote their own songs. So he began writing his own songs, although he rarely played them outside his own room. (One that he did sing for the family, a love song for a high school girlfriend, is remembered still as one of the most touching songs he's ever written.)

Then he entered his school's talent contest, which was his first public performance. Depending on the source—his unauthorized biographer Lauren St. John or his father Jack—Steve either finished third[1] or first.[2]

"I can't even think of the song he sang," Jack says, "but it was a Beatles song. And he was all fixed up in sort of a Buddy Holly getup."[3]

"He was playing pretty well, and we knew he could sing beautifully," Kelly recalls, "but nobody really took it seriously until he decided he was going to be in the talent show."[4]

His talent show performance having stoked a fire that was already burning fiercely, Steve, by age 14, began testing himself further by playing folk songs at coffeehouses in San Antonio. Encouraging his firstborn's ambition, Jack would drive Steve to the gigs and accompany him inside, since he was too young to be admitted to the clubs that served alcohol. Jack admired Steve's pluck and the good taste evident in his repertoire—"mostly folk and Beatles stuff"[5]—and down deep was hoping that the music might inspire the boy to focus anew on his schoolwork.

But schoolwork was getting to be a nuisance as far as Steve was concerned. The only class that engaged him on any level was drama. There he encountered Vernon Carroll, a teacher who got Steve involved in school productions behind the scenes: helping build sets, working the lights, providing musical backgrounds. Carroll understood Steve and actively encouraged his musical pursuits, introducing him to recordings the teacher thought were important for Steve to know about.

"That was the only teacher that didn't kick me out of his class," Steve says. "He turned me on to *The Freewheelin' Bob Dylan*. I had picked up on Dylan with *Bringing It All Back Home*, and he turned me on to the first couple of albums, which I hadn't heard."[6]

That was all well and good, but Vernon Carroll notwithstanding, school in general was becoming increasingly irrelevant to Steve, increasingly more dangerous to his emotional well-being, and an increasingly more troubling issue for his parents.

At home intense arguments over school erupted between Steve and his parents. Always supportive of their son's musical endeavors, Jack and Barbara hadn't lodged much protest against his appearance even when it flew in the face of school regulations. (At one point during Steve's junior high school years, the Earles met with other parents to discuss their concern that the school administration was spending more energy enforcing a rigid dress code than providing good classroom instruction.[7]) Jack and Barbara knew their own son: unlike some other kids who adopted the same social posture, appearance, and attitudes, Steve's rebellion had a purpose. He had already made music his life, and in him there was a restlessness to get on with the real work, which was not to be found in academia.

Jack Earle knew from experience how hard the world could be even if you had an education, and how unforgiving it was without one. He says he had only one message for Steve: "You gotta get through high school. You absolutely have to." But even as these words were coming out of his mouth, Jack had a sinking feeling that they were only words, words that were having no more impact on Steve than the school dress code. "I was seeing more and more that this wasn't gonna happen."[8]

At Holmes High School in San Antonio, Steve ran into a rigid dress code that forbade boys to wear their hair below their collar and girls their skirts above the knee. Steve was by then notorious for his rebellious behavior. Smoking and skipping class were the least of his malfeasance; he also had the inspired idea to publish his own underground newspaper, which featured on its first cover a caricature of Holmes High's vice principal. With his long hair and his bohemian attire, Steve found himself first among equals as a "freak," the lowest tier in the student caste system, with the kickers (the rich kids who dressed in the latest fashions and wanted for nothing) and the cowboys (who dressed the part, belonged to the Rodeo Club, and listened exclusively to country music) lording it over him and his kind.

"They hassled everybody" is how Jack Watson, a contemporary and friend of Steve's, remembers the intolerance that was visited on the outsiders. "Anybody that came even close to that Neil Young look was scary to parents. Back then, anybody that even remotely didn't look like they went to Harvard was scary. Steve caught as much hell as the rest of us did. They'd throw bottles out the window at you as we were walking. Beer bottles were a big one. Football players, varsity football players, they would jump you, eight or ten of 'em, and cut your hair with a pocket knife. That happened to me. And Steve caught as much hell as I did."[9]

To writer Lauren St. John, Steve described the environment as "a real division and it got violent," and limned a predatory scene of hunters and hunted. "Kids fought about it. I got my hair cut with a pocket knife three or four times on my way home from school. I got beat half to death just because I had long hair. It just happened in Texas in those days. And it didn't really change until Willie Nelson moved back to Texas.... In 1973, when Willie Nelson started having the Fourth of July picnics and these big gigs, all of a sudden Texas became, at least on that level, more tolerant."[10]

These years—from 1969, when he was 14, into 1974, when he left Texas for Nashville—are full of bittersweet memories for Jack and Barbara Earle. They saw their other four children progressing along fine in their lives in and out of school, but Steve's way was bumpy. He was testing them, testing himself, and testing the bounds of society. Although there is some disagreement as to when Steve started dabbling in drugs, both Barbara and Jack insist he was 14 when he smoked marijuana for the first time, after Nick had introduced him to it. Steve has told various interviewers through the years that he was 13 when he first tasted the herb. The only fact all parties agree on is that Nick was the catalyst. But when Steve was 13, Nick wasn't around. Shortly after graduating high school, Nick was arrested and sent to prison to serve a three-year sentence for marijuana possession.

"When Steve was 13, I was still at home," Barbara says. "Jack was real active in everything he did, and Nick was out of the picture that year, because he was arrested and away. But then Steve began to get out with the other older kids when he was 14. Jack and I both agree that if Steve were doing anything of consequence when he was 13, it would have been pretty hard. I just don't see how it would have happened."[11]

But Nick was around long enough post-graduation and pre-incarceration to lead Steve down another road entirely with regard to drugs. In addition to pot, Steve had also tried LSD (either with Nick or through contacts made on the coffeehouse circuit, where drugs were omnipresent and oftimes the center of an evening's socializing among friends), which turned out, thanks to a couple of bad trips, not to be his drug of choice. That was left for Nick to provide. One evening in San Antonio he took Steve to visit some friends who were gathered in a rundown hotel, all of them shooting heroin. Steve willingly joined the party, but not without some help.

"I couldn't inject myself," he says, "Nick had to do it for me. I didn't throw up, which most people do. I should have known I was in trouble right then. It kind of really agreed with me."[12]

By age 14 Steve was fixated on Nashville. Determined to get there, he and a friend lit out on the friend's Vespa motor scooter, on a southern route to Music City that would take them first, and inexplicably, through Houston. After the Vespa petered out, they hitchhiked into Houston. The two-week odyssey that followed found Steve jailed briefly for being caught shooting up speed in a gas station bathroom. The cops made him spend a night in an adult jail to send a message that this was the wrong way to go; his friend, who had ID on him that proved he was underage, was flown back home on his parents' tab. Steve roamed aimlessly for several days, part of the time with an under-age girl whose parents ultimately stepped in to bring her back home and leave Steve on his own again. Worse still, a group of boys out for some mischief spotted Steve hitchhiking and robbed him of his guitar.

While Steve was missing, Jack and Barbara were searching on their own. Jack remembered that Steve liked to hole up in the caves at Cibolo Creek, so he called the Schertz police and told them his missing son might be out at the caves. The next day the police reported that nothing had been found at the creek. Skeptical, Jack went to the caves himself and in one found Steve's old Boy Scout hunting knife, the remnants of a fire, and some candy and junk food wrappers, but no indication as to where he and his partner had gone. When his friend came back from Houston, he told Steve's parents where they had been, and off to Houston went the entire Earle family, packed into one station wagon.

"We started checking out some of these clues from other guys and what have you, and we'd ride with the police at night up and down all the streets and areas where he'd been seen," Jack recalls. "Then one day during the daytime we were just driving along in our car, and here he and a couple of girls come out of the woods crossing the road right in front of us. So that was that."[13]

Steve's explanation for what he'd done? "Mom, I didn't run away from home, I just don't have time for school."[14]

"His luck wasn't really good on the runoffs," Jack says. "He and a girl-friend ran away after that, and we realized it when the girlfriend's parents called and told us she was missing too. They were about 40 miles northeast of San Antonio, there was going to be a rock festival. So we just jumped in the car and took off, figuring that's where they'll be. We got up there and it turned out the rock festival hadn't happened because the city at the last moment got it shut down, they didn't want it. So okay, what does he do now? Then we were only 20 miles from Austin, and we figured that must be where he went. So we took off to Austin and as we drove into town we turned up Guadalupe, the drag there where you come to the University of Texas. And there he is and the girl, walking along. He had terrible luck."[15]

Barbara: "He just said, 'I think you're witches' and got in the car. Steve made it clear that he never ran away from us. And it's hard for people to understand. We've never been particularly careful to polish things and make things seem that they were perfect, because they weren't. But the big picture is that the family is very, very close."[16]

Steve returned to Holmes High, but after only a couple more months of failing or incomplete class assignments, he was expelled. Never telling his parents that he had been booted out of school, he spent the days hanging out with other ne'er-do-wells, smoking pot, and adopting the lifestyle of the comfortably numb. The police took exception to this attitude when they found the kids, but instead of arresting them, let them off with a warning. One policeman alerted Jack to Steve's truancy, and after asking around, Jack learned that his son had been kicked out of school. Moreover, he learned, from his son's own mouth, that school days were over for Stephen Fain Earle. He ordered Steve to see his mother's psychiatrist, a Dr. Kleck, who Jack regards as "one of our real heroes…he was just great. He really worked with Barbara when she was having some hard times there."[17]

After meeting with Steve, Dr. Kleck returned with one bit of advice for the parents: "Steve knows what he wants to do, and I think he has the talent to do it. He's going to do it one way or the other. Either you can oppose it and read about it, or you can help him out and he'll tell you about it, and he'll always come home."[18]

Freed from the bondage of academia, 16-year-old Steve went out on his own, although he was still tethered to the family. He got his own apartment in San Antonio, but Jack paid the rent for him. Nineteen-seventy was winding down as Steve was gearing up for his life's work, continuing to play solo and work out his songs in coffeehouses around town. He was also playing in bands, which afforded him an opportunity to flex his rock 'n' roll muscles and to gain some insight into the dynamics of arranging for multiple instruments.

Steve had been on his own for about a year when Nick came back into the picture. Having served 15 months of a three-year sentence before being paroled, he had returned to civilian life only to be busted again for selling a few ounces of marijuana to a federal undercover agent and was sent back to serve the remainder of his three-year sentence. (He had originally been sentenced to serve three three-year sentences, to run concurrently.) After serving his time, Nick came back to live with the Earles but stayed only a short while before meeting a young lady with whom he fell in love and soon married.

Right out of prison Nick formed a band called Hammer, which, according to Lauren St. John, "played Allman Brothers and Steely Dan songs and some original material."[19] Reuniting with Nick, Steve didn't hesitate to join his uncle in pursuit of fame and fortune. On the spur of the moment, Steve moved with him to Houston. Talented as he was, Nick was never to experience the glory he sought. For Steve, however, the move to Houston, where the seeds of a new musical order were just taking root, seemed like nothing less than destiny. In what other place, in what other time would this young man who treasured words, respected the integrity of a song, and held an abiding passion for what had come before him, find home? There, as in San Antonio and Austin, gathered a new breed of musicians. Disenchanted with mainstream country music, skeptical of where post-Woodstock rock 'n' roll was headed, these singers, writers, and players were determined to build something new on the very traditions they believed the Nashville establishment had abandoned.

chapter 5

Lone Star State
of Mind, 1970–74

I. Cosmic Cowboys

The early 1970s found country music in one of its transitional phases. The changes those few years wrought formed a template for both the industry and the music that would dominate country to the present day. For a genre steeped so deeply in tradition and often considered so conservative, country has birthed a surprising number of revolutions. Every previous stylistic convulsion in modern country music history—dating back to the emergence of Jimmie Rodgers and the Carter Family on RCA Victor in 1927—has yielded a pool of new artists whose fresh spins on tradition invigorated old styles with musical ideas from beyond country's borders. The most original and enduring new artists brazenly reference their influences but continue on, evolving individual styles that set new benchmarks. There is no place in the country vanguard for artists who diligently emulate, who bring nothing new, unique, or individual to the mix. Sounding like no one else—that's what this new generation was all about. From that quest for individuality, for difference, sprang an infusion of new approaches for a new generation.

An innovator who learned this lesson by accident was Texas native Ernest Tubb. After a tonsillectomy had forced him to abandon a stalled career as a rather shameless clone of Jimmie Rodgers and find a different route, Tubb emerged in 1941 with a monumental hit single, "Walkin' the Floor over You," the signal moment announcing an edgier, more rhythmically charged country offshoot called honky tonk. Within a decade, Hank Williams's work would become the genre's artistic apex, and adventurous artists such as Canada's "Singing Ranger," Hank Snow, whose original songs were fueled by sophisticated rhythmic patterns and imaginative lyrics, would follow. Then honky tonk spawned a second country-based offshoot (some detractors consider it a bastard child) called rockabilly. Two hundred miles west of Nashville and the epicenter of the country music industry, honky tonk was being perfected to a tee by visionary producer-entrepreneur Sam Phillips. In his Sun Records studio at 706 Union Avenue, Memphis, Phillips was rolling tape roll on an artist roster that included Elvis Presley, Carl Perkins, Jerry Lee Lewis, Johnny Cash, and Roy Orbison.

The often overlooked X factor in all these developments, of course, is the bifurcated audience, one segment comprised of older listeners who remain loyal to the artists they grew up with but rarely embrace the new guard as wholeheartedly as their established favorites; the other, younger and more restless for music that spoke their language, in style and in temperament. In his astute 1985 critique of country music history, *Nashville: Music City USA*, John Lomax III (grandson of John Avery Lomax; nephew of Alan Lomax and Bess Lomax Hawes; son of John Avery Lomax, Jr., the most distinguished family of folklorist-musicologists in American history) makes several salient points about the state of country music and its audience at the time Steve Earle—whose path Lomax III crossed most fatefully in the mid-'70s in Nashville—began his personal odyssey in Houston in 1970.

"What was wrong was that country music had little relevance to a rebellious generation that was spending the second half of the 1960s experimenting with social protest, drug use, and sexual freedom," Lomax observes. "In the eyes of the 15-to-25 age group, country music was square because it appealed to old whites and rednecks, two lily-white groups with few redeeming virtues for the young of the period ...

"The audience for country music then consisted primarily of old people getting older. Clearly, something had to be done. Some new fans were being recruited, but they weren't entering as fast as the older ones were dying off. In the late 1950s country had pulled itself out of the mudhole by upgrading recording facilities and adapting techniques from pop music production. These tricks were employed again in 1968, but the most important reason for country's upswing at the box office was the development of a whole new generation of artists and producers. From 1967 to 1972, country harvested a bumper crop of talented, younger artists. Such singers as Glen Campbell, Lynn Anderson, Hank Williams, Jr., Tammy Wynette, Conway Twitty, Charley Pride, Dolly Parton, Merle Haggard, Mickey Gilley, Charlie Rich, Barbara Mandrell, Kenny Rogers, Loretta Lynn, Crystal Gayle, Tom T. Hall, David Frizzell, Anne Murray, Tanya Tucker, Don Williams, Donna Fargo, Freddie Hart, Jack Greene, David

Houston, and Johnny Rodriguez either posted their first chart record or their first No. 1 during these six years."[1]

So by the time Steve set foot in Houston, the country mainstream was undergoing a makeover with a solid class of new artists, although the women Lomax III cites (with the notable exception of the gritty teen sensation Tanya Tucker) emphasized the pop elements in their music rather than the country. Among the generally high caliber of popular new male artists, Kenny Rogers, who would sell millions of records in his heyday, seemed no more country than Mister Rogers.

The young audience that was coming into country music wasn't entering by the front door. They were coming in through the side entrances, the emergency exits. Their conduit was rock 'n' roll, their conceptual visionary was Gram Parsons, a North Carolina native who campaigned for what he termed "cosmic American music," a blend of country and rock that Parsons introduced in his brief tenure as a member of the Byrds. His one album with the group, 1968's *Sweetheart of the Rodeo*, featured only two original songs, both by Parsons (the haunting "Hickory Wind" and "One Hundred Years from Now") amidst vintage country and folk numbers such as "I Am a Pilgrim," Woody Guthrie's "Pretty Boy Floyd," and two Bob Dylan songs. Parsons left the Byrds and took original founding member Chris Hillman with him, then augmented their duo with bassist Chris Ethridge and the masterful steel guitar player Sneaky Pete Kleinow, and emerged as the Flying Burrito Brothers. Dressed in sequined Nudie suits (with marijuana leaves on their jackets), the Burritos, thanks to Sneaky Pete's moaning and wailing pedal steel lines, trafficked in a classic honky tonk sound and spiced their original repertoire ("Sin City" was one of the evergreens that came out of this union) with covers by traditional country giants such as Merle Haggard, George Jones, and the Louvin Brothers. After leaving the Burritos, Parsons went solo, but he was barely getting started when he died of a drug overdose on September 19, 1973. In addition to a host of well-crafted, emotionally charged original songs, he gave country music another great gift in his 1972 discovery of Emmylou Harris in Washington, DC.

In 1968 the Byrds were not alone in championing country music. Bob Dylan emerged from seclusion following a reputed near-fatal motorcycle accident in upstate New York to record *John Wesley Harding*, a quiet masterpiece of country-folk full of parables and tormented visions; a year later he released a more lighthearted country effort, *Nashville Skyline*, which featured a very rural-looking Dylan on the cover, shot from below, holding his guitar by the neck, smiling broadly (a rarity, that), and tipping his hat. Johnny Cash also made a full-blown return to the upper echelons of American music with the success of his *At Folsom Prison* album, which catapulted him to well-deserved megastardom and allowed him to spread his mix of gospel, country, folk, and rockabilly to a national audience, thanks to a weekly ABC-TV variety show that found him bringing on guests from all realms of popular music who might not normally show up on network television (Bob Dylan, for starters).

From Texas in 1970 there emerged a solid class of new artists who were rejecting (not totally, but in large part) the country mainstream. One of those setting the pace in Austin was Dallas-born Michael Murphey (who later used his full name, Michael Martin Murphey, to distinguish him from the actor Michael Murphey), who was less an outsider than an insider with a saboteur's instincts. He didn't reject the establishment so much as figure out a way to maneuver within its framework while playing by rules partly of his own making. He wasn't merely testing the waters; he knew the waters well, having learned the nature of their ebb and flow at an early age. He was on the coffeehouse circuit playing original material by the time he was in high school and before going solo in his senior year performed with his friends Owen "Boomer" Castleman and Bob Jacobs in the Lost River Trio. By the time he was 18 he had his own TV show in Dallas.

Matriculating first to North Texas State College and then to UCLA in Westwood, California, Murphey continued writing and performing while studying classical literature, medieval and Renaissance history and literature, poetry, and creative writing. He started making a name for himself in the folk clubs, and in 1964 signed a songwriting contract with the publishing concern Sparrow Music. Another venture with Castleman ensued, this a band called New Survivors, whose other members were a bass player named John London, who had played on James Taylor's debut album, and another aspiring singer-songwriter named Michael Nesmith, who would find success not as a New Survivor but as a member of the Monkees (who recorded a catchy version of the Murphey-Castleman–penned "What Am I Doing Hangin' 'Round?"). The New Survivors recorded one unreleased album and disbanded. Murphey and Castleman then formed a duo, Travis and Boomer, which begat the Texas Twosome, who were joined by a third member, on banjo, a formidable instrumentalist named John McEuen, who became a founding member of the Nitty Gritty Dirt Band and remains a tireless champion of acoustic roots music.

It was in another duo with Castleman, the Lewis and Clark Expedition, that Murphey began to find not only a distinctive voice as a songwriter, but also a mission: to fuse country, folk, and pop and add to that blend the lore and poetry of the Old West, whose history had been one of the passions of his life. Murphey spent his childhood years riding horses on his grandfather's and uncle's ranches. As a youth he had absorbed his family's tall tales about the cowboys, Native Americans, notorious characters, and great deeds of the push westward and been enchanted by the cowboy songs his relatives sang to him. Out of this came a strong social conscience and a deep, abiding love of the land and nature, all of which informed his original material. After one unsuccessful album, though, the Lewis and Clark Expedition disbanded, Castleman going his way, Murphey retreating with his new bride to a bungalow in the pictur-esque mountains above the Mojave Desert.

The young man came down from the mountain in 1970 and moved to Austin, where he became one of the most popular artists in a burgeoning, fer-tile music scene that featured a raft of gifted singer-songwriter types working the Austin–San Antonio–Houston club circuit. Notable among the venues of choice were Austin's Armadillo World Headquarters, the Id, and the 11th Door; Houston's the Old Quarter, Sand Mountain, and the Jester. Murphey's co-conspirators included Willie Nelson, Jerry Jeff Walker, Guy Clark, the mercurial Townes Van Zandt, and bringing up the rear, a younger guard that included Houston-born Rodney Crowell and Steve. Murphey was referred to by the lo-cals as the "Cosmic Cowboy," and legend has it that a then-straitlaced Willie Nelson caught one of Murphy's shows at the Armadillo and was inspired to toss out his conservative suits and let his hair and his beard grow.[2]

But Murphey and the others weren't about just looking the part of out-siders. They were asserting a fresh view of country music. "When I went back to Texas and Austin in the '70s, everyone was pretty much listening to rock 'n' roll; but my idea, along with Willie, Waylon, and others, was to revive the songwriting ballad tradition of Texas and reconnect it to cowboy music," Mur-phey recalled in an interview with *The Performing Songwriter* magazine. "My music had been influenced by rock 'n' roll and pop music, too, as well as the modern country music of the day, but I couldn't get around the Western theme—it was all about loving the culture of my Texas roots. We were the hip, turned-on people of the time, but trying to salute tradition. This is what made Texas music different than anything else that was going on, because nothing else saluted tradition. Everybody else was trying to do something far out, and Texans were trying to reconnect with their roots in a turned-on way."[3]

In Houston the synergy between artist and audience was captured most vividly by Earl Willis in liner notes he penned for a live double album of a 1973 performance by Townes Van Zandt at a club called the Old Quarter, "sit-uated on the seedy side of downtown Houston … a sort of interface between various lifestyles in the late '60s and early '70s," according to Willis. "Here stoned-out freaks and professional types, blue jeans and blue collars, came together to enjoy the good music and cold beer along with other diversions that included free popcorn and a fresh air 'smoking' deck on the roof in full view of the county jails in the nearby courthouse.

"While the music varied widely in type and quality, when it was 'hap-pening,' it was superb. Of course, the musicianship was the basis for these memorable evenings, but the knowledgeability and the outspoken nature of the audience made it an important contributor to the event. Many a singer risked his songs against the 'passing of the hat'—in this case, a battered bed-pan—only to reap meager reward, indifference, and/or insult. On the other hand, when the music was right, the audience could be completely captivated. Perhaps this was why those performers who went on and graduated to more remunerative gigs still drifted back to play occasional sets at the Old Quarter. At any rate, one might find performers like Lightnin' Hopkins, Big Walter Jenkins, Jerry Jeff Walker, and Guy Clark playing in the little 38' × 38' room, and so it was that Townes Van Zandt came to play in July 1973."[4]

Having migrated to Houston with one dubious role model in Nick Fain, Steve almost immediately latched on to another in Fort Worth–bred wildcat, Townes Van Zandt. Born in March 1944 to an oil family, Van Zandt was handsome in a brooding poet's kind of way, with a thin visage, unkempt dark hair, and a mischievous smile. Two key events shaped his young life: first, when he was 12, he was forever changed by seeing Elvis Presley perform on *The Ed Sullivan Show*.

"That just flipped me out!" Van Zandt recalled in an article by John Kruth in *Sing Out* magazine. "He didn't quite seem real, you know?"[5]

Investigating the puzzle of Elvis inspired his second epiphany: "I realized you could make a living just playing the guitar. Elvis had all the money in the world and all the cars and girls he wanted."[6] Among the Christmas presents under the tree that year was Townes's first guitar, a gift from his father.

Much like Jack Earle, Townes's father moved the family around a lot, going from job to job, parking his brood for a while in Texas, traveling on to Illinois and Montana, landing briefly in Colorado, and stabilizing for two years in Faribault, Minnesota, where Townes spent his final two years of high school attending the private Shattuck Military Academy. According to Kruth, Townes's claims of receiving a rigorous prep school education at Shattuck must be taken with a grain of salt, given that he devoted considerable time and energy to being disruptive, with a peculiar fascination for demolishing dorm toilets with cherry bombs.[7]

As a young man and throughout his adult life, though, Van Zandt was given to pulling dangerous pranks on others and behaving irresponsibly. Those who were around him still tell the stories, and still laugh at the memory of how wild and free-spirited their friend was But Van Zandt was shadowed by emotional disorders: in his teens he had been diagnosed as manic-depressive with schizoid tendencies and had undergone electroconvulsive therapy that adversely affected his memory. In his sophomore year at the University of Colorado, his behavior became so aberrant that he underwent three months of insulin shock therapy, but he later told a journalist that his antics had merely been a ploy to get him out of the Selective Service draft at the height of the Vietnam War.[8] As an adult he became a heavy drinker and doper, sometimes going on weeklong benders.

At the same time, he began writing exquisite original songs, rife with startling, haunting imagery, a masterly, poetic use of the English language, and mesmerizing melodies and ambiance. From the early rock 'n' rollers he had admired and emulated, he moved on to the blues and worshiped at the altar of the prolific Texas giant Lightnin' Hopkins. He studied, and felt, the wrenching agonies Hank Williams described in his honky tonk masterpieces. Once he began playing live, he rolled out his original songs, the early ones being, as he said, "funny songs, not dirty songs, but funny barroom types just to get the audience."[9]

At the same time, the environment he was inhabiting spurred him to more somber meditations on wasted lives and lonely hearts. But it was hearing Bob Dylan's "The Times They Are a-Changin'" that called him to achievement. Now the song became the thing—the art of writing it, the integrity with which the craft was approached, and the quality of the content, the uncompromising honesty to say what you meant and to say it fearlessly but with a poet's vision, became his life's purpose. With that, he emerged transformed, an artist in full measure.

"You have to blow off everything else," he explained. "You have to blow off your family. You have to blow off comfort. You have to blow off money. You have to blow off security. You have to blow off your ego. You have to blow off everything except your guitar. You have to sleep with it. Learn how to tune it. And no matter how hungry you get, stick with it."[10]

Townes's uncompromising artistry, his offstage appetite for the edge, and his sweet demeanor beckoned others seeking to walk the same path. They saw in him someone who had an unflagging work ethic but had been touched by some mystical power that allowed him to operate on a higher plane than most mortals. Guy Clark was one of those, and he credits Van Zandt with inspiring him to begin writing songs and with transforming their music scene to one that cultivated original songwriters rather than interpreters plumbing the folk canon.

"I met Townes in Houston, we were both playing the clubs there," Clark says. "He had written about two songs, I think, and was hanging out with Jerry Jeff [Walker], married, supposed to be going to law school. Townes was bound and determined to have the blues. We got to be friends, and I really have to credit him because he is one of the main reasons I started writing. I had probably tried to write two songs before to no avail. But the first time I heard one of Townes's songs, it was so literate, you know, and yet musical. No one can be Townes, but you can use the same approach."[11]

As for the carousing and addictions that at the very least bordered on self-destruction, Van Zandt's friends were quick to put it all in perspective. Folk singer Eric Andersen observed that such behavior came with the artist's territory, was a common trait among creative types: "Whether they're writers, painters, or musicians, any incandescent talent or anybody who really feels deeply or sees far, within three feet of them you'll find a bottle or a vial," citing as examples of his assertion writers "from Proust … to Hemingway or Fitzgerald" and musicians from "Charlie Parker, John Coltrane, or Mozart.

"In Townes's case," he noted, "it was about maintenance. He wasn't getting high. He didn't enjoy it."[12]

To Guy Clark, Townes was a savvy addict who was purposeful in his pursuits. "Townes had a reputation for being wild, and he was, but I always had the impression he knew exactly what he was doing and how far it was goin' even when he was too drunk. He was always on the edge of control, but he'd lose it a few times. It was just his sense of humor, which was a real Texas sense of humor."[13]

Steve was so taken by Van Zandt that he became a half-assed valet, carrying Townes's guitar case around just so he could be close to him and absorb any stray wisdom he might offer. They were introduced to each other at the Old Quarter one night in 1972. Steve was playing the club, to an audience he recalls as numbering about eight, "and one of 'em was Townes," who kept up a steady stream of heckling banter between songs from his seat directly in front of the stage.

"I'm trying to play my set, and Townes keeps yelling, 'Play "The Wabash Cannonball!" And I'd just ignore him.

"He'd only yell between songs; he was nice enough to do that. So I'd play another song, and he'd yell, 'Play "The Wabash Cannonball!"' And I'd play another song, and he'd go, 'Play "The Wabash Cannonball!"'

"I finally had to admit that I didn't know the fuckin' 'Wabash Cannonball.' And he goes, 'You call yourself a folksinger and you don't know "The Wabash Cannonball"? So I played this song of his called 'Mr. Mudd and Mr. Gold' that has about 19 million words in it. And he shut up."[14]

Townes took Steve under his wing but didn't stop tormenting him with his "Texas humor." Speaking to an audience in Rotterdam in 1997, Steve explained how, during a period when he was making regular trips to Mexico, he gave Townes the use of his house in Tennessee with the stipulation that Steve would retain driveway rights, so he would have a place to park his truck when he returned home.

"During one of those trips Townes decided there was something lacking in my education," Steve said. "He asked me if I had ever read a book called *Bury My Heart at Wounded Knee*, which was written by Dee Brown. It was the first really honest book about what happened to Native Americans at the hands of my government. And I had to admit that I hadn't read it. And Townes went off and he dug around until he found his copy. He gave that and a copy of *War and Peace* and told me to go read them. Then he hid the keys to my truck. So I did some reading.

"After a while I finished them, and keep in mind that I'm living in a fucking truck, right, so there was a lot of batteries involved, but I got them finished. And he asked me what I thought about *Bury My Heart at Wounded Knee* and I told him I thought it was great—thanked him for making me read it. Then he said, 'What about *War and Peace*?' And I said 'Well, it was kind of long, but it was pretty cool.' And then he kept asking questions about *War and Peace*, always *War and Peace*, never *Bury My Heart at Wounded Knee*. And it dawned on me that Townes had never read fucking *War and Peace*. I think his plan was that I was gonna read it and I was gonna tell him about it. He said he never could get through the movie."[15]

Ultimately Guy Clark and Townes Van Zandt became the twin poles to which the other songwriters in the community gravitated. Both were dedicated to their craft, but whereas Townes saw his songs as being blessings bestowed by some higher power that summoned him unawares, Guy was more about the practical application of inspiration wedded to conscious craftsmanship. And that involved writing, rewriting, and editing until the finished composition (a product of painstaking editing, really) was precise, concise, right as rain.

As much alike as they were, they were also men of opposing ambitions: Townes, recalls John Lomax III, "just wanted to write songs and play 'em, that was the end of it."[16] Guy saw it a livelihood—get paid for what you do. Steve came down in both camps: no stranger by now to the temptations Townes embraced and even celebrated, and possessor of a growing résumé of unconventional behavior, he regarded Townes as his guide, even as he pursued the commercial success Guy was shooting for.

"Steve wanted sort of a Bob Dylan–sized success," says Lomax. "He wanted it all. He'd certainly paid the dues and he could entertain by himself, which, if you find an act like that, especially nowadays, you've really got something because most of them are a construct of one sort or another. I thought, This guy's going to make it if he doesn't explode or spontaneously combust."[17]

"You know what?" Rodney Crowell remarks. "In that early-'70s period, one thing I remember clearly is that I emulated Guy Clark and Steve emulated Townes Van Zandt. I say this with compassion, because for a young artist it's like, hey, emulate somebody until you get it yourself. I really thought that Steve built his persona off the way that Townes went about it. Ramblin', gamblin' Townes."[18]

II. "I took me a wife … "

In addition to working the Austin–San Antonio–Houston club circuit, Steve ventured further afield from time to time, most memorably when he signed on with a carnival and spent three months working in Colorado and New Mexico, always an outsider because "you're never really an insider there. There are people who have been with it for generations…. It's a completely different language."[19]

Apart from music, the abiding passion of Steve's life at this point was 16-year-old Sandra Jean Henderson, who had befriended him the first time he ran away from home. By all accounts, the passion, indeed the love, between them was deeply felt, but there were some serious obstacles to their romance blossoming—namely, her parents, who had money and an extreme disdain for the rakish, lower-class suitor—a musician, no less—sweeping their daughter off her feet.[20]

After Sandy turned 17 she and Steve moved in together, renting an apartment in a rough neighborhood near the Astrodome. Sandy got a job at Fox Fotos, Steve brought in a little cash from his gigs and from a part-time job at a car wash. Finally, Steve proposed to Sandy, she accepted, and wedding plans were afoot. They were married in June 1974 at Earle's Chapel, but the night before the wedding Sandy's father made an eleventh-hour effort to stymie the nuptials by offering Steve $5,000 to get out of town for good and leave his daughter behind.

Undeterred and insulted by Mr. Henderson's offer, Steve responded with a cutting "You don't think much of your daughter, do you? That's pretty cheap."[21]

After the wedding the newlyweds settled in Cibolo, near San Antonio, where they rented a house for $50 a month. Steve landed a regular gig playing the Roth Baron restaurant. For a while Steve's brother Mark lived with them after Jack and Barbara moved to Houston, where Barbara, now back in good health, re-entered the workforce at age 42, first by taking a job selling ads for real estate in the local newspaper, and then moving up to an apartment manager's job with Hall Properties. (She had worked in real estate when Steve and Mark were toddlers, as a secretary to a broker, and had started in sales when Jack was transferred to Louisiana. After Stacey was born she became a full-time housewife to the four Earle children rather than have to pay a housekeeper's salary that they could ill afford even with two incomes.) Steve's brother Mark joined the Air Force and was sent to Lackland Air Force Base in San Antonio for basic training. In November, a month after Mark's arrival at Lackland, Sandy went to Mexico with her family (Steve was not invited along) to help her sister get settled in a town where she had taken a student teaching position.[22]

Alone, more than a little miffed at Sandy for taking off on him, Steve let his wanderlust get the best of him and headed for Nashville, curious about the Music City scene and whether he could fit in. He stopped by to see his parents before he left, and Jack and Barbara appealed to him to reconsider.

"Why don't you wait?" Jack pleaded. "We'll get some money together for you."

"No, I'm ready to go," Steve answered. "I'll get a job right away."

Jack seized the opportunity to confront Steve yet again about his drug use. Although he and Barbara "both were pretty ignorant when it came to drugs," it was obvious that their son was indulging in some scary pursuits. Confronting Steve about it, though, was counterproductive.

"We had clashed a few times—it would get really ugly when I'd encounter him and face him up with it," Jack says. "We had a pretty good talk about it and he admitted that he was using drugs, marijuana, what have you, to some degree, about the time he went to Nashville. Of course, it was obvious that he was."

No matter Steve's bad habits, Jack and Barbara were not going to hang their son out to dry. Jack "scruffed up" $17 for his son—"it was one of our brokest times ever," he remembers—and Steve took off, making it to Jacksonville the first night, where he stayed with his grandmother, who was a dorm mother at a junior college. Before he left the next morning, she gave him $20.

"So he had an old guitar and $37 to get him to Nashville," Jack says.[23]

III. "And then he was just gone …"

Step out of the main gate at Randolph Air Force Base near San Antonio and the main drag of Universal City is right there. Now a growing community with a projected 2006 population of more than 16,000, it was considerably smaller in the early '70s, when Steve Earle was a semiregular visitor to a small burger joint where he would set up and perform for the customers dining al fresco on the patio. Although unscheduled, these performances soon became the talk of the town because Steve was a cut above most of the other musicians who would drop in to entertain the diners.

"In Universal City there wasn't much to do," recalls Jack Watson, who lived at Randolph Air Force Base, where his father was stationed and became friendly with Steve.[24] Steve befriended Watson, who was all of about 14 years old when they met through the auspices of Gary Tomberlin, one of Steve's closest childhood buddies and also a musician who played with Steve on occasion.

Watson remembers Universal City, which is located almost equidistant from Schertz, Converse, and Cibolo, as "one of these little three-stoplight towns. It's big now. It's one of those towns right outside an air base, it's a military town. And then there's all these country towns scattered around it. So we would all go into Universal City to the burger joint. We didn't even have McDonald's then; it was some little burger joint I can't even remember the name of, and Steve would play there. He'd show up at this one hangout, lot of young people would go there, and he was there. There's a grass area just outside the burger joint, and he'd just sit out there. There'd be sometimes 15, 20, 30 people sitting around, and we'd be listening to him. And there were other people that played well too, but he was pretty much the guy that everybody looked to already."

An aspiring guitarist himself, Watson was fascinated by Steve, and more than a little in awe of his artistry and spirit. He was spectral presence in town, never really close to any except Tomberlin, but somehow connected enough to know where the action was. Apart from the burger joint, he had a knack for materializing unannounced at parties being held out in the country, in huge open fields or at someone's home.

"He always knew where stuff was going on. He might show up and just play two songs," Watson says.

To Watson's ongoing fascination, Steve was forever on foot, hauling his guitar around wherever he went. "I never remember him having a car, ever. He'd walk. And he'd bring his guitar. It was not the Gibson that he plays now. He played a Martin, and it sounded good, man."

Neil Young's songs—and look—were a big part of Steve's modus operandi at the time. "I mean, this guy looked dead-on like Neil Young at the height of his popularity—and anybody that came close to that Neil Young look was scary to parents. And he was playing a lot of Crosby, Stills and Nash, Neil Young, and the Beatles. I remember Neil Young and the Beatles in particular. And he was real good at it, too. 'Cowgirl in the Sand' was one of his favorite songs then, and he did 'Ohio.' It was before the *Harvest* album."

And Yes, the English art-rock band, circa 1972, became an unlikely Steve Earle favorite too. "He liked everything," Watson emphasizes. "I remember when Yes came out—and he doesn't play Yes music—but he had this record under his arm, and me and this other guy are sitting in that burger joint, it's empty but me and him, and Steve comes practically running into this place and says, 'Have you heard this stuff!? You just won't believe it!' Just raving about this music, but I can't recall him ever coming close to playing anything like that; he just liked it. It was the *Fragile* album; he was totally freaked about it. I remember that clearly. He just thought it was something really magic."

More than anything, Watson, then an aspiring guitarist himself, remembers Steve for his mesmerizing interpretations of Beatles songs, especially "Eleanor Rigby." Steve came up with an arrangement on acoustic guitar that retained the lyrics exactly as they were sung on the Beatles' recording, but supplanted the song's orchestral parts with "a big, movable chord progression that would go up and down the neck and was real 'fat' sounding to cover the orchestra. It was like one of those three-finger power chords on the A and D strings. He would just move this thing around kind of like the metal guys do. That would cover that big part, and then when the singing came in he would start hitting the chords just like in the song. It was like a mix of what he had to do to cover the Beatles' band and then what he had to do to keep his singing covered with background, the right chords. That big introduction and big orchestrated part, that just all came out of thin air. It wasn't like anything the Beatles were doing, but it worked perfectly."

And to Watson Steve was a generous teacher. When asked how he pulled off this or that move on his instrument, "he'd show you the chords and how it worked. That's one of the reasons I really liked him, because he'd show you stuff and take some time. I was just learning. I could play some songs, but I wasn't even in the same ballpark with what he was doing.

"He was using alternate chords and tunings and all that early on. He knew five or six ways to play D, and just knew where to put 'em, where they'd be best suited—just like a jazz guy! He knew the voicing that he wanted. I learned a bunch from him that way. But he was already dropping his low-E string down to D and using different kinds of chords. You can play a country G chord with three fingers, or you can play it with four; and if you play it with four it just rings out like total Texas country, and it's fat. And they call that the 'Steve Earle G chord.' I've since met tons of people that know that, but he showed me that G chord and I thought, God, does that sound better! And then this movable C chord that you could make all kinds of other chords out of, he was using all that kind of stuff. And his right hand? The way he hit those strings with his pick? There wasn't nothing plain about it. His right hand is cool. He pulls a lot outta that guitar. Yes, he does. And I watched that a whole bunch. If you pay attention to what he's doing, you could pull a lot out too."

A couple of years into their friendship, Steve was "getting more into where he was gonna head," says Watson, meaning that Steve showed up for a club gig in Universal City "in a suit and a cowboy hat, his hair cut, looking like Hank Williams and playing that way—real hard-core country covers. Good, straightahead, three-chord country songs. But that right hand was just pumpin' 'em and makin' 'em strong. His voice was starting to go pretty hard-core Texas too—he started getting a big accent. There was always a little bit of an accent there, but I think he got up there in Austin running around with those Texas guys and became part of them."

On one memorable occasion during this transition to traditional country, Steve played "a little drunk bar with a corner stage." Appropriately enough, "he was real drunk, and I'd never seen him real drunk before. I'd seen him drink, and we'd pass a joint, but never where he wasn't like his regular self.

"He was doing a great job. The music was fantastic. I remember we stayed there the whole evening."

With Steve's blood alcohol level rising exponentially with each passing hour?

"Oh, yeah, people were worried about him, you know how girls can be— 'Oh, I'm so worried about him being so drunk,' and I'm just thinking, God, this is good shit, y'know. That just made it even better. We sat right in front of him, a couple of us guys that knew each other."

Apart from alcohol, it was, in Watson's recollection, "pills here and there, it was all common, you know," and not exclusive to Steve, who partook in the extracurricular activities with as much vigor as anyone. "Drinking, some pills, lot of hallucinogens—mescaline, LSD, everybody did it. It was just common.

But as far as things like cocaine, heroin, needles—never. Never. It was never talked about. It was never brought out. And we were all younger than Steve too. And he has a good conscience. I don't see him doing that to younger people, and I think that's why he didn't bring it up around us. I don't recall him ever encouraging us to do anything. He liked to smoke reefer, but beyond that, no. No. And usually it was him bumming the reefer off of us; believe me, I can't recall him ever even pulling out a joint."

Even without stimulants, Steve was "real high-energy all the time" and forever telling anyone who would listen about his game plan for making it in the music business. "He was just dead set," Watson recalls. "He would always talk like he was just gonna do it. It's like there was never any question about it. Never complained about nothing. I was not in his super inner circle or anything to know everything he ever said, but I never heard him complain about anything. He was always talking about what he was gonna do next—'I'm gonna play here,' 'I'm gonna learn this,' 'I'm gonna go meet this guy.' Always had something going."

Rather than Nashville, though, it was Austin that was on Steve's radar when he crossed paths with Watson. Austin was "the next step. I don't know what he was thinking, but that was definitely the next step he was gonna take— he was making trips up there. This is when Michael Murphey was playing around; Jerry Jeff Walker was coming on real hard; Willie was starting his Concert in the Hills. That sound was getting kind of big; it was taking off. People liked it."

True to his word, Steve went to Austin, "and he'd be gone longer and longer.

"And then," Watson says, "he was just gone."

Waylon and Willie and the Boys

I. The Boys

By the time Steve arrived in Nashville seemingly for good in 1974, his contemporaries in the Texas scene were finding their way into the national arena. Townes Van Zandt had been recording since 1968, beginning with his debut album, *For the Sake of the Song*. The album was produced by Jack Clement, who had cut his teeth in the Sun Studios in Memphis as Sam Phillips's house engineer starting in 1956 and was the guiding presence behind the scenes (including as a writer) on Johnny Cash's remarkable early recordings. Between 1968 and 1972 Van Zandt cut six albums, none of them hits, some of them freighted with ill-considered arrangements, but each and every one containing a few astonishing performances of beautiful, intriguing original songs. Among these gems: "For the Sake of the Song," "Tecumseh Valley," "Our Mother the Mountain" (the title track of his second album), and a vividly rendered tale of two enigmatic outlaws who meet uncertain fates, "Pancho and Lefty." Despite his prolific output, Van Zandt remained virtually unknown outside his circle of friends and fans in the Texas scene.

In 1970 the Nitty Gritty Dirt Band, cofounded by Michael Martin Murphey's former bandmate John McEuen, cut Jerry Jeff Walker's laconic ode to down-and-out hoofer Bill "Bojangles" Robinson, whom Walker had met in a New Orleans drunk tank. The single "Mr. Bojangles" entered the charts in early '72 and eventually rose to No. 9, making it the first Top 10 pop hit to emerge from the new generation of Texas songwriters. In 1972 Murphey himself made a splash with his first album on A&M, *Geronimo's Cadillac*. The title track (a Top 40 hit, peaking at No. 37), which referenced the ill treatment of Native Americans, brought considerable media attention Murphey's way and introduced music fans nationwide to the fertile new scene in east Texas. Handsome and literate to boot, Murphey was the image of the Lone Star State's new breed, his public persona sealed by the title of his second album, 1973's *Cosmic Cowboy Souvenir*. Three years later, a year after Steve put down roots in Nashville, Murphey hit it big with "Wildfire," a story song inspired by tales of ghost horses he had heard in his youth. The single was a smash, reaching No. 3 on the pop charts and dominating radio playlists coast to coast. Ultimately its success hurt Murphey critically, as the song's soft-pop arrangement, triumphant, catchy chorus, and Murphey's clear, soaring tenor disguised the tale's inherent mysticism; in the late '70s, when his pop career was foundering, he began doing solo shows, accompanying himself on guitar and piano, and in this stark setting, "Wildfire" took on a new gravitas, when it could be heard for the eerie invocation that it was.

Jerry Jeff Walker had been on record even longer than Townes Van Zandt, first recording for the Vanguard label in 1967 as part of the folk-rock group Circus Maximus. His debut album was issued in 1968 by Atco, its title track being "Mr. Bojangles." Born Ronald Clyde Crosby in upstate New York, he had moved to Austin in 1971 and he says, "the first time I set foot in Texas, particularly in Austin, I knew I was home."[1] The Nitty Gritty Dirt Band's hit with "Mr. Bojangles" did some good for his bank account and his career, as he signed with Decca/MCA in 1972 and released a self-titled album that included a powerful rendering of Guy Clark's dramatic tale of urban desperation, "L.A. Freeway." In 1973 he hit a high-water mark with a live album, *Viva Terlingua*, recorded in one night at a club in Luckenbach, Texas, with Walker and a freewheelin' Lost Gonzo Band simply roaring, unfettered and unholy, ripping it up on some Walker originals (including the timeless "Sangria Wine"), and bringing down the house with searing covers of Guy Clark's "Desperadoes Waiting for a Train," Michael Martin Murphey's "Backslider's Wine," and a song he made an anthem, "Up Against the Wall, Redneck Mother," by another young Texas songwriter just starting to make a name for himself, Ray Wylie Hubbard.

From a commercial standpoint, no new Texas-bred artist made more of an impact than Kris Kristofferson, who was a Rhodes scholar, son of a two-star army general, and former helicopter pilot in Vietnam with the Army Rangers. Kristofferson's ambition was to write literature of the lasting kind; during his stay at Oxford he had produced an essay on one of his chief literary influences, the poet William Blake. He took a detour, though, and came to Nashville, where he promptly knocked around for four years—working part of that time as a janitor at Columbia Records—before he got a break when Roger Miller cut his song "Me and Bobby McGee." He was still working as a janitor when he recorded his debut album for the Columbia-distributed Monument label. When the album started selling, a top Columbia executive reamed out his staff for letting Kristofferson get away to another label. To this another executive was reported to have protested, "But sir, he wasn't a very good janitor."[2]

But he was an inspired, fearless songwriter, and once he got rolling, he became a juggernaut, arguably in his early years the most important songwriter of his day apart from Bob Dylan. Artists everywhere were clamoring for Kristofferson songs, and the hits started rolling in: "Sunday Morning Coming Down" (Johnny Cash), "For the Good Times" (Ray Price), "Help Me Make It Through the Night" (Sammi Smith), "Why Me, Lord" (Kris himself), "Loving Her Was Easier (Than Anything I'll Ever Do Again)" (Waylon Jennings), and "Me and Bobby McGee" (Roger Miller, Janis Joplin, Waylon).

"He brought a new maturity and sophistication to country lyrics," was Waylon Jennings's assessment, "an explicitness to the verse-singalong chorus-verse-singalong chorus-bridge-verse two-choruses-and-out that was the standard country fare. Spelled X-plicit, meaning sex ... his songs were undeniably poetry, and he taught us how to write great poems. He changed the way I thought about lyrics ..."[3]

II. Waylon and Willie and ...

Nineteen seventy-four was a tumultuous year for country music, not least of all for a pocket rebellion by some of the established stars of the day who were outraged over the Country Music Association's (CMA) awarding of its Female Singer of the Year honor to the wispy-voiced Australian Olivia Newton-John, whose music had only the faintest of references to country and whose voice betrayed no country flavor whatsoever.

According to Bill C. Malone in his essential *Country Music USA*: "About fifty people met at George Jones and Tammy Wynette's home to create an organization that would 'preserve the identity of country music' and would be confined solely to entertainers (as opposed to promoters, record merchandisers, and other industry people). In the few years of its existence, ACE insisted that country music awards should go only to those people who considered themselves country, asserting that some musicians were merely opportunists who had hopped on country's burgeoning bandwagon and that many radio stations (such as New York City's WHN) adhered to a narrow selection of dubious country material. ACE encouraged radio stations everywhere to expand their playlists, and it sponsored concerts which were designed to give ignored performers opportunities to be heard."[4]

Ineffective and short-lived, ACE was seen as exclusionary and hypocritical. As Malone notes: "An organization that included Tammy Wynette as a charter member and Barbara Mandrell as one of its presidents could hardly be described as traditionalistic. It was easy for critics to argue, therefore, that ACE was primarily concerned with fostering a closed community among country musicians and that it was composed of jealous and parochial individuals who were trying to protect themselves from newcomers to the country field."[5]

As far as protesting the encroachment of pop on traditional country music, the most compelling arguments came from a select few artists, not in the form of an organized group like ACE, but rather by their insistence on doing it their way when they got into the recording studio. Bobby Bare had been in the forefront of artists demanding greater control over the content and presentation of their music, but it was Willie Nelson and Waylon Jennings—the former a Texan regrouping in Austin, the latter a Texan meeting the enemy from within its own gates in Nashville—who steered the outsiders into the commercial mainstream with stunning success.

Willie and Waylon were supremely suited to lead the contrarians. Both had labored long and hard in the '60s at major labels and come away with not much to show as solo artists. As a songwriter, Nelson had contributed mightily to the country canon with monuments on the order of "Crazy," "Hello Walls," "Night Life," and "Funny (How Time Slips Away)." As a solo artist, he had experienced middling success at best: between 1962 and 1974, recording for four major labels—Liberty, RCA, Monument, and Atlantic—he had 25 singles charted, but only two Top 10 hits, both coming in 1962 ("Touch Me" and "Willingly," the latter a duet with Shirley Collie). In 1973 he signed with Atlantic and delivered a bold stroke in the form of the album *Shotgun Willie*, which reflected his and the Austin scene's experiments in fusing traditional country—or infusing it—with elements of rock, pop, Southern soul, Western swing, and folk- and blues-style storytelling. It was fair to say that Willie, a generation ahead of the new breed in Austin, was on more intimate terms with his influences, being old enough to have seen, for example, a still-vital Bob Wills and the Texas Playboys up close and personal. *Shotgun Willie* also contained "Whiskey River" by Johnny Bush and Paul Stroud, which became one of Willie's signature songs and a concert favorite. More important, it foreshadowed his emergence five years later as an interpreter nonpareil with the Booker T. Jones–produced platinum blockbuster *Stardust*, comprised of Willie's folk, country, and jazz spins on pop standards from the pens of such great American songwriters as Irving Berlin, Hoagy Carmichael, and the Gershwins. He followed *Shotgun Willie* with a more challenging album, *Phases and Stages*, a concept album centered on the little murders of a failed marriage, with one side devoted to the wife's story, the other to the husband's. The album was suffused with melancholy and featured one of the most searing kiss-off songs ever penned in "Pretend I Never Happened" (a tale told from the wife's point of view); "It's Not Supposed to Be That Way," a blunt, mournful dissection of love gone awry; and, as the penultimate track, a deceptively warm waltz treatment of an overview of the soured relationship titled "Heaven and Hell." Disappointed and befuddled by the direction Willie was taking, Atlantic dropped him, but Columbia was there to catch him, and in 1975 was rewarded for the signing by Willie's daring *Red-Headed Stranger* concept album. Produced by Willie (totally in Texas, at Autumn Sound in Arlington, and mixed partly at his own Pedernales Studio in Austin), and based on his tale of a preacher who murders his wife and her lover, the album featured beautiful, poignant songs such as Fred Rose's "Blue Eyes Crying in the Rain" and Hank Cochran's "Can I Sleep in Your Arms"; a somber acoustic guitar-and-piano instrumental treatment of the venerable hymn "Just As I Am"; stark, acoustic-based arrangements; seconds-long snippets of expository numbers Willie wrote himself ("Denver" and the instrumental "O'er the Waves"); and some ruminative, bluesy singing on Willie's part that lent the whole affair an air of epic tragedy.

Bruce Lundvall, a record man in the classic tradition—meaning he had ears—had signed Willie to Columbia but was nonplussed when he first heard the record. Willie had been under contract for only three weeks when his manager, Neil Rushen, with Waylon Jennings in tow, brought the finished version to his office. After hearing it through, Lundvall told them, "This is pretty fascinating."[6]

In his liner notes to the 2000 reissue of the album, Chet Flippo documented Lundvall's account of how the meeting then unfolded: "It's not what I expected for the first record, and it's more like a collector's piece, in a way, in terms of its commercial potential, I thought, when I heard it. With that, Waylon jumped up and said, 'That's what this is all about. That's what Willie's music is all about. He doesn't need a producer. This is the way it should go.' I said, 'Okay, okay, hold on.' I said, 'Let me send a copy down to [Nashville CBS head] Billy Sherrill down in Nashville and I'll take a copy home and we'll talk on Monday.' So I took the album home and played it all weekend. I couldn't stop playing it and ended up loving it. On Monday I called Billy. He said, 'Oh, man, this is not a commercial record, you know?' I said, 'Billy, I love it, it's a very special record. But you're probably right, but this is something Willie really wants to do.' So Billy says, 'Yeah, man, this is what Willie's all about, so let's put the record out.' Which we did. I had a meeting with the entire Columbia staff. I played the album, after setting it up with this long speech about how special this is, it's an artistic endeavor, I said it may not be an important commercial record by Willie, but it'll be a valuable catalog album. And everyone thought it was nice ... and now, three million albums later ..."[7]

Born in 1937 and raised in Littlefield, Texas, Waylon Jennings had come into the business as a disc jockey after dropping out of school in 1953. That he should adapt so easily to the cross-pollination of styles that was going down in the late '60s and early '70s is unsurprising in light of his résumé: he had been a friend to Buddy Holly and member of Holly's last band (he gave up his seat on Holly's tragic final flight to the Big Bopper and suffered near-debilitating depression for a couple of years afterward). In 1964 he was signed to A&M Records and produced by the label's cofounder Herb Alpert, who heard in him the makings of a pop-folk artist, a fusion that informed his second A&M single, a lilting, evocative interpretation of Canadian folk icon Ian Tyson's "Four Strong Winds." Looking for a follow-up to his hit single "Detroit City," RCA recording artist Bobby Bare heard Waylon's "Four Strong Winds" and took it to Chet Atkins, one of the architects of the pop-fueled Nashville Sound, along with producer Owen Bradley, who had perfected his own country-pop fusion most memorably with Patsy Cline. Bare cut "Four Strong Winds," with Jerry Reed expanding on the acoustic guitar lick Waylon had played on his version, and it became one of the biggest country hits of his career. Atkins liked the crossover potential he heard in Jennings's voice and approach, and signed him to RCA. Over the next nine years he made regular appearances in the upper echelons of the country charts—1966's "(That's What You Get) For Lovin' Me" was his first Top 10 hit; 1967's "The Chokin' Kind" went Top 10; "Walk On Out of My Mind" was a Top 5 hit in 1968, the same year he ascended to No. 2—for five weeks straight—with "Only Daddy That'll Walk the Line," which couldn't dislodge Jeannie C. Riley's controversial smash "Harper Valley P.T.A." from the top spot; a cover of Chuck Berry's "Brown Eyed Handsome Man" peaked at No. 3 in 1970.

Like Willie, Waylon became deeply disenchanted with the Nashville system and its hard-boiled rules about what was and wasn't right for country music (even to the point of pulling a pistol on staff producer Danny Davis to express what he thought of Davis's dictatorial style[8]). Like Willie, he could hear a richer, more resonant—and more relevant—country music sculpted from non-country influences and being shaped in the studio by the artists and their bands, rather than by staff producers and the same core group of session players playing the same licks session after session.

"Our vision of country music didn't have any shackles attached to it," Waylon said. "We never said we couldn't do something because it would sound like a pop record, or it would be too rock 'n' roll. We weren't worried that country music would lose its identity, because we had faith in its future and character …

"To be real. To sing the truth, regardless of whether we were walking contradictions or not. We wanted the freedom to use any instruments we wanted, or not use them, whichever the song itself demanded. Why limit yourself? Country music is the feeling between the singer and the song. The instruments are only there to help."[9]

After his manager negotiated a new contract with RCA that gave Waylon the creative control he sought, the artist got to work on a long-awaited sound signature of his own devising, accompanied by his seasoned road band the Waylors (drummer Richie Albright, rhythm guitarist Larry Whitmore, Lee Miller, steel guitarist Ralph Mooney, Billy Ray Reynolds). From Steve Young came a rugged title track, "Lonesome, On'ry and Mean," and filling out the album were tunes that fit Waylon's broad-based vision of country music, such as a cover of Danny O'Keefe's laid-back 1972 pop hit "Good Time Charlie's Got the Blues"; Austin stalwart Mickey Newberry's "San Francisco Mabel Joy"; a rousing take on Roy Hamilton's enduring 1961 R&B gem "You Can Have Her," which was released as a single and peaked in the Top 10; and Kris Kristofferson's "Me and Bobby McGee," which had already been a hit—the final one—for another Texas product, blues singer Janis Joplin. Released in 1973, *Lonesome, On'ry and Mean* sold marginally better than its predecessors, but Waylon had made a larger point about doing it his way. Three songs on the album had been recorded before Waylon's new contract went into effect: "Gone to Denver," a Waylon–Johnny Cash cowrite, produced by Waylon's nemesis Danny Davis; and two by another RCA staff producer, Ronnie Light, namely, "Lay It Down" (with studio musicians and Waylon's peerless pedal steel player Ralph Mooney on the track) and Willie Nelson's "Pretend I Never Happened," the latter being released as a single and peaking at No. 6 in 1972.

All this was mere prelude to the pivotal event in Waylon's reinvented career and in this particular transitional stage in country music history. An aspiring, pudgy-faced Texas songwriter named Billy Joe Shaver had been banging around the business for a few years without much happening. Kris Kristofferson was on to him early, and in 1971 cut Shaver's "Good Christian Soldier" on his *Silver-Tongued Devil* album. The year Billy Joe came into Waylon's life for good, 1973, Kristofferson had followed up by producing Billy Joe's debut album, titled after one of the songwriter's winsome masterpieces, *Old Five and Dimers Like Me*. Billy Joe had been gently importuning Waylon for some time about giving his songs a listen, and Waylon had always found an excuse to avoid him. Finally, one night in a studio, Billy Joe laid it on the line to Waylon: "I got these songs and if you don't listen to them, I'm going to kick your ass right here in front of everybody."[10]

Holding his tongue and his temper, Waylon replied that he would listen to one, and if he didn't like it, they were going to part ways for good. Billy Joe proceeded to roll out "Old Five and Dimers," then another song, and another song, and another song, "a whole sackful of songs, and by the time he ran out of breath, I wanted to record all of them."

Thus was born *Honky Tonk Heroes*—an album produced almost entirely by Waylon and his contrarian running buddy Tompall Glaser and comprised of 10 songs, all but one written or cowritten by Shaver. ("We Had It All," by Donnie Fritts and Troy Seals, produced by Waylon and Ken Mansfield, was a lovely heartbreaker drenched in strings, kind of a sore thumb on an album of otherwise medium-cool, basic honky tonk band numbers, but it became a Top 30 single.)

"The only way you could understand Billy Joe was to hear his whole body of work," Waylon said by way of explaining how he arrived at the concept for *Honky Tonk Heroes*. "Billy Joe talked the way a modern cowboy would speak, if he stepped out of the West and lived today. He had a command of Texas lingo, his world as down to earth and real as the day is long, and he wore his Lone Star birthright like a badge. We all did."[11]

If it weren't for the Western feel of some of the songs, *Honky Tonk Heroes* would have sounded like a folk album. Jennings favored soft, lilting arrangements on Shaver's intimate, well-drawn portraits of down-and-outers and loners/losers making one more stand for something worth fighting for. The title song had an old-timey feel with a fiddle sawing away behind Jennings's precise, gently rhythmic vocal, until, midway, he picks up the tempo and the song rocks out to its end, with a snarling guitar, a moaning harmonica, and a steady pulsing drumbeat driving things to a big finish. "Old Five and Dimers

(Like Me)" was cast as a honky tonk heartbreaker, complete with a weeping pedal steel, but otherwise minimal instrumentation, with Jennings taking care to showcase the heart-wrenching tale of a man who's finding out that "everything ran out on me," in lyrics full of scintillating internal rhymes and plain-spoken insight into a desperate condition.

In the studio an interesting drama played out when Billy Joe took exception to Waylon's reconstruction of some of his tunes; he was especially teed off about the transformation taking place in "Honky Tonk Heroes." And he told Waylon about it, accusing him of "messin' with the melodies … screwin' around with the tune." Finally, Waylon, already a bit tense in the face of this opportunity to prove himself true to his word about what he could do if the RCA brass would just leave him alone, laid down the law to Billy Joe, to wit: "You are going to get your ass out of here and stop bugging me. I love your songs, but I'm starting not to like you worth a damn. Stand outside the studio, go for a walk, watch some television. I don't care what you do. When I get through, you can come back in. If you don't like it, I'll change it and do it another way, but now get the hell on the other side of that door."[12]

A truce was struck, a lifelong friendship ensued, and, as Rich Kienzle observed in the liner notes for the album's 1999 reissue, "after *Honky Tonk Heroes*, nothing was the same. Over a quarter century later, it stands as the landmark album that made Waylon Jennings Waylon."[13]

And to seal the deal, in 1974 Waylon's self-produced *This Time* album gave him his first No. 1 single, the title song.

"Suddenly we didn't need Nashville," Waylon said. "Nashville needed us."[14]

A beloved Nashville country music columnist, Hazel Smith, when asked in a radio interview what she would call the music being made by Nashville's new wild bunch, termed it "outlaw music," and the name stuck.

For all their stodginess sometimes, the labels can be crafty marketers. Seeing the way young people were embracing the rough-cut music being championed by Waylon and Willie, RCA Nashville President Jerry Bradley suggested to Waylon that he put together an album of songs cut by his friends, "an Outlaw anthology," according to Waylon.[15] RCA had the rights to Willie's back catalog; Waylon of course was in the fold and he demanded Tompall Glaser be included. Of the tracks Jennings assembled, some were a decade old, so he updated the vocals, added some new harmonies. He pulled some cuts from Willie's RCA album *Yesterday's Wine*; he included a 1970 duet he had cut with his wife Jessi Colter on "Suspicious Minds" and included Jessi's yearning "I'm Looking for Blue Eyes." Willie came in and cut duets with Waylon on "Heaven and Hell" and "Good Hearted Woman," and during the latter "was so high when he was doing his part that he was dancing a jig out in the studio."[16] Glaser cut an energized version of Jimmie Rodgers's "T for Texas," and from Glaser's MGM catalog Waylon licensed a thumping version of Shel Silverstein's "Put Another Log on the Fire." "Honky Tonk Heroes" was a natural choice for such a collection, and Waylon added a new cut of his own, "My Heroes Have Always Been Cowboys" (which would be a No. 1 hit for Willie in 1980).

Released in 1976 under the title *Wanted: The Outlaws*, the cover was a mock wanted poster of the Old West type with drawings of Willie, Waylon, and Tompall, all bearded and scruffy. The public ate it up: the album conquered the country charts, crossed over to pop in days when that was a rare event, and when the dust settled, *Wanted: The Outlaws* had sold more a million copies, the first country album to go platinum.

"To us Outlaw meant standing up for your rights, your own way of doing things," was Waylon's definition of the movement of the moment, adding: "It may have been why we didn't mind being lumped together, though we were all unmistakably individual. There's nobody like Willie Nelson. There's nobody like Kris, or Tompall, or Billy Joe. There's really nobody like me, and I know that. There's a loneliness and a pride there. Outlaws or in-laws, under the same roof that made us family."[17]

Phases and Stages

I. Alpha Male Ascending, V1.0

Steve returned from Nashville only to announce to his wife and family that he was moving back there. Sandy stayed behind, delaying her departure until Steve could get settled and find work.

But it was December, and the construction business, as Steve discovered, was slow. He wound up taking a job in a pizza parlor and finally saving enough money to send for Sandy more than a month later. (He also famously got work as an extra in Robert Altman's film *Nashville*, which gave him access to free food and drink whenever he was on the set.) Steve had been living on various friends' and acquaintances' floors and couches, but thanks to Townes Van Zandt and Guy Clark, he had a proper place for him and Sandy to stay. Townes and Guy had introduced him to a friend of theirs, fellow Texan John Lomax III, who had met both artists in Austin and would soon be managing Townes but was now making a living as a writer and publicist. Lomax had been hearing about Steve well ahead of his arrival at his home, thanks to Townes touting him at every opportunity. When Lomax heard Steve's songs for the first time, he thought Steve indeed merited Townes's high opinion of him—he's quoted in *Hardcore Troubadour* as saying, "He could have cut a record back then."[1] Indeed, Lomax was not the only person who ran into Steve in those early days who heard him say he would have a record deal before he was 21.

Not that Steve was in the wrong place at the wrong time to realize his dream. The energy and excitement the Outlaws generated had brought young people into the country fold, and the results were showing at the cash register: during the '70s country music would amount to a $500-million business in the $3.5-billion domestic record market.[2] The country industry was growing up and evolving.

Reflecting the emergence of feminism in America, female country artists were picking up on the self-sufficiency projected by their venerated predecessors such as Patsy Cline and Kitty Wells and asserting more control over their careers as well. Dolly Parton, Tammy Wynette, and Loretta Lynn were the pacesetters—great singers who also wrote their own songs and asserted themselves in the studio rather than simply go where the producer pointed them. The groundwork these women laid would eventually produce an industry in which females had a greater say in the shape of their recording careers and also assumed key roles at the labels, not only in publicity departments but in A&R, promotion, and marketing—and even at the very top of the roster, as when former publicist Evelyn Shriver was named president of Asylum's Nashville division. To this date, only as producers and managers are women woefully underrepresented, although an increasing number of distaff artists—from veterans such as Parton to younger phenoms such as Deana Carter (daughter of Fred Carter, Jr., one of Nashville's most sought-after sessions guitarists in the '60s and '70s)—are proving themselves to be as savvy behind the board as any male producer.

As artists enjoyed the fruits of the control Willie and Waylon had fought for, so did the old guard of producers who had helped build the modern Nashville recording industry begin to give way to young lions who were raised on rock 'n' roll but deeply respectful of country music's history. The pioneers and visionaries included Owen Bradley, who had discovered and/or produced Patsy Cline, Kitty Wells, Ernest Tubb, and Brenda Lee, among others, and had built the first modern recording studio in town. Chet Atkins, a masterful guitar player who ruled the roost at RCA, shared with Bradley a pop background with which he reinvigorated early-'60s country music by drawing on pop styles and arrangements—including strings—to create the Nashville Sound. Ken Nelson, the gifted staff producer at Capitol in Los Angeles, steered the hard-edged Bakersfield Sound of Buck Owens and Merle Haggard into the mainstream. These producers, along with Columbia's venerable Don Law, were gradually ceding control to young men determined to take the music into a new era: Billy Sherrill at CBS, who fused honky tonk and pop strings to create a "countrypolitan" sound that was making stars of Tammy Wynette, George Jones, and Johnny Paycheck in the early '70s; Larry Butler at Capitol, who would help shape the Kenny Rogers juggernaut of the late '70s; Mercury's Jerry Kennedy, a former session guitarist who had played with Elvis Presley; the colorful Chips Moman, whose legend was rooted in Memphis in the '60s, where his high-profile projects had included producing the 1969–70 sessions that put Elvis Presley back in the game in a major way; former Texas rockabilly artist Jimmy Bowen, who had built quite an impressive résumé in Los Angeles, where he produced major '60s hits for Frank Sinatra and Dean Martin. It seemed there was no more a shortage of outstanding producers than there was of new artist blood, and, as John Lomax III observed in *Nashville: Music City USA*, "It wouldn't also be out of the question to presume that these men were able to sense the upcoming changes in the popular music field."[3]

So a young man brimming with confidence to the point of obnoxiousness, in some estimations, and having the talent to walk it like he talks it, might be emboldened by his prospects in Nashville, circa 1974–75. The locus of his social life in those days was Bishop's Pub on West End Avenue near Vanderbilt University, and Guy and Susanna Clark's house, which eventually succeeded Rodney Crowell's as the place where songwriters and pickers would hang and test out their new material and, to some extent, each other. Willie, Waylon, Kristofferson, and their Outlaw bunch were notorious for ingesting copious amounts of amphetamines and cocaine and for being as likely to light a joint as a cigarette. For the Bishop's Pub crowd it was strictly "cheap whiskey and marijuana," according to Rodney Crowell, a Houston native five years Steve's senior, who had preceded Steve to Nashville by two years, arriving from Texas in 1972 and almost immediately insinuating himself into the scene at the Pub, thanks to Townes Van Zandt and Guy Clark befriending him. "Nobody had any money" for any of the more exotic drugs the Outlaws favored, he said.[4]

For nearly a year Crowell and Steve crossed paths at Bishop's Pub and became friendly. Rodney's first sighting of him remains a vivid memory.

"Skinny kid in a big black felt cowboy hat. When Steve first showed up he was a skinny cowboy; it was like he stepped right out of a Cormac McCarthy novel—when I was reading *Blood Meridian*, the kid in *Blood Meridian* made me think of Steve. Edgy. Finger in the light socket. Just this skinny kid from San Antonio. And obviously a real artist. He had a guitar-playing style then that was distinctly Steve's guitar-playing style. I could identify Steve's guitar playing anywhere; he has a certain way he plays that G chord and a certain way he uses his hand to deaden the strings that he was using all the way back then."[5]

But there was more; there was a certain subtle one-upmanship going on between the Texas troubadours, a complex game rooted in the genetic makeup of the Lone Star State's male population, especially those with an artistic bent. This ritual could not have been better cultivated than it was in the bacchanal that was Bishop's Pub.

A Conversation with Rodney Crowell

"That kind of Texas competition is not so much about ambition as it is about who's the alpha male."

What kind of place was Bishop's Pub?

It was an open-mike, pass-the-hat-folk club. I called it a combination open mike and soup kitchen. It was really a good hang there. A guy named Tim Bishop had a corner pub—it's now a restaurant called the Tin Angel—but it was Bishop's Pub back then. Tim had a '70s unisex hair salon on the left side and Bishop's Pub on the right. You come in and you sign up, you get your 20 minutes, and you pass the hat, and that was gas money and breakfast. I made friendly with Tim Bishop's girlfriend, and I'd come in the back door and she'd hand me a pitcher of beer and a hamburger. There was this guy, kind of cowboy singer, horse trader, guitar slinger from Colorado. He was the emcee. It was a hoot, man. Bishop's Pub was, in my estimation, as close as Nashville ever got to Greenwich Village. Me and a guy named Skinny Dennis Sanchez [*author's note: Skinny Dennis was immortalized in Guy Clark's song "L.A. Freeway"*] and another guy named Richard Dobson had this house where Townes Van Zandt and Guy Clark and those guys crashed. At Bishop's Pub there were sword swallowers, trapeze artists; John Hiatt, David Olney, Townes would play there on occasion, Guy on occasion. That's the first place I ever saw Steve.

Did your first sighting of Steve coincide with your first contact with him, or did you just observe him?

I sort of observed him. I don't know if we fell into conversation. He was ramblin' as much then as he would be later on. It was like, gee, he had all this energy, this really frenetic energy. But I remember him playing this song called "Ben McCullough" and another called "Darlin' Commit Me and I'll Play Parcheesi All Day with My Looney Friends." [*Note: As "Darlin' Commit Me" the song was one of Steve's early album cuts as a writer when it was covered by Slim Pickens on his self-titled 1977 album for Blue Canyon Records.*] Steve might have been 19, 20 years old then, and it was instantly obvious that he could write. So you know, it's that persona and the fact that he was a poet, a young poet. He just fell right into the fabric of what Bishop's Pub was.

How long a period of time was Bishop's Pub Bishop's Pub in the way you knew it?

As long as I lived in Nashville, 'cause I headed to California ... I bailed about the end of 1974, and '72, '73 Bishop's Pub was at its peak—'74 too. I'm not so sure that Steve wasn't in there—I know Steve was around and hanging around my house, and we actually had become conversational and friendly in 1974. But

I'd almost swear it was the latter part of '73 that Steve showed up around there. Jerry Jeff would come around now and again. I'll tell you who else was at Bishop's Pub, was "Please Come to Boston"—Dave Loggins. Dave was in and out of there. I want to think Lucinda [Williams] was in and out of there, 'cause I remember Lucinda was playing this song called "The Girl with the Watering Can" about a Renoir painting, and the first time I heard it it made me find out who this Renoir guy was. So in some ways Lucinda introduced me to Impressionist painting.

Did you know Townes before you came to Nashville?

Didn't know him before. I made Guy Clark's acquaintance and became friendly with Guy and his wife Susanna, and Townes was really close to both of them. He was in and out. Townes was so enigmatic. Townes was not as accessible as Guy, but incredibly enigmatic.

You said you got conversational and friendly with Steve fairly quickly. Did you guys talk about your aspirations? Did Steve articulate what he was going after?

No, that ain't the Texas way.

What is the Texas way?

It's more competitive than that. It's more instinctual. As I've gotten older and tried to cultivate the craft of artistry, it's become something I'll talk about. But you know, in the beginning it was just this instinctual thing. I think there was plenty of ambition and plenty of competition and a real Texas need to one-up each other. But it wasn't designed—that kind of Texas competition is not so much about ambition as it is about who's the alpha male. Townes Van Zandt was pretty much the alpha male. He was smart, he was strung out; he'd come into town and be upstairs kicking heroin and I'd be downstairs at Amy Martin's place at her big table—the Martin family was sort of the patrons of the street art around Nashville at the time, and we all began trading songs and playing and trying to figure out how to do it, and Townes would be upstairs kickin' heroin, and it was like, "Oh, God, Townes is upstairs kickin' heroin. Ooh, man, he's so cool." Then he'd finally show up and he'd be ready to get on another roll and just leave everybody in the dust. And you know, he was enigmatic and charismatic as well. In the early 1970s he was vividly on top of his game. It's very understandable that Steve would be drawn to that persona and that style. Whereas Guy Clark would be a little more accessible—Guy was like the arbiter of what real good songwriting was like and the curator of all these characters. It all evolved around Guy, 'cause Guy was the curator of all the wild spirits who were really just a group of songwriters trying to figure out how to do it. How to paint it. This is a long-winded way of saying a conversation about goals and stuff, it just wasn't the Texas way. It was so much more about the instinctual moment.

Would Steve have been drawn more to Townes because Townes was more out there, edgier, more flamboyant than Guy? Would that have appealed more to Steve at that time than Guy being more about the craft?

Yeah. Well, see, I learned from Guy about craft, and Guy was generous just in the process. It was all about writing really good songs. I'd say that Guy was a lot more generous than Townes. But Townes was the archetypal … he was part Dylan, part Ramblin' Jack Elliott, part Kerouac, and just really smart but instinctively just alpha male. I think by my nature, I was drawn to Guy, and Steve by his nature was drawn to Townes. But to be drawn to Townes was also to be drawn to Guy. Because these were two older guys who really had a sense of how to get it done. I would say people like me and people like Steve, we were really lucky to fall into that world, to be able to glimpse firsthand what was going on, how to do it. Steve came with a better handle on writing it than I did. My craft formed when I got here; I think Steve came a little more formed than me.

You've been talking about this Texas contingent that was around Bishop's Pub in the early '70s. A guy steps up onstage and does a song. Is there a distinguishing or a common quality that marks it as being Texas-born?

Basically Texas was the great deception. You know, Sam Houston got fired as the governor of Tennessee and he went to DC whining to President Andrew Jackson, "Aw, I got fired," drunk and maudlin. Andrew Jackson really wanted to get that Texas territory away from Mexico. "Oh, I got a job for you. I want you to go down to Texas, and I want you to scrape together a crew and let's have an uprising and get Mexico away from those damn Mexicans. I want that land. You guys'll get paid really good." It's like the Scots going over to Ireland. And so Sam Houston and Jim Bowie—Jim Bowie was a slave trader—they were all liars. They were drunks and liars. Shit, you know, Texans are the best liars in the world. So you've got a skill of lying coming from a tradition of just lying, dirty scoundrels, just the perfect foundation for being a songwriter. We're all liars.

Deeply rooted in history.

Yeah. Given the songwriters you associate with Texas, there is some search for truth in it but to deny that we're a bunch of damn liars would be to miss the point.

And Steve fit right into the tradition.

I suppose so.

II. Odyssey 1975–80

In October 1975, with Guy Clark's recommendation, Sunbury-Dunbar, a division of RCA, signed Steve to a publishing deal that would pay him $75 a week. Guy, signed to RCA, also brought Steve into the studio when he was cutting his debut album, *Old No. 1*, enlisting him to join a background chorus on his song "Desperadoes Waiting for a Train," his mates in the chorus being Rodney Crowell, Emmylou Harris, and Sammi Smith. Having admired Emmylou from afar when he saw her performing with Gram Parsons, he was beside himself to be face to face with her in the studio. "She gave me half her cheeseburger," he wrote in his liner notes in *Train a Comin'*.[6] "I wasn't the same for weeks." He then went on tour with Guy, playing bass in the band, Guy's rationale for hiring Steve being that if a fellow could play guitar, he ought to be able to play the bass. It was a ramshackle band, in that Guy was barely competent on guitar, Steve had no experience with the bass, and guitarist Champ Hood was trying to learn fiddle on the job. Clark: "We were *horrible!*"[7] When that first tour was completed, Guy put together a more experienced band, but took Steve out as well, and this time let him do some of his original songs in the sets.

Back home in Tennessee, Sandy was feeling more and more slighted, the distance between her and her husband growing as he devoted more time to the music and to the extracurricular activities around it. At a party one night, Steve met and immediately fell for a Tennessee girl, Cynthia Hailey Dunn. By the summer of 1976 Sandy had gone back to Texas, Steve had filed for divorce, and on January 21, 1977, Steve and Cynthia, nine months into their relationship, were married.

On the day of his marriage to Cynthia, a recording session was scheduled in Nashville, at the Creative Workshop recording studio. Elvis was in town for an album project and one of the songs he had selected to record was Steve's "Mustang Wine." For Steve, having Elvis record one of his songs was a better high than anything chemically induced. But it turned out to be every bit as ephemeral when Elvis failed to show for the session, leaving his band in the studio awaiting his arrival until they heard the news. His new piano player, Tony Brown, who had joined the group following a stint in Emmylou Harris's formidable Hot Band, put it succinctly: "Elvis was fucked up on drugs and couldn't sing. That's what we found out."[8]

Concurrent with that letdown was the news that RCA was selling Sunbury-Dunbar Publishing. Steve was still under contract and getting paid $150 a week, but the new L.A.-based owners made it clear that his songs didn't fit with the direction they wanted to take the company. Then living in a barely habitable cabin northeast of Franklin, Tennessee, he and Cynthia decided just like that to move to Mexico, to the picturesque and artist-friendly town of San Miguel de Allende, the same Central Mexico town to which Steve's first wife Sandy had journeyed a few years earlier to help her sister. For most of the two-year period of 1977–1979 Steve and Cynthia lived in San Miguel, their relationship marked by periodic bouts of drug-fueled feuding, both of them sharing what Steve referred to as "a mutual interest in drug abuse,"[9] Cynthia sometimes beating a retreat back to Tennessee when she couldn't take any more of Steve. When they were together, they tended to be on the move, and at one point wound up living in a trailer in Wimberley, Texas, near Austin. There Steve had the notion of becoming an integral part of the push to put the city on the music industry map, for both its studio and robust live music scenes. He found, though, according to *Hardcore Troubadour*, too many temptations: "It was too close to the border, and the dope was too cheap, and the girls were too pretty."[10]

This period also marked the beginning of Steve's obsession with guns. He and his friends often amused themselves by shooting up the surroundings around the trailer in Wimberley, and Steve began to make a habit of traveling with some kind of firearm.

Guy Clark told Rodney Crowell a story about how Townes Van Zandt got fed up with what he considered Steve's irresponsible handling of guns and decided to teach him a lesson. There are a couple of variations on the story, and it may well be apocryphal, but it has entered into Steve Earle–Townes Van Zandt lore and legend.

Crowell: "I think Steve was out at Townes's place with a pistol, wagging it around and talking about it. And Townes said, 'I'll show you what it is with a pistol,' and he took all the bullets out of the chamber but one, spun it, pulled the trigger, and he says, 'And if that doesn't prove my point,' and he spun it again, cocked, and pulled the trigger. Did it twice. And froze Steve. According to the way Guy told the story, just froze Steve. I never got it from Steve whether this happened or not. But I gather from Guy that that's what Townes told him. That's a great story; whether it's true I really don't know. I wouldn't put it past him. There again, that's the alpha male thing—nobody was gonna outdo Townes."[11]

In 1979, after Steve's publishing contact with Sunbury-Dunbar had expired, he and Cynthia moved back to Nashville. It was the endgame of their tumultuous marriage. Cynthia was getting deeper into cocaine and running with a crowd that practically worshiped the drug. Steve too started indulging, snorting it rather than injecting it as Cynthia's friends did. Then, out of the blue, he began to suffer debilitating reactions to the drug while on stage—dizziness, disorientation, difficulty breathing. Doctors recommended he adopt a healthier lifestyle that incorporated a better diet and regular exercise.

For two years he was unable to perform, and during that time took a regular job to generate some income. But the work he got—hanging billboards for an outdoor advertising company—wasn't exactly compatible with someone who was having dizzy spells. With his panic attacks persisting, he took the drastic measure of giving up all drugs, including alcohol. When Cynthia not only did not join him in his new sobriety but spent more and more time hanging out at her coke dealer's house, Steve gave her up too, ending a marriage that seemed destined to destroy them both. On Christmas Day 1979, Cynthia was hanging out at her dealer's house, and Steve, through the good graces of his father, who had sent him a plane ticket back to Texas, was at home with his family.[12]

III. Alpha Male Ascending, V2.0

While Steve was struggling to find a niche, both in Nashville and pretty much in his life in general, Rodney Crowell was on a near-unimpeded ascension to Texas alpha-male supremacy. Even before leaving Nashville he'd had a taste of minor success, when Jerry Reed cut Rodney's "You Can't Keep Me Here in Tennessee" and signed him to a publishing deal. After landing his dream gig as the guitarist in Emmylou Harris's Hot Band, he then found Harris championing his songwriting, first and to enduring impact on her 1975 sophomore album, *Elite Hotel*, when she cut a searing version of Crowell's wrenching country ballad, "Till I Gain Control Again." In 1978, on *Quarter Moon in a Ten Cent Town*, she turned to Rodney for two songs, "I Ain't Livin' Long Like This" and a witty, Cajun-flavored story song, "Leaving Louisiana in the Broad Daylight."

Crowell left Harris to make his move as a solo artist and formed a powerhouse group of his own to help get him there: the Cherry Bombs, as they were called, featured Crowell; Tony Brown, late of Elvis Presley's band after serving his tenure in the Hot Band; Richard Bennett on guitar; Larrie Londin on drums; Hank DeVito on steel guitar; Emory Gordy, Jr., on bass; Vince Gill or Albert Lee on guitar. Signed to Warner Bros., he released his first solo album in 1978, titled *Ain't Living Long Like This*, produced by Emmylou's husband and producer Brian Ahern. It generated only minor hits in the form of covers of Dallas Frazier's "Elvira" and of "(Now and Then There's) A Fool Such As I," a lovely, wrenching version done more in the country style of the Hank Snow original than the uptempo Elvis Presley classic. But with his debut album Crowell served notice that his was an expansive vision of country. Where his instincts had been leading him, Emmylou took him and validated his ideas about a style of country music that reflected the sensibilities of a generation raised on rock 'n' roll, and specifically raised on rock 'n' roll that had reached its creative zenith in the music of the Beatles and the productions of George Martin. An entire generation of rising country artists, steeped in the rock 'n' roll canon and tempered by the uncompromised traditionalism of the likes of Buck Owens and Merle Haggard, had heard the Beatles' 1965 masterpiece *Rubber Soul* for what it was: an acoustic-based, country- and folk-flavored interior monologue, its themes being the timeless ones of love (of the hormonally heated kind in "I've Just Seen a Face," of the dreamy kind in "Girl" and the breathtaking "Michelle"), jealousy (in the searing "Run for Your Life"), spite ("Think for Yourself," "You Won't See Me"), making up ("Wait"), with room enough for reflection on life's journey ("In My Life").

As a songwriter Crowell had been putting it together for years; now he took it to another level by assuming the producer's chair for the 1979 American debut album by Johnny Cash's daughter, Rosanne, titled *Right or Wrong*. On that and its follow-up, 1980's *Seven Year Ache* (between which he and Cash had fallen in love and visited the altar), he sculpted a scintillating fusion of tradition, both country and rock 'n' roll, fearless in melding Beatles-style textures and the robust sound of British Invasion–era recordings to an unmistakable country sound scape provided by some of the same stalwart musicians from the Emmylou Harris finishing school.

Then, in 1980, he had his first solo country hit, with his own "Ashes by Now," a merciless account of a love affair's end that crossed over to the pop chart's Top 40. Strictly as a writer, though, he made it, ma, when the Oak Ridge Boys topped the chart with "Leaving Louisiana in the Broad Daylight." All of this leaving no doubt as to the sure enough alpha male, Texas rules champion, in 1980.

IV. Squeeze Me In

In 1980 Steve and Cynthia were divorced, and by the time the decree was final, on March 10, he had fallen in love anew and was sharing an apartment with 21-year-old Carol-Ann Hunter, a free-spirited survivor of an abusive childhood who supported herself working multiple jobs, one of those being at a club called the Villager, where she had met Steve some two years before. They were married on March 22, 1981, in Nashville, and on January 4, 1982, their first child, a boy named Justin Townes Earle, was born at Baptist Hospital, where Steve's mother had been born.[13]

Upon holding his firstborn in his arms, Steve gained a fresh perspective on his own life and, if *Hardcore Troubadour* is to be believed, a sense of mission as well.

"I called my dad and I immediately apologized for every shitty thing I'd ever done," Steve said of that moment. "It was really instantly obvious to me, 'Oh, *now* I get it.' It's funny, parenting changes everything … How much you take that seriously, how much you rise up to it, is up to the individual."[14]

Nevertheless, the women in Steve's love life were beginning to resemble characters from Michael Ondaatje's novel *Coming Through Slaughter*, a quasi-fictional fantasia in prose and verse on a friend's search through New Orleans for the legendary turn-of-the-century jazz trumpeter Buddy Bolden. To paraphrase: "Their stories were like spokes on a rimless wheel ending in air. [He] had lived a different life with every one of them."[15]

Although he was still working odd jobs to make ends meet, Steve had experienced a bit of good fortune in 1981 when his former Sunbury-Dunbar publisher Pat Carter teamed with a former RCA staff producer named Roy Dea in a publishing venture called High Chaparral. Carter signed Steve, paid him $100 a week to write songs, cut demos, and pitch them to producers and/or artists seeking new material. Introduced to the Nashville tradition of cowriting, he began working with John Scott Sherrill on a new batch of tunes.

In 1980 John Travolta, who had become big box office on the strength of his performance in the disco-fueled 1976 smash *Saturday Night Fever*, starred in a film based on an *Esquire* magazine story about the off-hours antics of some bored oilfield workers in Houston. Titled *Urban Cowboy*, the movie was a flop, but the country music industry felt some positive repercussions from it. For a time, country was cool all over America, and its artists and its lifestyle were the subject of numerous learned, or gushing, magazine and newspaper articles. Western wear became the new fashion craze. But that's all it was—a craze, nothing of lasting impact on trend-conscious consumers.

"This mania of interest in country and anything country was, of course, more illusory and fleeting than factual or permanent," observed John Lomax III. "Like all fashion fads, the 'Western look' ran its course and was replaced by a new fashion trend. The novelty of country stars on television wore off through overexposure. The country discos evolved into 'dance' or 'new music' clubs. The country music star's lifestyle lost its allure for the masses after every major magazine ran a piece on 'the magic and mystery of life on the road.' (A 700-mile bus trip with 11 others in a 40-foot Silver Eagle loses its 'magic' after about 3 hours.) The national media solemnly pronounced the 'country music movement' to be 'dead' and moved on to other unsuspecting fields to find a new candidate for elevation into the next major trend."[16]

The *Urban Cowboy* soundtrack—which featured Bonnie Raitt, Jimmy Buffett, Joe Walsh, Bob Seger, Boz Scaggs, J.D. Souther, Charlie Daniels, Mickey Gilley, and the Eagles—sold well but yielded only one major hit single, a lilting honky tonk ballad titled "Lookin' for Love," by Johnny Lee, theretofore a self-effacing, obscure member of Mickey Gilley's band. The single had a three-week run atop the country chart and in late 1980 crossed over to pop and peaked at No. 5. (The only other cut to make a dent on the pop side was Anne Murray's "Could I Have This Dance," which peaked at No. 33 pop after having been a No. 1 country single.[17])

In search of his next hit, Johnny Lee cut Steve's "When You Fall in Love," and the single rose to the Top 10 of the country chart but failed to make a showing on the pop side. No matter—Steve may have missed by nearly five years his stated ambition of recording an album by the age of 21, but a Top 10 country single was something. Maybe not bragging rights in the alpha-male competition, but success enough to get him in the game.

Pink & Black
LSI, 1983

Produced by Roy Dea and Pat Carter
Recorded at LSI Recording by Al McGuire
Mastered at Masterfonics by Jim Lloyd

Musicians
Steve Earle: electric guitar, vocals
Pat Carter: acoustic guitar
Ron Kling: bass
Martin Parker: drums
Dale Sellers: lead guitar on "Squeeze Me In"

Songs
1. "Nothing but You" (Steve Earle)
2. "Continental Trailways Blues" (Steve Earle)
3. "Squeeze Me In" (Steve Earle)
4. "My Baby Worships Me" (Steve Earle)

The Johnny Lee single had a salutary effect on the whole of Steve's artistry. He essentially willed his panic attacks away and began performing again. After making the acoustic guitar his instrument of choice, he purchased an Aspen electric guitar and, for reasons he's never fully explained, began writing songs in a rockabilly style (perhaps hoping to capitalize on the success the Long Island, New York–based Stray Cats were having with a souped-up rockabilly sound centered on a powerhouse slapback rhythm and Brian Setzer's rousing vocals and sizzling, idiomatically eloquent guitar work). A couple of developments seem to have made an impact on his strategy at this point. For one, he had not been unaffected by the emergence of punk rock in the previous decade. In 1978 he had seen the Sex Pistols play in Austin, and though he judged them "not very good, but I thought it was kinda cool," the bigger point the band made on him was that playing music live was "supposed to be fucking *fun*."[18]

Second, a lightbulb went off when he ran into his new acquaintance Jack Emerson at a local punk club and found out Emerson was cutting an EP on the promising Nashville band Jason and the Scorchers. Melding punk attitude and hard country energy, the band advanced some razor-edged, guitar-based rock that drew from many wells: Southern rock, urban blues, honky tonk, Southern soul and, of course, punk. Illinois-born farm boy Jason Ringenberg was a dynamic frontman and forceful vocalist (dubbed by one wag "Jerry Lee Rotten"), and in guitarist Warner Hodges the band had an instrumental voice to rank with the best around. Hodges was as conversant with Keith Richards as he was with the Duane Allman–Dickie Betts–Rossington-Collins axis, and when the occasion demanded, he could fire off some hard-rock runs that compared favorably to the attack of Eddie Van Halen. The independent EP produced by Emerson, *Fervor*, was critically and commercially well received, leading to a major-label deal with EMI in 1984.[19]

Inspired by Emerson's example of bypassing the majors, Steve coaxed Carter and Dea into expanding operations to include a label venture, LSI, and to launch it with a Steve Earle EP. With Roy and Pat coproducing, and Al McGuire engineering, they set up in their own demo studio late in 1982 and cut four Steve Earle originals. They also assembled a backing band comprised of bassist Reno Kling and drummer Martin Parker from John Scott Sherrill's band, along with Carter on acoustic guitar and Dale Sellers playing lead guitar on one cut. Steve handled lead guitar and vocals.

Steve's voice was in the high-tenor range and heavily echoed throughout, not unlike any vocal that had been recorded at the Sun Studio in Memphis after Elvis's arrival in 1954. The lead guitar lines were robust and rich in twang, the product of many sources ranging from Duane Eddy to the Buckaroos' Don Rich and the Band's Robbie Robertson.

"Nothin' but You," the EP's opening cut, was a steady grooving, mid-tempo number, with Steve's narrator pledging his devotion to an unnamed female ("I don't wanna think 'bout nothin' but you") and offering a litany of rock 'n' roll/country girls that he would dismiss out of hand, including Chuck Berry's Maybellene and Sweet 16 (not Sweet Little 16, but everyone got the drift), Buddy Holly's Peggy Sue and the Yellow Rose of Texas. Except for its slinky, R&B-tinged groove, its bright melody and upbeat vocal bespeak an affection for the style of pop-rockabilly pioneered in Steve's terra firma, Texas, in the late '50s, courtesy Buddy Knox and the Rhythm Orchids. Not the most obvious of influences for an aspiring neo-rockabilly but an interesting touchstone in that Knox made wonderful, atmospheric records that were major hits in their day and had held up well over time, although Knox's solid contributions to the music were rarely recognized. Perhaps an accident of sequencing, "Nothin' but You," the first Steve Earle recording the general public would have heard, rooted Steve deep in the heart of Texas, not Nashville.

"Continental Trailways Blues," had a bit of a roadhouse feel about it, spiked by Steve's catchy top-strings walking line. Steve's first recorded road tune, the song depicts a down-and-out fellow, stuck in a bus station, eating food heated in a microwave, down to his last dime, and restless to get home to his woman. He traces his journey, marking his progress to Houston by way of Natchez, Mississippi ("bought myself a copy of the Natchez, Mississippi News"), all the while trying to "get some sleep and listen to that highway sound" (a lyric that would in part be recycled more dramatically a few years later), until at the end of the song, in a clever turnaround, he's back on the highway in the rain, "wishin' I was downtown / waitin' on a Greyhound …"

Side two kicks off with "Squeeze Me In," which features Steve chicken-pickin' lead guitar lines, breaking for a double-timed percussive shuffle, then pleading, "Darlin', squeeze me in!"; Sellers then enters with a serpentine, distorted electric guitar solo. Once again the main character in the narrative is on the road, trying to get a ride to his girl's house, vowing to be highway-bound come the morning and not hanging around "like your other man." Cocky but vulnerable, he closes by repeating the title sentiment, "Darling, squeeze me in," and the song trundles to a close.

"My Baby Worships Me" closes the EP on a bristling note. It's built around a supremely catchy, twangy, winding top-strings riff that drives the song forward. Steve's vocal is all attitude and drawl as he crows about how his woman subjugates herself to him, working on an assembly line and bringing her paycheck home to him, taking him out to dinner, making the payment on his Coupe de Ville and in all respects paying his way. It's a slight song lyrically, and the narrator's shameless sponging was not even vaguely autobiographical. But musically it cooks mightily, here and there summoning memories of Billy Emerson's Sun recording "Red Hot" but ultimately standing on its own as a convincing, visceral performance, the best on the EP.

The disc was packaged in a cardboard sleeve, like the EPs of old, with front and back black-and-white photos of a thin, mustachioed Steve attired in jeans, a conservative, light-colored sports coat and open-necked white shirt, his hair neatly coiffed, parted down the middle, and falling around the top of the collar. His name and the EP title were in bright pink lettering, with lightning bolts under "Steve" and "Earle," and below his name that of his band, which had been dubbed the Dukes.

With limited distribution, *Pink & Black* was not destined for any significant sales, but it did its job in another way. John Lomax III received a copy of it, was knocked out by what he heard, and took a copy to Rick Blackburn, the CEO of CBS whose signings in recent years included Rodney Crowell, Ricky Skaggs, and Rosanne Cash, all of them harbingers of a new musical order in country.

Blackburn loved what he heard and struck a $40,000 deal with Carter and Dea to license the *Pink & Black* songs and to cut six new numbers, all rockabilly style.[20] Steve's contract was vetted by a Nashville lawyer recommended by John Lomax III. After some discussion, Lomax, with some trepidation, agreed to be Steve's manager, even though he was still gun-shy after some bad experiences working with Townes.

The six new tracks included "If You Need a Fool," an Earle original that sounded like an early Carl Perkins Sun recording in its guitar style and in the clever lyrics—"they're just not making fools the way they used to," and "you can find me in the phone book under Blue," being two note-perfect examples of Perkins-style humor. "Open Up Your Door" was a straightahead rockabilly number featuring sharp, trebly guitar lines snaking through the number and lyrics in which he invokes a distinctly unreconstructed lower-class persona in the lyric "I won't let my dog sleep in your hallway / I won't spit my tobacco on your floor" after revealing the same character sufficiently articulate to sing, "in total submission I'm comin'" earlier in the song. It was the second original song in which Steve had made a class distinction, the first coming in "Nothin' but You" when he sang that the rich folks could "keep the whiskey, and the cocaine too."

Far and away the best of the new tracks, in "The Devil's Right Hand" Steve revealed how powerful a storyteller he could be when he transformed personal experience into a dramatic fictional narrative and mini-morality play all in one. All the entreaties he had heard about the dangers of fooling around with guns—and his seeming obliviousness to those dangers—informed the story of a young man who became fascinated with guns at an early age and disdained his mother's warning that "the pistol was the Devil's right hand." When he shoots a man dead after catching him cheating at cards, he pleads not guilty and explains how it was the Devil, not he, who did the dirty deed— "nothin' touched the trigger but the Devil's right hand."

Playing a Telecaster, Steve's licks are taut, trebly, and fraught with tension; the drums boom like gunshots, and the martial rhythm adds a patina of malevolence. Steve sings in a terse, rather uninflected voice, like a dispassionate anchorman reporting the day's news, his words and sanguine demeanor underscoring the main character's near-complete incomprehension of how depraved he had become. Mothers figure prominently in country music lore, of course, but whereas, say, Merle Haggard puts the blame on himself for his foul deed in "Mama Tried," Steve's character is free of conscience, a cold-blooded killer, neither blaming nor absolving his mother of any responsibility, nor taking any on his own. Even without parsing the narrative, "The Devil's Right Hand" was simply a powerful recording in all respects.

With minimal promotional support, "Nothin' but You" b/w "Continental Trailways Blues," was released as a single in October and peaked at No. 70 on the country chart. Its follow-up, "Squeeze Me In," failed to chart. Why one record succeeds and another of seeming equal or even better quality fails is one of the mysteries of the marketplace, or of marketing or of the stars, for those who choose to believe in such things. In the case of Steve's LSI recordings, their cool or nonexistent reception was simple to understand: not that the songs weren't good, or the singing, or the playing, but whereas the Stray Cats had added some modern-age thrust to their classic rockabilly, Steve's sounded not all that advanced from what the early Sun artists had done. It was, in a word, dated, a classic example of an artist so focused on digging into tradition that he neglects to look forward at all.

Told he would have to change producers and fashion something suited for the current market, Steve grudgingly agreed, because "no one else was offering me a record deal."[21]

From a list of label-approved producers, Steve was drawn to the name of Emory Gordy, Jr., whom he knew of as a bassist in Elvis Presley's TCB band, on Gram Parsons's first two albums, and with Emmylou's Hot Band. Supplanting the first incarnation of the Dukes was a formidable lineup of well-credentialed players, including one of the most beloved and versatile drummers in Nashville history, Larrie Londin ("the greatest drummer I've ever worked with," says producer Stewart Levine, who used Londin on the sessions for B.B. King's 1982 Nashville-recorded *Love Me Tender*); steel guitarist Hank DeVito, also a Hot Band alum; and Bobby Ogden, a long-term member of Elvis's band, his tenure running from 1968 through 1977, the year Elvis died.

The one Steve would get closest to, and who would loom largest in his legend, was the gentleman guitarist Richard Bennett. For a time Bennett became something akin to Steve's musical alter ego. There was an immediate connection between them when they met for the Epic sessions: "We found we had a lot of common musical passions," Bennett says.[22]

Born in Chicago in 1951, Bennett moved with his family to Phoenix, Arizona, in January 1960. He began playing drums at age six, but it was the guitar that most held his interest, dating from the moment he saw Elvis Presley perform on the Dorsey Brothers' TV show.

"I was always fascinated with singers who had a guitar slung around their neck, you know, be it Elvis or hillbilly singers; it's all one and the same, really."[23]

For his eleventh birthday, Bennett persuaded his parents to buy him a guitar, and "that was it." While still in high school he met and was taught by a popular local musician named Morris Skaggs, who had been a mentor to then-prominent Los Angeles session musician Al Casey (whose extensive credits include numerous Duane Eddy recordings, Jody Reynolds's "Endless Sleep," Sanford Clark's "The Fool"). Skaggs tipped off Casey to the guitar *wunderkind* in his instruction, and by 1968 Bennett was in Los Angeles playing on his first sessions. After finishing high school in Phoenix in June 1969, he relocated back to Los Angeles. Work, lots of it, seemed to drop out of the sky for Bennett— "playing on records from Peggy Lee and Johnny Mathis to Gene Vincent, whatever was around that day to do—the Partridge Family or Helen Reddy or whatever the hell it was that day, and sometimes three of 'em a day."[24] But it was a session with Neil Diamond that led to an enduring association that began in 1971 and continued through 1987, during which time Bennett also cowrote Diamond's 1979 Top 20 single, "Forever in Blue Jeans."

As a guitarist Bennett's influences weren't flashy players, but rather solid, imaginative, and precision-minded professionals conversant in many styles but rooted in country. He worshiped Carl Perkins and Elvis's first guitarist, Scotty Moore, but also admired the work of session giants Tony Mottola and Al Caiola. "And of course I loved Duane Eddy and I loved Chet Atkins, because I came up playing country music. People like Grady Martin were the absolute tops for me, and Hank Garland, Ray Edenton on the country side of things."[25]

"In Chicago I grew up listening to hillbilly music in the '50s," Bennett says. "So it was one of the first musics that really sort of moved me in a big way; even as a small child of two or three, I remember just being riveted by it. And moving to Phoenix, it was very tangible there, it was all over the place—they even had full-time country radio stations, which they didn't in Chicago at that time. So when I came up, starting to learn how to play guitar, I immediately gravitated to country music—well, it was pre-Beatles—but even rather than the Ventures, stuff like that. I really gravitated toward Webb Pierce and those types of artists. Because it was easy; it was an easy in, it was three chords, and I understood that much of it at that time. So all my years in Phoenix I didn't play with my contemporaries or play contemporary music. I played hillbilly music of the '40s and '50s. Yeah, I was very much in love with country music."[26]

Bennett established himself in Nashville in the early '80s. Unlike many of his friends in the L.A. scene who were relocating lock, stock, and barrel to Music City, Bennett still had his well-paying gig with Neil Diamond and a reason to remain based in L.A. Having been an original member of the Cherry Bombs, he was on Rodney Crowell's short list of players to work on what became Rosanne Cash's *Seven Year Ache* album in 1981, and then Jimmy Bowen, another former West Coast–based friend since transplantd in Nashville to take over the reins of MCA, began flying him in for sessions. Tony Brown had gone from Elvis to the Hot Band to RCA Nashville and then became head of A&R at MCA, working under Bowen, as was Emory Gordy, Jr. "They began calling me to come out and play on projects. And that's what I did."[27]

The Epic sessions with this group of premier players produced only one unsuccessful single release, a cover of John Hiatt's "The Crush" paired with Steve's "A Little Bit in Love," but otherwise may have been important only in encouraging Steve to be true to his vision of his music, as Townes had told him to be, and to introduce him to musicians who could translate his ideas into vivid sounds.

Apart from Steve's "A Little Bit in Love," the material for the Gordy, Jr.-produced sessions came from outside sources. British rockabilly fanatic Paul Kennerley, future husband of Emmylou Harris, had successfully melded the rockabilly sensibility to contemporary country arrangements. His "Cry Myself to Sleep," though, did not fit that description. Rather, it featured a distinctly surf-style guitar in the midst of the thumping rhythm, and Gordy further spiced up the arrangement with synthesized handclaps to give it a new-wave sheen. Dennis Linde's "What'll You Do About Me" had a hard country edge and a snarling, borderline confrontational vocal as Steve sings about a social misfit of a man who in essence stalks the woman he loves, threatening to scare off potential suitors with a 2×4, daring her to call "the lawyers and the fuzz," and vowing to shadow her until she gives in to him. Steve sings with the grim determination of a man on a mission, and the backdrop for his strategies is foreboding, thanks to the twanging guitars and the brooding beat. In 1987 Randy Travis would cut the song on his hit *Always & Forever* album, but producer Kyle Lehning gave the number a brighter arrangement than did Gordy, Jr., and Travis played the part of the cool, maybe even slightly goofy would-be paramour, reversing the dark tint of Steve's version and treating it as a humorous depiction of all-consuming love—no harm, no foul.

The cover of John Hiatt's "The Crush" kicks off with a passage reminiscent of "Elvira." Bouncy and upbeat, it too looks at a man who's as consumed by love as the protagonist of "What'll You Do About Me." Here, though, the B3 fills and good-time feeling lend it a Tex-Mex feel (apart from a bizarre synthesizer lick that crops up near the end), as if Doug Sahm had had a say in things.

Epic had enough songs in the can now for a full album, but had put its Steve Earle project on the back burner in favor of more commercially viable acts. Steve went back on the road, and back on alcohol and drugs, obtaining, through a connected friend, narcotic prescription medications such as Percodan, Bercacets, Tylenol #3s (Tylenol with codeine), and Tussionex.[28] As his drug use intensified, so did the distance between him and Carol, to the point where little Justin Townes Earle was the only link Steve felt to Carol. He was already romancing a new woman, a freelance writer named Macayla Lohmann. Steve and Carol were separated by the start of 1985, and Steve then picked up the pace of his courtship of Macayla. They took a sabbatical together to Steve's old stomping grounds in San Miguel, and while there he wrote another new song, a soft, stark tribute to the feeling that is always true to its name, "My Old Friend the Blues."[29]

Professionally he was in the midst of a split too, and a rebirth. Carter and Dea had dumped him when the Epic deal hadn't panned out, but John Lomax III steered him (with an assist from Merlin Littlefield) to Noel Fox at Silverline/Goldline, the publishing company owned by the Oak Ridge Boys. Fox had heard *Pink & Black*—had really *heard* it—and encouraged Steve to follow his muse. Steve, he recognized, was more than a songwriter; he was "a *writer*. He's so driven to write and report his findings here on earth."[30] Steve's response to Fox's confidence in him and to Fox's *laissez-faire* style was to write a pair of striking new tunes, "Fearless Heart" and "Goodbye's All We Got Left." Driving home to Texas for Christmas that year, he heard Bruce Springsteen's *Born in the U.S.A.* with new ears, and it clicked with him how the album and the live Springsteen show he had seen earlier in the year were synchronized: "I was intrigued by the fact that Springsteen opened the album with 'Born in the U.S.A.,' and that it was really a theme and an overture and he opened the show with it."[31] On that drive, two more songs emerged: "Guitar Town," envisioned as an album opener, and "Down the Road," a closer.

On the negative side of the ledger, in December Epic released the single of "What'll You Do About Me" (b/w "The Crush"). It peaked at No. 76. A second single, "A Little Bit in Love," didn't even make the chart. Then Macayla chose not to follow Steve back to Nashville from Mexico, where she announced she would stay.

Back in Nashville, Noel Fox was on the phone with Tony Brown, now the vice president of A&R at MCA under Jimmy Bowen's stewardship.

chapter 8

Me, Tarzan

J.D. Summer was the gospel version of Jimmy Bowen. One time there was a guy named Mylon LeFevre who played bass and always dressed so in style. He bought these shirts like Elvis wore, with the high collars, and J.D. told me, "If you ever buy one of those shirts like Mylon wears"—'cause Mylon and I roomed together in an apartment—he says, "I will fire you."

So Mylon talked me into buying one at a place up in Minneapolis, Minnesota. I said, "Mylon, J.D.'s gonna fire me, man."

He said, "Aw, don't worry about that shit. He's just bluffin'."

So I walk on the bus with this shirt on that I had just bought—and at the time I was making $150 a week and I couldn't even pay my bills, and this shirt was like an expensive shirt from the place where Mylon had bought his. So I walked in with Mylon, and J.D. sees me and he says—he called me Tarzan—he said, "Hey, Tarzan, come here." And he grabbed that shirt and ripped it off my body. The buttons were flying through the air. Opened the bus window and threw it out into the street. And what did I say? I said, "I'm sorry, man. I'm sorry!" He said, "I told you not to do that." I said, "I know, I know."

So I've been around some very benevolent dictator kind of people. Steve's the same way.

—Tony Brown

Difficult people didn't faze Tony Brown much, which may account for his swift rise up the executive ranks in the Nashville music business. At RCA (where he had replaced Roy Dea), he had a productive relationship with fiery president Joe Galante and had signed Vince Gill and Alabama. Though Gill's star would not rise for several more years—until he was signed to MCA by Tony Brown—Alabama would become the biggest and most honored group in country music history.

Then he moved over to MCA Nashville, where he was VP of A&R under the demanding, dictatorial company president Jimmy Bowen.

Life was full of colorful characters.

Born in Greensboro, North Carolina, raised in Winston-Salem, graduated from high school in Durham a Tarheel all the way, Tony Brown was always moving, in some definition of the word.

At age 13 he began performing publicly, playing piano and singing with his three siblings (two brothers and a sister) at his evangelist father's services. They traveled around the South in a station wagon with a "Jesus Saves" bumper sticker on the back of it.

"My father would preach hellfire and brimstone, and my two brothers and myself and my sister would sing. I've always been small for my age, but at 13 I looked probably 9 or 10. So when I learned to play a song during the church service … started to say all hell broke loose, but I can't say that. So it became like a big deal in church, during our appearances, that the little kid was going to play a song. That's how I got into wanting to be in show business. Back in those days I was only allowed to listen to religious music. I missed Elvis and all that stuff. The first album I bought, I'm kind of embarrassed to say, was George Beverly Shea, when he came out with 'How Great Thou Art.' He had the hit on that, if you want to call it that, from those Billy Graham crusades. Then when I got into seventh, eighth, and ninth grade, all the girls were into Elvis. I definitely heard of Elvis Presley and I saw the pictures, but I just didn't know what he sounded like.

"Eventually I'd walk into the band room or something, and they'd be playing the radio or a record—'Jailhouse Rock' and 'Love Me Tender.' And it didn't do much for me because I was into that quartet music. I grew up being around harmony singers, and the closest I came to anything outside of Southern gospel was hearing black gospel music in churches."[1]

From his family group Brown graduated to the professional circuit, spending seven years with J.D. Sumner and the Stamps, "a couple of months" with the Blackwoods, and nearly three years with the Oak Ridge Boys, up to the point where they signed with Columbia and left gospel for the country mainstream. After cutting a solo piano album of gospel standards, he joined Voice, which was Elvis's house band and, according to Brown, "just God-awful." He took the job not to get out of gospel music, "but just to be around such a big star as Elvis. I would hear that they would go to Beverly Hills or Graceland, and I just wanted to do that. That was sort of my segue into the secular music world.

"That was the last three years of his life when I was with him, and he was Elvis the celebrity, not Elvis the King of Rock 'n' Roll. So I ended up playing with the TCB Band, Ronnie Tutt, James Burton, and all those guys. But I was just as excited about playing with James Burton and Ronnie Tutt as I was playing with Elvis. I've always been into great musicians."

Tony Brown, during his tenure with Elvis Presley's band, sporting the style of shirt that so incensed J.D. Sumner: "I've been around some very benevolent dictator kind of people. Steve Earle's the same way."

On August 17, 1977, Brown was at the airport with the rest of Presley's band, getting ready to kick off another leg of a tour. In a moment, it seemed, a bright, sunny day suddenly turned dark and dangerous, "hurricane-level winds. Then we learned that the tour was off, but we weren't told why." The real news came soon enough.

"All of a sudden my importance seemed to have evaporated because, like everyone else in that tour, I felt like that when Elvis died, my career had died as well."

Not quite. Brown then stepped into a movement that he would have a significant role in shaping a few years later, after he had done his homework. He joined Emmylou Harris's Hot Band, where he forged friendships with not only Emmylou and Brian Ahern, but with Rodney Crowell, Emory Gordy, Jr., Hank DeVito, Ricky Skaggs, and Albert Lee, among others.

"These people were like musicologists," Brown says. "I had always taken my gospel piano playing for granted. They showed me how it fit into the big important picture of American music making. That to me was life changing; that was when I had an epiphany that I should learn about music and not about celebrity. With Emmy I found out about that whole country-rock scene and about Gram Parsons and how that all happened. And of course Emory Gordy and Hank DeVito and Emmy sort of turned me on to the history of country music and what was bad about it. That became my awakening to learning about who I had just been playing with, Elvis Presley, and how he wasn't near as good as he was in the beginning."

Moreover, Brown was a dutiful student of the process. He "took notes" during sessions, watching how Ahern worked with artists, and how Emmylou related to her band. When Rodney hired him to play on Rosanne Cash's first three albums, he had a chance to extend his education in the studio and be part of a new sensibility unfolding as Rodney and Rosanne fearlessly mapped out a broad-based musical palette built on country but referencing compatible sources in rock and pop (notably, the Beatles). These musicians were comfortable with acoustic music, they were at home with electric music; in a casual setting they might follow a workout on a Carl Perkins song with a rendition of a mid-'60s Lennon-McCartney tune, move on to a rousing take on "Jolé Blon" and temper it all with a Hank Williams gospel number. They were true eclectics, not dilettantes, who felt the music both viscerally and intellectually and played it with precision, to be sure, but never at the expense of passion.

They were the New Traditionalists, and their numbers would swell during the '80s, following the *Urban Cowboy* malaise, and for the better part of the decade the best music in America was coming out of Nashville. What the Beatles had suggested on *Rubber Soul*, what the Byrds, the Flying Burrito Brothers and Gram Parsons (with Emmylou) on his own had made explicit in the late '60s and early '70s was coming to beautiful fruition with the auspicious launching of Emmylou Harris's solo career with 1975's *Pieces of the Sky*. Her next album, later that year, the stunning *Elite Hotel* (which ranged from the Beatles' "Here, There, Everywhere" to Hank Williams's "Jambalaya"), would be followed by three more adventurous Ahern-produced/Hot Band–accompanied solo albums. She closed the decade with 1979's *Blue Kentucky Girl*, a return to traditional country stylings from a generational cross-section of writers (Charlie and Ira Louvin, Jean Ritchie, Nelson, and Crowell). Invariably, with this new blood on the artist side emerged another new breed of producers who spoke the same language as their young charges and may have been raised on rock but were country at heart.

Steeped in bluegrass, Ricky Skaggs (who had led Emmylou's Hot Band) returned to the high lonesome sound on his 1979 solo debut, *Sweet Temptation*, before being signed to Epic by Rick Blackburn. Although over time he would flirt with a more polished, pop-style sound, it was impossible for him to hide his roots, and his early- to mid-'80s output found him bringing traditional values to bear (and several of his Hot Band alumni to play) on a succession of first-rate albums: *Waiting for the Sun*, *Highways and Heartaches*, *Don't Cheat in Our Hometown*, and *Country Boy*.

In 1984 the mother-daughter duo of Naomi and Wynonna Judd released their self-titled debut album and proved themselves a formidable entity, thanks to Wynonna's gifts as a vocalist—she was conversant with and credible singing country blues, contemporary country, rock 'n' roll and gospel—and her and her mother's captivating harmonies, whether those be earthy ("Why Not Me," their first hit) or precious ("Sleeping Heart"). Producer Brent Maher enlisted Don Potter as the duo's musical alter-ego, and Potter became as integral to their sound and approach as Richard Bennett became to Steve Earle's.

At MCA Brown signed the folk-rooted singer-songwriter Nanci Griffith; CBS countered with Brown University–educated Mary-Chapin Carpenter, perhaps the most consciously literate writer of this generation of artists. Her insightfully drawn characters and finely crafted songs betrayed a poet's sensitivity and came with a feminist edge. Collaborating with her former boyfriend turned producer-arranger-bandleader John Jennings, Carpenter framed her diary-like music in a sound scape that embraced elements of folk, country rock, and rock 'n' roll.

As pure interpreters, both George Strait and Randy Travis made their stands for traditionalism, Strait under the guidance of the man who signed him, Jimmy Bowen, Travis with producer Kyle Lehning. Handsome and solidly built, Strait certainly profited from his sensitive hunk image, with his ever-present Resistol, tight Wrangler jeans, Western-style shirts, and of course a big, shiny belt buckle. But there was much more to him than style. Strait cut good, sometimes great, records, his sound incorporating elements of Western swing, honky tonk, country blues, rock 'n' roll, and pop, and these had a habit of landing regularly at or near the top of the charts. He could sing a tearjerker with the best of 'em, but the songs that most engaged him emotionally often dealt with concrete situations in elliptical terms ("The Chill of an Early Fall," about time passing and opportunities fading) or had a winsome, fatalistic edge ("Amarillo by Morning"). Moreover, he didn't just look like a cowboy—he had his own working ranch. He was authentic, in his love of country's roots and in his lifestyle. Strait's genuineness shamed a decade's worth of male country singers whose music was as empty as their ten-gallon, usually black, hats—or it should have. There's a certain stasis in Strait's recent work as he has retained largely the same formula that catapulted him to the top; still, he remains good for a few moving moments on any record he makes. Moreover, he has preferred to keep his own counsel, rarely doing interviews but emerging almost yearly to release another fine album and take it on the road for a well-received tour. He simply lets the music speak for him.

Randy Travis has pretty much done the same thing, although his track record is far spottier than Strait's. He emerged in 1986, channeling Lefty Frizzell and Merle Haggard, and produced by Kyle Lehning. His meal ticket was a pop-tinged style of honky tonk balladry that proved a commercial winner out of the box. He and Lehning were canny in finding the right material—musically and thematically (the issue usually was love, an enduring one)—and crafted a smooth sound out of honky tonk and pop approaches.

In 1986 another artist surfaced who challenged Steve Earle in championing a contrarian spirit. Kentuckian Dwight Yoakam emerged from the Los Angeles "cowpunk" scene with a blistering amalgamation of Bakersfield-style hard country, bluegrass, and rock 'n' roll, shaped in the studio by him and his own musical alter ego, Detroit native cum L.A. session veteran Pete Anderson. After teaming with Yoakam, Anderson beefed up what had been a traditional honky tonk approach with some Motor City muscle, notably with his sizzling, super-twangy guitar work and dazzling, atmospheric productions. Yoakam, in boots, painted-on blue jeans, a Nudie jacket over a white t-shirt, and a cowboy hat tipped low enough to cover his eyes (and his balding head, too), sang in a high, nasally whine, wrote (or cowrote with the likes of Rodney Crowell, Roger Miller, and the uninamed, country hitmaker of Greek extraction, Kostas) vivid, sometimes lurid, self-pitying tales of love and loss in which he invariably cast himself and his fate in apocalyptic terms.

Yoakam came on the scene via Los Angeles by way of his native Pikeville, Kentucky. He stopped in Nashville en route, hoping to get a break there, but he found the country music establishment hostile or indifferent to his roots-centric hard country, much as it had been in the early '60s to the hard-edged Bakersfield Sound pioneered by Yoakam's idols, Buck Owens and Merle Haggard. Frustrated, he migrated to California and insinuated himself into the L.A. punk and emerging cowpunk scene, never forgetting the backhand Nashville had given him. In a 1984 interview that expresses views he has never recanted, Yoakam said: "I was discouraged by the closed society in Nashville. There was very little sympathy for anybody trying to do something unlike what the record companies had in their mind as an appropriate country sound. The town has always been slow to recognize something outside their mainstream. Ricky Skaggs had his third gold album, and they're just now starting to sign traditional country musicians. So I decided to give the West Coast a try, because then there was somewhat of a hotbed of country-rock out here, in the recording studios at least, led by Emmylou Harris and others."[2]

Yoakam's first demos were cut in 1981 and featured a stellar bunch of L.A. session players, led by guitarist Jerry McGee (his credits includes stints with the Ventures and Emmylou Harris), pedal steel whiz Jay Dee Maness and pianist Glen D. Hardin (both alumni of Gram Parsons's and Elvis Presley's bands), mandolin-dobro virtuoso David Mansfield, Robert Wilson on bass, and Davey Crockett on drums. Four of these tracks—"It Won't Hurt," "I'll Be Gone," "Twenty Years," and "Miner's Prayer"—wound up on an Oak EP issued in 1984; this session also produced early versions of "Floyd County" and "I Sang

Dixie," which were later retooled for his 1988 masterpiece, *Buenas Noches from a Lonely Room*. Around this time, though, the signal event in Yoakam's career occurred, when his path crossed that of guitarist-arranger Pete Anderson, whose sense of mission and outsized ego were, incredibly, a match for Yoakam's own, as was the chip on his shoulder regarding the state of Nashville. The two hit it off, musically and philosophically, and one of the great partnerships in country music history was born.

Upon hearing Yoakam's early material, Anderson said he felt "the songs and voice were there, but it was like a diamond in the wrong setting. We needed arrangements." Anderson went to work, keeping things lean and mean with a basic band supplemented by fiddles, mandolins, steel guitars, and dobros, with the most well tempered use of strings this side of Owen Bradley. The music they made together looked eastward, but no further than Bakersfield, for its spirit (oh, there was at least a courtesy call to the Sun Studio in Memphis, in Anderson's judicious but devastating deployment of vocal echo), and evinced no regard at all for mainstream niceties.

Then there was Tony Brown, who unwittingly was getting ready to step into a moment in country music history that he would drive, both as executive and as producer. Before he could do that, he had to get up to speed on a number of fronts. To that end, his tenure with Emmylou and the Hot Band became, in his view, "a life-altering moment."

A Conversation with Tony Brown

"This is like a higher level of music here."

What did you take away from those years with Elvis?

I learned to never, ever be ashamed of where you came from, and that's what made him such a big star. He was a truck driver that became basically a style icon to this day, not to mention that he changed music. He wanted to sing gospel music, but he could never get into gospel. He used to come to gospel concerts. That's how I sort of got the job with Voice; everybody in Voice was ex-gospel singers that Elvis just loved. He hired them just to give them a job. But he never, ever was ashamed of his love for gospel music and black music, and also I learned that he knew the difference between mediocrity and excellence. That's why when Ronnie Tutt couldn't play, he would get Larrie Londin. And when Jerry Scheff couldn't play, he would get Emory Gordy, Jr. Of course, he never had to make that decision about James Burton.

I learned that even though he was a kind of fucked-up individual on drugs, he knew what he liked. He really had a musical depth, and that's what everybody bought into. I learned that he really climbed inside of his music and demanded that his musicians do the same.

The Elvis gig had changed my life; I elevated myself to another level of musician. And that's what made me sort of start learning, oh, that's good, this is great. Then Emmy turned me on to Rodney Crowell before I ever met Rodney, and after she had sort of given me the history of Gram Parsons; I started thinking, I bet for Emmy Rodney sort of fills that empty space that Gram left when he died. And I started learning about great songwriters, and Rodney was the first singer-songwriter that I got to know. That sort of turned me on to everybody else

I worked with later on, like Nanci [Griffith], and Steve Earle, Lyle [Lovett]; got turned on to that singer-songwriter thing because they just look at life a little bit different.

You say that Emmy and this group of artists around her talked to you about what was good and not so good about country music. Specifically what did they teach you?

It was about originality—like Haggard created and Buck Owens created something original. Dwight [Yoakam] sort of definitely drew from Buck, and so many people have drawn from Merle Haggard. When I got with Emmy I really wasn't into country music, per se. I loved those first two albums. I actually had bought *Pieces of the Sky* and *Elite Hotel*, and it really was because I knew that James and Glen D. played on them. Because they would always talk about Emmylou and how great she was. So I was in awe of those two guys. I was doing my research. I became like a record trivia nut—I read every engineer and songwriter credit, where it was recorded, that kind of stuff. I just started noticing, when the radio was on the bus as we were touring around with Emmylou, someone would say, "Turn that shit off. Let's play some good stuff." And there I was with everybody like Hank DeVito and Emmy and Emory and Ricky Skaggs—I replaced Glen D. in Emmylou's band, and Ricky Skaggs replaced Rodney—and of course Ricky came from the bluegrass world. I just learned I was around a bunch of elite musicians, and I thought, I'm just gonna glean from this, I'm just gonna pull from this, I'm gonna find out. There is a difference between X artist, whether it be rock or country, and another artist. And success doesn't necessarily mean it's excellent music. Over a lifetime, we all know what ear candy is and how you can just go for the dollar or you can sort of be more idealistic. And even back in those days as a musician, I wanted to play with great musicians, but all the great musicians I liked made big money. Elvis paid big money and so did Emmylou. And if you played with little country bands like Faron Young or you played with Tanya Tucker or you played with whoever else was about that time, that was a smaller level of a gig, and also, to me, a lower level of musical excellence, in my opinion. At least that's what I was learning on the bus. And how everybody was stealing James Burton's licks. Emmylou never got as huge as Crystal Gayle or people like that. And I was going, That's really weird. That opened my eyes. I liked a lot of Crystal Gayle's records that Allen Reynolds did in those early days; I really loved those early records of hers. But I was going, [Emmylou] is so much better, in my opinion. Wonder what the deal is here?

I became a very analytical person by being around those kind of musicians. Analytical about songwriting; analytical, if they weren't songwriters, about the kind of songs they did, the way they were recorded, how they sounded, who they toured with. In my mind Emmylou was a much bigger star than Crystal Gayle or Tanya Tucker. I was just thinking this is like a higher level of music here. It sort of turned me into an idealistic person.

Following Elvis's death in August 1977, Tony replaced Glen D. Hardin in Emmylou's Hot Band. A year later, with Emmy pregnant and off the road, Brown accepted an offer from RCA to head up a new pop label in Los Angeles called Free Flight. After her baby was born, Emmylou started playing shows on weekends, "all the different little clubs from San Diego all the way up to San Francisco." Rosanne Cash soon followed Emmy's model, and Rodney put together some of his ex–Hot Band mates, including Tony, to back Cash on the same California coast circuit. It was memorable part-time work.

"We'd go play Redondo Beach, and Linda Ronstadt would show up at the show, Billy Gibbons. That's when I experienced the rock 'n' roll life. We were living it; we just took the door, basically. I just loved being in that element, being around backstage with people I had sort of put on a pedestal."

In December 1979 RCA closed down Free Flight, and Brown moved back to Nashville to work as manager of the label's A&R department. In March 1980 he signed Alabama and, almost at the same moment, got a call from Crowell asking him to go on the road with the Cherry Bombs for the summer. Brown declined, saying he couldn't afford to leave his job. Crowell asked him how much he was getting paid between that time and the end of the year. Brown gave him the number—"I wasn't making that much money"—and Crowell offered to pay him that same amount for only six weeks of touring, "and you'll have a lot more fun."

Brown completed the contract with Alabama and resigned two weeks later. After touring with Rodney and Rosanne, and playing on Rosanne's first three albums, all produced by Crowell, Brown hit a wall when "Rosanne kept getting pregnant and Rodney couldn't have a hit."

Another fateful call came in '83, when new RCA chief Joe Galante rang him up, seeking a suggestion for "an A&R person with your kind of sensibility who runs in the circles you run in."

Said Brown, "What about me?"

"No," Galante said firmly. "You're a gypsy."

Brown gave that statement a quick evaluation and experienced another epiphany: "You know what? Rosanne's not working, Rodney's not working. And after playing in a band with Emory Gordy, Jr., Hank DeVito, and Vince Gill, and Albert Lee, I can't go down from that. So I'm retiring as a musician."

Galante offered Brown the job, and there Brown stayed for a bit more than a year, until March 12, 1984, in his recollection, when Jimmy Bowen, newly installed as the president of MCA Nashville and VP of the company overall, summoned him to MCA with an irresistible offer.

During sessions for a Hank Williams, Jr., album that he was producing, Bowen invited Brown to overdub some organ parts, "which turned out to be a secret meeting to tell me that he was taking over MCA. He said, 'I'll groom you to become a great producer like me.' And on his wall was Sinatra and Dean Martin, Strait, and I'm going, Gosh, I wish I could do that."

"Come to MCA and I'll make you a vice president," Bowen said, "and I'll let you coproduce Jimmy Buffett with me, and I'll bring Steve Wariner over and you can coproduce that with me."

Then Bowen added the final, unnecessary inducement: "I'm going to produce George Strait and Reba, Lee Greenwood, and you go out and find me the next big thing."

It was the opportunity to get behind the board that sealed the deal. At RCA he had been thrown bones—the veteran Norro Wilson gave him an opportunity to coproduce an album on rising star Steve Wariner, a Chet Atkins favorite. But thereafter Galante mostly resisted Brown's entreaties to let him produce, offering only vocalist Razzy Bailey and "whoever the acts were on RCA Canada that nobody wanted to produce." In Bowen's offer Brown heard an implicit promise that he could put his own stamp on the music in some way. He started his MCA tenure by signing his friend and former bandmate Vince Gill, who had run his course without a hit at RCA, and made Gill's MCA debut his debut as sole producer of a major-label project. Brown's career was unfolding like a verse in the old gospel song, "a wheel within a wheel."

"It all stems, actually, from the Elvis connection. The Elvis connection got me the Emmylou gig; the Emmylou gig is where I nurtured and discovered my musical taste and learned about the difference between good and excellent, and learned about what I did and didn't like and learned about blind faith."

A Conversation with Tony Brown

"The psychology of producing is what I learned from Bowen."

Was Jimmy Bowen your role model as a producer?

Bowen and Rodney Crowell. Bowen specifically told me he was going to teach me.

He brought you to MCA with the idea of taking you under his wing?

Right. He taught me about things such as, if wanted Amos Garrett to play on a song, why wouldn't you fly him in? As opposed to getting Reggie Young to do an Amos Garrett impersonation, which he could probably do. But why wouldn't you fly Amos Garrett in?

"Well, it would cost a lot of money."

He goes, "Can you put a price if you thought that would make the song? Why wouldn't you do that?"

I said, "Well, that would be great!"

"If you work for me, I'll let you do that. Everybody hates me because I fly in musicians and engineers from Los Angeles specifically because I think I need their help."

So that's one thing I learned from him. But before him, my heroes, I loved Brian Ahern's Emmylou Harris records, the first four; I loved Billy Sherrill's records, the Tammy and George, the Charlie Rich records—I loved how he sort of got that "countrypolitan" thing; and I loved Owen Bradley. I loved all the old cats. I started going back and listening and figuring out who played the piano on Patsy Cline and I started studying. And that was when I just started studying what was closest to me, which was country producers, 'cause by that time Emmylou had turned me on to country music. I was going, I actually kind of like some of this stuff. And I was so infatuated by session players after working with Emmy. I got infatuated with Reggie Young, Bob Moore, all the session players. So I would go over to the Quonset Hut [*the studio Owen Bradley built*], and somebody said, "This is where Dylan cut *Blonde on Blonde* and *Nashville Skyline*." And they said, "Last night Ray Price cut 'Danny Boy' and he put like a 20-piece string section on it. It's going to be a big hit." I said, "Gosh, I wish I could hear it." And this person, who was a publisher or something, knew the engineer who worked at the Quonset Hut, which was a Columbia studio. Columbia, like RCA, had their own studios. He was a Columbia engineer. They took me into the control room and played me the mix—they cut it the night before and they were already mixing. In those days they could turn a record around in a week. Now you gotta have ninety days or six months to get a record turned around. You gotta get it approved and go through the singles committee at the label, all that shit. They played me this song and I went, "God, this is cool! And there were like 20 strings in there!" Pig [Hargus "Pig" Robbins], and Pete Wade and what was that drummer that played back in those days?

Kenny Buttrey?

Probably Kenny Buttrey. Probably Bob Moore or Roy Huskey on bass. And Pete Drake on steel, Ray Edenton on acoustic. And I go, "God, I wish I coulda seen that!" And he'd go, "Oh, no, they don't allow people in those sessions. You can't just come in. It was cool, though. You shoulda been here." So then I started finding myself trying to sneak into control rooms when I heard so-and-so was recording. I remember Mike Nesmith. Remember when the Monkees were big? Mike started cutting his own records in Nashville, and I sneaked into RCA, the big studio they built next to Studio A, the studio Elvis recorded in, and hid in the corner and watched Nesmith record until they found me and threw me out. My heart was just beatin' so hard and I was hiding over in the back. I think Al Pachuki was engineering. I just wanted to be in the room with greatness. Of course, Mike Nesmith being one of the Monkees—it wasn't that I loved his music. He was just a star. But I did get to sit in there for a verse and a chorus. That's when I thought, I want to do this. This is so cool.

So when Bowen called up with that offer, you didn't have any second thoughts because of his reputation as a tyrant?

Well, at that time was when Hank, Jr., was cutting great records like *Family Tradition*, and Bowen was the producer. I loved those records. I heard all those stories, but I was thinking, Hell, Galante's not much different. But he's not a producer.

What's interesting about the Amos Garrett example is that Bowen, for all his reputation, the way he behaved, what he was telling you there was to spare no expense to make the music as good as it could possibly be. If it meant flying somebody 1,500 miles to do the lick the best it could be done, do that instead of just calling up a guy across town to come in and imitate that lick. Spare no expense to make the music the way it should be. It's an enlightened attitude in that it might cost more to bring in an Amos Garrett, but if it's a better record, everyone, including the label, might make a lot more money down the road. It was a decision based on art and commerce.

I remember the night Rodney brought in Hal Blaine to play instead of John Ware on a particular Rosanne song. And I'd heard of Hal Blaine my whole life, that he had played on more records than any drummer in the history of the world or something. And it scared me so bad that I went into the control room and asked Rodney—it was the one night Rodney didn't have Glen D. there. He'd have Glen D. and me there. He'd say, "Glen D. get on electric piano, Tony get on acoustic. No, y'all switch." To this day I'll switch guitar players. I like to hire electric and an acoustic. And one of the electrics will be sort of a utility guy and I'll just switch them. It's amazing how switching a musician will change the track.

So Hal Blaine came and played on the track and it scared me so much that I asked would he mind calling Glen D. because I couldn't play, my heart was racing. Rodney said, "Absolutely. You're doing fine. But I'll do that for you." So I learned from Rodney about those kinds of things. And how to not let pride bite you in the ass.

Another thing I learned from Bowen: most sessions are three-hour sessions with a lunch break or a dinner break. With Bowen, if they started at 10, there would be a lunch break at one; then a break at two, and at five a dinner break. Bowen did that and everybody thought he was being Mr. L.A. But he said, "T, the reason I'm doing that is because I've noticed so-and-so and so-and-so, whenever they go out for lunch or dinner, they go out and have a couple of glasses of wine and they come back a little tipsy and they don't play as good. And I don't like that. So I don't let 'em leave the building. I want 'em to stay in here. If they finish dinner early and there's a little overdub, if everybody's sorta getting hungry, I'll just shut it down and they can go eat in the lounge and I'll say, to the piano player or the steel player, 'Hey, when you finish eating, come back in here and let's throw that part on I was talking about earlier. You know, you just keep 'em all in the building and you don't lose your band.' And I said, 'That makes total sense.' But everybody to this day does that. A lot of people do it because it makes them feel like they're top-notch producers. I always thought, because there were a couple of guys that used to go and get a little tipsy, I kind of agreed that that's not a bad idea, man.

Stuff like that. The psychology of producing is what I learned from Bowen as much as musical things.

chapter 9

"Are You Ready for Me?"

I. "This guy's an opinionated son of a bitch!"

Noel Fox was on the phone to Tony Brown to pitch him on checking out Steve Earle's songs. He had set up a weekend retreat at the Gulf Shores, Alabama, Ono Island digs of Oak Ridge Boy William Golden, where he would be joined by Steve and songwriter Jimbeau Hinson. This, Fox thought, would be the ideal opportunity for Tony to find out what Steve the artist was made of.

Situated on the southern tip of Alabama, on the Gulf of Mexico, Gulf Shores has long been a popular Southern vacation spot, with an emphasis on sun and surf in the day and partying all night every night. It was called the Redneck Riviera, for obvious reasons, and for many years all anyone needed to know about the place was that the revered former Alabama and Oakland Raiders star quarterback and unabashed hedonist Kenny "The Snake" Stabler owned a bar down there. The parties never stopped with "The Snake" around.

But party central wasn't much of a lure for Tony Brown. When the invite was described as a way to meet Steve Earle in a more relaxed setting, Brown hesitated. He knew of the *Pink & Black* EP and had been rather turned off by the cover. He had seen Steve perform on Ralph Emery's "Nashville Now" TV show and had shrugged.

"He was basically a takeoff on Ricky Nelson and Elvis mixed together. More country than Elvis, but more towards like a Ricky Nelson–rockabilly kind of thing. It was aimed at being a rockabilly kind of direction," Brown recalls.[1]

On the other end of the phone Fox was adamant: "Man, you gotta hear the songs this guy Steve Earle is writing."

"I saw him on 'Nashville Now,' and I'm sorry," Tony said. "I had to compare him to Elvis, and there's no comparison."

"Naw, that's not what he really does," Fox said. "That was really sort of the direction the label sent him in. You gotta hear some of this stuff he's writing. I'm going down to the Gulf Shores with Jimbeau Hinson and Steve in a couple of weeks. Why don't you go with us?"

Brown agreed to go but began to doubt the wisdom of his decision on the ride down. "On the way there I learned a lot about Steve Earle, because he was the only one that could talk—we sure couldn't talk in between him talking. So I learned all his philosophy about how screwed up Nashville was, or the A&R at record companies."

Brown admits that Steve "scared" him with the force of his arguments. For starters, Tony is a diminutive man and a peace-loving type. Steve's soliloquies were rendered with a physicality that made Brown wary—that plus "his BO at the time."

As he endured Steve's tirade, Brown could only think to himself, This guy's an opinionated son of a bitch! He made that silly-looking album with the silly pink and black cover, give me a break.

Once on Ono Island, the tenor of the trip changed dramatically, thanks to Steve's ongoing romantic debacle with Macayla. Every night the phone would ring, and the next thing Brown knew Steve was yelling at someone on the other end of the line, and he could hear a female voice yelling back through the receiver.

After he'd slammed the receiver down to end the call, Steve would return to the gang hanging out in the living room, "and he'd write a song." Astonished at seeing this process up close and personal, Brown was beside himself: "I thought, This must be the way Kristofferson, Dylan—this must be the way it works. They write their lives. Autobiographical.

"I just realized Steve was a very opinionated person, he didn't really like record people, but when we finished the few days down there, he had written 'Fearless Heart,' 'Guitar Town,' 'Hillbilly Highway,' and he'd let me join in on 'Down the Road'—I might've helped out on the melody or the chorus or something. I was never a lyrics person, so I'm sure I didn't contribute anything lyrically."

Brown's account of the songs that came out of the Gulf Shores trip runs counter to the timeline in Lauren St. John's *Hardcore Troubadour*, but he's certain the songs he cites came to fruition during that first meeting with Steve on the Redneck Riviera. More likely is a scenario in which Steve rewrote songs he had started elsewhere and passed them off as brand-new, on-the-spot compositions. Regardless, it left Tony Brown impressed by Steve's potential.

Before they left Gulf Shores, Steve told Tony he was going to visit Epic upon returning to Nashville and play this batch of news songs to see if the label would pick up his option. Tony suggested an alternate strategy: "Don't play 'em this stuff! Play 'em anything but this stuff, because it's good shit! And if they don't sign you, I'll sign you."

Steve: "I'll hold you to that, y'know."

"At least don't play 'em 'Fearless Heart.' Don't play 'em that one."

"Trust me, man," Steve assured him. "They're not gonna like any of this shit. This is the kind of stuff they don't want me to write."

"And that's exactly what happened," according to Tony Brown.

II. Alpha Male Ascending, V3.0

The road to signing Steve led through Jimmy Bowen, whose pop credentials notwithstanding, was not unqualified to appreciate where Steve was coming from. Bowen had started out in Texas with his friend Buddy Knox and a rockabilly band called the Orchids (later the Rhythm Orchids, which included Don Lanier and Dave Alldred; Alldred eventually gained some regional recognition fronting a group called Dickie Doo and the Don'ts, which recorded for Swan Records). They recorded at Norman Petty's Clovis, New Mexico, studio, home to Buddy Holly. From their initial session they self-released a single (first on their Blue Moon label, later on their Triple D label), one side being Knox's song "Party Doll," the other Bowen's "I'm Stickin' with You." Roulette Records picked up the single but issued separate Knox and Bowen 45s, the A sides being, respectively, "Party Doll" and "I'm Stickin' with You." Both were million sellers in 1957. Limited as an artist—he sang in an uninflected monotone and, saddled with the standup bass he played, was pretty much stationary as a performer—Bowen cut several more sides for Roulette, none even coming close to being as successful as his debut, and then made his move into production. Following stints at the helm of the Chancellor and Liberty labels, he assumed a power position in L.A., producing Dean Martin to the tune of 26 hit singles and Frank Sinatra (including the session that yielded the classic "Strangers in the Night"), among others. Relocating to Nashville in the mid-'70s, he was mentored by original Outlaw Tompall Glaser, did a lot of homework on his own, and rose to the rank of major power broker when he took the reins at MCA. He reinvented the Nashville recording industry for the modern age: with the power of the buck at his command, he would lock up several studios for weeks at a time, as he oversaw multiple sessions by multiple artists. Technologically astute, he began the process of upgrading Nashville to a state-of-the-art recording center. An early champion of digital technology, he insisted the studios he used either lease or rent what was then the cutting edge of recording gear, single-handedly establishing the Mitsubishi X-800 32-track as the digital tape recorder of choice in Music City (it even was credited on MCA album covers), and Nashville as ground zero of digital's adoption as the preferred professional recording medium.

Jimmy Bowen knew who he was, understood the power he wielded, and generally made sure the rest of the business in Nashville recognized him as, without qualification, a big-time alpha male in the Texas tradition. Emory Gordy, Jr., for one, learned firsthand about this one winter when he was producing the Bellamy Brothers, under Bowen's aegis. Asking Bowen for permission to take off work on Christmas Day, not only because it was Christmas Day but because it was also his birthday, Gordy, Jr,. explained as well that "I don't want to make the Bellamys work on Christmas Day. So can I take the day off?"

Without hesitating Bowen replied, "Well, Emory, happy birthday to you and baby Jesus."

From inside a control room on December 25, Emory and the Bellamys heard the bells of Christmas Day their old familiar carols play.

So after listening to the Steve Earle demos that Tony and Gordy, Jr. (then working in A&R at MCA) had recorded at Silverline/Goldline, Bowen reacted as if there were a foul stench in the room. "I can't understand a word he's saying," the imperious Bowen announced. "Go out and cut one of these songs so I can understand what he's saying. And then we can talk about it."

Brown and Gordy returned to Silverline/Goldline and, according to Brown, "just put Steve through the rigors of pronouncing words better—of course, he loved the shit outta that." Bowen, though, lightened up when he heard the new demo. "Okay, you know what?" he said. "There's something here. I can see there's something here."

Bowen and Steve met shortly thereafter, following which Bowen summoned Brown to his office.

"Okay," said Bowen, "before we sign him, you gotta get his teeth fixed. We'll pay for it."

"God, Bowen, you're gonna get me killed!" Tony protested. "He's gonna pop me in the face!"

Told of Bowen's stipulation about his teeth, Steve was grateful. "Great, man, I've been wanting to get 'em fixed anyway," he said to Tony. "I couldn't afford it."

Even before starting work on Steve's first album, Tony had already gained an education in coming to a project with clean hands rather than preconceived ideas based on marketing concepts. And he had learned much about Steve Earle and the breed of artist he embodied.

Tony Brown: "Here Epic was trying to present him as this rockabilly sex symbol kind of guy—and Steve did have that kind of cool rockabilly look with his black hair and stuff, and he was pretty slim back then. But hearing those songs at Gulf Shores, I thought, This guy is the next Kristofferson, or Waylon, or

Cash, that's what he is. He's a songwriter first, and whatever he wears doesn't make any difference. He's really got something to say. I didn't even know or care if he wrote some of the Epic songs. I grew to like some of those early rockabilly kind of songs. I realized that was part of him too, but under no circumstances was Epic letting anyone know what kind of artist they had in Steve Earle. They were just trying to pitch an image of what they thought would be visually acceptable out there to fans.

"I realized down there at Gulf Shores that this guy was much deeper than I had anticipated, and I didn't even think he was deep when I saw him play those songs on 'Nashville Now.' I got the wrong impression. This is a good example for me that the first impression you give the world of an artist, even if it doesn't sell, should be the right impression of the artist—look at the history of Willie Nelson, Waylon. The labels painted them the wrong way—remember Willie Nelson and that crewcut, those suits and stuff? This is how a label's artist development really screws with artists, especially singer-songwriters. Artists who don't write their own songs, they'll do whatever it takes to get their foot in the door and get on the radio. Then a lot of times whatever image was created they build on it and become rich and famous, and eventually they sort of go off the radar screen and you never hear about them anymore. Whereas artists who are singer-songwriters—which I found I was being attracted to there in the beginning, like Lyle Lovett and Nanci Griffith—if they can have commercial success on their terms, when the commercial success is over, they can still have success on their terms doing other things. To this day Guy Clark and Lyle Lovett can play performing arts centers and all kinds of places and make good money performing their music to an audience that really appreciates their work, as opposed to playing empty houses to fans who have moved on to Kenny Chesney, Toby Keith, and whoever the latest artist du jour is in country music. So I learned a lesson about singer-songwriters, and what kind of artist Steve Earle really was, and thank God Bowen was a believer in that and supported it. Steve Earle would have never flown at RCA; he would have probably flown over at Warners, with Jim Ed Norman, but I don't know that there were many places he would have flown except with Jimmy Bowen."

Guitar Town
MCA, 1986
Producer: Emory Gordy, Jr., and Tony Brown
Associate Producer: Richard Bennett
Studio: Sound Stage Recording Studio with Mitsubishi X-800 32-track digital
Recorded by: Chuck Ainlay
Mixed by: Chuck Ainlay at The Castle
Overdubs recorded by: Steve Tillisch, Chuck Ainlay, Russ Martin at Emerald
    Studio

Second engineers: Russ Martin, Mark J. Coddington, Tim Kish, Keith Odle, Robbie Rose

CD Master tape prepared by Glenn Meadows and Milan Bogdan at Masterfonics using the JVC digital audio mastering system

Musicians
The Dukes:
Richard Bennett: guitars, six-string bass, slap bass
Bucky Baxter: pedal steel
Ken Moore: organ and synthesizer
Emory Gordy, Jr.: bass and mandolin
Harry Stinson: drums and vocals

Songs
 1. "Guitar Town" (2:33) (Steve Earle)
 2. "Goodbye's All We've Got Left" (3:16) (Steve Earle)
 3. "Hillbilly Highway" (3:36) (Steve Earle, Jimbeau Hinson)

4. "Good Ol' Boy (Gettin' Tough)" (3:58) (Steve Earle–Richard Bennett)
5. "My Old Friend the Blues" (3:07) (Steve Earle)
6. "Someday" (3:46) (Steve Earle)
7. "Think It Over" (2:13) (Steve Earle–Richard Bennett)
8. "Fearless Heart" (4:04) (Steve Earle)
9. "Little Rock 'n' Roller" (4:49) (Steve Earle)
10. "Down the Road" (2:37) (Steve Earle–Jimbeau Hinson–Tony Brown)

The album that became *Guitar Town* actually started, in a real sense, with Steve paying a visit to Richard Bennett in Los Angeles, a cassette tape in hand of rough versions of most of the songs he would record on his major-label debut. During sessions for his unreleased Epic recordings, Bennett had invited Steve to stay with him and his family if ever he found himself in L.A.

"And lo and behold, he made it a point to come out and stay with us for a week or 10 days," Bennett recalls. "I remember picking him up at the airport and him sort of wielding a cassette and saying, 'I've written this album and I'm gonna get off Epic,' and blah-blah-blah, as Steve does."[2]

Bennett remembers that he and Steve were barely in the front door of his house when Steve insisted he put the cassette on immediately. What he heard was "five or six" songs that would be the album "already finished and in place." Steve stayed with Bennett for a week, and the two of them wrote a pair of songs, "Think It Over" and a snarling stomp called "Good Ol' Boy (Gettin' Tough)."

"Think It Over" sprang from a "pretty well finished" melody that Bennett had composed but that lacked any lyrics. "It caught Steve's ear and he wrote lyrics for it." "Good Ol' Boy (Gettin' Tough)" started with a Bennett riff and "we kind of hammered it out and worked on what melody there is in the thing and the chord structure of it. And then Steve wrote lyrics to that. I remember us sitting in my garage workshop in Los Angeles, sitting across from each other with a couple of guitars, and it was pretty easy."

A couple of moments from that trip still stand out in Bennett's memory. One evening a musician friend of Bennett's showed up to hang out, "and Steve, never lacking any self-confidence, was telling this guy about this album he was gonna make, which of course ended up being *Guitar Town*. But we were nowhere close; he wasn't even signed to MCA, but he was already telling this guy, 'It's gonna be the most important album in twenty-five years in Nashville.' And I had to catch myself from saying anything. But both my friend and I had a chuckle about it after the fact."

Also on that trip, a night out for dinner took a downbeat turn when Richard observed Steve experiencing what seemed like an upset stomach or stomach cramps. He was "bent over and green.

"Man, what's up?" Bennett inquired.

"Let's go out and take a walk," Steve said, straining to get the words out.

"So we went out and walked around the block," Bennett says, "and he came clean that he was kind of coming off of heroin."

Back to Nashville Steve went, with a demo of "Gettin' Tough" and "Think It Over." A few more weeks passed, and Steve returned to Los Angeles, and to Bennett's doorstep. "Look, I want you involved with this album, and you just need to move to Nashville," Steve told Richard.

For Bennett, Steve's insistence on him moving to Nashville seemed fortuitous. Seventeen years of session work in L.A. had been profitable but enervating, and he was beginning to feel his day might have passed. But more and more he was taking to the idea of producing records, "and I thought Nashville might be a good climate to do that."

He called Emory Gordy, Jr., and, after some casual chitchat, "came clean" with him: "I want to produce records. Do you think I've got a shot?" he asked Gordy.

"There's never any guarantees," Gordy answered. "If you're at the point where you think you can make better records than other people are doing, then it's time for you to come out and take a swing at producing records."

With that, Bennett, his wife, and their two children packed up and moved to Nashville. Through Gordy and Brown, and his own reputation, he picked up all the session work he could handle. At the same time, he was working with Steve—who still wasn't signed at that point—at Silverline/Goldline on demos of what became the *Guitar Town* songs, with a band comprised of Gordy, Jr., on bass, Harry Stinson on drums, original Duke Ken Moore on piano, Steve on acoustic rhythm guitar, and Bucky Baxter on pedal steel. Baxter was an acquaintance of Steve's whom Brown considers "the ultimate yes man for an artist like Steve; he didn't give Steve any shit. Plus I think Steve liked his playing a lot. It was very simple, and Bucky did have a cool style. I just never thought of him as being the kind of musician that Harry Stinson is, or that Richard Bennett is; even though he did play with Dylan, I never thought of him in that way." Indeed, Brown brought in Paul Franklin to play steel on "Fearless Heart" and "Someday," but Steve insisted Baxter be used on the rest of the tracks.

Steve didn't treat these as throwaway sessions, either—he was intent on the musicians sounding like a real, seasoned band; not clean and perfect in the way of session players, but at once tight and freewheeling, intent on delivering the feeling of the songs first and foremost. "With Steve's thing—unlike most Nashville sessions, on which all the A team players play on—not only was it close to perfection with feeling, it really was about a vibe," Brown notes. In a deliberate, thoughtful process, the musicians worked up every element of each song until, in Bennett's estimation, "90 to 95 percent of what you hear on the finished record was in place by the time we went in to record it.

"There was a little eight-track recorder down there, so we could put stuff down and talk about it," Bennett says. "So we did our arranging and pre-production and rehearsed it in this little Silverline/Goldline studio. And it really came together that way as a band. Because we came in knowing what we were gonna do and were somewhat sure of ourselves, it just had a little bit of a flair about it instead of the usual cast of studio people thrown together, and there it is."

Bennett wasn't the only transplanted Angeleno playing on Steve's debut album. Drummer Harry Stinson, a Nashville native, had been making his living on the West Coast working with everyone from Al Stewart to Peter Frampton to blues queen Etta James, when he decided he was burned out on the road and in need of a change. A conservative fellow, Stinson was also feeling out of place in the L.A. music scene come the early '80s, "when it started to go to more punk and everybody was spiking their hair and piercing everything. I just didn't relate to that."[4]

On a memorable weekend trip to Nashville to visit his parents and family, Stinson was introduced to Tony Brown, who brought him in to sing some vocals on a Jimmy Buffett session, after which he strolled down the hall and wound up singing on a Pam Tillis session being produced by Barry Beckett. "It was an amazing weekend," Stinson says.

In the early '70s Stinson had made an effort to get established as a session drummer when he was still living in Nashville, but found it almost impossible to break into the game. Right out of high school he was on the road, drumming for Dottie West, whose son was a high school buddy and bandmate of Stinson's. "I liked going on the road, making fifty bucks a night and getting on a bus and playing on the Grand Ole Opry when it was still at the Ryman, and meeting Dolly Parton. I was in heaven."

But when he came off the road and tried to get work on Music Row, no one was taking. He sang on Eddie Rabbitt's first album, and then nothing. "It was tough, because it was the world of Grady Martin and Kenny Buttrey and people like that. So I left town, eventually ended up in L.A. and really went to school out there, so to speak."

He was drumming for Nicolette Larson the summer Tony introduced him to Steve. They talked about the upcoming album sessions for Steve's debut, and Stinson got the distinct impression that he already had been "scouted out," that the meeting with Steve was a mere formality in advance of him being invited to join the band. They gave him a tape of the *Guitar Town* demos and he listened to it while driving back to L.A. "I do remember thinking, This really is special music. If the record company doesn't get in the way and it gets out to people, this could have a chance; this could make a difference."

When he was hired for the session, Stinson understood his commitment would go beyond the recording studio: he wasn't simply a hired gun playing on an album who would then move on to another project; rather, he would become a Duke and go on tour with Steve when the album was released. He believes Tony Brown was using Emmylou's Hot Band as a model and "wanted to put a band together that would record and tour together, which was not the Nashville norm. And if some careers spun off in the wake of that, great, but he wanted it to be a band."

III. "Everyone knew what the thrill was"

With the musicians assembled at the Soundstage Studio ("using the Mitsubishi X-800 32 Track Digital," according to the album's liner copy), the actual sessions were almost anticlimactic. Brown and Gordy, Jr., were the credited producers; as the credited associate producer Bennett was a bit miffed. He had come to Nashville hoping to build a résumé as a producer, and here he was so close, but not quite there.

"I sort of never got what was promised to me," he says. "I was promised a third of the production, and a third of the production points, splitting it with Emory and Tony. As nice as that would have been, what I was really more interested in was a full production credit or a coproduction credit. That's really what I was aiming for, and that's really the reason I came out here, to chase production. Anyway, I sort of got screwed out of my point and got an emasculated credit in the end of it. But in the end, there's no bitterness, no hard feelings, because that did what I wanted it to do anyway. It opened up all the doors for me, as far as production. And it was a calling card as far as my guitar playing."

The work at Silverline/Goldline paid off in ways Tony Brown did not realize until they started up at Soundstage. It was, he said, the moment when he learned the value of preproduction.

"All those demos that we had done, which became the sketches for the record, saved us a lot of time, because all that stuff like working out the line Richard did on 'Guitar Town,' all that time was done in the demo, or preproduction, part of the record. So we could fly through stuff like that pretty quick. Little stuff like that; tiny, subtle, little changes. Those lines Richard was playing, he really worked and worked and worked on the way those lines played out. Once we got to the session, everyone there had played on the demos, so it went down pretty painlessly. And by that time Steve was feeling pretty good about everything. We had Chuck Ainlay engineering. Everyone on the project in the studio knew what the thrill was and knew what we were trying to accomplish sound-wise and arrangement-wise … so we were not in there struggling with an arrangement on the floor and being indecisive about shit like that."

"All the preparation that Richard and Steve and Tony did before I was involved," Stinson notes, "really cemented everything. They already had the map—as far as the parts, the keys, all that stuff, it was well mapped out. And that was the best way to record that album, in my opinion, because you weren't looking at a chart. You already knew it. And you could just relax and play. I think the best music comes like that."

Speaking about the chain of command between himself, Gordy, Jr., and Bennett, Brown doesn't intellectualize it: he was in the control room, Gordy, Jr., and Bennett were in the studio, "leading the band in the right direction." No one tried to get in the way of Steve's vision, though, being so careful to honor it that Brown says "Steve called the shots" during the session.

"He was in charge, and that's the way it should be for those kinds of records. If we'd cut a track and it was almost there, and Steve wasn't sure if he liked it or not, Richard and Emory knew what the problem was; it was usually about the guitar part Richard was playing—Steve played acoustic on all that stuff and broke strings on every pass. We'd have to stop and restring his guitar. The way he strikes the strings with his pick, as opposed to the flat part of the pick, he'd always break a string. On the last chorus you'd hear that 'ping'!

"But if the track was there except for that, we could always overdub and fix it later on. If it happened at the beginning of the track it ruined the song for the moment, because Steve pretty much led the band with his style of playing. He really did. No one plays like he does; in fact, to this day I'll be looking for … there's a tuning or a phrase that Steve plays … it's like an open fifth or something, I don't know what it is. But I'll ask an acoustic player does he mind doing that kind of a chord, and he'll say, 'I'm not sure what you're talking about,' and I'll put on 'Guitar Town' and say, 'Like this chord he's playing.' 'Oh, he's playing a root, a fifth and there's like a third in there.' I say, 'Well, whatever it is, make it sound like that.' And they go, 'Oh, shit, that's the stuff we learned when we were learning to playing the guitar, when you think you can't play.'

"Also, Steve would pedal things differently than anybody else. So his acoustic playing on that album became a real crucial part of the band having to climb in behind it and contribute to what he was laying down. And Richard and Emory, boy, they could get there. The pressure was on Emory and Richard, for the most part, and I basically listened to make sure the track felt like it was solid."

Stinson remembers an unusually egalitarian studio scene, with no discernible pecking order among the producers and musicians, and moreover, a camaraderie springing from the players' enthusiasm at being part of a special moment.

"Everybody seemed to work really well together and trust each other," Stinson recalls. "If somebody had an idea, they'd speak up. I don't remember anybody trying to run the show or anything. We all kind of had to come back to Steve, and if he didn't like it, it didn't happen. Everybody was playing in the same sandbox; everybody was really getting along."

IV. "You want a guitar solo? Here!"

During preproduction at Silverline/Goldline, Steve and Richard Bennett came to a mutual agreement that in the song "Guitar Town," because it was called "Guitar Town," and because the most obvious thing to do would be to feature a guitar solo in it, "that was the very thing we were not—*not*—going to do. And I was just a hundred percent with him all the way," says Bennett.

Rather than a guitar solo, the early rehearsals of "Guitar Town" featured Kenny Moore playing what Bennett recalls as "some kind of little Farfisa solo." After they actually recorded it that way, Emory Gordy, Jr., stepped forward with a blunt assessment: "I think it needs a guitar solo."

Bennett resisted, "sort of dug in my heels," and he and Gordy, Jr., proceeded to debate the point in a friendly but serious manner—"we had been in the trenches together since, God, the '70s"—until Bennett, finally ticked off enough to want to prove his point in more dramatic fashion, ended the discussion with a terse "Right. Okay."

Storming back to his guitar trunk, he "grabbed the most obnoxious thing I could think of first, and that happened to be a vintage early-'60s model Danelectro Longhorn six-string bass. I said, 'You want a guitar solo? Here!' And plugged in and played the first thing that fell out of my brain. And that was it. That was one of the few things that wasn't planned on that album. For the most part everything else was almost orchestrated, you know. That album, even though it doesn't sound it, it was very arranged. Except for the six-string bass solo on 'Guitar Town.'

"Of course," Bennett adds, without chagrin, "Emory was dead right; absolutely right."

A Short Course on the Danelectro Six-String Bass

In Steve Earle's recording history, no instrument has played a more critical role in defining his sound than Richard Bennett's Danelectro Longhorn six-string bass. In one breath Bennett may refer to it as "the most obnoxious" instrument he could think of, but it has also served him well throughout his career as a studio musician and looms large in his legend if only for the sound of a land without borders that it conjures on *Guitar Town* and on Steve's second album, *Exit 0*. If Steve wanted to cast himself in the role of the wandering minstrel, a populist loner taking the pulse of the people in the great out there and channeling the voices of the disenfranchised, the sound Bennett wrought for him could not have been more appropriate or more evocative.

Richard Bennett on the Danelectro six-string bass: "It's basically a guitar that's tuned an octave lower than a guitar. So if you can play a guitar you can play a six-string bass; it's the same fingering, just a full octave lower. 'Because They're Young,' by Duane Eddy—Duane played a six-string bass on that. Things like 'Theme from *The Magnificent 7*' and 'The Guns of Navarone' by Al Caiola, that's a six-string bass. And it was also used by people like Bert Kaempfert in those wonderful middle-of-the-road kind of things where you'd have a string bass sort of playing fairly static, a one and three kind of thing, and the six-string bass just dancing all around the foundation of the bass. And of course they used it for years and years in Nashville the same way. With a string bass and a six-string bass.

"So when I was coming up in Los Angeles, most guitar players carried a six-string bass in their kit, because often you were still called upon to use one. And even after the fact, after they quit using them, I still carried one. I would occasionally play it on things. I played it on the first Billy Joel album. There was a thing called 'Captain Jack' on the *Piano Man* album. The sort of menacing riff that goes through that thing is me on guitar and then I doubled it with a six-string bass. So I never quit using a six-string bass, but that's not to be confused with a baritone guitar, which seems to be *de rigueur* these days. But I don't care for the baritone. They're neither fish nor fowl, you know. The Danelectro is a wonderful instrument."

A Conversation with Richard Bennett

To Extricate, to Highlight, to Play

After Copperhead Road *was released, Steve talked in an interview about how happy he was to get to play guitar on his own album finally. Tony Brown has been so complimentary of your playing, but he hasn't put Steve down as a guitar player either. He has said that Steve wanted to play more guitar but that you had the right approach and he loved the riffs you developed. Steve obviously is proud of his guitar playing. How did you work out the guitar parts in the studio for* Guitar Town?

Steve's a very good guitar player. I really like the way he plays guitar, and I like the way he played guitar back then. Really, it was sort of common practice, and still is, that even if you play guitar and you're singing, for recording purposes it's more focused for you to stand up there and sing. And if you want to come back and do the guitar, great, but as far as getting the track and getting the vocal performance, it's just easier for everybody around to get that first. So that was my understanding of the situation. I didn't really think anything of it, and it didn't seem to be an issue. We would track and I'd usually put an acoustic guitar pass down for tracking, although some of them were electric passes. And then end up usually throwing on a second guitar part, either an electric or something else. I remember specifically Steve played acoustic guitar on "My Old

Friend the Blues," and I played the electric and solo and the whole thing went down live. To my recollection, on that album that was the only guitar playing he did. But it didn't seem to be an issue; if he was peeved about it, I wasn't aware of it. But I don't think he was.

I think it was well after the fact that it started to get under his skin—after the fact being the time when he rolled into Memphis to start Copperhead Road.

Yeah. And as far as the riffs and that business, I wish I could give you a percentage, but a very high percentage of that stuff was what Steve was doing when he was on acoustic and running these tunes down. We were learning the tunes essentially; a lot of these little riffs were sort of hammering away when he was banging away playing rhythm. He had this other little thing that he was intimating at as well. What I did was extricate that, highlight it, and play it. I mean I have to give so much credit to Steve on that stuff.

According to Tony, Steve would have the sketch of a riff—

Absolutely.

And you would develop it to another level.

Just highlighting it, really, is what I did on so many of the things. Not all of them, but a lot of them. "Someday" is a prime example. That riff that I've got going in there was something that he had sketched and was intimating at as he was playing rhythm guitar. He would sort of do that underneath. A lot of it was pulling the detail out of that and just playing it.

* * *

Ultimately, all the riffs, all the planning, all the execution were in service to the right cause: the songs. Steve's songs inspired a group of young but veteran musicians and producers to the pinnacle of their creativity, for the sake of a virtual unknown's recording debut. But in listening to the words Steve wrote, those around him came to believe in him and in his message.

"Well, listen to the songs," Harry Stinson says. "The songs, those are the vision to me. With that kind of material coming out of you, you've got to have a strong sense of yourself. And I think he did. And whether he actually went through it or not, he definitely could relate to that sort of white-trash/blue-collar lifestyle and to real people. What people were really going through. Country music was always—and I hate to put Steve in a country bottle here; I'm not trying to do that, because I think he's way farther out from that genre—but in Nashville, and even today it's still the same, everybody's chasing being a star and everything kind of gets manufactured, and it's really a Hallmark moment stretched into three minutes. I think Steve's music, based on the songs, shows what kind of sense of himself that he had."

V. Taking His Lonesome on Down the Road

Anyone who knew Steve Earle's rambling history when *Guitar Town* was released would easily have recognized him in its 10 songs. Those who knew nothing about him but listened carefully would have formed an impression, more accurate than not, of a man for whom the road was salvation, a path to something better than he had in the place he'd been, a long ways away from busted love affairs, dead-end jobs, and general bad luck. The character Steve paints is transient, troubled, and decidedly conscious of his station in life.

A recurring theme, then, presents itself:

"Guitar Town": "Nothin' ever happened in my hometown / And I ain't the kind to just hang around";

"Goodbye's All We've Got Left": "Maybe you'll run into me somewhere, some night";

"Hillbilly Highway": "I'm standin' on this highway and if you're going my way / You know where I'm bound";

"Good Ol' Boy (Gettin' Tough)": "I was born in the land of plenty / Now there ain't enough";

"My Old Friend the Blues": "Another lonely night, a nameless town";

"Someday": "I got me a '67 Chevy, she's low and sleek and black / Someday I'll put her on that Interstate and never look back";

"Think It Over": "I hope someday I'll find a way / I'll walk right out on you";

"Fearless Heart": "I admit I fall in love a lot / But I nearly always gave it my best shot";

"Little Rock 'n' Roller": "Hey, little guy, I can't believe you answered the phone / I guess I didn't know you could do that / God help me, have I been gone that long";

"Down the Road": "How's love ever gonna find you / If it ain't here, it's down the road."

It's not a flattering portrait he paints of himself, but it is an honest one, remarkably true to Steve's history and philosophy, even if, say, his own grandfather never lit out for Detroit on the Hillbilly Highway that took so many white, poverty-stricken Southerners to the Motor City to make a better life working in the auto factories, or his own hardscrabble family life is not as he describes in "Good Ol' Boy (Gettin' Tough)." He'd already been close enough to all of that to feel it and to be resentful of the way he, his family, and other working-class Americans were treated. And besides, he wasn't a documentarian; he was making art of his history. As a companion for a woman, he's forthright about his fecklessness, even apologetic for the hurt he's caused, but shows no inclination to change his ways. That said, he's as openhearted, even sentimental, about his feelings for the women he's loved as John Keats was in his

Steve performing in Austin during Farm Aid II, July 4, 1986.

short, tragic life. His expressions of love are moving in their plainspoken poetry—in time, his aching, simple love songs would become the most underrated aspect of his artistry, overshadowed by more incendiary, politically charged tracts.

Steve makes his presence felt from the first notes of the first cut, "Guitar Town," hard strumming an acoustic guitar before he enters announcing, in a clear, drawling tenor, "Hey, pretty baby / are you ready for me / it's your good-rockin' daddy down from Tennessee." At the end of the verse, following the words "guitar town," Bennett enters on the Danelectro, sounding a robust triplet figure and developing it before Steve enters for the second verse. Bennett dominates the arrangement with his twanging solos, which have an epic feel, but Ken Moore's washes of organ chords add depth. "Goodbye's All We've Got Left" again is keyed by Steve's solid acoustic strumming, and as this mid-tempo breakup song evolves, Bennett twangs along in the background, Moore interjects a keyboard commentary in between, and at the end of the verses the sound is beefed up with synthesized handclaps. There's a nice break before the third verse, when everyone falls away, isolating Steve's acoustic and Stinson's drums before the story begins again.

A bopping acoustic riff kicks off "Hillbilly Highway," preceding Bennett's entrance with some top-strings thump as Steve starts drawling the story of the coal miner grandfather who headed north to Detroit seeking a better day for his family. An ambiguous ending finds the narrator, after quitting school and whiling away his days at home, "just sittin' around playing guitar," out on the highway to an unnamed destination that he assumes everyone knows. But one of the most dramatic moments on the record occurs after the second verse when Bennett, playing a Gibson Les Paul recorded direct through the Mitsubishi digital board and double-tracked, enters like a sleeping giant awakened and in foul humor, moaning and groaning a single bent note and then letting out a discursive protest in a flurry of notes that seem to circle in on and around each other until Steve picks up the next verse. It's a riveting instrumental cameo, and he repeats it at the end, even expanding on the theme he's sounded as the song fades out with everyone singing "hill … billy highway!"

"Good Ol' Boy (Gettin' Tough)," one of the two Earle-Bennett cowrites, is a dispatch from the working class told in a rocking rhythm and featuring a hard electric riff from Steve and a driving guitar attack that would become something of a signature for him, surfacing again most dramatically on his third album, *Copperhead Road*. "My Old Friend the Blues" is a straightforward honky tonk–style tearjerker, complete with a moaning pedal steel and some aching harmony singing on the title sentiment. The lovely arrangement sprinkles some evocative piano interjections in between Bennett's rich solo, and toward the end the synth adds a nice orchestral flavor to the song's denouement. "Think It Over," the other Earle-Bennett cowrite, harks back to Steve's rockabilly incarnation and is as catchy a love song as they come, with Bennett adding the requisite slap bass lines, as well as a couple of solos on the Les Paul that summon the spirit of Elvis's stellar guitarist, Scotty Moore.

"Fearless Heart" finds Steve singing about the value of second chances in love in a dramatic narrative marked by the urgency of his plea for another go-'round, assuring the object of his affection that even if others consider him no good, he wouldn't ever hurt her. Ah, but there's a qualification, in another lyric that distinguishes Steve's writing from the usual: instead of envisioning fields of plenty in this reunion, he advises, "I can't promise this'll work out right / But it would kill me, darlin', if we didn't even try." Coming from a man who seemed always to leave himself an out in his romances, the lyric was both telling and prophetic. Here, again, Bennett sounds the solo that is the instrumental voice of Steve's anguished soul, this one a searing, trebly cry that comes screaming out of the second verse and proceeds to unfold in elegant cascades of notes up and down the neck of Bennett's Fernandes Strat, double-tracked, with a chorusing effect enhancing its steely grandeur. He returns again at the end, with a similar solo but bringing the song to a big finish with a twangy top-strings run.

"We struggled with 'Fearless Heart,'" Tony Brown recalls, "because it was the most anthem- and Springsteen-like song on there. I think Steve had a sonic vision in his head and it took us a while to finally arrive at. When Richard threw that cool solo in there, which was pretty different than anything on the album, we might have struggled with it. But I don't think we struggled all that hard. You know, when an artist knows what they want, and you have the musicians who are in the same place and sort of know what the thrill is, it's so much easier."

A sweet lullaby, "Little Rock 'n' Roller," sung by an absent father to his little boy, phoning in from "a truck stop on the Arkansas line," is as beautifully realized as its text is wrenching, Steve explaining to the child how he's going to be away "another couple weeks and another couple thousand miles." Bucky Baxter supplies a keening pedal steel solo at precisely the right moment to mirror the conflict Steve's character is feeling, the synth rises briefly for dramatic effect, Ken Moore strikes an ostinato riff on the organ, chimes surface, and Steve pours on the emotion in his vocal, dipping low in his register, biting off the ends of lines in a breathless tone, and finally, gently, softly singing, almost talking, "go to sleep little rock 'n' roller."

"That was a very kind of as warm and fuzzy as you'll ever get to hear Steve Earle, probably," says Tony Brown. "That track, as it was going down, it was really cool. It was not unlike that song that Springsteen did for the *Philadelphia* soundtrack. Steve Earle to me was Waylon, he was Cash, and he was Willie, but he was also Springsteen. He turned me on to Springsteen. We listened to *Born in the U.S.A.*; he's the one who got me to go out and see Springsteen. And if you listen to some of Springsteen's tracks, how he has a lot of things playing—like he has a theme probably on the guitar riff that the bass jumps on and the piano jumps on, and it's almost like an anthem—Steve has a lot of that kind of stuff happening."

A gentle, bluegrass-inflected shuffle (its distinguishing feature being Emory Gordy, Jr.'s evocative mandolin solos), "Down the Road" closes the story, not on the optimistic high of "Guitar Town," where it started, but rather on a note of weary resignation that at sunset the road beckons him again: "you start lookin' for a reason / to take your lonesome on down the road." If there were a final scene to this movie, it would be of the "$20,000 pickup truck" he sings of in "Good Ol' Boy" ("belongs to me and the bank and some funny-talkin' man from Iran"), easing onto the road, accelerating up a hill, and disappearing from sight as it descends on the other side, taking the man from God knows where to a destination unknown.

Tony Brown, producer and company man all at once, considered the finished album from the commercial standpoint and found it to have as much potential in that realm as it had aesthetic credibility. The bigger point he took out of the quality of the work, though, was what it said about Steve, beyond the fact of it proving his literary and musical gifts.

"I knew what a hook was. And all these songs had them. The intro to 'Hillbilly Highway,' man, that's a good intro. So I was thinking, Probably what we'll get back from the country program directors is that his voice doesn't sound like a country singer's, it sounds more like a Dylan or a Tom Petty. Most country singers, back in those days, they were singers. George Strait, George Jones, Randy Travis, they just were; it was pretty much singers, with a good baritone. They were singers who could do licks and little trills and all that kind of stuff like Jones did, or even Haggard in that beautiful baritone voice. Steve had that voice that's like Dylan and like Petty. He was singing on the note but with no vibrato—it was sort of an attitude, and country music has never been about attitude. I thought, That's what we'll get back from [radio]. Because you can't tell me these songs are not commercial or the tracks don't have hooks out the wazoo. If they were to play these songs in heavy rotation, I guarantee you they would be hits."

And then he names off the songs, as if in some kind of rapture—"Someday" and "Fearless Heart," "Good Ol' Boy," "Goodbye's All We've Got Left"— and goes quiet.

In comments made to author Alanna Nash in an interview published in her book, *Behind Closed Doors: Talking with the Legends of Country Music*, Steve pretty much confirmed Brown's sense of his commercial savvy.

Admitting "the album's kind of about me. It's kind of personal," Steve said he entered the studio "determined to make a record that you could put on the turntable and listen to. It was sequenced before it was recorded. I wanted it to all hang together, and so I sat down and wrote it in one time frame. And I write under pressure pretty well. I needed a kick in the butt, and this project was just the thing.

"The next one," he promised, "will be more political."[4]

As the result of a reference to it in the song "Guitar Town" ("there's a speed trap up ahead in Selma town …"), Selma, Texas, made the wrong headlines, kind of. In a AP news report published in the Jacksonville (Texas) *Daily Progress* on June 7, 1989, headlined "Selma Says Speed Trap Reputation Undeserved," city officials complained that Steve's song had resulted in the community of 650 getting a bad rap for its strict enforcement of traffic laws. Texas legislators had recently passed a law prohibiting small towns from funding more than 30 percent of their annual budgets from traffic fines. The new law was aimed at the infamous Patton Village, a community that generated some two-thirds of its budget through traffic fines. According to the AP report, "Selma City Administrator Margie Lubianski said her town took steps years ago 'to eliminate the reputation that the press has given us.'" The item claimed that $200,000 of Selma's $600,000 budget was generated by what was termed "public safety." CB operators had dubbed the town the "Valley of the Bears," but Lubianski objected, saying, "I guess it is an unfair image. I don't think that we're doing anything other than promoting protection." Former state representative Bennie Brock, who tried to pass laws to prevent Selma's police "from acting as roving municipal tax collectors," told the paper that despite the new state laws, "I slow down to 55 when driving through Selma."[5]

chapter 10

Odyssey: 1985–86

July 1985: As Steve's manager, John Lomax III had helped his client land the Silverline/Goldline publishing deal that reinvigorated his creative process (he told writer Alanna Nash, "Now I'm in a publishing situation where they make writers feel good about themselves"[1]); had put the *Pink & Black* EP on Rick Blackburn's desk and helped steer Steve to his first major-label deal with Epic; and had overseen his signing with MCA (Lomax's lawyer Dick Frank "negotiated the deal and got what we could considering we had little leverage," according to Lomax[2]). He had spent, by his own estimate, $50,000 of his own money to advance Steve's career.[3]

When Steve summoned him to Noel Fox's office, Lomax went figuring there was some business matter or other to attend to with regard to *Guitar Town*—business as usual.

"I came [to Silverline/Goldline] after hours to find [Steve] sitting at Noel's desk," Lomax says, "where he told me he had to 'let me go' as 'I can't figure out what it is a manager does.'

"All artists like to think their greatness alone makes their success possible and most hate to acknowledge any help from managers. I felt gypped."[4]

March 5, 1986: *Guitar Town* was released. Steve was 31 years old, 10 years beyond the age at which he had once asserted he would make an album.

At first, it seemed all the effort had been fruitless. No one seemed to care about *Guitar Town*, at least not anyone connected to country music. "Hillbilly Highway," released as a single, gained few advocates at radio, then dropped out of sight after struggling into the Top 30 of the country chart. And, as Steve noted in his liner notes to the 2002 reissue of *Guitar Town* (which included as a bonus track a lethargic live version of Bruce Springsteen's "State Trooper" recorded at a Chicago club in 1986), "the writers who normally wrote about country music were strangely silent."

Steve then described the twist of fate that came his way: "Rock critics, on the other hand, seemed to get it. Robert Christgau reviewed it favorably in *The Village Voice*. Dave Marsh wrote about it in *Rock and Roll Confidential*. Particularly over the top was Robert Hilburn in the *L.A. Times*. All the 'outside' press attention kept the record alive until *Guitar Town* itself was rereleased as a single. It reached the Top 10 in the country charts and a few weeks later the album went No. 1. Suddenly, I had a career."[5]

MCA first sent Steve out on a 10-day radio tour in May, with a Dukes lineup that included Bucky Baxter, Steve's buddy Reno Kling (from the *Pink & Black* sessions) on bass (Emory Gordy, Jr., had no intention of ever touring with Steve), Ken Moore, Richard Bennett, and Harry Stinson. Bennett, though, was only aboard for the radio tour, and then was off to other ventures. Just as he'd had his fill of session work before hooking up with Steve, so had he had enough of touring at the subsistence level. Years of traveling first class with and being paid first-class wages by Neil Diamond had taken the romance out of the extended grassroots-level campaign. Still Bennett found the "wonderful energy and momentum" surrounding Steve at that point made it "a curious little outing for me ... it was the fun thing to do, and because I was so intimately involved with the album, it was something I wanted to do. I really wanted to go out and do that."[6]

However, once discussion turned to doing a full-scale tour as a Duke, Bennett bowed out. Money—or the lack of it (he was accustomed to making anywhere from $1,000 to $1,200 a night with Diamond, in contrast to Steve Earle paydays tallying up to $75 to $100 a night)—was one issue, but more to the point was Bennett's refusal to be swayed from his career objective: "I didn't move to Nashville to go sit on a bus for a hundred dollars a night. And the fact of the matter is, apart from any of it financially, I had really come to Nashville to produce records, not to sit on a bus, not to go on tour. When push came to shove and it was offered up to me, I had to say no. And I think Steve got a bit bugged about that."[7]

Knowing Steve could never afford to take Richard Bennett on the road, and wanting his artist to sound as good live as he did on his record, Tony Brown offered Harry Stinson either one of his producer's points (Brown's version[8]) or "a small percentage, not a whole point" (Stinson's version[9]).

"It was important to me that Steve have that harmony vocal behind him and have that drummer driving it home," Brown explains. "It was important to me that when Steve played he sounded really good, and I thought an important part of Steve's music was about rhythms and about attitude. I gave Harry one of my points to go and play drums and sing with Steve on the road so Steve would have that support of the harmonies on songs like 'Someday.'"[10]

On the tour proper, Bennett was replaced by Bucky Baxter's friend Michael McAdam, who would have more than one tenure as a Duke.

I. "It's a whole new paradigm"

Acclaim from the rock press was one thing, but *Guitar Town* also made waves among Steve's contemporaries. Through her husband Rodney Crowell, Rosanne Cash knew something of Steve, but *Guitar Town* was her introduction to his music, and a release party for the album her introduction to him. *Guitar Town* had done nothing less than make her rethink her entire approach. Her Crowell-produced forays into fusions of traditional hard country and Beatles-influenced rock 'n' roll had produced a critically hailed debut (*Right or Wrong*, 1980, with three hit singles), a smash follow-up (*Seven Year Ache*, with three No. 1 singles), an ambitious effort that showcased her both as a fearless songwriter and an interpreter who could put her individual stamp on other writers' songs (*Somewhere under the Stars*), she returned from a two-and-a-half-year absence with *Rhythm and Romance*, released the same year as *Guitar Town*. The cover showed a strikingly remade Rosanne, in spiky hair and hot pink nails and lipstick, whereas on the back she was clad in a sleeveless denim vest and accessorized to the hilt, not the least of her accoutrements being a band of diamond bracelets around one wrist. The natural beauty she displayed on her earlier albums had been replaced by a hard, almost confrontational countenance, a real "hit me with your best shot" glare and a tough-chick image seemingly in homage to Pat Benatar. Only three tracks had been produced by Crowell (and those were co-productions with Dave Thoener, previously known only as an engineer whose résumé included work with John Cougar Mellencamp); the others were produced in Nashville and Los Angeles by David Malloy, whose credits included pop-country outings by Dolly Parton and Eddie Rabbitt. The Cherry Bombs were conspicuous by their absence (save for Vince Gill, singing some background vocals), having been replaced by a combination of L.A. and Nashville studio pros such as guitarist Waddy Wachtel, Tom Petty, keyboardist Benmont Tench, versatile R&B bassist Willie Weeks, and stalwart drummer Paul Leim. Some of the songs were among the finest she had ever recorded, including her self-penned "Hold On"; a piercing account of dying love cowritten with Crowell, "I Don't Know Why You Don't Want Me"; and the first overt recorded reference to her relationship to her famous father in the poignant "My Old Man" ("ask him how he remembers me / 'cause I want to know where I stand").

It was no accident that *King's Record Shop*, the first album she released post–*Guitar Town*, returned her to a rootsier sound, with an acoustic foundation as well as ringing electric guitars, honky tonk piano, and Crowell's elegant, multitiered productions that were rooted in country but enhanced by gospel-style background choruses and discreetly deployed string arrangements. The supporting cast included several impressive new faces on the Nashville scene, notably solid drummer Eddie Bayers, bassist Michael Rhodes, and one of the most inventive guitarists to emerge in years in Steuart Smith, whose feel for the texture and narrative line of a song translated into the most striking and unpredictable solos. Veteran Southern soul and country producer keyboardist Barry Beckett was also on board, as was the remarkable fiddle virtuoso Mark O'Connor and Earl Scruggs's son Randy on acoustic guitar on a hit version of Johnny Cash's "Tennessee Flat Top Box," a song Rosanne didn't even know her dad had written until someone in the studio told her so. All in all, it was a return to the forward-looking sound and style of her first three albums—honest, lean, and emotionally charged—a potent assertion of the sensibility and voice that made her one of the most important singer-songwriters of her generation.

Guitar Town, she says, "made all of us feel redundant. I'm not kidding; it made me feel redundant. It was like a tidal wave came through Nashville, and it was so refreshing. I remember this reporter coming up to me at the record release party. There was a huge buzz, tons of people there, lots of press, and this reporter comes up and says, 'Do you think he has the potential to be a star?' And I said, 'Doesn't matter. He's already changed everything. It's a whole new paradigm.'"

Richard Bennett was the key for her. "I can't underestimate how important he was. Really without Richard there would be no Steve back then. And that's not to diminish Steve's greatness at all, but Richard was, and is, genius. The way the whole thing coalesced, it was the perfect time for Steve, but it was the perfect time for Richard too, and the fact that they met at that moment is genius. And it's Tony's [Brown] brillliance to know to bring Richard into the album. That's like the sum being greater than the parts, and the parts are pretty great.

"It reinspired me, and it made me want to strip down and get rid of some of the treacle, that keyboard shit. Steve's songs were so rooted. Everybody, including me, was doing just syrupy, overkill pop. It was kind of the malaise of that particular time period. Then Steve just came out with this really fresh, rooted music."[11]

II. Chasing the Dragon

Pam Lewis had moved to Nashville from New York in 1984 to work for Joe Galante in RCA's publicity department. Born and raised in upstate Red Hook, New York, she had entered the business straight out of college ("a woman's college in the middle of nowhere on the Finger Lakes") with an economics and marketing degree and a minor in communications and French, taking a position in publicity with the then-fledgling MTV. Country acts would come to town and she'd attend shows with a photographer friend, and through that access became acquainted with Nashville heavyweights, including Joe Galante and Tony Brown. When she got a call from RCA Nashville offering a job in publicity, she took it, because "I had been at MTV for four years and kind of peaked. There was no place for me to move at that point."[12]

There was another issue that affected her in her work at MTV too—rampant drug use in the office. "I was kind of sick of the whole drug thing at MTV. Walking into peoples' offices and an amount of cocaine on the desk; the whole seediness of it. I knew some people who got really whacked out on it, and I was just kind of, I don't want to do this anymore. I wasn't heavily into it myself, but I knew a lot of people and I saw what it did to their lives."

Within a year, after losing her job at RCA on a day when four others were fired, she opened her own publicity firm, Pam Lewis Associates, working out of her home, at one point making no more than $500 a month "and happy to get it."

Impressed with her intelligence and energy, Tony Brown hired Pam as an independent publicist to supplement the company's in-house staff in pushing *Guitar Town*. She was entering a volatile environment, owing to the internecine warfare over Steve Earle. In Steve's corner were Tony and, at least partly, Jimmy Bowen. But the marketing and promotion departments didn't share Brown's high opinion of Steve's prospects or his music.

"We were meeting resistance within the company," Lewis recalls. "This was Tony's baby, and I have great respect for Bruce Hinton [Brown's counterpart in the A&R department], and I have great respect for Sheila Shipley [head of promotion]. But Sheila did not care for [Steve]. And you know, he stunk; he had body odor. He wouldn't shave, he wouldn't use deodorant. You weren't supposed to look like that. You were supposed to be an artist and you were supposed to clean up, and you know, they had people like George Strait that they were working with. And here's Steve basically telling everybody to go to hell, and he didn't care one way or the other what they thought. And he'd come in and he'd have had a couple of drinks. He would start off lunch with me with three Jägermeister shots. That was like standard, on an empty stomach. He'd have gotten up at 11 and we'd be eating by noon, and the first thing in his stomach was three shots of Jägermeister. And chain smoking. I had never been around anybody like this."

Friendships with Emory Gordy, Jr., and Tony Brown led to her being invited the *Guitar Town* sessions at Soundstage. She had already heard the demos for the album, and to this day says she prefers those over the official release, "because it was rawer."

In the studio she found "something really wonderful taking place. It was an alchemy experiment and it was all coming together and the byproduct was going to be something fabulous."

She also found something else she had never seen before: heroin. Steve, whom she knew through their mutual friend Richard Dobson, another Texas songwriter, and who always called her by her last name, approached her one night at Soundstage. "Hey, Lewis!" he said. "You wanna check this out? We're gonna chase the dragon."

"I had no idea what he was talking about; I was so naïve. [The heroin] looked like cocaine that somebody had spilled coffee on. It was brown cocaine, is what it looked like. That was kind of shocking to me. Also there was something kind of thrilling about it—Oh, I'm really in the music industry now."

III. Working It

Steve may have been at war with some segment of the MCA machinery, but that didn't stop him from working his own album like the most dedicated company man. In the August 5, 1986, edition of the Houston *Chronicle*, Marty Racine traced his path over the preceding months.

"On the West Coast he's headlined showcase clubs. He's opened for the Bellamy Brothers and George Jones. He's played stadium dates with Waylon Jennings, shared a theater stage in Phoenix with Charlie Daniels, co-billed a date with the Long Ryders and even opened for punk rockers the Replacements at the Ritz in New York."[13]

As Racine noted, the itinerary reveals a smart marketing plan that booked Steve with a pair of standard mainstream hitmakers, a honky tonk legend, a Southern rock trouper, a retro country band, and a punk rock–influenced group. Whatever others might have heard in his music, Steve knew where he belonged.

"I'm a country act, there's no doubt about that," he told Racine. "Some people consider me to be a traditionalist, but I'm definitely not a revivalist. I'm a traditionalist in the sense that I believe country music should say something. But I don't think there are any rules about instrumentation."

Most telling, for an artist who had no truck with the niceties of the industry machine—"the whole notion of Steve Earle going to media training is laughable," says Pam Lewis[14]—Steve comes off in the Racine piece as an artist sincere in his desire to be accepted by the establishment, as long as the establishment accepts him on his terms. At the same time, he evinces a market awareness that Nashville still hasn't figured out on its own.

"I hope that country radio realizes what I'm trying to do for country music. It's real important to me, and a young audience is real, real important for country music. The younger audience is not going to go see George Jones. Country music needs younger buyers, people whose priority in their lives is to buy records. And [in] the traditional demographics in country music, that's not true."[15]

IV. "What he wanted was a cruel, pure relationship ... "
—Coming Through Slaughter

"Cynthia and I split up, and I didn't use for a while until I met the woman who became my third wife. She worked in a bar, so I started drinking beer. I also discovered and started taking prescription opiates, when I could get them. I had some problems with my teeth by that time, probably brought about by my drug use, so I got a few prescriptions from dentists and I remembered how much I liked opiates."[16]

In the winter of 1984 Steve, then still legally married to Cynthia, met and was soon courting a 24-year-old red-haired beauty named Lou-Anne Gill, who by day worked at the William Morris Agency as an assistant to the vice president and by night tended bar. She was married to a musician, who left her shortly after she met Steve. At about the time *Guitar Town* started picking up steam, Steve and Lou-Anne were inseparable. And then she announced she was pregnant by him. On January 7, 1987, she gave birth to Steve's second child, a boy named Ian Dublin Earle. Steve's divorce from Cynthia was not yet final.

V. Alpha Male Ascending, V4.0

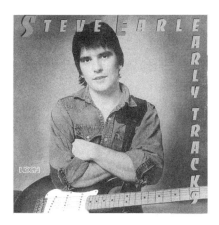

Its sales spurred by Steve's late-September appearance on "The Tonight Show," *Guitar Town* topped the country chart on November 8, 1986, on its way to selling 300,000 units. Hoping to cash in on the album's success, Epic finally released Steve's Emory Gordy, Jr.,–produced sessions for the label under the title *Early Tracks. Rolling Stone* named Steve Country Artist of the Year, and in early '87 he learned he had been nominated for two Grammy Awards, for Best Male Country Vocal Performance and for Best Country Song, "Guitar Town."

By then, Steve was on to more important matters: his follow-up to *Guitar Town*, recording of which had commenced in December 1986, at Emerald Sound in Nashville, again with Tony Brown and Emory Gordy, Jr., producing, and now with Richard Bennett receiving, as per Steve's insistence, a full coproducer's credit as well.

VI. Trust in Twang: Origins

Ray Kennedy: "I met Steve when I first came here, just hanging out at different publishing companies. What you did, when you finally got a few cuts under your belt, you'd go hang out at different publishing companies. One was Pete Drake's late at night. You'd always see David Allan Coe there, Marshall Chapman, some of the musicians that worked there, and they'd be there until four in the morning. And there was Combine Music, which was where Kristofferson wrote, John Scott Sherill, David Lindley, a lot of really cool writers. Steve was part of that whole Texas scene. I got to know Guy Clark. had a house and I let people come rehearse there in my living room; Guy would come over with his band and rehearse in my living room. I used to have picking parties at my house, and all these musicians, singer-songwriters, and players would come over and we'd play until the police showed up and shut us down. I did that about once every other month, for years. But you get to know everybody, and Steve still says to this day that when he got his deal on MCA and put his first band together, most of the band got hired in my house at one of my potlucks, late 1985 after they did *Guitar Town*. A lot of those guys were playing at that party and Steve showed up and said, 'I'll take this one and I'll take that one.' That's where he met a lot of those guys.

"But back then we were never really good friends. It was more acquaintances."[17]

Alpha Males (Gettin' Tough)

I. Mind Games

Immovable objects and irresistible forces met whenever Jimmy Bowen and Steve Earle crossed paths, whether the crossing was in fact physical or philosophical and from a distance. The two prototypical Texas alpha males rarely had face-to-face encounters, preferring instead to send their billets-doux to each other through the intermediary Tony Brown. Being caught in the crossfire lent Brown a more balanced perspective about the two principals' motives; he understood the overriding issue and learned how to work both sides of the street.

From his initial lukewarm response to Steve, Bowen had become a believer in, if not an outright cheerleader for, the artist. The turnabout came when he saw Steve perform some of the *Guitar Town* songs at a local club called the Cannery for a show to be televised on the Nashville Network. After Steve's brief set—he performed "Guitar Town," "Someday," and "Fearless Heart"—Bowen told Brown, "T, I'm glad I stuck with you on this Steve Earle kid. He's got it, man. At the microphone you can tell, man, he's got something to say, and by God, you better listen. I see what you saw in him. I'm glad I didn't screw up and run him off. I get it; I totally get it."[1]

Bowen wasn't the type to buddy up to Steve Earle, though. However much he had enjoyed the success and esteem *Guitar Town* had brought to his label, he was a man who knew to plan ahead. Before Steve had begun touring in support of his first album, Bowen had urged him to get to writing for his second album, warning him that he was going to find it hard to come up with songs while he was on the road. Steve bristled at Bowen's suggestion that he would ever have a problem finding something to write about or time to write it. Neither man seemed fully to understand the other.

"Bowen was just a badass," Brown says. "He used fear as a motivator, and it worked most of the time. And the bottom line is Bowen's whole deal was, 'Cover your ass. Think ahead.' As soon as you finished one album, he would say, 'Book the studio for the next album.' And he would calculate. In the case of a George Strait, he knew we would probably do two singles for sure. So he'd say, 'First single will take this many weeks, and you'll have three weeks before we put the next single out, and if it goes three deep you'll have the album in the can. But if it doesn't, you'll be ready.' And you better be ready 'or I'll fire you.' He always thought way ahead and that was his way of threatening Steve. I mean, Steve had an attitude about him too, so those two guys in the same room was pretty fun to watch, actually."

With Steve's second album tensions between artist and executive reached the boiling point, not over music, as Brown points out, but over "bullshit stuff."

The album cover, for instance.

Steve had come off the road and immediately headed for the studio to start polishing his latest batch of new songs, some of which he had already tested out in front of concert audiences. (A CD of his first appearance on "Austin City Limits," *Live from Austin, TX*, recorded on September 12, 1986, but not released until 2004, features six new tunes that would wind up on his second long-player.) When Tony came around, Steve told him he knew what he wanted to title the next LP and what he envisioned as its cover art.

"*Exit 0* is the title," he told Tony.

And that means what?

"There's an exit between Nashville and Louisville that's Exit 0 and that's what I want to call the album. And I want the cover to be the exit sign." With that he produced a Polaroid photo he had taken of the big green Interstate road sign with white lettering.

"This is what I want it to look like," Steve said. "I want to hire a photographer to take a great picture of this road sign or have a road sign made that looks just like the road signs on the Interstate. On the road sign it'll say 'Steve Earle and the Dukes.' And that's the cover."

"And of course," Brown notes, "Bowen went ballistic."

Figuring Steve was going to get his way, the art director at MCA Nashville sent a photographer to take a shot of the road sign and then did a mockup of the cover based on Steve's idea. Upon showing it to Bowen, she discovered the depths of his disdain for the cover concept. Then Bowen summoned Brown, ordering him to apprise Steve that his road sign would never be seen anywhere but on the Interstate.

The issue wasn't the drabness of the cover shot, or even the absence of an artist image. Steve wanted the Dukes to play on the album and to be credited on the cover, in order to convey to the public that he and the band were an inseparable unit, that there was a correlation rather than a distinction between the studio and the concert stage.

"With *Exit 0*, the argument wasn't so much about using session players, because most session players don't really play the Steve Earle songs right anyway," Brown explains. "They wouldn't sound the same. The deal was, he wanted to use his band, and he insisted that the album title be *Exit 0*, Steve Earle and the Dukes. And we said, 'We have a little problem with that, because that means if you get a CMA or a Grammy nomination, you're no longer a male vocalist, you're a band, you're Steve Earle and the Dukes. He didn't care. He went, 'Tough shit. That's the way it's gotta be.' He was doing that thing, 'I'm sticking up for my guys.'"

Brown was conflicted because deep down he tended to agree with the thinking on the awards issue. As a band, Steve and the Dukes would have to compete with the trophy-gathering juggernaut that was Alabama; as a male vocalist nominee, he would "stick out of the pack.

"So we were thinking about those kinds of situations, which he didn't really give a shit about. He thought we were feeding him a line of bullshit, that we were actually not supporting his idea of the band being part of his vision of the album."

Tony set up a dinner meeting with Steve at Jimmy Kelly's, one of Steve's favorite dining spots, and requested they be seated in a private room downstairs, where they could talk at a safe distance from eavesdroppers.

Tony began. "Hey, Steve, Bowen told me to tell you that there is no way this cover is gonna fly."

Steve: "Oh, really?"

From the other side of the table Tony saw the anger rising silently in Steve. And then: "*You hillbilly faggot!*" he screamed at Tony, his angry gesticulations upending his plate and launching the steak across the table into Tony's lap. After a moment's pause, he offered an "I'm sorry, man," and then, voice rising again, spat out a message to take back to Bowen: "Just to let you know, man, there won't be a fuckin' record unless that's the cover!"

"I went back and told Bowen that the meeting did not go well," Brown recalls of his understated report to the label chief.

Bowen gave in, and the road sign shot adorned the cover of *Exit 0*. Steve's legend has been spun to make his act of defiance heroic and principled, but in fact Bowen had practical Business 101 reasons for giving up the ghost. As Brown points out, "When you get with labels, what you realize is they need it. Everybody has their projections and they needed Steve's record to come out at that time. So you give in by default, you know. Better to have a Steve Earle record with a shitty cover than miss a release and miss billing several million dollars. Then you have Irving Azoff calling and going, 'Hey, Bowen. You missed your projections by about five mill. What happened?' So you just go ahead with it."

Exit 0
MCA, 1987
Produced by Tony Brown, Emory Gordy, Jr., and Richard Bennett
Recorded and mixed by Chuck Ainlay
Additional overdubs recorded by Russ Martin
Second engineers: Russ Martin, Mark J. Coddington, Tim Kish
Preproduction engineer: Andy Byrd
Studio: Emerald Studio with Mitsubishi X-800 32-track digital
Mixed at Masterfonics
Mastered by Chuck Ainlay and Glenn Meadows at Masterfonics using the JVC digital audio mastering system
Digital editing: Milan Bogdan

Musicians
The Dukes:
Bucky Baxter: steel guitar and vocals
Steve Earle: lead vocals, acoustic and electric guitars, harmonica
Reno Kling: bass guitar
Mike McAdam: six- and 12-string guitars, vocals
Ken Moore: organ, synthesizer, vocals
Harry Stinson: drums and vocals
with:
John Jarvis: piano
Emory Gordy, Jr.: mandolin
Richard Bennett: acoustic guitar, electric guitar, six-string bass
K-Meaux Boudin: accordion

Songs
1. "Nowhere Road" (2:27) (Steve Earle–Reno Kling)
2. "Sweet Little '66" (2:38) (Steve Earle)
3. "No. 29" (3:30) (Steve Earle)
4. "Angry Young Man" (4:24) (Steve Earle–John Porter McMeans)
5. "San Antonio Girl" (3:06) (Steve Earle)
6. "The Rain Came Down" (4:11) (Steve Earle–Michael Woody)
7. "I Ain't Ever Satisfied" (4:00) (Steve Earle)

8. "The Week of Living Dangerously" (4:26) (Steve Earle)
9. "I Love You Too Much" (3:37) (Steve Earle)
10. "It's All Up to You" (5:42) (Steve Earle–Harry Stinson)

Unlike his boss, Tony Brown wasn't worried about Steve being able to deliver some quality songs for his second album. He had heard sketches of tunes in progress, and Steve had already written what he considered "the centerpiece" of the new album, "a Zen truck driver song" titled "Nowhere Road."

"He would play me on the guitar things he was working on," Brown says. "You know some writers and artists have a work ethic. Steve is always thinking what's next. He's already thinking about his next move. Either he's writing a book or he's writing a song or writing something. So I was thinking, Even if he writes it and we don't like it, he won't give a shit. He'll want us to like it, but if we don't like it, his take on it is that we're stupid. Those kind of artists—and Steve was definitely one of those artists—you almost have to have a bit of arrogance to pull off what you're going to say. He wrote a few songs that might be considered ditties, but he's always got a social comment, he's got a platform, what he's saying about the working man or politics or religion or something. I just didn't worry about him."

The music for what became *Exit 0* was every bit as mapped out as the *Guitar Town* songs had been, but this time what had been demo sessions for the first album were now designated "preproduction." It was a ploy on Brown's part to keep Steve from falling further into debt with the publishing company and at the same time to keep some change in the artist's pocket.

The game is that a songwriter's demos are financed by the publishing company, which then applies the demos' cost toward the album's overall production costs. "It's really sort of an accounting issue," Brown explains. In Steve's case, this bit of linguistic legerdemain meant he wasn't billed for studio time or the cost of the musicians, "and Steve was cool with that.

"Most writers," Brown adds, "their draw isn't that much. The draw is basically an advance against future performance or mechanicals. In Steve's case, he wasn't writing the type of songs that were No. 1 for five weeks. So we didn't want to tap into that any more than we had to, because he lived off his publishing draw. In Nashville, it takes two or three albums before an artist makes a dime, because the label's subsidizing not only the record, but the videos and the touring, and they're not making shit. By calling it preproduction the record label became the bank for Steve putting down the songs that he was writing, and it gave the publishing company a reason to stick with him. So we wanted Silverline/Goldline to stay involved. That was merely a way of funding Steve's creative process, where it did the least damage to his bottom line. He wasn't making that much money in the beginning. That's all that was about."

Brown recalls the *Exit 0* sessions "going smoothly," but both Bennett and Stinson were starting to notice what Bennett calls "chinks in the armor" in the midst of what was otherwise a fairly routine album project.

Bennett: "I remember one incident. I remember him blowing in and I think it was Emory and I or Tony and I, maybe all of us, we had already begun a few overdubs. Steve blew in late and out of his knapsack pulled a pistol and kind of slammed it on the control board. I don't want to see any fucking guns. I said, 'Put that away or I'm leaving.' And he did. There's no place or time for that. Apart from the occasional deal like that, it was, again, very enjoyable. Steve, despite his bad-boy thing, was always a pleasure and a joy to work with in the studio. Was open to any suggestion and would try anything, and the best one would win out; it wasn't always his idea that won out. A joy to work with."[2]

Another issue loomed larger for Bennett, though. He finally got his co-producer credit "and my little point," but he was miffed to find that on the session credits he was grouped with musicians who had played only a part here or there on a song (including one "K-Meaux Boudin" on accordion, who in fact was keyboard player Ken Moore), whereas Bennett had shouldered most of the guitar load. New Duke guitarist Mike McAdam, who had come on board to replace Bennett in the touring lineup, got the main credit but in fact played on only a couple of songs.

"It was giving with one hand and taking away with the other," says Bennett. "In this business, your calling card is the last thing you've done or what's currently out there. You know, the guitar-playing thing was very important to me, not out of ego, but simply because that's my stock in trade; that's how I make my living. So I got the production credit, but I got short-shrifted on the guitar thing. It was an 'and also with' kind of thing.

"When the reviews came out, *Rolling Stone* was all over the place about how great *Exit 0* was—this, that, and the other; 'and the fabulous guitar playing of Mike McAdam.' Well, Mike didn't play, hardly at all. There again, it's just another little dig. But that was it. Because I wasn't a Duke in fact on the tour, I was an also-ran on the record."

Harry Stinson found the dynamic between Steve and the various Dukes to have been altered by the post–*Guitar Town* acclaim showered on Steve, and consequently, Steve feeling his oats because of all the praise directed at him. Which made *Exit 0* "a bit more difficult to record" than *Guitar Town*, in Stinson's estimation, "because things weren't innocent anymore. Steve was creating a stir, there was more of a press buzz going on, egos were a little bit bigger by that point. It was just natural stuff that happens. He was famous, the whole deal was already considered a landmark in some ways, everybody in Nashville was kind of jealous and wished they could be a part of it, all that stuff. So egos get bigger and a little more bullshit goes on."[3]

That said, the album betrays no signs of any internal stresses on Steve or the band, but it does plow some of the same turf as *Guitar Town* in sound, style, and themes. The acoustic guitar riffing that kicks off the first song, "Nowhere Road" (the "Zen trucker's song" that inspired this collection of songs), evokes the opening of "Guitar Town," but the sound gains added body from Ken Moore's high-spirited Farfisa organ fills and Bennett's whimsical, resonant electric interjections. A bittersweet, nostalgic look back on a common laborer's glory days as a celebrated high school football player in "No. 29" evolves from a soft, acoustic ballad into a synth-laced, pop-inflected story song, Bucky Baxter's moaning pedal steel lines adding eerie commentary along the way, and those synth lines surface so discreetly and so tenderly about midway through. "Angry Young Man" trades on an insistent harmonica line, Steve's feisty shouts of "Whoop! Whoop!" and Bennett's atmospheric, swirling electric lines, as Steve rolls out a son's plea for his mother's understanding of why he had to get out their stifling small town, although he reveals that the cruel world outside has him contemplating robbery as his next career move. Jabs of Farfisa and a meaty double-tracked electric guitar solo set the stage for a bouncy Tex-Mex-flavored love letter to a "San Antonio Girl." Both "Angry Young Man" and "San Antonio Girl" reintroduce familiar characters from Earle's troupe, those being men who recognize their fate as loners, by chance ("San Antonio Girl"—he can't imagine the object of his affection "up in New York City" so "I'm gonna leave you alone in your own little world") or by choice (in "Angry Young Man," the son reports, "I told my mama the day I ran / This ain't no place for an angry young man").

In a Steinbeck-inspired narrative, "The Rain Came Down," its thumping arrangement as steely and grim as the story's main character, Steve sings of a struggling family's migration to a life farming 40 acres on a government grant, six children needing to be fed, prospects diminishing with the turning of the earth, until the law shows up to seize the property. Strength comes to the narrator through the spirit of his deceased grandfather, which inspires him to make a stand— "you can take my machines, but you ain't taking my land." It's the first reference in song Steve has made to his beloved granddaddy Booster Earle, who had indeed been dead now for 23 years, as had the grandfather in this song. "The Week of Living Dangerously," despite its dramatic title, is something of a roadhouse rocker with a bit of Cajun flavoring by way of K-Meaux's buoyant accordion solos, with some added comic effects supplied by Bennett's fanciful walking lines, which at one point are so deep they sound like a tuba solo, and a rollicking piano sortie by John Jarvis redolent of "The Killer," Jerry Lee Lewis, complete with some pumping passages and exuberant glissandos. Next comes another upbeat rocker, "I Love You Too Much," furiously driven by the twanging guitar and the howling organ, a hiccupy vocal that seems an homage to Elvis's "Baby, Let's Play House," and an opening guitar riff that fleetingly references the Rivieras' surf classic "California Sun."

A cowrite with Stinson, "It's All Up to You," closes the album and returns the story line to the wandering, self-sufficient loner, walking to a horizon that heralds a new beginning. "Don't stop to look behind you," Steve urges in a somber arrangement that kicks off with a stark, moody acoustic guitar riff and broadens out to feature pounding drums, crying pedal steel lines, and a single, sustained dark chord from the organ. At the close, the other instruments gradually fall away, and all that's left on the track is that lonely chord, rising, rising, and then abruptly ceasing, the silence it leaves embodying the void in the character's life. In that moment the song spins on its axis, light fades to dark, with oblivion the only off-ramp at Exit 0.

II. "What does that mean, 'Nowhere Road'?"

Tony Brown was excited about *Exit 0*. Good songs, with lots of hooks for radio, great playing, gritty vocals from Steve. Something to build on in the aftermath of *Guitar Town*'s success. He took the master in to play for Bowen, Bruce Hinton, Sheila Shipley, and promotion man Scott Borchetta. Smart and personable, Borchetta was MCA's man in the trenches at the time, interacting with radio daily, visiting the stations, and providing the ground-zero reports of each new release's prospects for airplay based on early reaction from program directors.

Brown began the meeting. "Guys, this time we've got some radio stuff here," he said. " 'Nowhere Road' is a slam dunk. Check this out."

What Brown heard in "Nowhere Road" was "a hook and a guitar lick that sounded like radio to me."

Shipley had a comment in the form of a question: "What does that mean, 'Nowhere Road'?"

Brown became flustered, taken aback that he was already on the defensive. "Oh, uh … I forgot, the lyrics maybe aren't mainstream, but … well, it means what it means. It means what you want it to mean."

"I don't know what that is," Shipley responded.

Stunned, Brown tried to square his enthusiasm for *Exit 0* with his colleagues' disdain. Had they heard the same record? " 'The Rain Came Down,' 'San Antonio Girl,' I thought, Those are really songs that country radio will gravitate to. It seems obvious to me."[4]

It didn't quite work out that way. *Exit 0* was released on May 18, the reviews were generally favorable, but country radio was casting a wary eye on the album. "Nowhere Road" began making some headway on playlists, but when some rock stations picked up on the Springsteen-like anthem "I Ain't

Ever Satisfied," the country stations started dropping "Nowhere Road," leaving it for dead after it had peaked at No. 20. Steve's catchy love song to Chevrolet's powerful SS 396 model, "Sweet Little '66," died at No. 37 on the country charts after some car dealers complained about Steve's putdown of Hondas and Subarus in the lyrics ("when your Subaru is over and your Honda's history … "). In *Hardcore Troubadour*, Steve explained the lyric passage with typical bluntness: "I hate Hondas and Subarus, that's why I wrote the song in the first place."[5] The album made it into the Top 20 of the chart but didn't come close to matching *Guitar Town*'s No. 1 ranking.

A heated contretemps between Steve and Jimmy Bowen—one of their rare face-to-face encounters—in which Bowen dismissed *Exit 0* as "watered-down rock" and "bastardized country,"[6] convinced Steve that his vision and the MCA brass's vision of him could not have been more disparate. In the August 1990 issue of Tower Records' *Pulse!*, speaking to writer Harold DeMuir, he recalled his confrontation with Bowen and stated his belief that Bowen had a vendetta against Tony Brown and against him, "because I didn't do what he asked me to do, which was to cut an album with two or three things that would be tailor-made for country radio, and then I could do whatever I wanted with the rest of the record. I think he just assumed that I was so ambitious that I'd be willing to do that, but I see an album as an overall work, and I'd rather not make records at all than make records that way. I had absolutely nothing to lose at that point, so there was no reason not to hold out."[7]

III. Everything Put Together Falls Apart

Steve Earle: *"Around that time I started traveling, which brought me to places where there was good, cheap heroin. Suddenly I was going to New York, and I was going to L.A., and Amsterdam. I didn't use needles during this period. I smoked heroin when I was in England. That was how almost everyone did it. If it was highly refined white heroin, I would snort it. I had a pretty steady habit going. I could lay down, however, if I was going someplace where there wasn't any drugs. And usually before tours I would kick. I would usually come back off a tour strung out, depending on where we played. If there was plenty of heroin, and it was easy to get, then I'd come back strung out."[8]*

With a No. 1 album and a follow-up, albeit lesser, hit on his résumé, Steve now took to the highway, leading the Dukes on what was to be a full-blown international tour. They played New York to rave reviews, generating favorable comparisons to Bruce Springsteen and the E Street Band. In Canada, Steve was treated like the Second Coming—"he was a rock star up there," Tony Brown says.[9] North of the border *Exit 0* sales soared from day one, and before long the album was certified platinum (a lower standard than in the

United States, with 100,000 units sold qualifying as platinum). The Canadian division of MCA embraced everything about Steve Earle, including the cover of *Exit 0*.

"Steve felt the love up there, so he didn't give them the shit he gave us down here," Brown says.[10]

It was also in Canada, where drugs were plentiful and the laws more lax than in the States, that Brown saw Steve "doing really bad things. Seriously getting strung out after shows."[11]

Will Botwin, whose Side One Management in New York had been retained after Steve had fired John Lomax III (and whose clients included Rosanne Cash and Rodney Crowell), began having second thoughts about staying the course, telling Steve, "Your life is getting so out of control that I'm not sure I want to keep doing this."[12]

The drama of the tour hit a dubious pinnacle of sorts on New Year's Eve, 1987, when Steve's guitar tech, a childhood buddy of his named Chip Phillips, became drunk and unruly while they were in Dallas to ring in the New Year as the opening act for rockabilly pioneer Carl Perkins. After his set on the outdoor stage in an area rich in nightclubs and bars known as Dallas Alley, with his parents and other band members around, Steve and Chip started scuffling when Steve thought Chip was making a move for a security guard who had upbraided Chip earlier for hitting on his girlfriend. Steve began pushing Chip toward a waiting cab, hoping to get him out of the area before anything bad happened between him and the security guard. As he was struggling to get Chip into the cab's backseat, the guard, an off-duty Dallas police sergeant named Lonnie R. Allen, came on to the scene to find what looked like a fight erupting. Without asking questions, he rushed up behind Steve and immobilized him by pressing his nightstick hard against his neck, causing Steve to faint.

Jack Earle saw his son in distress and reacted. "I tried to get the cop off of him. I didn't realize it was the police, because all I saw was a white shirt and dark pants, and I was trying to pull him off of [Steve] because I thought he was killin' him."[13]

Steve came to in the back of the police car, handcuffed and groggy. He was held at a police station until 4:00 A.M., then was charged with aggravated assault, a felony, and arraigned. He posted bond and was released later in the day. His police blotter was filling up: back in late September, preparing to fly from Norfolk, Virginia, to Atlanta for a show, he was arrested for gun possession after an airport security check revealed the presence of a Colt .45 automatic in his carry-on bag. By mistake he had taken the wrong bag with him to the airport and sent his regular carry-on on ahead with the band in the bus.

Just as '87 had gone out on a sour note, so did '88 dawn with dissension.

Fed up with Steve's drug habit and drug-induced bad behavior, Harry Stinson announced he was quitting the Dukes, no matter the extra financial inducement Tony had given him to go on the road. The final straw came when he was told that an Australian tour had been planned, but the money was so slight he would have to take a pay cut—and he was making only $125 per show as it was. (Of an account in *Hardcore Troubadour* that Steve became disenchanted with Stinson after the drummer refused to play an encore following a two-and-a-half-hour set at the Cannery in Nashville on January 2, Stinson says forcefully, "I have never refused to go out on stage at any time. That is total bullshit; I don't know where that came from." To *Hardcore Troubadour*'s assertion that Steve considered him an MCA spy, Stinson responds again with "total bullshit," and adds, "Steve probably really remembers that. Who knows what was going on in his head?"[14])

Tony Brown was the first to hear of Stinson's discontent. "Harry called me one day from the road, and Steve was really getting bad on the junk. Harry said, 'Listen, I can't do this anymore. I'm gonna throw in the towel. If you want to pull back what you've been giving me—'

"I said, 'You know what? You'll get it as long as I get it. But it slowly gets smaller and smaller. Just understand that. Just because you did it, I think you being out there with him helped, when you played live it helped everything about Steve's career, and it helped sell records and it was an important thing. I appreciate it.'

"'Well, I'm coming home,' Harry said. 'I can't take it anymore.'"[15]

"Basically I was done with the heroin abuse," Stinson explains. "I did not partake and I just couldn't handle it. I felt like [Steve] was lost and I wasn't speaking to him anymore, and he wasn't speaking to me. And so I had enough. And he wanted us to go to Australia for like six weeks and no money and I said I couldn't do that. I couldn't see making my bills. And I felt like I had put up with enough at that point. Everything just reached a head. It really affected me. It took awhile for me to recover from being on the road with all that going on. It kind of threw me for a loop. It was time for me to go or it probably would have done more damage to me psychologically. I was not partaking of any drugs, but being around it? I remember being with Etta James, and you know, you're living the blues. You might be doing a show and getting paid for it, but when you're traveling with Etta, it's the blues lifestyle, and it rubs off on you. And it can affect your aura and everything else. The cumulative effect was getting to me."[16]

Livid over this turn of events, Steve fired bassist Reno Kling, who had been rooming with Stinson in order to avoid the drug scenes on the road. He threatened to fire Bucky Baxter for fraternizing with Kling and Stinson. And he ordered Botwin to cancel the Australian tour. A couple of months later, when they were in rehearsals for Steve's third album, Mike McAdam quit the band in a huff over Steve auditioning other guitarists to join the sessions.

Then there was Lou-Anne. Ultimately, there was no Lou-Anne. On July 6, Steve and Carol's divorce had become final; later that month, a curiously restrained Steve married Lou-Anne, and by November of that year they were separated. At the end of the year he learned he had become a father for the third time, but not by either of the women now in his life. The mother was a groupie with whom Steve had enjoyed a moment's pleasure in a bus at a Hank Williams, Jr., show.

Almost for the entire duration of his courtship, engagement and marriage to Lou-Anne, there had been another woman. Steve had fallen, and fallen hard, for Maria Teresa Ensenat, a beauty of Cuban extraction who was a rising star in the A&R department at Geffen Records, her burgeoning reputation as a talent scout burnished by her signing of Guns N' Roses. After she fell in love with Steve, she terminated a three-year affair she had been having with an A&R colleague at Geffen, but the ongoing ill will between her and her former lover was intolerable. In April of '88 she resigned from Geffen and moved to Nashville to live with Steve, bringing along her younger sister Grace, a former publicist for Slash Records who had been hired as Steve's personal assistant.[17]

Tony Brown remembers being introduced to Teresa Ensenat. The occasion was memorable. Brown and some friends took Steve out on the town for a bachelor party the night before he married Lou-Anne. Steve showed up with Teresa on his arm.

Tony pulled Steve aside at one point. "Man, are you sure you should be doing this?" he asked.

Steve seemed amused. "Am I scaring you a little bit, man?"

Brown: "I was thinking, This is rock 'n' roll. This is the way they live. This guy is fucking wild. At that point I didn't even know about the junk. I knew he smoked a little pot and he loved to drink Jägermeister, which I realized later on in my life how bad that shit was."[18]

Exit 0 also marked the end of Steve's platonic and business relationship with publicist Pam Lewis. He fired her after she had arranged to have him interviewed by *Hustler* magazine, a publication he claimed to abhor. (He later granted *Playboy* an interview, though.) For Lewis, her firing was no more traumatic an event than Stinson's resignation had been for him. Like Harry, Pam had had enough.

"Do I think [*Hustler* is] the pinnacle of literary excellence? No," Lewis explains. "But for the exposure it was fine for him to do, and it was certainly his proclivity. So what are you getting so moralistic about? It was huge exposure at the time. We had quite a bit of control over the article. I think I even engineered where we would do a Q&A; I can't remember now. But he was a typical artist. Steve would say something, then it would appear in print and he'd say, 'I never said that.' And like every journalist that ever talked to him never got it right. They can't all be horrible. When you are very outspoken and very colorful, sometimes when you say something and you see it in print, it looks a lot more glaring. And this happened regularly. Then he would get mad at me, saying, 'Why did you have me sit with this son of a bitch? He didn't quote me right.' So that would happen also. That coupled with drug use and alcohol and everything else, not sleeping for days. At the time I'm sure [being fired] bothered me a great deal, but I'm sure there was a part of me that was relieved."

This ungainly development closed out a wild ride Lewis had taken with Steve. She looks back on the Lou-Anne debacle and remembers "weirdness" all around.

"[Steve] was fighting with his ex-wife, there was this battle over seeing [his son] Justin; then he was dating Lou, then he married Lou; and then she had a kid, a little girl, and they had kids together. It was like, Wow, I didn't know people lived liked this.

"There was all kinds of weird stuff. Just screaming and yelling and her calling me asking, 'Were you with Steve at three o'clock today?' And I'm like, Okay, either way I answer it's not going to be right. And then Steve would be, 'Why the hell didn't you tell her you were with me at three o'clock!?' I'm like, 'I didn't know! Give me the script! I'll follow the script!' I didn't know. Stuff like that would happen. I didn't know where he was going, what he was buying, and who he was with. I was just trying to get his record heard and make him a star. I cared about him. But that's the kind of weird stuff that was going on."

One night Lewis confronted Steve about his marital mishaps, suggesting that he should "just fuck around if that's what you want to do. Why do you keep getting married and then have to make alimony payments? And having kids and complicating your life?"

Steve's answer became one of his standing jokes as the years wore on, to wit: "I'm not afraid of commitment."

"There was total drama all the time around him, with his personal life and the women in his life and his inability to be faithful," Pam says. "You know how that is—it's like somebody will ask you a question and you'll answer it honestly and then they're like, 'Why did you tell them that?' Because they're cheating, or they really didn't go to the market, or whatever. They really took that money and they bought drugs. And you're just innocently answering a question, and the next thing you know everybody's mad at you. That's the kind of junk that would be happening."[19]

chapter 12

Copperhead Road

Tony Brown has a vivid memory of a moment in time, early 1988:

"I was working in one of the SIR rehearsal rooms with someone like Kelly Willis, or just listening to her band rehearse. And Steve was in the building, and he said, 'Hey, man! I just thought of a good idea for a song. I'm gonna write a song about all the cats that went to Vietnam, they were moonshiners—all the cats were moonshiners and their sons got drafted to go to Vietnam. The ones that made it back from Vietnam, when they got home, their parents had quit making moonshine because they got arrested or something. But all these kids came home, the kids of moonshiners came home and started growing dope. They went to all the places where they had hid all the moonshine stills and started planting dope, and all the moonshiners' kids were dope growers. And that's what "Copperhead Road" is.'

"I said, 'That's wild. Have you written that song yet?'

"He said, 'I'm working on it. I don't have the chorus yet.'

"I ran into him at some place, right in the middle of a restaurant, and he just started singing me the song, as only Steve would do. Singing and spittin'. You have to watch yourself when you talk to him, because he spits at you. I'm dodging his spitballs and saying, 'God, that song is incredible.' To this day I have people look at me and say, 'That's the best song he ever wrote.'"[1]

Though to Steve's musician peers *Copperhead Road* lacked the craft or beauty of *Guitar Town*, fans and some of the press considered it an indisputably great album. Conceived, executed, and issued in a spirit by turns and all at once chaotic, duplicitous, toxic, selfish, comical, unnerving, and exhilarating, *Copperhead Road* brought Steve to a crucial crossroads. It marked the end of Tony Brown's journey with Steve, and for Brown, a refocusing of career objectives; it marked the onset of Steve's journey into the dark side of drug addiction and megalomania, a time when he seemed to be working at the height of his powers even as he was marshalling the forces of his artistic *Götterdämmerung*; it was the end of a seasoned Dukes lineup that had taken Steve to the upper echelon of critical, professional, and public acclaim and the dawn of a reconfigured Dukes that lacked their predecessors' experience or the chops but played with a wild rock 'n' roll abandon that suited Steve's evolving vision of his music; it was a time when Steve's romance with Teresa Ensenat was in full bloom, electric and impassioned even as he was sowing the seeds of its destruction.

It was positively Dickensian—the best of times and the worst of times—the aftershocks of which would leave Steve stripped of everything save the love of his family. By his own admission, he would reach a depth at which he could count but one friend left in his life. Only then would he begin to crawl from the wreckage he had created in his headlong plunge into self-immolation.

I. The Memphis Yin-Yang

Copperhead Road
Uni/MCA, 1988

Produced by Steve Earle and Tony Brown
Digitally recorded by Joe Hardy at Ardent Studios, Memphis, Tennessee, except for "Johnny Come Lately," recorded by Chris Burkett at Livingstone Studios, London, England
Mixed by Joe Hardy at Ardent Studios
"The Devil's Right Hand" *arranged by* Garry W. Tallent
Drum programming on "You Belong to Me" by Chris Birkett
Second engineers, Memphis: Mark J. Coddington, Tom Luane
Second engineers, London: Julius Croaol, George Shilling
Preproduction engineers: Andy Byrd, Dale Brown, Jack Burke
Mastered by Bob Ludwig at Master Disc

Musicians
Steve Earle: vocals, guitars, harmonica, 6-string bass, mandolin

Donny Roberts: guitars, six-string bass
Bill Lloyd: acoustic guitar, 12-string electric guitar
Bucky Baxter: pedal steel, lap steel, dobro
Ken Moore: synthesizer and organ
John Jarvis: piano
Kelly Looney: bass
Custer: drums
Neil MacColl: mandolin on "Johnny Come Lately"
Background vocals: John Cowan, Maria McKee, Radney Foster
The Pogues (Terry Woods: cittern; Philip Chevron: guitar, vocals; Jem Finer: banjo; James Fearnley: accordion; Spider Stacy: tin whistle, vocals; Shane MacGowan: banjo, bodhran; Daryl Hunt: bass; Ardren Ranken: drums) played on "Johnny Come Lately."
Telluride (Sam Bush: mandolin; Jerry Douglas: dobro; Mark O'Connor: violin; Edgar Meyer: bass violin) played on "Nothing but a Child."

Songs
1. "Copperhead Road" (4:29) (Steve Earle)
2. "Snake Oil" (3:30) (Steve Earle)
3. "Back to the Wall" (5:28) (Steve Earle)
4. "The Devil's Right Hand" (3:03) (Steve Earle)
5. "Johnny Come Lately" (4:09) (Steve Earle)
6. "Even When I'm Blue" (4:14) (Steve Earle)
7. "You Belong to Me" (4:24) (Steve Earle)
8. "Waiting on You" (5:10) (Steve Earle–Richard Bennett)
9. "Once You Love" (4:40) (Steve Earle–Larry Crane)
10. "Nothing but A Child" (4:25) (Steve Earle)

Richard Bennett had no reason to suspect anything untoward was going on. Everyone was back at Silverline/Goldine, beginning preproduction on Steve's next album project, *Copperhead Road*. In fact, one of the songs he helped Steve sketch out for recording was the title track. Another was a powerful song of love, yearning, and commitment, "Waiting on You." Bennett had written a rough version of the song a few years earlier, on the night, in fact, when he and his family had arrived in Nashville from Los Angeles.

"I pulled in with a U-Haul and everybody got in this rented house and was so weirded out to be in Nashville after this trip across country," Bennett recalls. "My little kids and my wife, they just went off to bed. It was like three in the afternoon, and they just went to bed. I had this little guitar, and I wrote the melody of that song. And then Steve and I finished it up later."[2]

A third song, the title of which now escapes Bennett, was mapped out as well. After that one was completed, Bennett returned to the studio the next day to news from Emory Gordy, Jr., that their services were no longer required. Steve had fired them both. The only explanation Steve ever offered was "Bowen doesn't want you anymore; he wants me to do it." Bennett didn't buy it then and doesn't now.

"I think the fact of the matter was that Steve saw an opportunity to save two points, if you will, and him jump in there as producer and get a part of that while still keeping Tony, the company man, on his side, there with him. Which is of course a smart thing to do. That's what I suspect happened. Nonetheless, the two or three songs that I began preproduction on, lo and behold, they sound on that album just like what we preproduced."[3]

Bennett is not far off the mark in his suspicions, according to Brown. *Copperhead Road*, Brown says, was the moment when Steve "wanted to go a different direction, and he wanted to be in charge.

"Now that I look back on it, I think that he felt as though [Bennett and Gordy, Jr.] really controlled the way the first two records sounded. And he liked those records. But Steve came up with a lot of those little riffs on those records, and Richard perfected them. Richard was our Carl Perkins. So I think Steve wanted to take all that stuff back. He decided to do it in Memphis, and not with Richard and Emory. I think they understood it as a creative decision Steve had made, no hard feelings. I think he let me hang around probably because I'm with the label and we got along good, and he realized I really respected his intuition and let him go with it. I think I stayed for that reason."[4]

As for the band, Steve was looking for more of a "rock 'n' roll kind of approach," Brown says, and so replaced Bennett with Donny "The Twangler" Roberts, from Webb Wilder's band; Kelly Looney on bass; rocker Kurt Custer (who later became a member of Lynyrd Skynyrd) on drums, Bucky Baxter returning on pedal steel; and on acoustic and 12-string electric guitars, Bill Lloyd, who partnered with Texan Radney Foster in the New Traditionalist duo Foster and Lloyd, whose 1987 debut album had yielded four hit singles, three in the Top 10, one in the Top 20. A solid, seasoned pro based in Nashville, Lloyd, with roots in pop and traditional country, proved to be an anchor for Brown during the sessions, the producer being otherwise "skeptical about the cast of characters we had put together.

"I was a big fan of Donny's from Webb Wilder, but I didn't know if Donny could turn on a dime like Richard, between takes or something. And I didn't know if Kelly could carry the weight that Emory carried on Steve's songs. The only thing that gave me any comfort was Bill Lloyd. I knew that he was a world-class musician and had a lot of the same kind of respect for the kind of guitar playing that Richard does, that harkens back to the Everly Brothers and those kinds of cool rhythms, and he owns some great guitars. Having Bill Lloyd on the sessions gave me a real comfort zone.

"But my job was really just to make sure it got on tape. Because Steve was not only the artist; he pretty much carried the biggest stick in the recording process on all the albums I worked on."[5]

. . .

In late 1987, at Kiva Studios in Memphis, Joe Hardy was engineering a Jim Dickinson–produced session for the Rock City Angels, a band signed to Geffen Records. One day he noticed Dickinson in conversation with a bearded visitor in sunglasses who was all black leather and denim, his long, greasy hair falling below his shoulders. This visitor, who was voluble to an annoying degree, was accompanied by a beautiful young woman with exotic features. Dickinson told Hardy the couple was in Memphis scouting out studios and that the woman worked in Geffen Records' A&R department.

Later, during a break in the session, Hardy retreated to the lounge, where he found Dickinson's friends hanging out. Almost immediately he got into a "heated debate" with the bearded man "over the root causes of the Civil War.

"I'm an arrogant loudmouth, and he's an arrogant loudmouth," Hardy says. "I was taking the states' rights position, and we would always square off. I got forced into the conservative role, even though I'm not very; compared to him I suppose I am. And when he left Dickinson said, 'Man, you should have been nicer to him. That's Steve Earle.' I said, 'Who the fuck is Steve Earle?' There's no country music in Memphis; I was way out of it. Steve's an ideologue, but he's not bitter or humorless about it, and apparently I made an impression and he liked me. I suppose it was about six months later that he decided to do *Copperhead* and wanted to do it at Ardent. Steve remembered me, and Tony knew me, so that's how I ended up as the engineer on that job."[6]

. . .

Going to Memphis to record was anything but a whimsical decision on Steve's part. He wound up booking sessions at Ardent Studios on Madison Avenue, a facility with a long and rich history of recording rock 'n' roll. Ardent's founder-owner John Fry started the business in his garage and built it into a world-class facility, always state of the art, always artist-friendly in its amenities. Fry's own production credits included what became the legendary Big Star sessions (for the band Alex Chilton formed post–Box Tops), and he drew talented people to his staff. Joe Hardy and fellow Ardent engineer John Hampton were two of the best in the business. A steady flow of top rock 'n' roll, blues, and R&B artists came through Ardent and a few months later would be sending gold records back to be hung on the walls—it was the home recording base for ZZ Top in that band's glory years; Stevie Ray Vaughan recorded there, as did B.B. King. And Steve Earle, for *Copperhead Road*. Depending upon the perspective being

Steve performing in Nashville, December 1987.

offered—either Joe Hardy's or Tony Brown's—what happened at Ardent over the course of a few weeks in spring 1988 was either a wild-assed free-for-all fueled by drugs, guns, and outsized egos (Brown's take) or a fairly routine Memphis recording project (Hardy's take).

For Brown, Steve's drug use had escalated to a disturbing level—rather than discreetly partaking out of sight of everyone else, as he had during *Guitar Town* and *Exit 0* sessions, he was using openly now, and making a show of it. During the mixing with Joe Hardy, he pulled out a bag of heroin and offered some to Tony, who politely declined. Throughout the sessions Brown had noted that Steve's behavior had become "very strange"; seeing Steve being so brazen about his heroin use had given rise in Tony to a real crisis of conscience. The Memphis sessions were an expensive undertaking—in addition to the production costs, everyone was living in a house rented for the duration of the sessions—and having ceded almost all control to Steve, Tony began to think of himself as "an enabler, no better than him."[7]

Brown's unease with what was going down was only exacerbated by Steve's casual disregard of the control room as sanctuary. If anyone of note was working at or visiting Ardent, Steve would invite them in to hear what was going on in his session. R.E.M., for example. Peter Buck wandered over one day to hang out in the control room with Steve. The entire lineup of a Memphis-based rock band wandered in on another day. All the hubbub was a distraction to a disciplined producer such as Tony Brown, who felt further alienated from the process by his unfamiliarity with the abilities of the musicians on hand.

"On those first two albums, I knew everybody as well as Steve knew them. I played on the road with Emory. I played on the road with Richard. I'd worked so many sessions with Harry on drums and as a background vocalist. And the tracks we used Paul Franklin on—and John Jarvis—I knew all the players, I knew what we could accomplish. On those sessions I had to deal with making sure the session guys didn't play too generic or too slick. That's easier to do than to have musicians whose limits you don't know. It's the difference between edginess and sloppy."[8]

Not the least of Brown's worries was the lack of preparation before the fact. Other than the songs Steve had mapped out with Bennett before firing him, and the known entity that was "The Devil's Right Hand" ("I was glad he finally decided to recut that," Brown says), the rest of the material had yet to be shaped. "We went in pretty cold. I think [Steve] might've got with the guys and rehearsed the arrangements and stuff. But it was not as good a sketch of the songs as we did for *Guitar Town* and *Exit 0*. Those albums became pretty much carbon copies of how we sketched them out in preproduction."[9]

Then there was Steve's penchant for raining verbal abuse down on Brown, as if deliberately testing his coproducer's patience. One such incident occurred when two key MCA executives visited Ardent to check up on the sessions. David Simone (pronounced Si-monee) and MCA Director of Promotion Bill Bennett were teaming up to relaunch the company's dormant Uni rock label (for which Neil Diamond had cut some of his early hits and which had once had Elton John on its roster as well). They appeared at Ardent on the day Steve was recording his vocal on the mesmerizing, hymnlike "Nothing but A Child," a duet with Lone Justice's Maria McKee that closes *Copperhead Road* on a heartfelt and calming note. (Steve had written the song originally for an Oak Ridge Boys Christmas project.)

Listening to the playback, Steve told Tony he thought it sounded "pretty good."

"You know what, Steve?" Tony responded. "There's still a little more time. I think you can sing it better."

Steve erupted. *"Hey, listen here, you little hillbilly faggot!!* I'll tell you when it's there! I'll do it again just because … just because!"

After Simone and Bennett departed, Brown, aggravated and testy, let Steve know he didn't appreciate being called a "hillbilly faggot" again, and especially with visitors in the studio.

Steve laughed it off. "Aw, man, that's why I like you, 'cause you can take all that shit. I don't mean it to be mean; I just mean it like a joke."

"Okay," Brown said warily.

"That's why I like you, man, 'cause you can take that shit," Steve repeated.

"Doesn't mean I like it," Brown snapped.[10]

What Joe Hardy saw, on the other hand, were sessions that were "rowdy, boisterous, and fun, like Steve had had a big weight lifted off him."

Steve's casual approach to preproduction seemed to Hardy to conform to the standards of a regular Memphis session—set it up and go. It was an approach that had worked often to history-altering effect in the Bluff City, dating back to Sam Phillips's Memphis Recording Service sessions.

Hardy: "In Memphis, the music stands are there to hold up an ashtray; nobody uses charts, nobody would know how to read one. So Steve would go in and play the songs on acoustic guitar, play a cassette, and then the band would just follow his lead. There was thought put into it as far as everybody knowing their parts, but it wasn't orchestrated at all, not planned out at all. I talked to Richard Bennett about the first two records. I know that Steve was always frustrated that they wouldn't let him play guitar. And Steve plays great. The kind of artist that he is, it's incomprehensible to me that he wouldn't be playing—once you've written the song, your part is always right because that's the song. So I think he was real happy—I mean, he was just ecstatic to be able to play and [be in charge]. Tony was more of an executive producer. He would come to look at stuff and hang out for a couple of days. He would lay out in the courtyard at Ardent and try to get some sun, and Steve would put up signs that said, 'Producer Erectus,' like Tony was a museum exhibit. It was all lighthearted fun."[11]

And what Tony Brown considered distractions—namely, the unannounced studio guests—Joe Hardy thought of as business as usual. His résumé included Southern soul projects cut at the Stax studio—the Bar-Kays' floating membership, for example, numbered up to a dozen musicians, and typically a good number of each one's friends and relatives would be hanging out and enjoying the good vibes going down in the studio. Peter Buck showing up for a Steve Earle session, or a four-man rock 'n' roll band wandering in for a quick look-see and hang with Steve? To Hardy, "That was nothing. Memphis is light-years from Nashville; it's just a whole different way of looking at things. I do appreciate their work ethic in Nashville, and I like going in at ten and getting off a six. I like that. But that's just not Memphis. When I first heard about it, it seemed insane to me. I used to go into a Memphis session on a Monday and get off on a Thursday, because people would come in all day—Ardent booked by the day. Well, a day is 24 hours, isn't it? So that's what would happen—of course, there were substances to help you get through it.

"All I'm saying is, it's a matter of perception. To Tony, they may have seemed chaotic; to me, they seemed routine."[12]

II. Alpha Male Ascending, V5.0

The music was coarse and rough, immediate, dated in half an hour, was about bodies in the river, knives, love pains, cockiness. Up there on stage he was showing all the possibilities in the middle of the story. —*Coming Through Slaughter*

It opens with what sounds like a bagpipe out of the Scottish Highlands, an angular swirl of anguished, piercing notes rising above an ominous droning note. Before the bagpipe line fades out, a drum booms like a cannon shot, and a forcefully strummed mandolin emerges from the mix. The drum settles into a heartbeat-like pulse, the mandolin riffs on ceaselessly, and then Steve enters, identifying himself as "John Lee Pettimore / same as my daddy and my daddy before." His granddaddy, we learn, is a seldom seen presence "he only come around about twice a year"—but when he does, he brings with him the tools of his trade as a moonshiner. Granddaddy, we're told, has also become adept at eluding the revenue agent who "wanted [him] bad" and would chase him down, but "never come back from Copperhead Road." The second verse recounts a similar scenario involving moonshiners and the law, but this time centering on his father and his uncle, who are carrying forward granddaddy's legacy.

After Steve ends the verse singing, "You could smell the whiskey burnin' down Copperhead Road," the band as one emits a rat-a-tat-tat roar—four shots' worth—Steve barks a guttural "Hey!" and the song soars into rock 'n' roll orbit, Steve's snarling guitar lines swirling angrily around the mix, Custer hitting the drums with fearsome strength.

In the third and final verse, set in the present, the narrator is singing about himself, a Vietnam veteran ("they draft the white trash first around here") back from two tours of duty. He's not running moonshine, but rather the product of "seeds from Colombia and Mexico." In the sky above his fields are DEA helicopters; he wakes from fitful sleep screaming, visions of the Vietnam horrors engulfing him, and sounds a warning: "I learned a thing or two from Charlie, don't you know / You better stay away from Copperhead Road."

Thus "Copperhead Road" sets the stage for *Copperhead Road*. All the themes of the album's first half are contained within this single song: the legacies passed down from one generation to the next—indeed the implied veneration of the preceding generation's values, including an anti-authoritarian attitude; actions defined from the vantage point of the lower class ("white trash"); the unapologetic deployment of violence as protective coloring; and an acute awareness of history as it affects one life—the narrator's. It's an incredible bit of songwriting, compressing an exhaustive breadth of time, detail, and character in four and a half minutes, like a novella in song. Even the music carries the weight of history: the bagpipe line (which is actually played by Ken Moore on a synthesizer that Joe Hardy calls "the goofiest-looking thing; it was like a Casio or something … the worst piece of shit") and the mandolin coming right after it establish the *mise- en-scène* in the Scottish-Irish music that is at the root of American country music, along with a style of Southern-influenced rock 'n' roll that evolved from traditional country and incorporates elements of Southern boogie and blues in its relentless, driving sound. It meshed perfectly with the cover image, which again was not a photo of Steve, but rather of a skull and crossbones set against a camouflage background, the skull having fangs and blazing yellow eyeballs with red pupils. On the back cover, though, the remade Steve is shown clad in motorcycle boots, lived-in blue jeans, a sleeveless work shirt. Bearded, straight hair hanging limp below his shoulders, cigarette in his mouth, sunglasses hiding his eyes, he holds a Western-style jacket of the sort he sported back in his *Guitar Town* days, poised to toss it away, along with all it represents.

The next two songs, the seemingly benign honky tonk–influenced "Snake Oil" and a hard-edged, slow-boiling story song, "Backs to the Wall," take dead aim at the unconscionable economic agenda of the Reagan administration. In "Snake Oil," the huckster scumbag narrator posits his magic elixir as a cure for everything from drought to joblessness, points out that the president "knocked 'em dead in Libya and Grenada too," and assures one and all that " 'tween me and him, people, you're gonna get along just fine." In the roiling "Back to the Wall," two friends—one "doin' good now," the other homeless, alcoholic, and living under a bridge—get together to hash out the state of things. Afterward, while driving home, the better off of the two characters reflects on the night's conversation, his thoughts turning to "what's been going down"—specifically, jittery Wall Street types trying to put a positive spin on the day's bad news, "or maybe they just don't care," and a sense of the dispossessed's rising anger as they "feel the tables turnin'." As if to say, "the revolution starts … now."

Now the groundwork had been laid for two of the most extraordinary pieces of music Steve would ever write and record. From his debut LSI recordings he resurrected "The Devil's Right Hand," keeping the basic structure intact but adding ballast and firepower in the form of these rock-centric Dukes— Custer, as he has throughout but most especially here, makes a statement with his gut-shaking, cannon-shot punctuations—and a grittiness in the vocal treatment courtesy Steve's slightly ragged singing, a byproduct of vocal cords that were damaged in the New Year's Eve close encounter with the off-duty policeman's nightstick. In the earlier version the narrator seemed almost a victim of his own naïveté, and Steve's clear, ringing tenor voice effectively made of him a pathetic, if conscious-free, character. Nearly five years' life experience and one nightstick across the throat later, Steve paints a far more malevolent portrait of a character who might well be the embodiment of a society that has dulled itself to the casual violence consuming it, both physical and verbal. The narrator understands what a Colt .45 can do ("…called it a peacemaker, but I never knew why"), but he's clever enough to absolve himself of any responsibility by twisting the intent of his mother's admonition that the pistol was "the devil's right hand."

If it doesn't fit, you must acquit.

"My granddaddy sang this song / Told me about London when the Blitz was on"

On September 7, 1940, at approximately 4:00 P.M., 348 German bombers with an escort of 617 fighter planes began raining bombs on London in an effort by Nazi madman Adolf Hitler to force the British into surrender. Two hours after the first wave of bombers, a second wave struck and continued pounding the city until 4:30 the following morning. For 57 consecutive days London was bombed by the Germans, and the attacks were sustained through May of the following year. On May 11, 1941, Hitler called off the Blitz and ordered his Luftwaffe air force eastward to prepare for Germany's ill-fated invasion of Russia; the previous night, May 10, had been the deadliest night of all, with some 3,000 Londoners killed in bombing raids.

America's respected World War Two correspondent Ernie Pyle described the initial attack as "a night when London was ringed and stabbed with fire," and observed: "There was something inspiring just in the awful savagery of it."[13]

"There's nobody here, maybe nobody knows / About a place called Vietnam"

On April 30, 1975, the Vietnam War ended when the Saigon government announced its unconditional surrender to the Vietcong Army of communist North Vietnam. In a final scene of desperation and chaos, the last of the U.S. military in Vietnam, trailed by U.S. embassy employees, raced up to the embassy roof, boarded waiting evacuation helicopters, and were airlifted out to safety.

"I was crying and I think everyone else was crying. We were crying for a lot of different reasons," said Major James Kean, one of the last evacuees from the embassy roof. "But most of all we were ashamed. How did the United States of America get itself in a position where we had to tuck tail and run?"[14]

Casualties in the Vietnam War: 1 million Vietnamese combatants, 4 million civilians killed; 55,926 Americans killed, 2,300 listed as missing in action.

There were no parades for returning Vietnam vets, only a legacy of shame that has still not completely worn off 30 years after the fall of Saigon. Filmmakers found no John Waynes to kick ass on the sands of Iwo Jima; instead, the horror and insanity of Vietnam were embodied by psychopathic, deeply scarred characters such as Tom Berringer's monstrous Sergeant Barnes in Oliver Stone's *Platoon*, whereas the plight of the returning (and damaged) vets was vividly, searingly depicted in Stone's *Born on the Fourth of July* and Ashby's *Coming Home*.

"We're gonna drink Camden Town dry tonight"

Located in the North London borough of Camden, Camden Town was founded in the 1790s by Charles Pratt, the Earl of Camden. The devastation caused by the Irish potato famine in the 1840s resulted in an influx of Irish immigrants into Camden Town, which was already in the process of being transformed from a bucolic, rural enclave into a bustling mini-metropolis as a result of ongoing canal construction and the building of a railroad link to the town. That process was completed in 1850 with the opening of the Camden Road railway station. Come World War Two, the railway termini at Camden Town became an important strategic target for German bombers.[15]

"I'm an American, boys"

The grandeur that is "Johnny Come Lately" begins with four simple ringing chords strummed on a 12-string acoustic guitar and Steve's growling introduction, "I'm an American, boys … " The scene, as he later reveals, takes place in a Camden Town pub, and he's singing in the voice of his granddaddy, an American GI buying rounds for the townsfolk, gently criticizing America's former isolationist policy ("it took a little while, but we're in this fight") but assuring those assembled that we're staying "'til we've done what's right." As he nears the end of the verse, his guitar is joined by a rolling swirl of notes from a lone banjo (played by the Pogues' Jem Finer). When the second verse begins, the entire band kicks in, and the Irish dominate: the song gains the celebratory bravado of a rock 'n' roll Irish reel, an absolutely captivating burst of energy issues from the track, and when everyone comes in on the chorus—which describes a heavily medaled American GI returning home to waiting crowds at the train station in San Antonio—the force of the music mated to the lyrics is transcendent and triumphant, setting the stage for an instrumental passage of heartbreaking beauty fashioned from a round of crisp, vibrant ensemble interplay. Floating majestically over it all is Spyder Stacey's haunting tin whistle, its airy flight and timeless melody evoking a sweep of Irish music ranging from the canon of the great eighteenth-century Irish harper Turlough O'Carolan to the melodies that made their way overseas to Appalachia and points south and southwest, providing solace for troops from the Alamo to Antietam. The second and third verses find the narrator meeting the love of his life in a field canteen, painting her name on the nose of his plane ("six more missions I'm gone"), and spending a long night with her during the Blitz, which inspires one of Steve's most elegant lyrics, "death rainin' out of the London night / We made love 'til dawn," a juxtaposition of terror and tenderness so succinctly and viscerally imagined it takes the breath away.

Granddaddy then extols his P-47 Thunderbolt single-engine fighter as "a pretty good ship," sings the praises of his "North End girl," and vows to take her back to America with him "as soon as we win this war." Another stomping instrumental break ensues, setting up the final verse, which cuts to the present day, with the narrator summarizing the story his granddaddy has told him, "how he married Grandma and brought her back home." From that sentiment we learn the narrator is a returning G. I., standing on a San Diego runway, "couple Purple Hearts and I move a little slow," but the hope of being greeted by waiting crowds of well-wishers is dashed by the spectacle before him—no one is there. What next? Not the anticipated rage, but rather a curious kind of vocal shrug on Steve's part, as if to say, "Huh. How 'bout that?" Until he sings "maybe nobody knows about a place called Vietnam" and leans hard into the last word, almost spitting it out, his frustration finally boiling over into bitter sarcasm. The song closes out with several stanzas of the instrumental theme we've been hearing throughout, Spyder Stacey again and again taking flight on the tin whistle, which begins to sound like a haunted soul seeking a safe place, until, with the track fading, someone lets out a weary, resigned sigh, barely audible but nonetheless chilling as a coda.

Recorded at Livingstone Studios in London, with the great and volatile Irish punk band the Pogues in tow, "Johnny Come Lately" was testimony to the power of Steve's vision of *Copperhead Road*. "He was bound and determined to make that happen," says Tony Brown of the overseas session, "and he did."[16]

Steve had met the Pogues a couple of years earlier at London's Abbey Road Studios during sessions for the band's epochal *If I Should Fall from the Grace of God* album. When Steve decided to try to line up the Pogues to accompany him on "Johnny Come Lately," he had his management contact the Pogues' management with the request. His audacity in approaching the band with such an offer impressed the slightly mad musicians, according to Pogues' guitarist Philip Chevron. Because to come into the Pogues' world was to invite humiliation if you didn't have your act wrapped tight.

"The approach came to us from his office, saying he had written this song that he thought was his response to a Pogues song from an American perspective," says Chevron. "We knew straight away that for anyone to make that kind of a jump—and he'd already done it—it must be good; otherwise it would be really stupid to make the jump and be embarrassed by the song. So we actually said yes to it on spec, without even hearing 'Johnny Come Lately,' because we knew that to have the confidence to say 'I've got a song here I think the Pogues can do,' the guy's gotta be good, he's gotta know what he's doing. And it was, it's a great song, and it's very clever from the point of view of how you interpret what the Pogues were doing as a sort of London Irish circle of the damned. Some lived in London, some still lived in Ireland, some had never been Irish, but they all converged on this sort of London Irish milieu in Camden Town. I think Steve got that pretty much straight away— Camden Town is mentioned in the song as a place where his grandfather goes to raise Cain. So it struck us as being an honorary Pogues song."[17]

At the studio Steve dealt with engineer Chris Birkett on the particulars of setting up for the session, while ordering Tony to be sure ten cases of Guinness dark beer were in the studio for the Pogues.

"I was in charge of making sure the Pogues had plenty of beer because they wouldn't come to the studio unless they had lots of beer," is Tony's assertion.[18]

Otherwise, the session for "Johnny Come Lately" took about a week's time, only one day of it actually spent in the recording studio, many nights of it spent on stage making music, and, in the case of Steve and the Pogues' Spyder Stacey, on the town and roaring drunk. It was an incredible odyssey, by all accounts, that produced an astounding performance in the studio once the red light came on.

A Conversation with Philip Chevron

"Anyone who walked into our lives in those days, they joined the band."

At the time you heard about the session for "Johnny Come Lately" were you familiar with Steve's music?

To some extent I was familiar. And I kind of knew by reputation that he was this rock guy who did country music, or this country guy who did rock music. So I was aware of him. And also, I have a huge soft spot for Texas music in general. I'm a major Doug Sahm fan. To me Doug is better than Elvis, because he was the greatest composite of Americana, blues, and soul. Most of the people I admire most in American music are Texans, so I would have been aware of Steve's work, but not as much as I would have liked to have been at the time.

It's an amazing song. It wraps up 30-plus years of American history in three and a half minutes.

In some ways it also resonated for me as something of the Second World War and the American presence in England, where—what was the phrase they used?—"overpaid, oversexed, and over here"—but obviously the American GI presence in England was usually welcomed. They brightened up the place and raised merry hell, and it was great. With all the British men away at the war, American servicemen had quite a good time as well with the English ladies. So it somehow involved that, even though that wasn't what it was about. But it sort of spoke of an earlier generation, and as a songwriter I identified very much with his writing strategies of using the freedom of the pop song structure to switch between the past and the present, sometimes blurring the distinctions as the song progresses.

What form was it in when you first heard it?

I was trying to remember that. I really don't know. To be honest with you, things were moving really quickly at that point. In the context of recording "Johnny Come Lately," it was like the maddest year of our lives. The previous December we had the hit single "Fairytale of New York," Top 3 in Britain, and it made such an impression in England that when our album came out in January of '88, it went straight into the Top 3 and suddenly we were big stars in Britain. We had gone from being this cult band to being a serious contender. We booked a show at Town & Country in Kentish Town on St. Patrick's Day, and tickets went so fast we kept adding more shows and playing St. Patrick's week. This became partly a celebration of St. Patrick's week, partly a celebration of what the Pogues represented in London—not just the Pogues, but here for once was a positive Irish presence in a country where Irish racism had been rampant for three decades. It was unusual for people to stand up and say, "I'm Irish!" So those gigs at Town & Country were pregnant with meaning and consequence for all of us, and for the audience. And the Pogues responded in the only way they know how in moments of great consequence, and that's to party their way through. At the same time we were aware that this was the most extraordinary week— also, two film crews came in to film all of this. "Hey, the Pogues are doing a week in London. We should make a film of it!" So we had one crew making a film of the show, another one making a documentary of the Pogues, which includes footage of the "Johnny Come Lately" session.

In addition to that I was guesting on an album called *For the Children*, a project to raise money for children for a nonsectarian effort for Northern Irish children. I was involved in that and so was Shane [MacGowan] and so was Terry Woods. And in the midst of all this, Steve was going, "When are we going to do this recording?"

We told him, "Believe it or not, the only time we can do it is that week, because that's the only time we're in London long enough to sort of focus on it." So we had this mad situation where we were sound checking in the afternoons, going to the studio, doing the gig, going to a party and staying up all night, going back to the sound check, back to the studio, and all the events are kind of jumbled up that week. Meanwhile, a film crew were taking me off to Camden Town to a record shop I used to work in to show me in my old environment showing people Beach Boys records and stuff. And Shane was taken off somewhere else to show how he was writing his novel and got the call to be in the Pogues. Everyone had these little scenarios where the producer or director had decided he wanted to get to know us. So all this madness was going on as well.

Somehow into all this Steve Earle walked—anyone who walked into our lives in those days, they joined the band. It's a simple as that. It wasn't sufficient that you just hung around and waited for your bit; I think we learned "Johnny Come Lately" at the sound check the first day and Steve came on that night with us and did we performed it for the next two or three days. Mary Coughlin was also involved in those shows; Kirsty MacColl was involved; Joe Strummer; couple of people in a band put together by a guy who used to be in the Specials. It was Mad Dogs and Englishmen, like a Joe Cocker revue or something. But it was organic and natural and still in keeping with the Pogues wanting to celebrate their moment of great triumph by bringing their friends along. Somehow it just seemed okay to do that. So Joe Strummer came on and did a couple of numbers, including "I Fought the Law." Kirsty sang "Fairytale of New York" and "Dirty Old Town," I think. Steve came on and did "Johnny Come Lately"— the Pogues Revue. And it was wonderful. What are these people gonna do? Sit backstage drinking? Get 'em workin'! Get 'em out there onstage!

Steve tells this story about how we got so accustomed to him coming out and doing "Johnny Come Lately," and every night Terry Woods introduced him, [raspy, high-pitched voice] "And now, from the great State of Texas, to perform a song we just recorded called 'Johnny Come Lately,' ladies and gentlemen, Steve Earle!" and then one night nobody walks on. At this point Steve's on his way back to the States and no one's told Terry. He and his producer Tony Brown had pissed off that day, seriously hung over, three nights of partying with the Pogues, and we didn't know Steve was gone.

But anyway we kept the song in the show—Spyder sang it for months, years after that. It was in the show for a long time; it was Spyder's kind of spotlight number. And it proved that it's a Pogues song in a funny sort of way because it blended with everything else.

The only reason I remember any of it is because of the documentary—it was captured on film.

What was the scene like in the studio when you got down to brass tacks?

It was funny because we took the view that Steve did: let's get it nailed down right. Let's get a feel going. Essentially it was the band playing live, including Shane, who was experimenting with rhythm banjo at the time. I was the guitarist. Steve was playing acoustic guitar, Jem Finer plays banjo, James Fearnley, accordion, Terry Woods played cittern, and Shane MacGowan played this kind of rhythm banjo. Shane was determined not to be left out of it.

One account of the session claims Shane showed up four hours late.

That's entirely out of context. Shane showed up whenever it was time for him to be there. The drummer turns up first and gets the sound on his drum. The bass player turns up—these people have to be there. I assure you, everyone was there when it came time to press the button and record. Neil MacColl, who plays mandolin, is Kirsty's half brother. I didn't know who Neil MacColl was, just somebody who was backstage and had joined the band that day, y'know.

Steve made a couple of adjustments to the arrangement as we went along, he did a guide vocal as we were putting it down. I'm not sure, he may even have used some of the guide vocal in the final mix. But I know that everything got down very quickly, with a minimum of messing around.

That's Tony Brown's recollection, too, that once you got down to it, it happened fast.

I think so. Anything that needed to be touched up or patched up, he did it right there.

Did you have much interaction with Tony?

I know more about Tony since then than I did then. I've since realized he's a major, major producer, one of the top three or something. But like all the best producers, his job was not to impress himself but to translate the atmosphere onto tape; to capture bits that were good about it and make sure we didn't lose any of that. I have to say he did a great job, but he wasn't somebody who was garrulous and voluble. He was doing the job. I could tell also he was noticing when something was slightly out of the ordinary that would work—like Shane on the banjo and Tony going, "How can I make that work?" And actually getting on with doing it, where other producers would say, "Look, Shane, maybe we can think about the banjo later, maybe we can overdub it," hoping to get him to go away. But Tony, to give him his due, was responsible to people and that's where a good producer needs to be to get the best Pogues. With our eccentricity, self-absorption, whatever, you have to be able to see and pick up on what we're doing. That takes intuition. So he probably was working very hard but not looking like it. Tony was like a swan, paddling underneath but calm above the water.

When Tony talked about this part of the album, he tried to get me to believe his only job was to bring in ten cases of Guinness to get the Pogues through the session.

The results speak for themselves. I think he did a real good job on that. It's easy to say, "Oh, I just supplied the beer," but it's the hardest band in the world to produce and that's why so few people did it. Really, Elvis Costello lasted for an album and a half, and that was enough for him. Steve Lillywhite had enough of us and refused to do the third album—the second was too painful for him. So literally, in that case, always the perpetual Plan B—call up Joe Strummer, he'll do it. I missed a tour in '87 because I was in the hospital, and Joe was literally called two days beforehand and told he was going on tour with the Pogues. "Oh, okay, I'm not doing anything else this week, so fine." They had to sit there and teach Joe the show, four hours. And equally, when we couldn't get anyone to produce us for anything, the last days before we booked into the studio and still couldn't find a producer willing to take a risk, Joe was called and told, "We've got a job for you, Joe. You're going to produce our new album." And when Shane left, Joe was the obvious choice for lead singer. He was never able to refuse us. Which was kind of good and kind of painful for him at the same time. Had he thought about it for longer than 10 minutes, he might have said, "Uh-uh." So I know how hard it is to produce the Pogues, and also I've been there—before I joined the band I produced a few tracks.

How was Steve during the actual sessions?

To me he seemed perfectly normal, so I don't know. I was aware that he and Spyder were spending nights staying up, but that was a bit much for me. I have my limits. But I was aware that he and Spyder had forged this brethrenship of staying up all night. But I certainly wasn't part of it. But nothing Steve did was getting in the way of the work in the studio.

That was the first time on record—of course, it was only his third album—when he addressed the Irish connection at the roots of his music. He's since referenced the Irish roots of his music on almost every album.

It's definitely there, and it's something I'm very interested in, it's something Terry Woods is very interested in. Terry Woods learned Irish music through Appalachian music. Wasn't hearing the great Irish fiddle players or pipers; that wasn't the music he was seeking out. American folk music, and it was that that drove him back to Ireland. And also Woody Guthrie and so on. I'm very much aware of that in my own musical journey. It's partly about how Irish music moved around the world and back. In some ways, the Texas connection, that story hasn't been completely told. I was actually down in San Antonio a couple of weeks ago myself, talking to Sean Sahm, Doug's son. He never heard of the Pogues, which is brilliant, because I was able to explain the Pogues, that essentially it's like Irish music given a punk rock kick up the ass. The connection is there. David Crockett played fiddle at the Alamo. The late influx at the Alamo, a lot of those boys were Irish. Also at San Jacinto, where the Alamo damage was redressed, the marching tune there was "Will You Come to the Burgh," which is based on an Irish tune and has become part of the standard American folk repertoire and was brought to America by the Irish. In the Texas-Mexico wars, there were Irish on both sides. That's because there were Catholics who felt exiled from America by the Protestant majority and had gone to the Mexican side because they were Catholics. Most of the Alamo people were adventurers, pirates, slave traders—basically people who had run out of luck and had to move on further forward. To me, there's a lot of those loose ends that have not been tied up, and it's the one area Doug Sahm didn't actually quite explore. And it's interesting to me that Steve is exploring it as a Texan. It's interesting to me how he's been making that connection from the other side.

I think you can't actually understand American music unless you acquire some understanding of Irish music. Inevitably, Irish music has tended to be more the foundation of American music. I grew up in Ireland with a huge distaste for Irish music. Because it was part of official Ireland, it was in the same league for me as Gaelic Games and the Irish language and the Catholic Church—they were all part of the official Ireland that they tried to propagate as this new society, but a very sort of rural society and a very reactionary society in many ways. They felt they needed to embrace Irish culture in all its forms in opposition to British culture. You can't do that. The Irish country has an imperial culture and having embraced that culture through people like Oscar Wilde, Winston Sheridan, George Bernard Shaw, the Anglo-Irish art form is very much a cornerstone.

Even the Chieftains were beyond the pale for me to listen to. They looked like schoolchildren, like they were part of the official doctrine of Irish thinking. The breakthrough didn't happen for me until the early '70s when a band called Horslips came along. They had long hair and looked like they might smoke the occasional joint. They were obviously a rock 'n' roll band. But Horslips was a freak of nature. They didn't mean to be a band; they got together for a commercial and they needed some guys who looked like a band. And they had such fun, they thought, Wouldn't it be a good laugh if we actually did become a band? Then they discovered that one used to play guitar, one played drums. When they got good at it they hadn't been able to articulate and say, "What we're doing here is illustrating that rock 'n' roll is based on Irish music." Young people reclaimed Irish music through Horslips, reclaimed it through long hair and spangly suits and platform shoes, and they looked like *they* might smoke the occasional joint. Horslips opened the door to Sion O'Riorden, the Dubliners. So all of this is relatively new.

Steve Earle came in at an interesting point, only a decade or so later, and it was still wide open, discovery and rediscovery.

In February 2005, I took the Amtrak train from Chicago to San Antonio, a service which takes around 36 hours. Arriving at San Antonio station behind schedule at 2:00 A.M. or so, and although I was not anticipating a welcoming committee ("they'll be waiting at the station down in San Antone / When Johnny comes marching home"), I was struck by how romantic the scene still was, the gleaming silver train proud against the sky. And I became painfully aware that I was already watching a scene from America's past, with the rapid demise of passenger trains in the U.S.A.—and at a time when they are environmentally friendly too—Steve Earle's lyric is already nostalgic. The capacity to contain the future past in a contemporary lyric that already plays with time, is quite remarkable.[19]

* * *

As the lyrics suggest, "Johnny Come Lately" is a song rooted in family history and lore. The main character, Granddaddy, is modeled after Jack Earle—not Steve's father, but Steve's father's nephew, who served in the 8th Air Force in World War Two, his entire tour of duty spent in England. While there he met and fell in love with a beautiful Welsh girl, Mair Thomas. As soon as the war was won, Jack Earle (bearing the same name as Steve Earle's father) married Mair Thomas (bearing the same maiden name as Steve Earle's mother) and brought her home to America.

"You know, we talked a lot and Steve would be there when we talked," says Jack Earle, Steve's father. "And she's such a great person and loves to talk, so she was sort of one of Steve's favorites, and that was just one of the stories of the Earles as we progressed along."[20]

* * *

The second half of *Copperhead Road*—always underestimated because the first half is so powerful and politically charged—turns inward to the state of the heart. It's a collection of love songs gritty, tender, and longing, a side of Steve Earle that still tends to be overlooked.

"In a sense he's stereotyped about doing the angry or political stuff, and they forget he writes great love songs," Tony Brown observes. "He's just a good songwriter, period. Melody—all those little riffs that go through his songs, they were his riffs. Maybe Richard gets credit for playing them, but they were Steve's riffs, and to me that's what's so great about the first two records we did together. It showed me that this guy sort of drew from the same place that Carl Perkins drew from, and the Everly Brothers drew from, really drew from music, and then he got into the attitude thing because that's what the critics focused on, and he ended up being the angry young man."[21]

"Even When I'm Blue" and "You Belong to Me" are two fierce love songs, the former keyed by the six-string bass made memorable on *Guitar Town*, the latter by its hard, twanging drive, and both remarkable for their clear-eyed and openhearted sentiments. "Even When I'm Blue" is about an imagined lover, long sought, never found but surely out there, not a product of blind love, but of something transcendent and uplifting, "like a beacon in the night." "You Belong to Me" is sung to a woman he feels he's let down because "none of my dreams came true." Faithful to his own story, he's still plugging away, a knight in rusting armor with, in a beautiful phrase articulated in chivalrous terms, "a heart inside here entrusted and sworn to you." Steve's cowrite with Richard Bennett, "Waiting on You," is a big, thunderous production that begins with a sighing wash of synthesizer before the band enters with a thudding roar, the guitars ring out, the drums blast a shot here and there, and Steve sends out the lyrics with gripping urgency—he sings of his patience in waiting for the lover he wants, "a whole lifetime, just a lifetime," as if that's a small price to pay. The song brings it all together: the band's energy and empathy, along with Steve's commitment to the story line. Even more remarkable, the arrangement keeps shifting in texture, from verse to verse it seems like something new is coming into the sound scape—there's a chiming, Byrds-like guitar, then a swoop of organ underneath it, then an acoustic line will surface amidst the din. As the aural representation of a soul in need, it's powerful and persuasive. "Once You Love," a cowrite with Larry Crane, is an age-old story of the man who has everything but love, then finds it, then loses it, and "still calls her name out after all these years." It's a simple message about how love, or the need for it, never subsides, and this message is lent added poignancy at the close by Bill Lloyd's evocative 12-string electric guitar solo, baroque-like in its torrent of pristine, cascading notes. As it fades out, an acoustic guitar line emerges, and Steve begins the beautiful country lullaby, sung with Maria McKee, that brings *Copperhead Road* to a hopeful, humanistic conclusion. Ascribing to the birth of the Christ child a hope for humankind's survival, Steve extends that sentiment to the wonder and promise every mother and father finds in their newborn, "another chance allowed." The backing band on this track was Telluride, a bluegrass supergroup comprised of Sam Bush on mandolin, Mark O'Connor on fiddle, Jerry Douglas on dobro, and Edgar Meyer on bass violin, thus accounting for a sound as robust and personable as it was precise.

When it was all done, and he listened back to it, Joe Hardy was astounded by what he heard. Or more accurately, by what he heard that he believes he had never heard before: *Copperhead Road* was so advanced a vision that it was a genre unto itself.

"I think what I was taken by more than anything was the quality of the songs—I thought the songs were just great songs," he says. "If another band—and they had happened to be a rock band—had cut 'The Devil's Right Hand,' it would still be a great song. The genre was irrelevant. Even though I didn't think it was country, I didn't know what it was. And, you know, unfortunately I'm in the music business; I love the music and hate the business. But I know one of the things that just drives A&R people crazy is marketing. They want a loaf of white bread or a loaf of rye bread; they don't want it mixed up. I guess I was wondering, What in the hell are they gonna do with this? Because I would listen to the rock station, or the R&B station, and I just hadn't heard stuff like this before. Really, I'm not too sure there had been stuff like this before. As much as people talk about David Allan Coe or Merle Haggard being the godfather of new country, that's really not the case. I don't know, I just thought it sounded like some new, weird thing. It certainly didn't sound like Springsteen. I know a lot of people compared him to Springsteen, but that's only true from a populist, philosophical base."[22]

III. Aftermath

Jimmy Bowen's reaction to hearing *Copperhead Road* was, according to Tony Brown, immediate and blunt: "He said the album was a piece of shit."[23]

But Bowen had a plan: he would offer the album to Irving Azoff, who headed MCA and was based at the West Coast headquarters. "If he wants it, he can have it. But if he doesn't take it, it's not coming out," Bowen told Brown.[24]

Not long after, late one night, the phone rang at Tony Brown's home. He answered it and heard a familiar voice on the other end. "Hey,T. It's Irving."

Irving Azoff, calling in the dead of night. Which turned out to be commonplace because he liked Tony and cultivated his friendship. Sometimes their calls would be about some serious business issue, sometimes they were, in Brown's words, "just idle chatter."

On this night, serious business was afoot.

"Hey, listen," Azoff began, "Bowen wants me to take that *Copperhead Road* album of Steve's. Bowen said it's a piece of shit. I listened to it and I told Bowen—now I just told him this—'cause I know if I told him I liked it, I know Bowen, he won't let me have it. So I told Bowen I agreed with him, but I'd put it out anyway. But I want you to know I love the record. So when Bowen says, 'Irving took the record, but he thinks it's a piece of shit too,' count your lucky stars."

In a meeting the next day, Bowen told Brown, "You're lucky. Irving agrees with me that the album's a piece of shit, but he's gonna take it."

Brown never told Bowen of Azoff's strategy, but this incident became another chapter in the ongoing education of Tony Brown, record man.

"I thought, So this is how the game at the top is played. Yes sir!"[25]

Even though he was losing one of his prize artists—and his other Texas artist signings, Nanci Griffith and Lyle Lovett, would soon join the exodus from MCA Nashville to the West Coast pop division ("it was a domino effect," Brown says[26])—Brown supported Steve's move to Uni. "It looked like a good opportunity, and I thought, Shit, I want this record to be heard. I love this record. So I'm for it. I totally supported it. Everybody at the label was pretty much disillusioned with Steve's vision of himself. I didn't blame him; I'd get the hell out of here too."[27]

Uni released *Copperhead Road* on October 17. The reviews were over-the-top positive, and, according to Brown, the album sold a million units worldwide.

The year hurtled to a close in typical colorful fashion. On September 13 Steve was arrested at the border on his way back from Canada. He was charged with jumping bail in the case involving his alleged assault of Sergeant Lonnie

Allen on New Year's Eve. It was all a mistake, though—a Dallas bail bondsman had misread the dates on his calendar and had erroneously identified Steve as a fugitive from justice. Steve spent six hours in custody in Detroit before his lawyers straightened out the matter. On September 20, in Dallas, he pleaded no contest to a reduced charge of resisting arrest and received one year's unsupervised probation (to be expunged at the end of that period providing no new charges were filed against him) and was fined $500.

"I reached a point a long time back where I realized I would never reach a plateau where everything would be all right," Steve told *Rolling Stone* reporter Holly Gleason in a January 26, 1989, feature headlined "Steve Earle: A Bad Boy Settles Down." "So by eliminating false hope, you don't have those unattainable expectations. It just makes everything easier to deal with, because you're coming at it from a more realistic perspective."

Admitting to having "a real hard year," Steve told Gleason, "it seems to be winding down. My energy seems to be going more into music now and less into bullshit—lawyers and stuff. I'm starting to apprehensively look forward to this album and tour."[28]

In early 1989, in a quiet ceremony in his attorney's office in Franklin, Tennessee, Steve married Teresa Ensenat.

IV. Alpha Male Ascending, V6.0

In March 1988, Rodney Crowell, now signed to Columbia, released his fifth solo album. Coproduced by Crowell and Tony Brown, *Diamonds & Dirt* was the byproduct of a template Crowell had devised in the summer of 1985, when he and some musician friends had gone into the Garage Studio in Nashville to cut some new songs he'd written. The sessions were free-spirited and productive, the results of which "pointed clearly in the direction I knew I wanted to go and illustrated beautifully the method to use getting there; work fast and don't think," Crowell recalled.[29] It was the same strategy Steve Earle adopted for the

Copperhead Road sessions in Memphis. In Crowell's case, the upshot was a masterful exhibition of stellar songwriting craft, tradition-rooted arrangements with a contemporary rhythmic thrust, adroit lyrics that were clever and penetrating in a single phrase, and the most engaging vocal performances he had ever put on tape, proving himself over the course of the album as skilled a heartbreaking balladeer ("The Last Waltz") as he was a raucous belter ("Crazy Baby").

Not the least of the album's virtues: a stunning ballad of love and longing, "It's Such a Small World," performed as an intense duet with his wife Rosanne Cash. *Diamonds & Dirt* generated an unprecedented five No. 1 country singles, sold 1.2 million copies and elevated Crowell to a plateau of commercial viability and aesthetic credibility hitherto unknown to his generation of Texas alpha male songwriters.

chapter 13

The Hard Way: A Reality

I. Stacey

In February 1989, with the *Copperhead Road* tour kicking off, Steve summoned his sister Stacey to Nashville. He asked her to bring her two children and take care of his house while he was on the road. In return he would not charge her rent and would support her financially.

It was the second time around for Steve and Stacey as roomies. After becoming pregnant at 15 and giving up her baby for adoption, Stacey, at Steve's invitation, found a home with Steve and Cynthia in Wembley, Texas. "He always took good care of me," Stacey says of her brother.[1]

Now in a failing marriage to Michael Mims and facing a mountain of debt besides, she did not want to be a burden to anyone, regardless of the magnitude of her problems. She declined Steve's offer of financial support and instead found herself a job working in the Fairview Elementary School cafeteria. At home she cared for her two boys by Michael, Chris and Kyle, as well as Steve's two sons.

"The mothers would drop them off and they'd stay four or five days and I just kept the house functioning," Stacey says. "That was my part in Nashville. He was helping me get on my feet on my own, and I was helping him being the nanny and the housekeeper."[2]

Stacey and Steve had often smoked pot together when they were hanging out, and Stacey was aware that Steve was overly fond of alcohol, but what she saw when she got to her brother's house unnerved her.

Stacey Earle at Steve's home studio, rehearsing with Dukes guitarist Zip Gibson for The Hard Way tour, 1990.

"That's when I found out, Whoa, we have a problem. I always knew he did use. But that's when I started noticing needles laying around. That's when I went to his wife, Teresa Ensenat, and I said, 'I think he's injecting.'

"This was always a big factor in our family—yes, Steve used drugs, but he would never use needles. Steve was always afraid of needles. That was even discussed by my parents. That's how open it is—like I said, addiction does not shock our family. But he's a smart user. He is, otherwise he'd be dead as a doornail. He's very sensible about it.

"But I went to Teresa and I said, 'I think he's eight-balling. He's using speed and he's injecting. He's using a needle.' I think they got into it and he came to me and said, 'You don't know what you're talking about.' He fought me on it, and I think he lost a little trust in me there.

"Picture it: it's like me, Chris and Kyle and J.T. (Justin Townes), and there's needles laying everywhere, blood I'm washing off the mirrors, washing it off the walls. And the spoons—I'm feeding kids with cereal spoons he'd been using to cook crack."[3]

On her own, Teresa had become concerned enough to try to do something to bring her husband to his senses. In addition to the heroin and the crack, he was downing Tussionex prescription cough syrup in alarming quantities while on tour. Attempting to organize an intervention, Teresa enlisted in the effort Steve's best friend, Rick Steinberg, himself a recovering addict; Patrick Earle, Steve's younger brother who was now working as his production manager; and Jack and Barbara Earle, who agreed to drive up from Houston in an effort to save their son's life. Someone, believed by the family to be Teresa, also called Lou-Anne Gill, whom, unbeknownst to Teresa, Steve was seeing again on the side. She in turn, the family believes, alerted Steve to the plan afoot. While the Earles, Teresa, and Steinberg were waiting for Steve to meet them in a hotel room, the phone rang. It was Steve calling to say there would be no intervention, but if Jack and Barbara wanted to spend the night at his house, they were welcome.

"So we did," Barbara says. "He was still our son and we still loved him. We couldn't make him do what we wanted him to do."[4]

Steve wasn't home when Jack and Barbara arrived. Jack found him at Lou-Anne's house and pleaded with Steve to get professional help. Steve insisted he had everything under control.

"Well, there was really no talking to him," Jack says, "as far as discussing that aspect of it. Of course, we were terribly concerned and trying to figure every possible way we could to turn that around."[5]

Steve also told Teresa he wasn't returning to their home. "The intervention made me so angry that I left the love of my life," Steve says.[6] Devastated, Teresa returned to Los Angeles and took up residence in a hotel as the first step toward piecing her life back together post–Steve Earle.

Stacey, on the other hand, battled her own demons, the ones she was born with. Her epilepsy, long dormant, returned with a vengeance in her late teens and upended her life. She was so burdened with simply getting through a day that she was barely cognizant of her older brother's achievements. Music was the calm in the storm that was her life.

"I knew nothing of the music industry. I knew what a songwriter was, because I grew up with songwriters coming in and out of our household. I knew that Steve had *Guitar Town* out; I knew that it was playing on the radio, but I wasn't one of those kids that knew what the Top 10 hits were. I didn't know really any of how that worked because I was 17 and raising children. People don't seem to understand that. You lose reality on what's normal for 17- to 29-year-old folks who might be keeping up with the latest music, going to the record stores, what is the Top 10, what is the next hit? Those things did not function in my mind. One, because maybe three years of that was dealing with a serious, serious seizure episode and raising two children at the same time. I mean, for me that was hanging on for dear life. Every time it would happen I would feel like, Oh, I'm dying! And then just working every day. I was a baseball coach and all these things. But I loved playing guitar and I loved singing. Maybe because it was the only thing I could afford to do, I don't know."[7]

II. Hey, Joe

There were moments during the recording of *Copperhead Road* when Steve Earle and Joe Hardy connected. When Tony was out of the studio or back in Nashville for a respite, Steve and Joe would be left alone to do his guitar overdubs or some other bit of business that involved only Steve being there. Invariably, after trying something, Steve would ask Joe what he thought of it. They would bounce ideas off each other, and Steve saw and heard in Joe's style an approach he liked.

Joe Hardy: "I did some stuff that I don't think [Steve] had heard before, especially on the mixes on *Copperhead Road*, like echo on the kick drum, sort of oddball stuff that the Nashville guys wouldn't ever have thought to do, because they would have been fired. I don't want to sound too self-congratulatory because some of it if I heard it now I would hate—but he really liked it. I think at the end of that record he thought my contribution had been more than an engineer, less than a producer, and that he thought I deserved a shot to coproduce with him. Because really, it's hard for anybody, especially if they have a substance abuse problem, to produce themselves. And Steve rightfully deserves first credit on *The Hard Way*, but I held up my end of it too."[8]

A Kentucky native, Hardy found his career path taking shape while attending Centre College in Danville, Illinois. There his college roommate was the brother of Andy Hummel, Big Star's bass player. Determined to be an engineer, Andy Hummel enlisted his brother's band as guinea pigs and would have them come to Memphis, where he oversaw their recording sessions. Eventually Hardy dropped out of college and moved to Memphis with a couple of other band members—"the ones who were serious"—and was signed to John Fry's Ardent Records label, which was distributed through Stax, but lost the deal after Stax went broke in 1975. Hardy had started engineering some at Stax and eventually engineered some projects at Ardent Studios. The latter developed into a job managing Ardent, which allowed him to record his own music after everyone had gone home for the night. His big break, so to speak, came in producing a couple of hit albums for the Christian rock band DeGarmo and Key. The Christian music scene became a small profit center for Ardent, and Hardy eventually found himself engineering and playing bass on sessions for the Blackwood Brothers, whose keyboard player was Tony Brown—"always real, real nice to me."

At Ardent he found his dream sound—"an acoustic guitar loud. Andy Hummel miked up my old Martin and you could crank it up. And it was just unbelievable to me that you could hear an acoustic guitar at the same level as a Marshall. So I was floored by acoustic guitars, always—I think they're the ultimate rock instrument."

But his ideas about sonics were formed, as they were for many of his generation and since, by the Beatles' albums. A self-professed "Beatles nut," Hardy took note of the Fab Four's progress from album to album, and "it was obvious something was happening—from 'I Want to Hold Your Hand' to 'Strawberry Fields,' something really happened there"—and from that developed a heightened awaremess of audio-as-texture. "Do you remember the first time you heard 'Itchycoo Park'? What the hell is that!? It was the coolest sound. Or Hendrix's stuff—I used to wear headphones to listen to 'Third Stone from the Sun,' over and over and over, just couldn't believe it—and had no idea how to make stuff sound that way. I just knew I would sure like to."

III. Tony, Exitus

Tony Brown had signed Steve and overseen the trajectory of his career from obscurity to acclaimed outlaw country rocker. He had given him a degree of autonomy in the studio that was almost unprecedented for a developing artist in the Nashville system. And he had been a cool customer in tolerating Steve's excesses and insensitive behavior, as well as an advocate for him when Jimmy Bowen seemed bent on chewing him up and spitting him out.

So it came with some shock, and a little relief, when Tony found out he was no longer Steve's producer of choice. The manner in which this news was conveyed to Tony, though, showed Steve still oblivious of anyone's feelings but his own, and seemingly ungrateful to another key person—as John Lomax III would confirm—who had believed in him and extended themselves on his behalf.

It happened on a night when Tony and Steve were on a NARAS-sponsored panel session at Belmont College in Nashville. An audience member posed a question to Steve: "Are you and Mr. Brown going to be working together on the next album?" Not making eye contact with Tony, Steve responded with a cocky, "Well, he doesn't know this yet, but I guess he will when I answer the question. No. I'm doing the next one by myself."[9]

The news slammed into Tony's gut, but to the attendees he betrayed no emotion. It took him hardly any time at all to breathe easy. He was ready to put some distance between himself and the least popular artist on the MCA roster.

"You know what? My reaction was, like Emory and Richard, I guess, it's time. I knew he was headed that way anyway. I was kinda relieved, because I was thinking, He's only going to get worse with his habit. And as a record executive I might have to step up and be a bad guy, and God knows I hate that kind of shit. So I was not unhappy to step aside.

"I totally got into Steve and would've stood by him had he wanted to use me on the record after *Copperhead Road*, but he chose to do it himself. He should do his own records, because basically we're just liaisons between the engineer and him, and the musicians; we're team players with him, but he really wants to do it himself. And that's where it ended up."[10]

IV. Guns, Drugs, Bikes, Love, and Family

A revised Dukes lineup joined Steve for *The Hard Way*. Donnie Roberts was gone, and so was Custer. Returning from an earlier incarnation of the Dukes, circa *Pink & Black*, was guitarist Zip Gibson, and the new drummer was Craig Wright, who had no prior history with Steve. Despite the triumph of *Copperhead Road*, Steve elected to return to Nashville for *The Hard Way*, setting up shop in the high-end Sound Emporium studio on Music Row. For mixing they went back to Ardent in Memphis, where Joe Hardy was on familiar turf, and stay there for the recording of "When the People Find Out," which would feature the local Christ Missionary Baptist Church Choir, led by former Stax keyboardist Lester Snell, backing Steve.

Fully in charge now, Steve's behavior was brazen on more than a couple of fronts. When it came time to record, he was all business, focused and intense, delivering some of the most assured performances of his brief recording career. But he was no longer even attempting to be discreet feeding his addiction—to the point where even the easygoing Joe Hardy became upset—and he was manifesting what seemed to some to be a treacherous infatuation with weaponry, stemming from the times he armed himself for drug-buying forays into some of Nashville's more dangerous neighborhoods. "It's not the heroin that's dangerous," he told Hardy, "it's the buying it."[11] Joe may have been unsettled by Steve's blatant drug use in the studio, but he was blasé about the gun. "I'm a Southern guy; we're comfortable with guns, so that didn't bother me at all."

But Hardy threatened to quit the project when Steve started shooting up in the lounge, in full view of anyone who would walk in. It was one thing for jaded music industry types to witness such a spectacle, but when ex-wives and children were around—and they were around a lot, as Hardy recalls—it was over the line of acceptable behavior, even by rock 'n' roll standards.

"*The Hard Way* was more chaotic than *Copperhead Road*," Hardy says, "just because we were recording in Nashville and there were eight million wives and it was more of a family thing. Which was all fine with me. But the needle thing, with kids walking in, I thought it was stupid.

"Back in the lounge, where people came to hang out, that's where all the people who were coming over would walk in. And to see someone sitting in the lounge shooting up … I mean, we live in America and he has a right to do this, but I got pissed about that.

"But as far as him, he was always absolutely on top of his game, I thought. Focused about everything, ready to work—he would be tardy occasionally. Like we'd be doing a vocal comp; Steve would never do more than three vocals. He'd say, 'Fuck, I can't sing anyway. Make whatever you can out of those three.' And he'd get on his bike and split to go buy dope. Teresa Ensenat [with whom Steve had reconciled] and I would stay in there and comp his vocal. Well, she would get really weird and anal about it, whereas I think Steve didn't really give a shit. We'd get done and might have to wait an hour for him. And that's about as bad as I remember it getting."

As for preparation, Hardy found Steve ready to work. He had done some rough demos at home and "he had some machine stuff he had overdubbed and he was trying out guitar synthesizers. I think he was exploring all kinds of stuff."

Teresa was back at Steve's side again in the studio. She had been an unobtrusive presence during the making of *Copperhead Road*, but she got more involved on *The Hard Way*, as Hardy recollects.

Hardy sensed that Teresa "desperately" wanted the marriage to work out, and he also noticed that she kept her frustrations with him to herself during the sessions. Steve, who told Hardy he was smart enough to beat heroin, would make jokes about his addiction constantly, and sometimes at Teresa's expense.

"Oh, Teresa's tired today," he would crow to Hardy. "She didn't know what it's like to have sex with a junkie!"

But for the most part the sessions were smooth and professional. Steve and Teresa were "all business," Hardy says, noting that whatever might have been going on in their personal relationship was kept well away from the recording studio.

"She looked bummed on some days," Hardy recalls, "but Steve was just sailing through the whole thing. I've never seen Steve act depressed, ever. But there was obviously some shit going on, I just didn't think it was any of my business. The other thing is, ex-wives would come over all the time. I just don't know how Teresa handled that. I think she was just trying to keep her mind on the work."

Then there was the matter of a Harley-Davidson motorcycle that Steve drove into the Sound Emporium loading area and started breaking down, piece by piece. Not only did Hardy shrug off the ever-growing pile of parts nearby, he found a way to use them productively—ever resourceful, he recorded the engine and used the sound on "This Highway's Mine (Roadmaster)."

(Stacey remembers the studio "covered in motorcycle parts," but was amused by Steve's biker flirtation. She regarded it as harmless, except on the rare occasions when he tried to ride one of his four Harleys. "He wasn't one of those people that rode 'em regularly. He wasn't real stable on it, but he could pull it off. I actually got on the back with him and rode from C&S Harley out to [his home]. I would say we were very lucky to get there. Because he was higher'n a kite and doesn't ride that much. As soon as he got one, it had to be dismantled and someone was painting a new tank for it with skulls on it. It would get so taken apart that he'd have to go in and have it put back together."[12]

Not the least of the fine performances on *The Hard Way* came from the most unlikely source—Stacey Earle, making her recording debut, and singing like her life depended on it in a blistering duet with Steve on the incendiary rocker "Promise You Anything."

It began when Steve heard Stacey at home, scrubbing away on guitar and singing the Suzanne Vega song "Luka." It was the only song she knew. "I want you to try and sing a song with me," he told her.

Fearless but quaking inwardly, she consulted with Chip Davis, Steve's guitar tech, who gave her a quick vocal lesson in singing harmony, "because I had never really sang harmony."

In the session, she stumbled on the first two passes—"I couldn't get the cue in." Then Steve stood in front of her and directed her where to come in. On the third try she nailed an amazing performance—her Southern drawl was alluring and urgent all at once, full of unbridled sensuality and go-for-broke passion.

"I was just so terrified," she recalls. "But I nailed it on the third take. That's all I did."

"She was scared to death," Hardy concurs. "It was toward the end of the sessions, and I don't know if she'd really sung before. I thought she sang great, but she was just unsure of herself because she hadn't done it before. The part is killer, that song is great. That's just a pop song, I think."

Steve then asked Stacey to accompany the band on *The Hard Way* tour, and through the good graces of Zip Gibson, who charted out all the songs for her, she learned the set list, practiced diligently before the tour started, then hit the stage with "notes taped all over the floor, and they didn't come off the floor until about halfway through the tour."

Bitten by the bug, Stacey returned from the tour and started playing open-mike nights around Nashville, hoping to find the same magic her brother had been born with.

The Hard Way
MCA, 1991

Produced by Steve Earle and Joe Hardy
Digitally recorded and mixed by Joe Hardy at
    Sound Emporium, Nashville, Tennessee,
    and Ardent Recording, Memphis,
    Tennessee
Overdubs recorded by Mark Coddington
Preproduction engineers: Peter Keppler and
    Mark Coddington
Mastered by Bob Ludwig at Masterdisk Corp., New York, New York

Musicians
Steve Earle: acoustic guitar, electric guitars, mandolin, mandoblaster,
    6-string bass, guitar synthesizer on "Billy Austin," percussion program
    on "This Highway's Mine," harmonies on "Justice in Ontario" and
    "Hopeless Romantics," motorcyle

The Dukes:

Bucky Baxter: Mullins pedal steel guitar

Ken Moore: organ, synthesizer and string arrangements on "Esmeralda's Hollywood"

Zip Gibson: electric guitars, vocals

Kelly Looney: bass, vocals

Craig Wright: drums

Also

John Jarvis: piano

Lester Snell: organ on "When the People Find Out"

Patrick Earle: percussion

Stacey Earle: harmony on "Promise You Anything"

William C. Brown, Susan Jerome, and Patricia Snell: background vocals on "Close Your Eyes"

The Christ Missionary Baptist Church Choir, Memphis, Tennessee, directed by Lester Snell: background vocals on "When the People Find Out"

a bunch of white people directed by Skott Nelson: background chorus on "Regular Guy"

Songs
1. "The Other Kind" (5:09) (Steve Earle)
2. "Promise You Anything" (2:43) (Steve Earle–Maria McKeee–Patrick Suggs)
3. "Esmeralda's Hollywood" (5:58) (Steve Earle–Maria McKee)
4. "Hopeless Romantics" (2:43) (Steve Earle)
5. "This Highway's Mine (Roadmaster)" (3:53) (Steve Earle)
6. "Billy Austin" (6:13) (Steve Earle)
7. "Justice in Ontario" (4:14) (Steve Earle)
8. "Have Mercy" (4:40) (Steve Earle)
9. "When the People Find Out" (4:10) (Steve Earle)
10. "Country Girl" (4:10) (Steve Earle)
11. "Regular Guy" (3:15) (Steve Earle)
12. "West Nashville Boogie" (3:08) (Steve Earle)
13. "Close Your Eyes" (4:43) (Steve Earle)

V. "My daddy's worst fears realized"

From its first booming notes on the album opening "The Other Kind," an in-your-face declaration of independence by an unreconstructed outsider, *The Hard Way* promises to be punishing, brutal music. It fulfills its promise and then some, especially at the outset with "The Other Kind" and the ferocious, howling road song "Promise You Anything," both beautiful blasts of deep-into-the-red rock 'n' roll, no pretense to be anything but, except perhaps for the subtle mandolin stylings in "The Other Kind." Even when some calm sets in, by the third song, the ominous "Esmeralda's Hollywood" (cowritten with Maria McKee), the thumping of the drum that gives way to gunshot-like reports set against wiry, serpentine waves of acoustic guitar licks only thickens the foreboding atmosphere. In this tale of a prostitute who dies on the streets of Hollywood, to the concern of no one around ("it was just like any other day"), a string quartet emits a rising wail evolving into a roiling storm that evokes a death rattle at the fadeout. No sooner has the storm subsided than a drumroll and a thundering of guitars enter to announce "Hopeless Romantic," a rare, cynical look at romance, although the line "nowadays everyone knows that it's cool to be blue," seems more an indictment of modern mores by a man who is struggling to believe that his warrior heart will not be left wanting.

Another thunderous kick of the bass drum, and an exhale from Steve that sounds like someone punched him in the gut, announces "This Highway (Roadmaster)," wherein a former drug dealer turned, perhaps, avenging road angel sends a warning that the man and his machine— "I run on desperation / she runs on gasoline"—are on a vengeful mission to reclaim "my kingdom now."

Some cite Bruce Springsteen's stark, acoustic *Nebraska* album as the inspiration for *The Hard Way*. But if Springsteen figures into the concept, it's more *Nebraska*–meets–*Born in the U.S.A.* Steve's songs—roaring and intense—depict characters loose on the land, plunging headlong into futures they can't envision. They scramble to meet their fates, encased in "aluminum and steel"; collectively they are "my daddy's worst fears realized"; and their word is ephemeral. "I will promise you anything" is sung so triumphantly against a hurricane blast of rock 'n' roll grandeur that it implies nothing so much as heartbreak and disappointment ahead.

Against this backdrop of desperate characters, Steve gets specific and merciless on "Billy Austin" and "Justice in Ontario." "Billy Austin," which rolls out deliberately and stately on the strength of Steve's ragged vocal and his finger-picked acoustic guitar, tells the story of a 29-year-old half-breed Cherokee Indian from Oklahoma on death row. Just hours before his execution, he reflects on how he killed a gas station employee during a robbery and was hustled through trial, convicted, and sent to await his final day. A wash of synthesized strings enters about halfway through, and later, spooky, echoed rim shots, as Billy Austin prepares to take his final walk. At the end, Steve turns the narrative around to confront the listener, "Could you pull that switch yourself, sir," after we've heard the convict admit to his crime and his lack of remorse. "Could you still tell yourself / that you're better than I am," he asks at the end, before one final, booming rim shot leaves the question hanging in the air as the track goes dark.

Stacey Earle remembers the night Steve wrote "Billy Austin" as "very eerie." She was in the kitchen cooking a meal, and Steve "was down in the basement, surrounded by his needles and spoons, and the house he lives in is way out there in the middle of nowhere. It's dark, it was a very eerie night to hear 'Billy Austin' come up from the bottom of the basement steps."[13]

Of the key line, "Would you pull that switch yourself, sir," Joe Hardy told Steve he didn't like the word "sir" in there. "Yeah," Steve said, "it's Springsteen." And it stayed.[14]

Billy Austin is indisputably guilty but suggests that others sharing death row with him may not be. "Justice in Ontario," which at least borders on Philip Chevron's definition of the Pogues' music as being "Irish music being given a punk rock kick in the ass," thumps along on a soundscape rich in snarling guitars, pounding drums, and blasts of B3 chording. Its story was inspired by the real-life murder of a man in a bar fight, which was pinned on members of the Satan's Choice Motorcycle Club. The bikers convicted of the crime did not do it, but another SCMC member did, admitted as much on the stand, and yet went free. Given that backstory, it's a wonder "Justice in Ontario" isn't an angrier tune. Instead, Steve simply lays out the facts like a reporter and lets the horror of the injustice speak for itself minus any of the moralizing of "Billy Austin." He suggests, though, a history of lynch-mob mentality—a rush to injustice—in Ontario by opening the story with a verse about Jim Donnelly ("no angel sure"), who, a century earlier, was murdered, along with his entire family, by a mob avenging unspecified crimes. "Have Mercy," following "Justice in Ontario," reprises the gunshot drums, snarling and twanging guitars, and a desperate "Esmeralda's Hollywood" ambiance. But this story concerns a search for what the narrator—a white, dedicated family man—considers "mercy," which comes from the ministrations of a black prostitute. For her, though, mercy comes at the point of a pawnshop pistol "made of cold, blue steel" that she turns on herself. The seediness of the whole scenario, most especially the white man's seeming lack of conscience, is unsettling, to put it mildly.

"When the People Find Out" makes one of the most exhilarating transformations in all of Steve's recorded work. It starts out as a bouncy country ditty, a dobro leading the way against a thumping rhythm, as Steve drawls the first verse of a song about duplicitous behavior. But in the choruses it kicks into overdrive, spurring a gospel choir to shout in unison "Where you gonna run to / when the people find out that you lied," and the song is transformed into a gospel housewrecker, with the band kicking hard and the choir shouting its part and clapping in time.

The Christ Missionary Baptist Church Choir of Memphis was led by Lester Snell, whom Joe Hardy considers "the world's greatest keyboard player." Snell had stepped in as Stax's house keyboard player following Isaac Hayes's departure, and there had formed a friendship with Hardy.

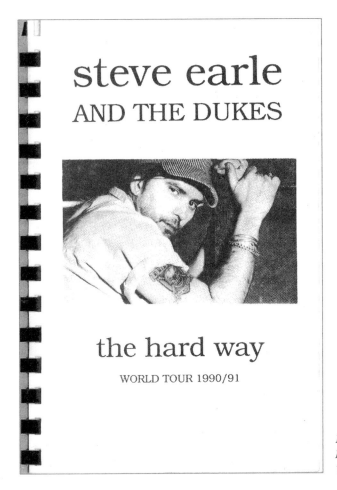

steve earle
AND THE DUKES

the hard way

WORLD TOUR 1990/91

Band members' tour book, The Hard Way World Tour 1990/1991.

Hardy: "I'd known Lester forever and used him on a lot of stuff because he just played with such incredible feel. And he's a musician—he can do string arrangements, he's just great. But Lester is a man of God, so on Sundays he plays at his church. So one day I just asked him, I'm a white boy, I don't know what goes on in black churches on Sunday, except it seems to last a long time and they dress up a lot. So I asked him, 'What's the deal? Do you have a choir?' 'Yeah, yeah, we have a choir.' And I talked to Steve about using some Memphis people on some stuff. I don't consider Steve a country artist in the slightest. I can hear it on maybe his first two records. But he wasn't country at all, and I thought, and still think, that unless you have a black person on your record it's not a real record. I don't know if that's a Memphis thing, or reverse racism, but it just sounds insane to me. It's not right; it's not in the natural order of things. So he was all for it. We had to contribute 200 bucks, or 300 bucks to the church; Lester brought 'em all over; they all brought robes, so it was all purple, satiny. The only problem was the guys couldn't sing. So we split 'em up and politely lied to them and said, 'We're gonna do the 50 women first and we'll do the guys second.' And that's what we did. Altogether maybe 60 or 70 people. They all started clapping at the end. I prompted Lester to have them clap on the last chorus. And Steve was totally into it; I think it was probably a unique experience for him."

With a decided Tex-Mex flavor in its swing and accordion-powered riffing, "Regular Guy," in all its bounce and ebullience, is a pointed barb at the Reagan administration (again), with Steve singing in a jolly, lighthearted voice, portraying a fellow who didn't vote in the last election because he finds politicians aren't worth "a trickle-down dime … one man's promise is another man's lie." Similarly, "Country Girl" uses a bopping rhythm track and a bit of an early-'70s Stones feel (and in the background, every so often, the sound of a thunderclap) to relate the story of a simple country girl who goes to the big city and charms everyone with her Southern drawl to the tune of all the pink champagne and cocaine she can handle—until, after a night of revelry, she encounters a bag lady talking to her cart, and the country girl sees her future clearly. It's a character study, open-ended, leaving the lass at a crossroads in life but offering no clue as to which path she chooses. "West Nashville Boogie" has the feel of a toss-off, but that's deceptive. It's fierce Southern boogie fuels a song about class warfare and resentment that has been growing since the narrator was a "white trash" kid being bussed to school on the rich side of town and being made fun of by the bigoted offspring of wealthy parents.

The album-closing ballad, "Close Your Eyes," retains the thunderous drums from earlier cuts, but the rich organ chords and the tender mandolin lines that set up a roaring chorus transform it into a Southern soul gospel workout featuring an angular run of pedal steel phrases in the instrumental break.

The last lines on this, the last studio recording Steve would make for nearly four years, reference a common bedtime prayer, a key sentiment of which—"If I should die before I wake"—"echoed all night through my head."

At the time it seemed like an appropriate ending to an album full of waking nightmares. Then he proceeded to make that phrase not a conditional tone, but a reality.

Odyssey:
Lost and Found

*We had no order among ourselves.
I wouldn't let myself control the
world of my music because I had no
power over anything else that went
on around me, in or around my body.*

— Coming Through Slaughter

The record of the *Hard Way* tour, literally and figuratively, is written in the tracks of the live album *Shut Up and Die Like an Aviator*, recorded over two dates, October 5 and 6, 1990, in London, England, and in Kitchener, Ontario, Canada.

Shut Up and Die Like an Aviator
MCA, 1991

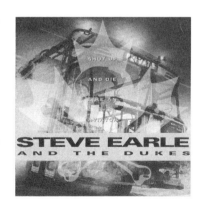

Produced by Steve Earle
Recorded by Ron St. Germain
Recorded live on October 5 and 6, 1990,
    in London, England, and Kitchener,
    Ontario, Canada
Live recording coordinator: John Alexander
Live digital recording: Comfort Sound
    Mobile Unit
Sound company: Sunn Sound
Mixed by Ron St. Germain and Steve Earle
Mixed digitally at Studio 55, Los Angeles, California
Mastered by Bob Ludwig at Masterdisc, New York, New York

Musicians
Steve Earle: lead vocals, electric and acoustic guitars, 6-string bass, mandolin
The Dukes:
Bucky Baxter: steel guitar, electric and acoustic guitars, 6-string bass
Zip Gibson: electric guitar, background vocals
Kelly Looney: bass, background vocals
Stacey Earle Mims: background vocals, acoustic guitar, percussion
Ken Moore: keyboards
Craig Wright: drums
Background vocals on "Fearless Heart": Custer

Songs
Intro
 1. "Good Ol' Boy (Gettin' Tough)" (Steve Earle–Richard Bennett)
 2. "Devil's Right Hand" (Steve Earle)
 3. "I Ain't Ever Satisfied" (Steve Earle)
 4. "Someday" (Steve Earle)
 5. "West Nashville Boogie" (Steve Earle)
 6. "Snake Oil" (Steve Earle)
 7. "Blue Yodel #9" (Jimmie Rodgers)
 8. "The Other Kind" (Steve Earle)
 9. "Billy Austin" (Steve Earle)
10. "Copperhead Road" (Steve Earle)
11. "Fearless Heart" (Steve Earle)
12. "Guitar Town" (Steve Earle)
13. "I Love You Too Much" (Steve Earle)
14. "She's About a Mover" (Doug Sahm)
15. "The Rain Came Down" (Steve Earle–Richard Woody)
16. "Dead Flowers" (Keith Richards–Mick Jagger)

It begins with an introduction that sounds like someone surfing TV channels, landing on one long enough to get a headline and then moving to another. There's a story about Mohawk Indians erecting a blockade of a bridge into Montreal to protest a land dispute with Canadian authorities; another blurb about a stay of execution for an inmate on Wyoming's death row; and another announcing that Saddam Hussein had declared Kuwait an Iraqi province. Then *click*, and an audience applauds and shouts before the band kicks into the first thundering notes of "Good Ol' Boy (Gettin' Tough)." The band sounds great— tight and driving, playing big and bold—especially guitarist Zip Gibson, whose soloing proves to be as inventive as it is electrifyingly charged—but Steve's voice is a ragged shadow of its former gruff self. At times he struggles to stay on key. He doesn't sound much better when he speaks. The set is an overview of his career up to that point, from "Guitar Town" to "The Other Kind" and "Billy Austin," with three covers: Steve, in his best performance on the album, offers a bluesy, attitudinous reading of Jimmie Rodgers's "Blue Yodel #9," and accompanies himself on acoustic guitar; a draggy version of Texan Doug Sahm's early Sir Douglas Quintet hit "She's About a Mover," Steve's voice so worn by this time that it sounds like he might not make it through the number; and a set-closing, altogether appropriate take on Jagger-Richards's "Dead Flowers." Here Steve again conjures an evocative atmosphere with his deliberate strumming of a 12-string guitar before the entire band weighs in come the first chorus. If Steve had been up to matching the power of his band, *Shut Up and Die Like an Aviator* would have been a great album. Instead, it's a sad document of an important artist's decline.

"After *Die Like an Aviator*, it was coming to an end," Tony Brown remembers of his reaction to hearing the album for the first time. "When I heard it I knew that I got out at the right time. That's the worst record I think I've ever heard. Steve couldn't sing; he was so hoarse, he could barely talk."[1]

Meanwhile, *The Hard Way* failed even to crack *Billboard*'s Top 100 Albums chart; a single, "Back to the Wall," peaked at No. 37.

I. Odyssey, 1991–1994

Jack Watson, Steve's buddy from Universal City, Texas, had been keeping up. He'd been floored when *Guitar Town* came out—"I saw it in the record bin and it was an actual record. Then I started seeing him on television. Now I'm coming unglued. I'd say, 'This is the guy I used to follow around. This is the same guy I walked around in the gorge with, that I listened and learned about guitar from, I'm real proud of him.'"

Watson wanted to reach out to Steve but thought better of it. He had, after all, been keeping up. Word got around. "I was afraid to call him up. He was such a charismatic person and I'd heard about all this heavy doping. I said, 'You watch, man. I'll just go right down the toilet with him if I find him.' I always looked up to him a lot, and I imagine if he was doing something, I'd sit down next to him and do it too."[2]

* * *

Between *Guitar Town* and a tour she did with Steve "around *Copperhead Road*" (*Hardcore Troubadour* claims it was after the release of *Exit 0*), Rosanne Cash saw the difference in Steve. He was "kind of spiraling down. I loved him. I had a real soft spot for him. But you can't help anybody like that. They gotta go through it. And I kind of knew that at the time. There's nothing you can say. This guy's gotta go through it, and you hope he survives."[3]

One night Pam Lewis got a call from Steve. He needed a ride somewhere; where to he wouldn't say exactly. "I think I probably had a notion we were doing something we probably weren't really supposed to be doing. But he was busy talking, being incredibly engaging, saying, 'Turn here, turn here, turn here. Stop.' And we were in this really shitty neighborhood, and I'm like, 'What are we doing here?' And the next thing I know people are walking up to his side of the car, and I'm going, 'Oh, my God!' Again, I was naïve. I'm in a red Honda hatchback. Pretty obvious car. I said to him, 'I can't believe you did that!' He said, 'Aw, it'll be a story you can tell your grandchildren.' And he just laughed his ass off and took his drugs."[4]

* * *

Steve Earle: "Around this time, I made another record [*The Hard Way*] in really bad shape. It's a pretty good record but kind of dark and scary. The next tour, though, was a nightmare. I played a lot of shows really sick and I was having to take drugs before I went on stage for the first time. I had never sunk to that before. I waited until after the show. I had a habit, but I started getting sick at 10 o'clock at night. We were playing mostly theaters and arenas by that time, so the shows were earlier. By 10 o'clock, my body wanted to know where the dope was."[5]

* * *

Native Nashvillian Mark Stuart, an exceptional guitarist who was trying to carve out a career in music for himself, was a Steve Earle fan from way back. He was introduced to Steve's music in the early '80s, when Steve and the Dukes were booked at an annual summer event called the Last Chance Dance, which featured a lineup of college rock bands. The bill Mark remembers witnessing was headlined by the White Animals; the other two acts preceding them were Jason and the Nashville Scorchers, and Steve Earle and the Dukes.

"It was really weird because it's the first show I ever attended where I saw slam dancing. The first act to come on was this three-piece rockabilly band, and it was this skinny, clean-cut-looking guy and they all had on matching Western suits with bolo ties. It was Steve Earle and the Dukes, and he was doing this rockabilly stuff. The Stray Cats were really happening at the time, but aside from that, doing rockabilly was really antiquated. And the audience that was there hated it—they absolutely hated it. It was just so square, what he was doing. But I really dug it. I thought something really unique was happening. He was a guitar player and it was three-piece, but he didn't really do solos. His songs were more about the songs, and not a lot of flashy guitar playing. I thought, This guy's really good; I'm gonna keep my eye out for him, I really like his songs.

And the next act to come on was Jason and the Nashville Scorchers, as they were called then, and they were outrageous—it was like a punk–meets-hillbilly thing and the audience went crazy."[6]

About a year later, he saw an ad in the paper for a local club, with Steve Earle listed as an upcoming headliner. Remembering Steve from the Last Chance Dance, Mark went to see what had become of the rockabilly kid so despised by the college crowd. The change was startling.

"The difference was it was a four-piece band. I'm not sure who the lineup was, but probably Mike McAdam had been added as a lead guitarist, and Steve was now on an acoustic guitar most of the time. When they came out on the stage in a small club called Bogie's, the Western bolo ties and all that were gone and he was in like a T-shirt and jeans, and he had bandanas tied around his wrists. It was more earthy, more blue-collar-looking. Once again it was all about the songs but more so because Steve was now on acoustic guitar and he seemed to be more at home on it, and the sound was more well rounded with the four-piece.

"I'm really absorbed by music and I've always really studied lots of artists and learned from them. I've always been drawn to singers and songwriters and guitar players, and that's what I decided I wanted to be. Some of those guys are better players than they are singers or writers. Some are better singers, maybe, some of them are better writers. So all my heroes are people from John Fogerty to Buddy Holly to Carl Perkins to Paul Simon to Woody Guthrie to Bob Dylan to Tony Joe White to John Prine, Chuck Berry. Steve was for me one of the last guys I came about in my career that I sort of adopted as one of my heroes, really—this is before I knew him. I really got into his songwriting and thought, Man, this guy is one of the greatest songwriters I've ever heard. I really followed his career there for several years in the late '80s. He was one of my favorite artists, and I was covering his songs at these bar gigs I did. And I was telling people, Man, you gotta check out this guy's writing. He was just to me a great songwriter and an artist I was really proud of because I'm from Nashville and Steve had came out of the Nashville machinery. I was proud of the fact that Steve made this bold move in his career where he was projected as a rocker. It was the first time somebody out of Nashville had really been that recognized as a rocker. The only other artist that I kinda felt a little bit like that about was Jason and the Scorchers, because they got the big record deal out of Nashville as a rock act, but they didn't quite get over the hump nationally like Steve did."

Mark Stuart had seen Stacey Earle open a concert for Steve in 1990, and was impressed by her songs and charming stage demeanor. In February 1992, he saw that she was hosting an open-mike night at Jack's Guitar Bar, "a little dive, really, in south Nashville." He went specifically to see Stacey perform. He introduced himself to her there, and that night they had their first date together:

he took her to eat at the Waffle House. Afterward, at her place, they started singing songs together; before the year was out they were living together. Then Steve Earle, whose songs he had admired and touted to anyone who would listen, came to live with Mark and Stacey. Mark began an odyssey he was unprepared for but undertook, never flinching in the darkest hours, never abandoning the man who would become his brother-in-law, ultimately finding enough common ground with Steve to be part of the solution rather than part of the problem. The ultimate solution always lay with Steve, but Mark Stuart, who did not ask for this assignment, and had no personal or professional history from which to draw wisdom, performed like a champion.

Mark Stuart: The Years of Madness

"Steve was really a disturbing soul"

What was going on with Steve at the time you and Stacey got together?

At that time Stacey and Steve were sort of estranged. In fact, I think she had gone a really long time and not seen him or talked to him, maybe even as much as about a year. And her kids were living with their dad. So she was in Nashville pursuing her music career, and she did not have her kids with her, which would turn out to be the only time ever, for probably about a year. And we got involved, started dating, and wound up moving in together, really, shortly afterwards. Steve was just absolutely absent.

A few months later he showed up at our place. That's when he entered my life, at some point in '92; I can't tell you exactly when, but it was several months after me and Stacey met in February. Steve was really a disturbing soul, because he was at the rock bottom of his drug addiction problem, and he was skin and bones. He looked awful. He had no music career at that point; he had just dropped off the planet. I had no background at all with drug addicts. I didn't know how to deal with it, and I dealt with it I guess the way most people do— I tried to help him. And you really can't help them; they have to help themselves. But I did things, like I gave him rides, I loaned him money, we let him stay with us. In fact, it was probably a year and a half there where he basically lived with us, slept on our couch, was there just about every day. I got to know him quite well during that period because I was around him so much of the time. We talked a lot about music. Stacey even told me right off, the first couple of days that me and Steve were meeting, she said, "It's amazing, he talks to you like an equal," and apparently that was not the norm. Apparently, he figured he knew more than the other guy, but he really talked to me like an equal when it came to music. We were both huge Beatles nuts; we talked about Beatles stuff a lot, and we played guitars sometimes around our house when he actually would be capable of sitting up and being calm enough to put a guitar in his hands. He played me a couple of songs that he had written not too long before that. I guess it was like the genesis of whatever his next record would be. And those songs were "Hurtin' Me, Hurtin' You" and … I can't remember the other one, but both of those songs wound up being on the album *I Feel Alright*. And immediately when Steve got to know me, he saw that I was a really strong guitar player and then he found out I also played piano and a little bit of mandolin, and he started targeting me to be in his next band. And I had my own band at the time, and I played with Stacey all the time around Nashville. My plans were for my own career as an artist to take off. It wasn't really happening, but I was hoping it would. But I kind of had in the back of my mind, well, if things aren't panning out and Steve gets his act together, I'll probably go out and do that because it'll pay really good money and I'll probably get some experiences through Steve that I hadn't had yet. It turned out that way [*laughs*]. I wound up going out on the road with him, but that was a few years later, in '96, '97.

But he started targeting me to be in the band, and we interacted quite a bit musically during that period, because really nobody else was. He wasn't around anybody in the music industry. I sometimes laugh when I read interviews with people who talk as though they were around him during that period, and some of them are established artists, and I know that they weren't. He literally spent 24 hours a day in our house or on the streets pursuing his drugs. It was actually quite a nightmare for us.

How was Stacey reacting to Steve's presence in the house?

It was kind of strange. They had been away from each other for a long time, and he was kind of uncomfortable being around Stacey, because he didn't know whether he was welcome. So I wound up kind of entertaining him a lot of the time. And also, his problem was so apparent and so overwhelming that Stacey couldn't really deal with it a lot of the time. She would purposely be in the kitchen and me and Steve would be in another room, and I would try to accommodate him and keep her away from all of that. He was bringing in the drug paraphernalia and the drugs, and he was bringing pistols and stuff like that into our house, and he wouldn't take a bath. It was the life of a drug addict.

Was he doing the drugs openly in the house?

Yeah, he would do it right in front of us, and it would cause Stacey to have seizures. I remember one time, I didn't have a lot of money. I made my living as a musician playing local gigs. I had a bar band and I did a solo thing like at sports bars, and I did private parties and stood up there all night long singing Creedence and Beatles songs, and getting paid for it, and that's how I paid my bills and got by. When I didn't have gigs like that, I would play around Nashville in the showcase rooms doing my original music for, like, six people. So I didn't really have a lot of money, and when I would loan Steve a few hundred dollars for drugs, it was a huge chunk of money for me and I would have to harass him to get it back.

I remember one time we went out to his house and he hadn't been to his house in a really long time. He was living on the street or at our house. I made him take me out there and give me collateral.

What was the collateral?

Well, there was a little metal stand you put a mandolin in. Some guy had hand-made it. It was a clever little gizmo. And he gave that to me and said, "You can hang on to that." And I still have it to this day. He paid me the money back, but I wound up with the stand.

What was the band you were playing in?

I kinda changed the names of my bands a lot. It was typically the Mark Stuart Band, but I had a band for awhile called the Long Gone Daddy, which I kinda lifted from the Hank Williams song, "I'm a Long Gone Daddy." I had Mark Stuart and 356 for awhile, and I got that from Shoeless Joe Jackson's batting average, which was .356. I'm a big baseball nut. So I was doing that all the time and I was at the top of my game as a musician all the time because I was constantly playing four-hour gigs.

Toward the end of his downward spiral, he was in a treatment center in Chattanooga, Tennessee, on a methadone program. Were you around him much during that time?

Constantly. I was constantly around him then.

What was he going through, and how were you trying to handle it?

The first thing he did was he got on a methadone program, which really wasn't the answer. It was sort of like a temporary quick-fix answer to his problem, but it wasn't the answer. He was having to go to Chattanooga, where he could go into the state of Georgia and get a higher dosage of this methadone. It was a legal operation; there were different laws from state to state, apparently, so in Georgia you could get a heavier dose of this methadone. A side effect of that is this huge fluid buildup, you gain a lot of weight. That's why Steve got to be so fat. He went from skin and bones to Humpty Dumpty overnight. And I used to drive him down there, because they would only dispense the methadone once a week, I believe it was, and he would want to be there when the doors opened on that day he was able to go get it. Somebody would have to drive him down there; many times I would do it. Actually he got popped two or three times by the authorities for sitting in a parking lot doing drugs. He wound up getting thrown in jail, like forced to go to jail and rough it out and detox in the worst atmosphere I can imagine. That's when he really cleaned up and wanted to live and didn't want to die. And he would have died. It's amazing he didn't.

And all through that period I went to visit him, went to see him in jail and talk to him through the little window and all that. I made him a crossword puzzle about music.

How did he feel about where he was and what had happened to him? Did he express regrets? Was he defiant? How was he handling it?

I think he wanted to live and I think he decided it was time to make a change. I think most people who have reached the pits of hell that he reached don't make that decision; it's almost impossible to make it. And somehow he dug down inside and made the call. One of the disappointments was that he had been a really horrible person to have to endure, but after he got clean he still, to me, continued to be kind of a jerk. I hate to say it, but to this day we have a very weird relationship.

When he got out, did he come back to stay with you and Stacey?

No, he didn't. In fact, at the point that he went in—I should clear up—he had already reunited with his ex-wife Lou Gill. She was also using drugs, so both of them were using drugs, and that probably was the attraction in him going back to her. So he had reunited with her, and in fact remarried her. I always call her the Grover Cleveland of his wives. She was number four and six. But they were living together and married again, and they had a very, very horrific household going there, because they had kids and they were using drugs and all that. What happened was that after he cleaned up he was still married to Lou, but she continued to use drugs and he had turned his life around, so it was only a matter of time before that marriage fizzled.

You and Stacey must have been worried that when he went back to Lou-Anne Gill he would also go back to the drugs.

To this day I am absolutely amazed that Steve has cleaned up and not ever used drugs again. Because if you could have seen the two or three years there that I did, where he was at his lowest, I would have never believed, a, he would have survived and not died; and b, I would never have believed that he would have cleaned up to begin with; and c, I certainly would not have believed he would have cleaned up even for a period of time and not gone back and just returned to it, because I think most people do. And you know, we have our fingers crossed in that regard, because even though it's like eleven years down the road or whatever it is, he really is always an addict. And it'll always be something he'll have to battle to not go back to it.

When you were visiting him in jail, did music ever come up?

He had a fear in fact that if he wasn't doing drugs he couldn't write. That there was a block or something. I think he discovered that wasn't really true.

I remember him talking about that a lot, talking about he was kind of scared to death about whether he could get the juice back and be able to write something. When I talked to Steve during that period, nine times out of 10 our conversations were about music, because that was the one thing we had in common, and I'm sure it's the only thing I have in common with the guy.

What an ordeal to live through.

Oh, it's remarkable. You know, he one time went out to—this was probably in '93—he went out to record a song with Joe Walsh, "Honey Don't," a Carl Perkins song, for the *Beverly Hillbillies* movie. The talk was, Joe Walsh and Steve Earle together, that's probably not a good combination. Sure enough, he disappeared out in L.A. after doing the session. He just disappeared; no one had heard from him for several days. We were thinking the worst, because he was supposed to fly back to Nashville.

It turned out, because I had been going down in Nashville and grabbing him by the collar and pulling him out of these crack houses down in these ugly parts of town that I had never known about before, that I was the only person that could go and pull him out of these places sometimes. My appearance was such that I could walk around that part of town and carry myself like I belonged and it looked like I did. But actually I had never been in that culture before, and it was pretty scary. But I would go get him out of there.

So the idea was for me to fly out to L.A. and find Steve. And I was actually up for it, but it was terrifying because at that point I had never been to L.A. And that was like just crazy to me. But I was the guy elected by the family, "Mark's gonna have to go out there and find Steve, he's probably holed up in a crack house somewhere." And it turned out he finally called and turned himself in. He had totaled a rental car and fled from the scene. He had gone out to the Joshua Tree National Park and probably was real close to not being with us. He probably was contemplating suicide. I know he had mentioned it to me a time or two in Nashville. So he was really at rock bottom. At that point is when Stacey said her parents, probably for the first time, realized just how bad his problem was and that something was gonna have to be done. And talk of an intervention was starting to go around.

Stacey Earle: Deeper and Deeper into Hell

"I would sometimes put a mirror over his mouth to see if he was breathing."

So this intervention. It was '92, '93. We were living on Benton Avenue in Nashville, and [someone I knew with a medical background and access to prescriptions] had given me some shots to give him in case he OD'd. It's an adrenaline-like substance. And they showed me how to give the shots—and this was at the point where I would sometimes put a mirror over his mouth to see if he was breathing. 'Cause he would be down for so long.[7]

I have to put you into the environment. I mean, we had a SWAT team at our house the night he stole guns. We had our neighbors wanting us to move because they were tired of finding needles in the bushes. They were afraid their children would get hold of them.

What happened, Steve had stolen a gun from [Lou-Anne Gill's] mom. And that very day, it's really weird—he was smoking crack continuously and then he would shoot eight ball. And then he was using Dilaudid. He would go down and then come up. He sat at this little square table that I got from Jack's Guitar Bar. Mark and I had a single-bed mattress and a couch and this little square table—that's all we owned. And he sat at this table with the drug paraphernalia, just going after it all day and all night. There was one night I woke up, the fire department had to come because he left the gas stove on all night. I just happened to wake up and smell the gas in the house and evacuate it.

But anyway, he had stolen the gun, and I didn't know about it. My seizures were getting really out of control and I finally figured out, it's the crack smoke. I was having too many in a day. I told Mark, "I just need some time away. Let's go to a hotel, and we'll tell Steve we're going to a movie." I looked at Mark and said, "Just make it stop, just for a while, please." So we got in the car and drove to a hotel off Metro Center. And we checked into the motel and I told Mark, "I'm worried about him. Why don't you call him and see if he's doing okay and tell him we're about to go into a movie?"

So Mark called him and Steve says, "Don't come home. The police are coming, and I don't want you to come home. I've got a gun." We're sitting there going, "Oh, shit." I said, "Steve, what's going on?" He said, "I stole Lou's mom's gun and she's sending the SWAT team." I called my mom and dad, and said, "Okay, here's the situation. I don't know what to do." My dad's recovering from a heart attack. My mom said, "Call Steve's attorney. Call him now and find out if there's a way we can get a 24-hour commitment." There's 24 or 48 hours where you can have someone committed and everyone can think what to do.

So I called his attorney. He called, and sure enough, the police were coming. He arranged it for Mark and I to meet the police and the SWAT team two blocks from the house. I wanted to let them know Steve would not harm a fly. He has held many guns in his hands and never shot a soul. So we met the police on the way and sat there and told them, "Just ask him to come out and he'll come out."

So they put us in the back of a police car and we drive around to the front of the house. Well, guess what? I'd never been in the back of a police car before. You can't open the doors. So Mark and I are locked in. Next thing I know, we see them on their knees surrounding our house, and on the front porch banging on the door, demanding him to come out. They can't hear him, but he can't come out because it's a double deadbolt. We always left out the back door. He can't unlock the door. And we're banging on this window in the car, but they can't hear us, saying, "He can't open the door! He can't open the door!" But finally they figured that out and they go around back and enter—the door was just open in the back. So we're sitting in the police car, and 45 minutes later we see Steve walking down the street. It's like 12 degrees outside. They come and get us and take us in the house, and I say, "What did you do? You agreed to take him into Vanderbilt Hospital for 48 hours." They go, "Well, he didn't do anything wrong. Is this your home?"

I said, "Yes, it is."

He said, "Well, you have 20 minutes to clean up all this drug paraphernalia or we'll put you under arrest."

I said, "What??!! I told you we need him for 48 hours. My parents are getting on the plane, they're coming."

He said, "Whose gun is this?"

I said, "That's Lou Gill's mom's gun. That's the gun you're after."

Then he said, "Whose gun is *this*?"

Another gun, I didn't even know it was there. I said, "I don't know."

He goes, "Well, do you want it?"

I said, "No! I don't want it!"

See how crazy all this was? And then it tore my heart up to see him walking down the street. I said, "You just sent him out in the cold. He thinks I don't want him. What did you tell him?"

"We just told him you wanted him out of the house."

"No! I did not say that!" So that had to hurt his feelings.

That's the picture that was going on.

Things cooled down, he was back in our house, and it was Christmas. Mark had been pulling him out of crack houses. And his only vehicle was ours— we had so many warrants against our vehicle. I made a wrong turn down Second Avenue and the cops would come chase the vehicle saying, "Hey, Steve!" But it was me, I would be running from crack dealers trying to sell me drugs. They knew my car well. I told Steve, I said, "Steve, look, why don't we go out to your house and let's have a Christmas, a real Christmas. And think about getting clean. [I found a drug rehab professional who's agreed to come with us.]"

I couldn't believe I got my nerve up to talk to him about it. And the cool thing is, he said, "Okay."

I said, "Wow. Great. That was easy."

So I cleaned the house up, because other drug addicts had been living out there and it was really a mess. It's a beautiful home and it was just disgusting. Mark and I put a Christmas tree up, bought groceries, got [the rehab specialist] lined up. It was gonna be Mark, I, and a friend who doesn't use drugs. We were all gonna go out there. I think the biggest mistake was, I booked an airline ticket to fly [to Texas] on Christmas Eve, to spend five hours with my children, and then be on the noon flight home Christmas Day. Be back just long enough to spend a little time with the kids. I had sold a Chet Atkins guitar that was given to me on the Hard Way tour to buy my airline ticket and to buy the kids some Christmas presents. I got $700 for it.

So I had my airline ticket, had the house cleaned up, and I went and picked Steve up at the crack house. I said, "Steve, we're gonna do this?"

And he said, "Yeah, we're gonna do this."

I said, "Is there anything you want? Want some chocolates?" He was really into sweets—opium addicts, their thing is sweets.

So we went by Kroger [*a supermarket*] and I ran in to get some things. When I came out, he was sitting in the driver's seat. I went, "Steve, what are you doing?"

He said, "If I'm gonna go out there, let me go back for one more rock."

See, I had never been out with Mark to purchase the rock. I said, "Okay." I get in the car and we start driving deeper and deeper and deeper into hell. We pull up, first thing I remember is young children, almost my boys' age, with their fists in the windows. And one handing it to him and Steve sticking it in his mouth and throwing it back at him and saying, "That's soap!"

My heart just dropped. I thought, My God, they're gonna shoot us. Because they were young, and those are the ones that kill. Because they're young and they're dumb.

About that time an older one comes out. Even in desperate times, Steve did have some morals to him—he didn't like purchasing from the kids. A little older one came out, and just as he was sticking the rock in the door, Steve threw the money out, a police car pulled right up on our rear. And my heart's thumping again. How are we gonna get out of this? But you know what? They just followed us out. Didn't stop us. And I knew they had my license plate number.

So we get the rock and we head up to the house. He smokes it on the way out there. I'm going, "Please, we don't need me having a seizure in the car." That's insane, to put yourself or your family in that position.

I guess it was getting close to 10 or 11 o'clock, and he's starting to get sick. And he's yelling at me from the bedroom, starting to get into panic mode: "Stacey, you don't know what you're doing to me!" He's crying, "I'm really sick. You don't know what you're doing!"

I said, "No, we're gonna make it. We're gonna make it."

But it's getting worse as time goes on. Before my flight, all hell was breaking loose. He tried to get in the car and go. I ran out, out of desperation, slit the tires on the car and said, "No way! No way!"

We get him back in the house and I said, "No one's going anywhere!"

So he goes back in the house and he seems to settle down a bit, goes to sleep. Mark takes me to the flight. I fly home. And Mark calls me, I'm not in Houston more than four hours, and says, "He's gone."

I screamed, "He's gone!"

"He's walking to Nashville."

There's a snowstorm and Mark can't leave for a day and a half. I fly back in and it's just all over with. And Steve is really angry with me. But yeah, maybe I didn't know what I was doing, but I was trying to do something. Even Teresa came. I called her. It was so wrong, but it was true. I told her, "He still loves you. And I need all the support I can get." And she came. Mark and I picked her up, and I could feel how uncomfortable she was; Steve was trying to get close to her. We lost her by seven o'clock that night. Then when I heard the song "We Never Said Goodbye," I meant to tell him she said good-bye. Mark and I ran down to the store and came back and Teresa was at her car loading it, and she said, "I can't do this. Tell him I said good-bye. I can't do it. I won't be back." So for four and a half hours it was Teresa, I, Mark, [three friends], and Steve. It just didn't work.

* * *

Pam Lewis made an effort to reach Steve, to get him to clean up. Her conduit was Townes Van Zandt, whom she was now representing as a publicist. Steve Earle horror stories were all over Nashville in the early '90s—as were his guitars and Harleys, all of which he had sold off or pawned to support his drug habit—and Pam thought Townes might be the person who could bring Steve back to the world.

Over the phone she pleaded with Townes. "Come on. You've been hooked on heroin. Can't you go talk to him? He loves you; he respects you. More than anybody I can think of."

"Well, let me think about this," Townes said. "He's pretty smart. He'll figure this out."

What they figured out was a ruse in which Townes would go out to Steve's house ostensibly to record in the home studio Steve had set up. A friend of Pam's had told her about the studio, but had added: "[Steve's] so screwed up he can't even use the studio." This same friend had once found Steve on the street, a needle sticking out of one of his arms.

Townes drove out to the house. Answering the door, Steve stood and stared at Townes for a few seconds, shaking his head. "I must be really bad if they're sending you," he said.

When he returned to his own house, where Pam was waiting with Townes's wife, Townes announced, "Mission accomplished. I don't know if I did any good."

"What happened?" Pam asked.

"Well, we sat around and shot the shit and we got drunk together."

"Well ..." Pam said.[8]

* * *

In Houston, Barbara and Jack Earle were beside themselves with worry. They had seen Steve when he was working on *Copperhead Road* and finally realized the severity of his drug problem. Now that he had gone off the deep end, worry consumed their days.

Barbara Earle: "I called Stacey almost every day during that period, and I'd say, 'Have you seen Steve?' I was living in Houston and I was working, and she'd say, 'Well, I haven't seen him today.' And I'd say, 'Would you please go find him and let me know how he is?' And she'd track him down, and I never gave her any peace about it. It wasn't fair, but she was the one there in town and I had to know that he was still alive. So she was the one I tormented with it, and Steve doesn't even realize that."[9]

* * *

Teresa Ensenat filed for divorce from Steve on April 28, 1992. The divorce became final on November 17, 1992. On September 13, 1993, Steve married, for the second time, Lou-Anne Gill. It was marriage number six for Steve.

* * *

Steve's police blotter gained new entries. September 29, 1992, arrested for failing to appear for jury duty in July; May 1993, charged with a misdemeanor for driving without a license and for having a "heroin-looking substance in the ashtray" and a needle in the glove compartment.[10] In September 1994, the same year he had attempted to clean up by enrolling in a methadone program in Chattanooga, Tennessee, he was sentenced *in absentia* by Judge Tom Shrive in Nashville Criminal Court to the maximum of 11 months and 29 days and fined $2,500 for failing to appear at a September 2 hearing on the May 1993 heroin charge. He turned himself in, was remanded to the Criminal Justice Center, where he suffered such severe withdrawal symptoms that he was transferred after eight days to a hospital in Fayetteville, Tennessee, to undergo a clinical detoxification program.

Steve Earle: "After I finished my 28 days of treatment, I had to go back to jail. You know, there's dope in jail, so I was faced with it in my unit three days after I returned. I just pretended that there wasn't any dope in jail, 'cause there's not supposed to be. I went to meetings—whatever meetings were available to me. Then I got out. They released me at midnight with the smelly clothes I went to jail in, four and a half months later. My clothes had been marinating in there, and I reached in my jeans and there was 40 dollars in my pocket, and I was in downtown Nashville. All I had to do was walk four blocks. Instead I made a phone call and didn't even leave the lobby of the Criminal Justice Center. And now I go to meetings every day when I'm in Nashville, and to meetings on the road."[11]

. . .

Drug addicts do not recover unless they want to recover. Steve's years of madness ended with him choosing life. Day by day during his incarceration and treatment, with the help of his family's expressed love and support, he climbed back into the world and embraced the 12-step program that would become the backbone of his drug-free existence and of his artistic resurgence.

Even when he would have been physically incapable of writing and recording music, there were wheeler-dealers who sensed a profit in him. Joe Hardy, coproducer of *The Hard Way*, remembers being approached by "an A&R guy of some sort" to do an album with Steve while Steve was still in jail. Hardy declined the offer. "I just didn't want to do it. Maybe Steve could have used the money, maybe I wasn't fair in not asking him about it. It just seemed exploitive to me in an odd way."[12]

The "A&R guy of some sort" whose name Hardy could not recall may have been Steve's old buddy, the sound engineer William Alsobrook, who, according to *Hardcore Troubadour*, had made several visits to Steve in Chattanooga with an idea to record an album with him "on the road somewhere, wherever he's hiding out."[13] (Steve would later remember Alsobrook as "my best friend for years and in my darkest hour he was my only friend."[14]) Alsobrook's former employer, Owsley Manier, had partnered up with a former label executive named Steve Roberts to form the independent Winter Harvest label. In the summer of 1994, Manier and Roberts had approached Alsobrook about doing a record with Steve. A deal was struck, not for some "fugitive" album. Rather, this would be a legit studio recording, a bare-bones acoustic project of songs drawn from Steve's repertoire that had never seen the light of day except in live settings now and then. A contract was signed on November 11, and on November 16 Steve was released from jail. On January 4, 1995, he was at Magic Tracks Recording Studio in Nashville, inspired to do a rootsy, acoustic album modeled after Emmylou Harris's heralded *Roses in the Snow*, and preparing to reclaim all that he had thrown away over the past three years.

. . .

Steve Earle: "When I was locked up, I was getting ready to go off on this boy that stole my radio. My partner Paul [Carver] asked me where I was going. I said, 'To get my radio—and then go to the hole for a little while.' He looked at me like I look at my 13-year-old sometimes and said, 'No, you ain't. You're gonna sit your little white ass down and do your little time and then you're gonna get out of here and make a nice record.'"[15]

Resurrection

*"His shoulders were like
huge rounded humps of
self-defense."*

With a mane of wavy brown hair swept back on his head and hanging below his collar, wire rim glasses, and a thick goatee, Norman Blake looks like either a distinguished professor of English literature or a character who just stepped out of a nineteenth-century daguerreotype. Along with his beloved wife Nancy and too many stringed instruments to count ("but it's more than one," he says in his deadpan fashion) he resides in the northwesternmost corner of Georgia, directly below the Tennessee state line and right beside Alabama, where the three states abut.

"It's sort of mountainous here," he says in his dry Georgia accent, "the end of the southern mountain chain. They go about 50, 60 miles further south."[1]

The town is Rising Fawn, Georgia, and the Blake place is about three miles from where Norman was raised. "I've been here all of my life, basically, with the exception of seven years that I lived in Nashville and two years that I spent in the army. But Nancy and I have lived on this place for 28, 29 years. We built the house, we're responsible for it, yes. It's a three-story large frame house, old Southern style, with porches all around. Sort of just a big farmhouse, really."

Norman, who enunciates precisely, chooses his words carefully, and is often given to understatement, is one of the world's greatest stringed instrument players. He plays country music for a living "because it's what I've done all my life and it's what I do best. And it's certainly what I love the most and it has the highest element of truth I think of most any music. I think most genuine country music has a high truth element in it; it covers most any situation that people get into. It's real-life stuff."

One of Norman Blake's best friends is another string master of great repute, Peter Rowan, who, like Norman, has made a stand for traditional roots music, especially bluegrass. Rowan is a former Bill Monroe Bluegrass Boy, and no more solid credential could be had for a roots music advocate.

In the fall of '94, Rowan took a trip to visit Blake in Rising Fawn, and the two men shared a memorable evening together over music on old 78 rpm records that Norman was playing for Peter in an upstairs room.

"Norman played me 78 after 78," Peter recalls of that night, "saying 'Pete, you'll like this one here,' and he'd play me that one. A lot of those tunes ended up on a record that I did with Jerry Douglas called *Yonder*. So what was happening with Norman is that we were listening to this old stuff, like 'Lullaby of the Leaves,' just fantastic old 78s that Norman has been collecting. And thinking, Wouldn't it be great if we could make music that was just original acoustic music, something we could be part of? Too bad this isn't what's going on these days, because this is what we play."[2]

A couple of months later, Peter got a call from a man who identified himself as Bill Alsobrook from Nashville. "How would you like to do a record with Steve Earle?" Alsobrook asked. Another string virtuoso, Sam Bush, had been booked to play with Steve, but a wrist injury had forced him to bow out.

Rowan was amenable to the idea, even though he knew Steve was or had been in jail, and that "all of Steve Earle's great guitars were in pawnshops all over town, to be had for a song.

"I think Bill Alsobrook had convinced him to go ahead and make a record of acoustic music of him at his most raw. Because rock 'n' roll had just about killed him."

Rowan, who had begun his career in Nashville in the '60s, then had moved away, returned to town in 1984. Around that time, he met Steve Earle for the first time through the auspices of attorney-turned-manager Ken Levitan.

"I met this kid in black slacks and a white sport coat, and it was Steve Earle. But in Nashville everyone's on their own trajectory. I was writing songs with Pam Tillis when suddenly she got a phone call, or made a phone call as we were going from lunch to the songwriting room. She said, 'I gotta go.' Next thing I know she's a country music star and I didn't see her for another year.

"With Steve it was much more like a karmic thing. I'd see him around town. Of course, Steve is definitely wrapped up in his own circle of rock 'n' roll destiny. I bought the first record; I thought it was really cool. But I didn't understand him as a person. But every contact I had with him had something to do with something deep. The next time I saw him was at a gas station on West End. And he told me, 'Did you now that Flaco Jiminez's father had died?'"

"I said, 'No!'

"He said, 'Yeah, I went down to San Antonio to the funeral and I bought flowers and I put your name on 'em.'

"I said, 'My God, man.' That's evidence of a deeper connection. Our paths are always crossing in a meaningful way.

"Then he went to the dark side. Became obsessed with the whole process— the thing is, Steve is such a strong guy. He was almost throwing himself against a brick wall just to see how strong he was. I mean, the wall was never going to break."

So in January 1995, "in the middle of a freezing winter," Peter Rowan found himself at Magic Tracks Recording Studio with Steve Earle. On one side of him was Norman Blake, who had also been recruited for the session, on the other was the most highly regarded standup bass player around, Roy Huskey, Jr. Peter had known Roy for years from session work and from playing around Nashville, notably and most memorably at Peter's regular bluegrass night at the Station Inn with a group called Crucial Country, whose lineup shifted according to which hot picker was in town on gig nights but boiled down to "basically bluegrass players ripping it up with everything from Bob Marley tunes to Bill Monroe tunes and my tunes."

Peter looked at Norman and smiled. "How did this happen?" he asked. "We're making that record I was talking about."

When Peter first laid eyes on Steve that night, though, he was shocked. It was a Steve Earle he had never seen before. "Physically, he was almost like deformed. His body had bulked up hugely; his shoulders were like huge rounded humps of self-defense. He was having dental problems. He was missing teeth. He'd been beat up; he'd been in jail; he'd been on heroin.

"But personality-wise he was hot as a pistol."

For his part, Norman was seeing the only Steve Earle he had ever known— it was their first meeting. In a typical Norman Blake construct, he says simply, "I don't believe I had ever met Steve before this. We were just called in to do the record."

Steve may have been away from the studio for a while, but he hadn't forgotten the lessons he'd learned along the way. When it came time to record, he did exactly what he had done in Memphis for *The Hard Way*—set it up and go. Preproduction amounted to Rowan, Blake, and Huskey listening to Steve run through a tune, playing it afterwards, and then recording it.

"He sang 'em through, we played 'em through, we recorded 'em" is Rowan's memory of the five days at Magic Tracks.

Blake was looking for one thing: getting the right sound on the instruments. Then it would all fall together; it was only matter of "really listening and getting a real intimate thing going to where everybody can hear each other; just really listening to what's going down and getting it to where you've got a real good recording to start with before you get to the point of we can fix it in the mix or EQ it. You know, really getting the instruments miked right and that kind of thing. And not being afraid to have a little leakage and things like that on a record like this. Not being so sterilized."

"We met in front of microphones," Rowan says. "We were all around different microphones, and Steve was in the room. We were all in the room playing with each other. But that's what I'd been talking about with Norman, that immediacy. Which of course has translated well through the years, even through *O Brother, Where Art Thou?* That sense of rawness. The acoustic music tradition has a sense of the moment and the rough edges are still there, which is one of the great things about it. I mean they don't sound like rough edges but they're all there; they're not all squeezed out. There's no attempt to overly smooth out things on *Train a Comin'*. Which is great, because it has bite. But Steve's passion—he was so wanting to live and yet he could sing funny songs about 'my hometown,' great lyrics, 'Ben McCullough,' then the great Townes Van Zandt song, 'Tecumseh Valley,' oh, my God!"

The pattern was to record and play back the performance for everyone to critique on the spot. Every warm-up, every performance was taped, "just as a reference point," according to Rowan. Typically Norman would point everyone in the right direction after a playback: if they had come close to nailing the song, he'd announce, "Well, it's not quite believable yet." If he judged the performance to be unacceptable, the pronouncement from on high was "That's a little unbelievable."

What Blake was waiting to hear was "everybody just kinda looking for something, freedom in their own structure, so to speak. In other words, you know basically what you're supposed to do, but you're looking for your own artistic freedom inside that framework—people like Peter and I, who have certainly played our own music, you're looking to express yourself in a way that is you, but you're still doing it to contribute to something like what Steve's doing. But you're expressing yourself in your own way too."

By all accounts, Steve began to feel his oats as the sessions went on, taking charge and dispensing with the tentativeness both Blake and Rowan saw in him at the outset. There was good reason for Steve to be cautious. These weren't the Dukes, his old pals in debauchery. In the four years he'd been away, he'd endured the fear of being unable to write songs in a sober state. Finally, he felt he was back at square one in his career, with one last chance to make it right. He was suffering, physically and metaphysically. Both Blake and Rowan saw that suffering, and both saw him overcome it in a show of strength that's burned in their memories.

"I thought that he definitely was not well," Blake remembers. "He was having trouble with his teeth at that point, and in some pain. And there was a small lack of confidence in what he was going to do or needed to do. I think he was just there to do it and didn't know really which direction it was going to go in.

"As it went on, he gained confidence rapidly and became much stronger in what he was doing. It started off a little on the shaky side, just from the fact that he was medicated and not feeling very good. But very rapidly as we went into it, I think his confidence came fast and he was able to rise to the occasion and go on and do a great job."

"So there we are in the studio with the core," Rowan says. "It was like finally I really got to meet Steve. All these years he had been part of my life, and this was the meeting with Steve. He'd been up hard against it, and we had a great exchange. I learned a tremendous amount from him, and I think he learned from me too. As we made the record it was all live takes. It's really a sense of confidence, and Steve hadn't lost his confidence. He'd lost his teeth and he'd lost his instruments, but his sense of confidence was outrageous. It was great performances, live performances, maybe a line or two overdubbed where he got off-mike or something, but they're all live performances. I didn't have enough confidence in myself, and Steve was very much like, 'You asshole. What are you equivocating about?' That planted a seed in me to not sell myself short. Nashville will make you sell yourself short if you don't have that overriding confidence, you know."

"It was not the standard studio thing where you just hire some musicians to come in," Blake points out. "He knew everybody was on his side and was trying to do what needed to be done. It worked, in the long run. He recovered real fast."

Once the album was done, Steve took the band right out on the road, where at each stop he was greeted by thunderous ovations and crowds eager to share the experience with him again. In Los Angeles, at the Troubadour, the fans surged towards the stage, so close they could reach out and touch Steve. Norman kept scooting his chair back about six inches after every song, saying to anyone who would listen, in a typical Norman Blake construct, "I don't believe I'm gonna be too close to the front of this stage."

According to Rowan, Norman was the only hard sell in the group. Steve—of whom Norman once said, "he's a lot of fun, but he's kind of opinionated," leading Rowan to burst forth with a hearty laugh and note, "The joke is that Norman is so opinionated in a classic kind of way"—approached him with the offer to go on tour, explaining, "There's $50,000 in it for you and you just have to be out for three months and be on a bus with …" Norman, in a typical construct, replied: "No, you know I don't believe I'll be going on that tour." Clearly, something or someone persuaded him to change his mind.

To Rowan, the first tour with Steve, and a second leg, was about more than making music. That was a big part of it, of course, but it was the offstage camaraderie that has stayed with him all these years later. The long rides, picking in the back of the bus, Norman playing "for about 12 hours without stopping," introducing Steve to Beat poet Lawrence Ferlinghetti's City Lights bookstore in San Francisco, where "Steve walked out with a couple hundred dollars' worth of books," whiling away hours in the bus reading Kerouac and Ginsberg to each other, "and the years fall away with every mile," as Steve sang in "The Other Kind."

"It was a moment frozen in time," Rowan says. "We were like kids. Steve looks at all things with equal light of possibility. He's not discouraged by things that might make me turn a little sour. Which is great. Which is just to say that there was a brief moment in time when we were both taking a breath of the same air and it was a wonderful time."

. . .

Pam Lewis came back into Steve's life briefly at this juncture. In the years since she had worked on *Guitar Town*, both she and Steve had seen the heights and depths of their profession. Pam had gone on to become partners with Bob Doyle in a management company, and one of their early successes was in launching the career of their client Trisha Yearwood, who, steered largely by producer Garth Fundis, became one of contemporary country's premier interpretive singers. Another of their early clients was a complete unknown no one in the business cared to listen to: Garth Brooks. Eventually, everyone listened to Garth, to the tune of making him one of the best-selling artists of all time— not just in country but in all of popular music. Garth's success was such that he begat an entire new genre of male country artists, the "hat" acts, so called because they all wore the same broad-brimmed cowboy hats Garth favored. Some of them—Clint Black and Alan Jackson—proved to have real staying power and for good reason: they could write, play, and sing with authority and credibility. Too many, though, went for the safe, middle ground, had a formulaic hit or two and settled into the lower tier of country stardom, having no lasting impact or influence.

Brooks was the exception in that his outsized ego matched the magnitude of his record sales. Behind-the-scenes horror stories of his power plays abound in Nashville, but in public he always put on a humble act, and the public ate it up. His music was nothing special—he sang in a baritone drawl with a bit of a Southwestern accent, favored syrupy ballads and hard country drinking and partying songs, spiked with flourishes from the worst of '70s and '80s arena rock. (In interviews Brooks would often wax rapturous about Styx and Kansas, and at the peak of his popularity he cut a version of "Hard Luck Woman" for a Kiss tribute album that was some kind of monstrosity, with Brooks growling the lyrics in a voice that no one could have recognized as his.) His arena-rock-influenced live shows were notable for their physicality (he seemed to enjoy swinging from ropes at one point, for instance) and their fireworks.

It figures that Steve Earle would have little use for an artist as compromised as Garth Brooks. In *Hardcore Troubadour* he offered a withering assessment of the '90s phenom: "Well, he really can't sing. He really can't carry a tune in a bucket. His records need a lot of work. He really is tone deaf. He's one of the worst singers I've ever heard in my life. I think Garth Brooks is kind of evil just because he sucks so much energy and money out of the business. But, you know, that's country music, and I don't have anything to do with what they call country music. I haven't since my second record."[3]

Pam Lewis and Bob Doyle's thank-you for steering Brooks from obscurity to the pinnacle of the entertainment world was to be fired by him. Brooks cut a wide swath through the executive ranks at Capitol Nashville too, maneuvering to have his friend Pat Quigley, whom one industry observer derided as "Garth's beer salesman," installed as label president. Quigley had in fact been an executive at Labatt's Beer, and he immediately wrote his name large in the country music hall of shame by suggesting to a staffer that Patsy Cline be flown into Nashville to cut a duet with Capitol artist John Berry. "Well, that may be a little hard," Quigley was told, "since she's been dead for 30 years."[4]

Pam went back to where she started, rebuilding her independent publicity business and doing a lot of soul searching. When Steve Roberts and Owsley Manier approached her about working on several of their Winter Harvest projects, including *Train a Comin'*, the personal work she had done served her well, because she found Steve to be "bratty, adversarial, and difficult. I think he was punishing me. And his manager [John Dotson] was being difficult, very obstructive. When someone wanted to interview Steve, it would take days to get an answer. Things like that. But we got through it.

"I had gone through my own transitions in life, and I was reading a lot of metaphysical books, and I was trying to really get my own act together and be more insightful and patient. By that time we were in our late twenties, early thirties. Steve's older than I am. But you get to an age where you do some soul searching and you get a little wisdom. I wouldn't be devastated, because I realized, This is a guy who's gone through hell and back."[5]

Pam did succeed in getting Steve to do some press for the new album. One of the best of the interviews from that time was with Chris Morris in *Billboard*'s March 18, 1995, issue. In it Steve described *Train a Comin'* as "exactly the record I needed right now. No major label would let me make this record, coming back after four years especially. I always wanted to do it. It was a low-pressure record, at a point in my life when I needed a low-pressure record."[6]

He had to tweak Norman Blake a bit, of course, describing the fact of Blake even leaving his beloved Georgia as "a coup because Norman is, shall we say, set in his ways. There's nobody that does what he does better than he does it. Norman is a flat-picking acoustic guitar player, but he can play anything with strings on it, and he really became a utility man on this record."

Later on he would be blunt and forthcoming about his drug addiction, but at that early stage of his recovery he recoiled from the subject, saying, "it isn't anybody's business." Rather, he offered an eloquent appraisal of the changes wrought in him during his visit to the Seventh Circle.

"At 40 it becomes clear—especially if you get to be 40 the way I did, defying gravity—that what's important is your life and your wife and your kids. There is an edge in things you do when you're younger, and you think it's life or death. But if you survive long enough, artistically and otherwise, it suddenly dawns on you one day that you didn't have to go through maybe all the shit that you went through, but there ain't nobody in the world that could have told you that when it was goin' on. It's just that simple."

About that wife, a little more than a year later Steve filed for divorce from Lou-Anne, thus ending his sixth marriage.

Train a Comin'
Winter Harvest, 1995

Produced by William Alsobrook and
    Steve Earle
Executive producers for Winter Harvest:
    Owsley Manier and Steve Roberts
Recording engineer: Wayne Neuendorf
Additional engineer: Mike Elliot
Recorded at: Magic Tracks Recording
    Studio and Masterfonics, Nashville,
    Tennessee
Mixed by Wayne Neuendorf at Masterfonics, Nashville, Tennessee
Second engineers, Masterfonics: David Hall and Keith Boden
Mastering and editing: Mack Evans at Magnetic Technology—Nashville,
    Tennessee

Musicians
Steve Earle: guitar, high-string guitar, harmonica, vocals
Norman Blake: guitar, dobro, fiddle, mandolin, Hawaiian guitar
Peter Rowan: mandolin, mandola, gut string guitar, vocals
Roy Huskey: acoustic bass
Emmylou Harris: vocals

Songs
  1. "Mystery Train Part II" (2:31) (Steve Earle)
  2. "Hometown Blues" (2:41) (Steve Earle)

3. "Sometimes She Forgets" (3:01) (Steve Earle)
4. "Mercenary Song" (2:39) (Steve Earle)
5. "Goodbye" (4:57) (Steve Earle)
6. "Tom Ames' Prayer" (3:02)
7. "Nothin' without You" (3:02) (Steve Earle)
8. "Angel Is the Devil" (2:12) (Steve Earle)
9. "I'm Looking through You" (2:28) (Lennon-McCartney)
10. "Northern Winds" (1:40) (Norman Blake)
11. "Ben McCulloch" (4:10) (Steve Earle)
12. "Rivers of Babylon" (B. Crowe–J. McNaughton–G. Reyam–F. Farian)
13. "Tecumseh Valley" (4:28) (Townes Van Zandt)

In the annals of comeback history, Steve's return from oblivion, especially when seen in the context of the work he's produced post-rehab, seems every bit as remarkable as Elvis's 1968 ascension from mediocrity and irrelevance back to his customary regal standing. As if acknowledging at least this much of a connection between Steve and his first musical hero, *Train a Comin'* begins with an obvious Elvis reference in the title of its opening song. "Mystery Train Part II" begins with a bouncy mandolin line that's playing before the recording starts and fades in, then is joined by the deeper mandola, and is borne ceaselessly to a frantic conclusion. The lyric seems fairly straightforward, about a train rumbling through the countryside and the singer's longing to be on it. Given Steve's recent history, though, the lyric, "She ain't bound for nowhere … engineer don't seem to care …" hits close to home as a summary of the years of madness that preceded this session. Rowan joins in on a soaring harmony chorus, helping kick off Steve's comeback on a triumphant note.

From 1977, "Hometown Blues" (Steve's note: "Went home to Texas and no one remembered me but the cops") begins with Steve announcing "apologies to Thomas Wolfe and Doc Watson" before kicking into a lilting, old-timey melody that happens to be driving a harsh indictment of the old hometown, where his friends are gone and the changes have unsettled him. In a lively singsong chorus, he notes that "my heart lies in broken pieces / scattered along the way." Which in turn sets up a jolly, angular solo spun out by Norman Blake on Hawaiian guitar.

A beautifully crafted portrait of a lonely woman who won't admit to her longing for companionship, "Sometimes She Forgets," from 1979, is a classic country tearjerker, made doubly poignant by Blake's earnest, song-length fiddle solo and Rowan's rustic, trilling mandolin lines supporting Steve's drawling vocal. The punch line is the song's comic relief—Steve encourages a male suitor to go for it "'cause sometimes she forgets."

Clearly, three songs in, Steve has made a statement that *Train a Comin'* is going to be a modest, back-to-the-basics exercise. The drug-fueled fury of

Copperhead Road and *The Hard Way* has given way to craft, feeling and folk-flavored storytelling. This is the sound of an artist marshalling all his gifts at their most fundamental level—language, structure, style, point of view in a minimalist environment—and finding his voice again, his mojo.

In keeping with the tenor of the project, the atmospheric "Mercenary Song" is a soldier of fortune's account of how he and a couple of friends joined up with Pancho Villa's army, advising that they "fight for no country, but we'll die for good pay." There are no great revelations—when the fight is over in Mexico, they're looking to go to Chile, "heard tell there's some trouble down there." Again, evocative guitar work rules the day, with exotic atmospheres courtesy the tune's Spanish flavor, especially in the melody lines fashioned in tandem by acoustic and gut-stringed guitars played by, respectively, Steve and Norman Blake. And the high-stepping, Guy Clark–style chorus is a delight, a pure, jubilant celebration of the mercenary's ethos.

As "Mercenary Song" marches out, the first, tentative, finger-picked acoustic notes of "Goodbye" emerge, haunting and winsome. Written when he was in the Buffalo Valley rehab center, "Goodbye" is a heartbreaking farewell, apparently to Teresa Ensenat. Steve sings it gritty and breathless, sounding at a couple of points as if he's struggling to find the words to express regret over losing a great love and at the same time thrashing himself for the debacle he caused and can't come to terms with because he doesn't even know if he was "just off somewhere, just too high" even to remember how they parted. Rowan on gut string, Blake on dobro, and Steve on harmonica surge into the chorus, as if the song might break open to a more hopeful place, but as quickly as it rises, so does it recede back to the stark, lonely sound of Steve's finger-picking and ragged vocal, a forlorn soul on the lost highway.

"Tom Ames' Prayer," circa 1975, is a classic, strutting story-song about an Old West bank robber who finally gets caught and sent to jail, but escapes before his hanging and walks out into the street with his pistols cocked, ready to go out in a blaze of gunfire rather than at the end of "Parker's rope." Midway through, Blake fashions a fleet-fingered acoustic solo as energizing as it is exquisitely conceived and impeccably executed. Later on the disc Steve rolls out another epic story-song in "Ben McCullough," also from '75, one of those songs fondly remembered by the Bishop's Pub crowd. (Born in 1811 in Tennessee, raised in Arkansas, the real Ben McCullough is considered a heroic Texas patriot for his service at the Battle of San Jacinto—he didn't arrive in time to join his friend Davy Crockett at the Alamo—and as a member of the Second Congress of the Republic and of Texas's First Legislature. A brigadier general in the Confederate Army, he was killed while leading a division in the Battle of Elkhorn Tavern on March 7, 1862. His body was returned to Austin, where it is buried in the State Cemetery.[7]) Set in the Civil War—Steve's first venture into the lore of the War Between the States, which he would explore in more depth later—

"Ben McCullough" tells the story of brothers who enlist in Ben McCullough's infantry and come to hate everything about their plight (one brother is killed at Wilson's Creek), especially Ben McCullough for leading them into misery and horror. Rich in detail and overflowing with venom, "Ben McCullough" plays out in dark, foreboding tones, Steve perfectly embodying and expressing the rage his character feels toward his commanding officer's base inhumanity, sounding almost gleeful when he spits out the final sentiment of the chorus— "when you die, you'll be a foot soldier just like me / in the devil's infantry."

"Ben McCullough" is set up by an expressive, longing guitar solo by Norman Blake, 1 minute 40 seconds of angular poignance that sounds like thunderclouds gathering. Blake's intricate approach to the tune finds him employing pull-offs, trills, and ominous strands of triplet figures on the bottom strings in stating, restating, and augmenting the composition's main theme. Titled "Northern Winds," the song was originally an untitled march Blake found in *The Northern Fiddler*, a traditional fiddle tune book from Northern Ireland.

"I just called it 'Northern Winds' for identification's sake," Blake says. "It was just a traditional piece that seemed like it fit in that spot."

Blake came up with it when Steve asked him if he had something that would be suitable as a prelude to "Ben McCullough." It's in a standard tuning, but Blake doesn't play it standard; instead, he approaches it "in a very nontraditional way. I played it more abstractly and it would not be at all like it was in the book, as far as mood or tempo or that kind of thing."

From 1980 Steve dusted off a traditional country-styled love song, "Nothin' without You," featuring Emmylou Harris adding keening harmony on the choruses, and Rowan and Blake offering lonesome, heartbreaking solos on mandolin and dobro, respectively. From what Steve refers to as his "vacation in the ghetto," circa '92, came the whimsical ragtime-style "Angel Is the Devil," to which Steve gives a robust ambiance with his 12-string guitar, while Blake weaves a fanciful mandolin solo throughout the arrangement.

The collection is rounded out with three covers, all of them telling: Lennon-McCartney's "I'm Looking through You," from the momentous *Rubber Soul* album, is done at a slightly slower tempo than the original's, but Rowan's mandolin and Blake's dobro enhance the country flavor that was suggested in the Beatles' arrangement. ("I had heard that song, but that's about all," Blake says, adding in a typical Norman Blake construct, "That's a far cry from where I live.") With Emmylou Harris sitting in again, the band cooks up a countrified version of the Melodians' reggae gem "Rivers of Babylon," which Steve sings with gripping intensity, as if the song speaks both to the spiritual renewal he's undergoing and to the social conscience that would soon become a dominant feature of his resurrection. Finally, a delicate rendering of "Tecumseh Valley," Townes Van Zandt's account of a wayward girl whose broken dreams lead her first to prostitution then to suicide. Roy Huskey, Jr.'s bass, which has been the pulse of *Train a Comin'*, thumps softly throughout, like a softly beating heart; Steve finger-picks a melody on acoustic, Rowan adds rich texture with the gut-string guitar, and Blake emits an eerie cry on the dobro. This is where Steve came in: a beautifully structured tale, characters defined in terse, vivid phrases, a landscape described succinctly as the setting for a story that gathers momentum with each sorrowful verse until the inevitable, heart-wrenching concluding scene and a subtle but stirring closing line—"Fare thee well Tecumseh Valley"—that heightens the senselessness of the tragedy.

When the song fades, Steve is back where he started as an artist, schooled in the fundamentals of his craft by a demanding mentor; having mastered those fundamentals, he is ready to set his sights on the world again and, with clear vision and a fearless heart, to take its measure.

Trust in Twang: Calling Ray

Ray Kennedy: "When Steve disappeared for a while, a lot of us were really concerned about him. One of my really close friends, Alice Randall, is a songwriter who became a screenwriter and then a book writer; she's one of Steve's closest friends too. Alice and I used to go to these functions together, like when Steve would be doing something at the Country Music Hall of Fame, signing a guitar, giving a speech about something. Sometimes Alice would go out on the road with Steve, and she'd tell me what was going on with him. We'd start seeing some of his guitars showing up in pawnshops, and some people would actually buy them and put the guitars away with the idea of giving them back to Steve at some point. At one point I ran across a six-string bass that was custom made for him by Joe Glaser. I called Joe and he came and bought it and at a later date returned it to Steve. That's kind of cool that Steve had that kind of support.

"When he finally did go to jail and go to treatment and get out of treatment, the person that was managing him, John Dotson, had been kind of co-managing me with Dale Morris. John suggested to Steve to call me. Steve didn't know that I had this great studio down on Music Row. So he called me and said while he was in jail he wrote some songs, and wanted to record some demos. Those first couple of demos were the beginning of that record *I Feel Alright,* and that's how that kind of unfolded. Day one of recording the first demo, which was the song "Feel Alright," we recorded it and mixed it and went home with a finished cut for that record. Within a couple of days A&R people from the different labels were showing up at the studio; people started coming after him. Which was pretty funny, because they just kind of sat in the corner and watched us work."[8]

Tough Love

In the hectic year following *Train*'s release in March 1995, Steve put some old business to rest (pleading guilty in November to a 1994 crack cocaine charge, he was sentenced to a year's probation, required to do a show at a local prison, and to attend Narcotics Anonymous meetings), reaped the rewards of his sobriety, and laid the foundation for his future as an artist. His business dealings frustrated those he dealt with, but when it came to music he was on top of his game in a way he had really never been before. As the year progressed, it was clear he was seizing his second chance with the vigor of a man determined to make good on it. Whatever self-doubt he had harbored about his abilities when he was at the lowest ebb of drug addiction had largely evaporated. In resurrection, he flourished.

The year looked like this: across-the-board critical acclaim for *Train a Comin'*, as well as a Grammy nomination and a Nashville Music Association nomination for Best Folk Album; positive, sometimes wild-eyed reviews for the acoustic tours he did in support of *Train*; an invitation from actor-director Tim Robbins to write a song for the soundtrack of his film *Dead Man Walking*, which produced the stirring "Ellis Unit One"; no less than 17 recordings of his songs by other artists.[1] And, on September 11, a memorable night at Nashville's Bluebird Cafe, performing an acoustic set with his Texas alpha male mentors, Townes Van Zandt and Guy Clark. A benefit for the Interfaith Dental Clinic organized by Clark's wife Susanna, the concert was a night of tall tales, poetic musings on the state of the heart, and communiqués from the deepest part of these Texas troubadours' worldly souls. For the most part Guy Clark was wry and sardonic, Townes Van Zandt bemused and laid-back, and Steve, by contrast, edgy, intense, political. Townes had a wonderful moment with a humorous introduction to "Katie Belle," and the subsequent tender, lyrical reading of same, then Steve mesmerized the audience with a touching version of "Valentine's Day," his declaration of pure love. Clark had rarely been better than he was on "Randall Knife," a self-penned recitation with minimalist guitar accompaniment documenting conflicted feelings summoned by his father's death. Townes's reading of his classic "Pancho and Lefty" heightened the narrative's irony to a degree that had escaped the song's most famous interpreters, Merle Haggard and Willie Nelson. An uncredited Emmylou Harris popped up singing ethereal harmony with Clark on "Immigrant Eyes" and returned again to add a spectral presence to Earle's fierce set closer, "Copperhead Road," the

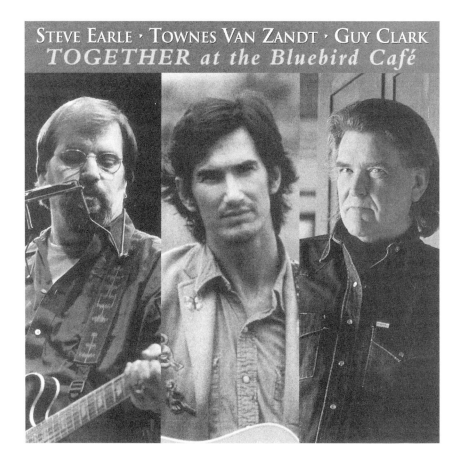

third in a trio of stunning performances that closed the set, the first two tunes being "Mercenary Song" and Townes's "Tecumseh Valley," both from *Train a Comin'*. (The concert was released on CD in 2001 on the American Originals label as *Together at the Bluebird Cafe*.)

But there was trouble brewing on the label front. *Train a Comin'* had been resequenced without his consent, and Steve's response was to blast his copy to pieces with a pistol.[2] Then he saw that his liner notes had been edited, also without his consent, and he was enraged. Peter Rowan witnessed it all.

"I have never seen anybody so pissed as Steve when they edited his liner notes. He was outraged. I said, 'Well, what does it matter, really? You're saying what you want to say.' He just looked at me as if to say, 'You fool. You can't let these people do that to you.' And I guess that's when he got his back up—that's the confidence."[3]

The ultimate upshot was that Steve reconnected with his buddy Jack Emerson, who had launched Jason and the Scorchers from his Praxis operation in Nashville to a deal with EMI and ensuing national acclaim. With Jack's credit card and a second mortgage on his house,[4] he and Steve bought *Train a Comin'* from Winter Harvest in February and formed a partnership and label, E-Squared (Emerson and Earle). After months of negotiations, a five-album deal was struck with Warner Bros. to distribute Steve's E-Squared recordings. (Brad Hunt, a good friend of Emerson's who had been senior VP and general manager of Elektra Records in New York before running the Zoo label, facilitated the deal and became a consultant to E-Squared but was no fan of Steve Earle the businessman.) Steve, however, was thinking of building E-Squared into an artist-friendly label, producing acts he liked and releasing them on his own imprint; Warners wanted no part of that. Hunt's persistence and knowledge of the industry paid off when he did the necessary politicking to get E-Squared an independent distribution deal for its non-Earle product through the giant ADA distribution company.

Leaving Winter Harvest also meant leaving behind bitterness on the part of the label's principals, including his friend Bill Alsobrook, who in 1998 sued Steve and E-Squared for $120,000; a year later, with the suit still pending, Alsobrook died suddenly of a heart attack.

Alsobrook's death prompted a heartfelt tribute from Steve, who on May 25, 1999, wrote: *William Alsobrook was my friend for 25 years. He took care of my instruments and equipment on and off the road. He was there almost every minute of* I Feel Alright *and* El Corazón. *He coproduced* Train a Comin' *and facilitated the continuation of my career in many, many ways. He knew more about music than anyone I ever met. He was my best friend for years and in my darkest hour he was my only friend. I miss him very much.*

See you when I get there, brother,
Steve[5]

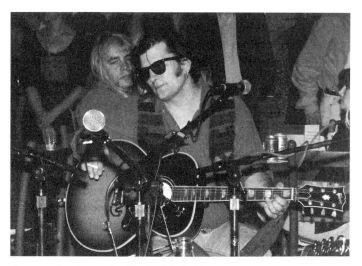
Steve performing at the Bluebird Cafe, Nashville, 1997.

Owsley Manier, Steve Roberts's partner in Winter Harvest, was hurt and bitter at how the Steve Earle saga had played out. He felt the label had taken a chance on Steve at a time when no other would—true enough—and that Alsobrook's reward for coming up with the concept and pinpointing the right musicians for *Train a Comin'* was to be dumped. "Steve can say what he wants about it, that's fine, but Bill did come up with those players and Steve had never been in a direction like that before. And the songs were perfect for it. And that was after a lot of contemplation and thinking about a direction to go in to reemerge. So it was unfortunate."[6]

In 1998, when Steve was preparing to make a bluegrass album with the Del McCoury Band that Warners didn't want, E-Squared struck a deal with former Warners chairman Danny Goldberg to have its recordings distributed through Goldberg's new label, Artemis. A year later, Emerson was out at E-Squared— "forced out of the situation," Hunt alleges, livid at the memory of Steve's treatment of the man who helped him get back on his feet. With disdain he refers to Goldberg as "the great white hope [who] became the sugar daddy that Jack had been up to that point."[7]

Ever the entrepreneur, Emerson moved on to start another label, but he was a sick man. Afflicted with a degenerative lung disease that had been developing over a period of time, he had gone to the hospital at the University of Alabama at Birmingham in September 2004. Hoping to get on the list for a heart transplant, he was instead turned down because his illness was too far advanced. In November, according to Hunt, "he was sitting on his bed at home. He'd just made the rounds, had talked to his sister in Seattle, and fell off the bed and died while he was on the phone with his mother."[8]

People who knew Jack Emerson often refer to him leaving behind "a legacy of love." Brad Hunt concurs and says no one should be more thankful for that legacy than Steve Earle.

"When nobody—I mean *nobody*—believed in Steve, Jack was the only guy. Not that Steve couldn't have come back on his own, but Jack shortened the process by a ton. [Steve] would have had to make some independent records, prove he was staying clean, and that could have taken a long time. Jack shortened it by years."[9]

Steve delivered a tribute to Emerson at the funeral, and two weeks later returned to play a benefit to raise money for Emerson's widow.

• • •

I Feel Alright
E-Squared/Warner Bros., 1996

Produced by Ray Kennedy and Richard Bennett (Tracks 1, 5, 8, 9, 10, 11, 12)

Recorded and mixed by Ray Kennedy at Room and Board, Nashville, Tennessee

Produced by Richard Dodd (Tracks 2, 3, 4, 6 & 7)

Recorded by Peter Coleman at Treasure Isle, Nashville, Tennessee

Mixed by Richard Dodd at Room with a V.U., Nashville, Tennessee

"You're Still Standin' There" produced by Ray Kennedy and Richard Bennett; Recorded by Ray Kennedy at Room and Board

Mixed by Richard Dodd at Room with a V.U.

Assistant Engineers: Dan Leffler and James Bauer

Mastered by Bob Ludwig at Gateway Mastering Studios, Portland, Maine

A&R: Jack Emerson, E-Squared

A&R: Joe McEwen, Warner Bros.

All songs written by Steve Earle

Recorded in a Magnetic Field

Musicians
Steve Earle: guitars, harmonica, vocals
Richard Bennett, Ray Kennedy: guitars
Kelley Looney, Garry W. Tallent, Roy Huskey, Jr., Ric Kipp: bass
Custer, Greg Morrow, Rick Schell: drums
Ken Moore: organ
Richard Bennett: harmonium
Custer, Richard Bennett, Greg Morrow, Dub Cornett: percussion

Custer and Logan, the Fairfield Four (Mark Prentice: musical director),
    Lucinda Williams: vocals
Siobhan Maher: Ms. Williams's stunt double
Strings arranged and conducted by Kris Wilkerson
Carl Gorodetzky, Pamela Sixfin, Richard Grosjean: violins
Lee Larrison: viola
Robert Mason: cello

Songs
  1. "I Feel Alright" (3:04) (Steve Earle)
  2. "Hard-Core Troubadour" (2:41) (Steve Earle)
  3. "More Than I Can Do" (2:37) (Steve Earle)
  4. "Hurtin' Me, Hurtin' You" (3:21) (Steve Earle)
  5. "Now She's Gone" (2:48) (Steve Earle)
  6. "Poor Boy" (2:55) (Steve Earle)
  7. "Valentine's Day" (2:59) (Steve Earle)
  8. "The Unrepentant" (4:31) (Steve Earle)
  9. "CCKMP" (4:30) (Steve Earle)
 10. "Billy and Bonnie" (3:39) (Steve Earle)
 11. "South Nashville Blues" (2:28) (Steve Earle)
 12. "You're Still Standin' There" (3:24) (Steve Earle), with Lucinda Williams

Even before he started work on *Train a Comin'*, Steve was preparing for a new album, one he thought would signal his comeback (and the one that in a sense became his comeback in terms of representing his music as he saw it developing), the one for which he had written some songs before going back to jail and since coming back to the living. For undisclosed reasons, Steve was not going to produce the new album—perhaps because he was already in the midst of the *Train a Comin'* sessions and had a full plate on the production end—and so it was that Jack Emerson, along with another veteran executive who had joined the E-Squared team, Dub Cornett, reached out to hands old and new for this chapter of Steve's legacy. The old hand was Richard Bennett, who was teamed as coproducer (much to his dismay again—"once again the emasculated credit"[10]) with a new hand, Ray Kennedy, a casual friend of Steve's from picking parties around town and at Ray's place and himself a former chart-topping country artist and stringed instrument master. From the start, though, the plan included another producer, Richard Dodd, who had interesting credits to be working with a rootsy artist like Steve. Dodd put his recovering and somewhat shaky artist through his paces as had no one before him. Though Dodd was responsible for only five tracks out of the 12 planned for the album, his take-charge approach and the nonnegotiable demands he placed on the conduct of the sessions seemed to be exactly what Steve needed at this delicate point in his recovery.

I. "He looked like an accident waiting to happen"

Born in Bedfordshire, England, Richard Dodd began an apprenticeship as an engineer at the Recorded Sound studio in 1970 and rose to the rank of chief engineer rapidly, within only two years. In 1974 he engineered a No. 1 record for Carl Douglas, "Kung Fu Fighting," and moved into the producer's chair for projects with the highly regarded traditional Irish band Clannad. A reunion with George Harrison, with whom Dodd had worked in 1978 on a solo project, led to his involvement with Harrison in the soundtrack to the box office debacle *Shanghai Surprise*, starring Sean Penn and Madonna. From there it was an introduction to Jeff Lynne, work on the first Traveling Wilburys album, and then an engineering role on Tom Petty's Grammy-nominated *Wildflowers* and *Echo* albums. In 1991 he moved to Nashville, because it was close to equidistant from his two main places of business at that time, Los Angeles and Radley, Hertfordshire.

Dodd's ideas about recorded sound were shaped more by instinct and trial and error than by conscious emulation of and admiration for anyone else's approach. He knew what he liked, and he found his way into a style in his own manner.

"After awhile it happened that I was emulating certain people, and I didn't know them. I never bothered to find out how anything was done or who did it; I wasn't interested. There was a goal, a target for me to aim at, and I'd find my own way of doing it. And in the process I'd be copying people; I didn't invent anything. I discovered things on my own that had already been discovered. To that end, if you want to put a name to it, Joe Meek. The Beatles—the engineer, the producer, the artists. That whole thing was what I heard, and I would find ways of doing *that*, whatever *that* was. Short of being brilliant at writing songs, that was fuel to spur me on."[11]

Joe Meek, tone deaf, brilliant, and disturbed, was a genuine sound visionary whose productions had a unique sonic presence that was the envy of most every pop music professional who heard them. Working with rudimentary gear, he eventually began building his own compressors, which were well advanced beyond what was commercially available and are still manufactured through the joemeek company in England. (The company, which Meek had nothing to do with founding, uses his designs. Or, as the company's mad scientist Ted Fletcher puts it, "All those years I worked for Joe, he was always accusing me of stealing his designs. And now I am.") Meek first made his mark in 1962 with a wild, careening production of the Tornadoes' instrumental homage to the satellite "Telstar," which topped the chart in America for three weeks; in October 1964, the Honeycombs, a British quartet boasting an oddity in the form of a female drummer, Ann "Honey" Lantree, had a No. 5 single with the Meek-produced rouser, "Have I the Right?" Meek had an enviable track record in

England, and beyond his commercial work he engaged in advanced, thematic, sonic experiments quite unlike anything else in the pop universe. Due to limitations in the recording technology available to Meek, some of his experiments haven't aged so well. Still, a conceptual *magnum opus* such as 1960's *I Hear a New World: An Outer Space Music Fantasy*, with Meek and a group of musicians he billed as the Blue Men, stood apart in its day for its ambition, sonics, and unselfconscious sincerity, something akin to a musical counterpart of an Ed Wood movie, although much better executed. Meek committed suicide on February 3, 1967, the anniversary of Buddy Holly's death, killing himself with a gunshot to the head after shooting his landlady to death.

Richard Dodd came to Joe Meek long after Meek's death. "I found out that the records I liked, a lot of them were made by him. And you know, it's like I realized I like the sound of the guitar on the Honeycombs' 'Have I the Right?' And it wasn't until 10 years ago that I found out that the kick drum sound was Joe stomping in the bathtub. It wasn't the girl playing the drums! Yeah, wonderful things.

"I just didn't realize what I liked, who they were," he says of his education in sound style. "Obviously Phil Spector was easy to spot. The Beach Boys were easy to spot. The Beatles. I liked Stevie Wonder before I knew that he was responsible for more than just writing and singing and playing. It was an ignorant discovery.

"Spectacular little moments like Del Shannon's 'Runaway.' Not knowing what I liked, I could go back now and analyze it, but I don't care to. The whole sound, the whole package was important and inspired me. A funny thing is when I was doing a project for a Japanese artist and in my mind I had 'Jailhouse Rock' when I was creating the drum sound for and aping the whole intro. I was never satisfied, could never get the sound big enough. I settled on what I had. Long after I finished it, I actually had a listen to 'Jailhouse Rock' on a studio system, and it's the wimpiest drum sound ever! In my mind, it was incredible. So I take an influence and allow it to trick me, I allow the essence and the spirit to influence me, and I strive for that. It gets left behind, of course; you never can capture anything."

Asked what he likes about producing, Dodd answers with a tart, "Not very much." He endures it, he says, because he's drawn to "the challenge. If I don't do it, somebody else will, and they'll do it wrong. It's a way of me contributing, hopefully, helping somebody fulfill something. I was about to say 'vision,' but I don't think that's right. There's been a few occasions—not many, to be honest—when I've had a moment when I know what the end product's going to sound like before I even start. Funny enough, one of them was with Steve Earle. He played me a song and I knew how it was going to sound. In fact, I said to him, 'I'll do it if you'll let me do it exactly the way I want to do it.' And he said, 'Yeah.'"

At the time Jack Emerson and Dub Cornett called Richard Dodd's manager with an offer to produce Steve Earle, Dodd had never heard of Steve Earle. Told of the offer, Dodd weighed the two options he considers in cases when he doesn't know an artist or an artist's work: he could investigate both and make a decision based on the available information, or he could remain ignorant but intrigued and gauge his feelings in the course of a face-to-face meeting with the subject. With Steve, he chose the latter, "and that was a shock."

"Oh, my God. He had just come out of prison. He looked dreadful. He was very large, with a huge growth growing out of one of his arms, left arm I think, about the size of a baseball. Teeth going every way, what teeth he had left. He sat across from me in the interview, I suppose is what it was; he interviewed me and I interviewed him. Both his legs were going at different times, shaking and everything, with a Diet Coke in his hand, saying how he was completely cured of drugs and in control of everything. He looked like an accident waiting to happen. I was desperate to get out of there; I didn't want anything to do with him. I don't like the drug thing, and I'm not that deeply rock 'n' roll. I've been around it, I've just chosen not to be part of it. It was a relief when he said, 'Can I play you something?' So I thought, Yeah, I can listen to some music and say I don't like it or I'm not the right person, and then leave."

After hearing some demos Steve had put on tape, Dodd was impressed almost to the point of speechlessness. But suspicious too, given Steve's recent history.

"When did you record these demos?" he asked. "Are they 10 years ago when you were straight?"

"I did them just a little while back. Since I've been out," Steve answered.

Then, Dodd says, "I kind of beat him up in a way. I'll do that one, and I'll do that one," he told Steve, citing the songs that most grabbed his attention. "I'll do that one if you let me do it the way I hear it. And I want to do another one because I thought you sounded like Elvis," Dodd thinking this would be as close to producing Elvis as he ever got.

"Well, if you do those two, I'd like you to do these two as well," Steve replied, then tried to wheedle a bit more out of Dodd, musing, "Maybe these three."

Dodd resisted. "No, I'll pick two, you pick two."

"Okay." Steve became quiet.

"And another thing," Dodd demanded, "you've got to do it live."

"What do you mean?"

"You've got to do it live in the studio."

It was a protective measure on Dodd's part. His experience with drug addicts was that "they get jacked up and you could spend days waiting for them to turn up for a session." So he reiterated: "You have to be there with the band, you sing live, we cut it live. And that's it. No fixes, you've gotta go for it."

Steve didn't hesitate. "Okay, I can do that."

"Okay," Dodd said, "let's do this one first, and if that goes well, we'll book the session and do everything."

Dodd recalls, "So we did the one I was strongest to do, and that worked out pretty well; I enjoyed it a lot." The one Dodd was "strongest to do" was the beautiful, aching love song "Valentine's Day."

It begins with a deliberate, stark finger-picked figure on acoustic guitar, and Steve entering strong but sorrowful, singing, "I come to you with empty hands," apparently having forgotten Valentine's Day and thus having only "my love" to offer. After the first verse the gospel quartet the Fairfield Four come rumbling in—and rumble they do, with low, resonating notes like rolling thunder; on the chorus, ascending with an elegant, upward glide, comes a string section, in an arrangement by Kris Wilkerson that brooks favorable comparison to the subtlety and understated beauty of a Nelson Riddle chart. In the song as it unfolds, Steve is apologizing for overlooking material manifestations of his love and offering instead something of more lasting value: "I hope my heart will do." The strings, ever lovely, pour on the ache, and the Fairfield Four maintain their low, ominous, wordless hum until the end, when they join Steve in burnished four-part harmony that evokes the precision beauty of the Ink Spots on the words "Valentine's Day" as the song eases to its close. To this point in Steve's recording history there is no more beautiful moment than "Valentine's Day," even if him oozing sincerity about his motives doesn't square with the record of his own love life. ("'Fearless Heart,'" Richard Bennett quips, "that pretty well tells the story of the Steve Earl school of romance."[12])

The session developed according to Dodd's timetable. He ruled the studio, brooking no ego trips from Steve or anyone else, and demanded punctuality, especially of Steve, of whom the producer was still wary. After outlining his idea for the arrangement, and getting Steve's approval with "Okay, let's try it," Dodd met with Kris Wilkerson. She presented her interpretation of the arrangement he had described to her earlier, "and it was nothing like what I'd asked for, but that was my fault obviously in conveying what I wanted." Dodd went through it again, and Wilkerson came back with a version he liked even better than what he had suggested before. Then he booked the Fairfield Four for a day's work.

Then to Steve he laid down strict instructions: "Steve, at 11 o'clock you come in and we put guitar and voice down—the definitive guitar and voice. And 'round about two the singers will come in, and perhaps five, the strings will come in. Then we'll be done."

Steve turned up at the appointed hour, but his performances were tepid. "We'd try a few takes, have a break, try a few takes, have a break." The Fairfield Four came in as scheduled, and by 1:30 P.M. "Steve had an audience in the control room." Which seemed to be the key, because after Dodd told him that the next take had to be a keeper "because I've got a lot of people invested in this day," he nailed it on the next go-'round.

The Fairfield Four then listened as Dodd explained what he wanted them to do on the track, "and they did their thing; took awhile."

Seems there was some communication problem between Dodd and the Fairfield singers. Their musical director, though, understood what Dodd wanted, "which is just as well, because I couldn't understand a word they said. They were lovely. They were suspicious of this little English white boy telling them what to do. I must admit, at the time mentally I 'settled' for what they gave me as their interpretation of what I asked for. I later found out that they knew better. I thought they were just ignoring exactly what I wanted and doing what they could do, but they were doing what they do do, which was the right thing. So cheers to them."

As for the use of strings on "Valentine's Day," Dodd found Steve totally amenable to the idea, "a complete pussycat," in fact. "He was nothing like what he is now," Dodd says. "He was desperate for someone to take him serious again, I think. So I had my way with it, really."

"Valentine's Day" went down so well that Steve and Dodd moved on to the band tracks—"and I said, 'No overdubs, Steve'"—and those went smoothly too, to the point where an enthusiastic Steve Earle suggested, once again but this time more successfully, that they do a fifth song together. In three days they had completed all the work on the four remaining Richard Dodd–produced cuts that would appear on the succeeding album, *I Feel Alright*, a telling title if ever there was one. Steve even allowed Dodd to select the band to accompany him, there no longer being a formal Dukes lineup. He brought Greg Morrow in on drums, Richard Bennett (a favorite of Dodd's) had already been enlisted as a guitarist, Roy Huskey, Jr., returned on bass for "Poor Boy," but otherwise that slot was filled by the E Street Band's Garry Tallent, now a Nashville resident.

Of those songs—"Hard-Core Troubadour," "More Than I Can Do," "Hurtin' Me, Hurtin' You," and "Poor Boy"—the only one that was a bit of a struggle was the turgid, moody "Hurtin' Me, Hurtin' You," a recycling of an oft-told tale in Steve's canon, him screwing up (and screwing around), explaining that it wasn't intentional ("I never meant to be cruel and untrue"), and coming to some level of self-realization in the aftermath of his duplicity (see title sentiment). As the song develops, Bennett interjects snippets of twangy pull-off notes, hits a hard chord in the chorus, settles into the background again with minimal comment, until the song starts building to an angry pitch in the final verse. Then, Bennett's guitar starts wailing like a saxophone—indeed, it even has a sax tone—and takes the music roaring into the a final, halting chorus in which Steve, sounding exhausted and breathless, affects the aural equivalent of crawling across the finish line.

"That was a long overdub," Dodd recalls, "by virtue of what I asked Richard to do. He was up for it, but it took an hour."

As he did on *Train a Comin'*, Steve used the first three songs of *I Feel Alright* as a personal state of the union message, celebrating his return from the depths and reasserting his strengths as a craftsman. On the album opening "Feel Alright," against a background of jangly and processed guitar sounds (a Ray Kennedy touch that Dodd believes is his influence—"Listening to things Ray had done prior to our meeting and things he has done since, I think the use of the compressor—or the overuse of the compressor—might be my fault"), Steve fairly wallows in rubbing his survival in his detractors' faces ("find a place to hide away and hope that I'll just go away—ha!") in a performance that underscores the quiet confidence he had gained by the time he started working on the Ray Kennedy– and Richard Bennett–produced tracks. "Hard-Core Troubadour," with its edgy, vaguely south-of-the-border flavor and an arrangement and melody inspired by Bruce Springsteen's classic "Rosalita" (from which Steve even lifts a lyric near the end) both announces his resurrection and pokes fun at his slacker ways ("He'd come to make love on your satin sheets / Wake up on your living room floor"). It is a pure, triumphant, semi-autobiographical romp fueled by Bennett's rich, jangly guitar (he even tosses in a twangy quote from "Guitar Town" to close the track) and Steve's life-affirming performance. An appeal to an old lover he can't forget, "More Than I Can Do" takes off on stomping mid-tempo rhythm, insistently strummed acoustic guitar, and a wailing harmonica. Steve details all the reasons he's not giving up on the love affair, a background chorus adds soaring harmonies, and the story's climax reiterates the narrator's unstinting focus on reclaiming his lost love, closing out the trifecta of songs on the same positive, upbeat note at which it began, minus the gleeful revenge factor of "Feel Alright." The amiable "Poor Boy" is a bopping little neo-rockabilly tale with a class sensibility about it, as Steve sings of a boy from the other side of the tracks falling for a girl from "up there." Undeterred, he holds out hope he might become her chauffeur, if only for a chance to adore her blue eyes in the rearview mirror.

The remaining tracks introduced Ray Kennedy to the Steve Earle story. He came in essentially with Richard Bennett, unbeknownst to Richard at the outset. Richard had arrived home one afternoon to news from his wife that Steve had called. Upon returning the call, Richard learned that Steve wanted him to produce his new studio album, the one he would record after he finished mixing a new acoustic album he had recorded. Initially reticent even about returning the call, fearing Steve might still be a junkie, Bennett found him quite the opposite: "He sounded pretty damn good." Steve dropped off a cassette of some of the songs he had written, and after hearing them Bennett was excited again. He agreed to join the project, but only after making it clear that he was to be the producer, period, no co- stuff. "I had really quit coproducing with people," Bennett explains. "I just wasn't interested, for a number of reasons. I had a certain way I liked to do things. I was just headstrong enough at that time that I didn't feel I needed to compromise anymore."

Next time he spoke to Steve, he was told Ray Kennedy had to be given a coproducer credit because the sessions in part were being held at Ray's Room and Board studio (the Richard Dodd tracks were recorded at Treasure Isle). Still, Richard loved Steve's music, so he accepted the coproducer credit and went to work.

More than anything else, Richard was heartened by the changes he saw in Steve, who had gone from being "very dark" when last he had worked with him (on *Exit 0*) to "being the ol' Steve again." In the studio, it was like the old days, the good times, "very loose—we'd all become looser about things. You know, he wanted a little more than *Exit 0* or *Guitar Town*, and we wanted to leave some loose threads laying around. And of course at that point it was just given that he was playing guitar—which was perfectly fine. My job was to find something to complement or to add to what Steve was doing. It was a lot of laughs, a lot of fun. There was never a tense moment that I remember. It was really a little bit of a homecoming. It was nice to go back and do it."

The ultimate team player, Bennett gave Kennedy great latitude as a co-producer—the seven tracks bearing their credit often have sonic touches that have since become a signature of Steve's albums, which are also co-produced, but by Steve and Ray. As Bennett asserts, *I Feel Alright* really is the comeback album, for it's here that the groundwork is laid for everything that followed.

"Now She's Gone" has a slightly Irish feel in its rustic ambiance; Steve's 12-string is jangling like it was lifted from a Byrds track, and Bennett is adding an amazing bit of depth and atmosphere with a calliope-like harmonium solo he plays in tandem with Steve's wailing harmonica. And the story, about a girl

"I feel alright" — Steve in 1996, post-rehab, reclaiming his life and his art.

who "took to running wild," reads like Steve's saga transposed, as she tears through people's lives, walks away from the wreckage but still leaves behind at least one man who's ready to forgive and forget. "The Unrepentant," ferocious, stomping, and foreboding, with Bennett fashioning some startling, snarling guitar lines around Steve's dramatic reading, might have been a *Hard Way* outtake. In it, a nefarious character "stands at Hell's door with a bad attitude and a .44" engaging the Devil in his dark, unnamed mission. The guitars here are as fierce as any on *The Hard Way*, the drums (Custer is on the Ray Kennedy–Richard Bennett tracks) are blasting those familiar shots from way back and Steve perfectly embodies the desperation driving the story's main character to his inevitable—even foreseen—destruction. As the song fades out with a fillip of guitar feedback, we hear the first resonating notes from a National Steel guitar, Delta blues licks, and then droning on behind it, a single, sinister organ chord; the harmonium appears again, interjecting a single longing chord. Singing "CCKMP" (for "Cocaine Cannot Kill My Pain") in a weary, bluesy drawl, Steve summarizes the darkness of the previous near-four-years in a few terse verses that describe an addict's free fall into the abyss as he seeks a better high, from cocaine, then heroin, which he describes as "the only gift the darkness brings." The final verse affirms what everyone has learned in their efforts to help him— Steve sings, "leave me alone until these blues have gone." The music intentionally drags, the sound is purposely muddy, and the song, which has only four short verses, doesn't completely fade out until the 4:30 mark—reflecting the addict's distorted space-time continuum, his woozy quest for a more righteous and numbing high. "Billy and Bonnie" is a bouncy country ballad about a couple of wild kids who meet at "the dirt track races" and go on a kind of Bonnie and Clyde rampage, robbing a Texaco station and killing the attendant. In the end, Bonnie saves her skin by ratting out Billy, and as he's led away, Billy promises to meet Bonnie in hell. Mandolin is the predominant instrument in the mix, but the country flavor is spiced with a touch of rock 'n' roll courtesy guitar and a pulsing organ—it's hard not to hear it as Steve's contemporary upgrade of Flatt and Scruggs's "Foggy Mountain Breakdown," from the film *Bonnie & Clyde*. Delta-style 12-bar blues and a National Steel—finger-picked and played with a slide—are the defining elements of the steady rolling "South Nashville Blues," which is a quick 2:25 of casual reportage from a character who goes out on the town with a pistol and a $100 bill, hell-bent on getting locked up again, and suggests that prison is the only place he's really comfortable. Bouncy and bright, with a folksy vocal, the song's engaging ambiance could make a listener forget that Steve's portraying a cold-blooded killer on the prowl. "You're Still Standing There," an engaging folk-rock duet with Lucinda Williams, closes the album on a bright note, even though the song describes a mixture of loss and hope as the narrator describes his life and the memory of a former lover that "cannot keep me warm, but it never leaves me cold." Lucinda, who manages to sing on key, seems to be straining to keep up and her performance is not nearly as assured as Steve's, but the buoyant melody, Steve's Dylan-ish harmonica solos, and subtler elements such as the tumbling notes from what sounds like an electric 12-string guitar buried in the mix following Lucinda's verse, all combine to make the moment one of soaring passions. Not a bad way to leave a listener, when you're on the road home.

II. Trust in Twang: Ray

Ray Kennedy likes to tell anyone who asks not that he was born in Buffalo, New York, but rather that he was born "43 degrees,1 minute, 41 seconds north, 78 degrees, 9 minutes, 31 seconds west—look it up."[13] His father, Raymond A. Kennedy, was a mover and shaker of an executive, at one time serving as a vice president of Sears, a vice president of Dean Witter, and president of Discover Card, which he had founded as an offshoot of the Sears charge card. Because of numerous relocations during his childhood, Ray feels he never really had a hometown. His childhood map looks like this: "Buffalo to Boston, which was my early childhood; to Philadelphia, to northeast Philadelphia, where I went to junior high school and high school. To Washington, DC, and back to Philadelphia, to west Philadelphia, then to Chicago. By that time, my dad had become vice president of the company and was at the Sears Tower. But I had left home by then and gone out west to Oregon." Lower Moreland, Huntington Valley, Pennsylvania, was an especially rough high school where "half my class carried guns. Back then if you didn't carry a switchblade or carry a gun you weren't normal. Sniffing glue in the bathroom and dropping LSD in chemistry class—basically '60s upbringing."

In 1971 he matriculated to the University of Iowa, where he was accepted into the school's prestigious writing program, headed by Kurt Vonnegut, Jr. But between the time Ray registered and the time he showed up on campus, Vonnegut had resigned. One semester later, Ray was on his way to Portland, Oregon, to visit a girlfriend. He stayed seven years, during which time he attended college (Portland State, Portland Community College) by day and by night played in bar bands—"dragging myself to a nine o'clock music theory class every morning, studying music theory the old-fashioned way, then at night playing guitar in a band. But it was fun. I was young; I could do anything back then."

Ray describes his musical influences as being "kind of all over the map— Beatles, Stones, Hendrix, Cream—anything that was guitar oriented was intriguing to me. Any band that had a great guitar player in it was where I was. Also Buffalo Springfield, the Byrds and Poco and the Eagles, Gram Parsons— today it's called country-rock, but back then it wasn't. I was very caught up in that whole taste of jangly 12-string guitars. The Byrds were my favorite.

They had a unique sound, and they were considered the American Beatles. And I think that's how I kind of discovered country music, through the back door with people like Gram Parsons, Chris Hillman, Roger McGuinn, Dylan."

Through a friend who owned a record store, Ray delved deeper into country music history, going back to Bob Wills, up through the years with Hank Williams, Lefty Frizzell, Webb Pierce, George Jones, Merle Haggard, Buck Owens, Johnny Paycheck, "just kind of on and on, the whole early history of country music in the '50s and '60s. Things that had a lot of character and rawness to 'em. I never liked anything that was slick. I'm still like that to this day—country music that's got edge and got character and got a sound to it and an attitude. And of course along came the discovery of Willie and Waylon and the whole Texas scene, and from that the Texas songwriter scene of Guy Clark. And that's where I discovered that songwriting is where it all starts. And I discovered that most of my favorite acts were songwriters, like Haggard. And it just kind of grew from there. As a songwriter my angle and point of view shaped itself more towards traditional country, but old traditional country. I came to Nashville in 1980, kind of on an experimental six-month plan. Always knowing I could go back to Oregon. I didn't know anybody, just kind of went around knocking on doors, met a few publishers; within a few months I had a few songs cut."

chapter 17

A Clear Field

He loved it.
His mind became the street
—*Coming Through Slaughter*

Steve may have had no use for the post–New Traditionalist mainstream country music scene—he would dismiss the most popular female artist of the day (and the best-selling female artist of all time), Canadian Shania Twain, as witheringly as he had Garth Brooks, calling her "the highest paid lap dancer in Nashville"—but it hardly mattered. An entire new generation and genre had arisen that embraced him as one of its avatars. It was called, variously, alternative country ("I think that means 'out of tune,'" Tony Brown observed) and Americana; it had an eloquent journal of its times in the magazine *No Depression*; and even came to have its own trade group, the Americana Music Association, complete with an annual convention and an album chart. Americana embraced the honesty country music had always been known for—as Norman Blake would have defined it, for instance—but which had been diminished in the mainstream recordings coming out of Nashville, too many of which now favored '80s-styled power ballads or arena rock flourishes, and style over substance. At the older end of the Americana spectrum, seasoned hands such as Steve and Emmylou, whose bodies of work established a benchmark of craft, integrity, social conscience, and stylistic eclecticism rooted in folk, country, and early rock 'n' roll traditions, set the pace for younger bright lights who followed their lead—Uncle Tupelo, for instance, which split into Sun Volt and

Wilco, and kept making intriguing—and in Wilco's case, challenging—music in new configurations; Whiskeytown, which begat the solo careers of two formidable singer-songwriters in Ryan Adams and Caitlin Cary; and the Chicago-based Freakwater, which seemed to be channeling the Carter Family's rustic dread and longing in haunting original songs written and sung by Catherine Ann Irwin and Janet Beveridge Bean.

The consciously retro approach of Americana ultimately seemed a tip of the hat to the populist traditionalism of James Talley, who emerged from nowhere in 1975 with *Got No Bread, No Milk, No Money but We Sure Got a Lot of Love*, a powerful album of classically styled traditional country and country-folk tunes, his original songs bespeaking a poet's eye for the telling details of the common man's struggle. He came by his populism honestly. Born in Oklahoma to a family that knew only struggle, Talley had lived in the belly of the beast of want. He grew up not bitter but rather with a deep affection for those who made something, anything, of nothing, especially in the face of obstacles designed to keep them hidden in society's underbrush. He had seen the triumph over this in his own family. His mother, who stressed to her son the importance of education as a way up the economic ladder, was herself a role model for young James—in the '30s she had put herself through Oklahoma A&M (now Oklahoma State University) and become a teacher.

"In high school, I started playing the guitar and discovering that I had a passable voice and could carry a tune," Talley recalled in liner notes he wrote for his 2002 album *Nashville City Blues*. "I gravitated toward folk songs, because they told such vivid stories about America. My mother had been raised very poor on a small Oklahoma farm north of Stillwater. My father was the son of a small-town merchant; his father owned a general store in the tiny town (population 300) of Welch, Oklahoma. They met during World War Two when they were working at Oklahoma Ordinance, a gun powder plant near Pryor, Oklahoma. We did a lot of traveling and moving around when I was young. When I was three years old, my parents moved all the way to Washington state, and when I was eight we moved to Albuquerque, New Mexico."

Talley followed his mother's footsteps and attended Oklahoma State, but after his father (who had worked for many years at the Hanford plutonium plant in Richland, Washington) suffered a heart attack and the bills mounted, James returned to Albuquerque, where he graduated from the University of New Mexico. A succession of jobs followed, including an eye-opening one as a caseworker for the New Mexico Department of Welfare, which assigned him a caseload of indigent Chicano families, "who had little or no education, and even less hope.

"They were cast about and buffeted this way and that by society," Talley recalled. "I had studied the Great Depression years in college, and had absorbed all the stories my parents had told me about that period. I had seen the faces of the Okies immortalized by the Roosevelt-era Farm Security Administration photographers; but what I saw at my welfare department job let me know that for some people, things had changed very little during the 30 years since the Depression. What I saw as a caseworker changed my whole view of life in the United States; and to this day those images are stamped indelibly in my memory."

Moving to Nashville, where he hoped to get a record deal, Talley found the music industry's movers and shakers inhospitable to his music. So he cut an album on his own and began selling it out of the trunk of his car; a local radio station began playing his beautiful song "Red River Memory," an executive at Capitol Records heard it, advanced Talley some funds to pay his musicians, and in June 1975, *Got No Bread, No Milk, No Money but We Sure Got a Lot of Love* was released. After getting a boost from a couple of key reviews, the album, and Talley's career, started going places—he even wound up playing for another avowed populist, President Jimmy Carter, at the White House (thrice, in fact). Talley's gifts didn't diminish over the course of three more acclaimed Capitol albums, but country music did in its Urban Cowboy era, and by the late '80s Talley was a part-time musician and studying to be a full-time real estate agent in Nashville. Still, he kept a flow of new recordings coming out, releasing four albums overseas on the Bear Family label. In 1999 he formed his own label, Cimarron Records, and issued a rousing collection of Woody Guthrie songs, reconsidered in James Talley style, titled *Woody Guthrie and Songs of My Oklahoma Home*; a year later he followed that with a full-on band album, searing and impassioned, of straightforward, plainspoken original tunes, *Nashville City Blues*. His resources for funding Cimarron are limited, to say the least, so its releases are infrequent. But Talley has never stopped writing, and in 2004 issued a live album of performances recorded at a concert in Italy. Titled *Journey*, it included four potent new songs, including one of the most insightful commentaries on the root causes of the 9/11 tragedy any artist has put to song, "I Saw the Buildings," as well as a powerful story song about the tragic demise of Chief Joseph of the Nez Perce tribe, and a mystical, haunting evocation of the spirit of the great Sioux warrior Crazy Horse, "Somewhere on the Edge of the World."

As stated in his *Nashville City Blues* liner notes, Talley's driving philosophy speaks to the essence of the artists under the Americana umbrella, who do not reap the riches of their mainstream brothers and sisters, but have reason to believe their calling is honorable and vital.

Talley: "My hat goes off to those who have not made a fortune from their music but who have continued to have something to say, and have persisted and survived: Steve Young, Guy Clark, Townes Van Zandt, and many others. It's harder to create, it takes more effort, without the comfortable cushion of financial success. Who is to say what will last into history; what will be important, what will be a footnote? The music making millions in profits today may well be tomorrow's footnote. The music business, like the health care business, has been taken over by marketing people with MBA and law degrees, by corporate America. These people can quantify, they can read computer sales printouts, and make decisions based on numbers, but can they create? Can they feel? Do they have a vision? Can they recognize dreams? Can they see what is important in the long run, or do they even care? Is that their job? Most of the music that will last from today may well be some of the most obscure right now, rather than what is fed daily to the public over corporate-controlled radio stations. Everything cannot be reduced to its lowest common denominator. Everything cannot be foretold with numbers. Time will tell, as it always does."

· · ·

January 1, 1997, 44 years to the day when his hero Hank Williams died, Townes Van Zandt, in failing health, suffered a massive heart attack after returning home from surgery to repair a broken hip.

Peter Rowan had known Townes since 1978, when they were booked together to play an Irish pub in Cambridge, Massachusetts. He likened him to Ralph Stanley's brother Carter in the encouragement he gave other artists. "Men like that took your measure by the fact that you were doing something similar to them. And they showed a lot of respect—even if my own confidence wasn't that high, they showed me a lot of respect. It was like a boost in confidence, you know."[1]

Rowan has a photo of him and Townes onstage "somewhere down in Arkansas, in the hills." He is struck by the look on Townes's face, one familiar to him; a look that "telegraphed this sense of mortality and at the same time there was a little vibe of immortality. If you said, 'Well, Townes, see you in the morning. Wanna have breakfast?' He'd just look at you like, 'Pete, you know there's no tomorrow.' He'd just give you this look and it would just shoot through you, like, 'We can't even bullshit about tomorrow.' Scary.

"He knew darkness, but he was kind, that's the thing," Rowan says. "Totally kind."

Steve held nothing back in extolling his hero and mentor, referring to Townes as "the best songwriter in the world" and adding that he suspected a conspiracy in the timing of his death, being on the same day as Hank Williams's. "At least I knew he would have dug that," Steve said. "That was the way he was. It's very, very hard for me to imagine the rest of my life without Townes because he's been in it since I was 16 years old. He was the purest folk singer I ever saw.

"He was my teacher, he was my friend, I named my oldest son after him and he was the best I ever saw."[2]

· · ·

Near the end of January Steve kicked off a two-month solo tour of Europe that proved momentous on several fronts. For starters, in tow with him on the tour was his 14-year-old troubled son Justin, who was on his way to being a mini-Steve. As punishment for stealing his gun, Steve sent Justin to the Three Springs "boot camp" for juvenile delinquents (such work camps were at that time a growing trend in the American penal system), where Justin got a taste of life on a chain gang. The experience didn't change his behavior—Justin was a holy terror on the tour, "an out-of-control 14-year-old boy," says Steve.[3] For his part, Steve disposed of the two guns he owned and became less NRA friendly than he'd been back in his years of madness when, he says he was lucky "I didn't kill someone when I was out running around carrying guns all the time and out of my mind on dope."[4]

He also stepped up his opposition to the death penalty, which had waned during the peak years of his addiction. In 1996 he had been introduced to members of Journey of Hope: From Violence to Healing, an organization comprised of relatives of death row inmates and death row inmates that had been found innocent.[5] After hearing their stories, talk about the inhumanity of the death penalty became commonplace in his interviews and in his onstage comments. It wasn't as if his knowledge was only secondhand, either. In the early '90s he had corresponded with several death row inmates, one of whom, Jonathan Wayne Nobles, would become an important player in Steve's story, however briefly.

At tour's end in March, Steve sent Justin home with a friend and made his way to Galway, Ireland, located on the western reaches of the Republic of Ireland. Founded in the twelfth century by Anglo-Norman settlers, Galway is rich in the arts and universities, as well as natural beauty—a stimulating environment for an artist. Steve rented a house on Connemara Road and settled in. It was a good ride—he began writing, one of the first songs being a tribute to Townes, "Fort Worth Blues," gently finger-picked in Townes's style, describing a nomadic—and apparently unsatisfying—lifestyle that never cured the longing for home. It references a pastoral scene on Galway Bay, and reels off Paris, Amsterdam, and London as towns that always came up wanting, never erasing the hometown blues. By mid-May Steve had written the bulk of what would be his next album.

* * *

Trust in Twang: Meet the Beatles

"Rubber Soul ... that's where the real true genius stuff started"

Ray Kennedy: "I guess I've just lived and breathed Beatles musical since I was a kid. I think the exceptional thing about them is they were a true case of musicians who came from working-class families that were very good and very competent, but none of them stood out as being potential solo artists. But they definitely had some pretty amazing synergy together as a band. What they did together as a band was way beyond what any of them could do individually, and it just grew and grew. In the early days their songs were fairly rudimentary kind of rock 'n' roll, teenage music; and then, over a very quick period, it got very sophisticated. The reason I think it did is that they were the first band to come along and, because they were so successful they were able to indulge themselves and basically live in the studio for eight years, I don't think any band before that ever had that opportunity. They found themselves at home at Abbey Road Studio 2, and basically they just camped out there. And if you look at their discography, you'll see that in 1964, there were five records that came out—*Meet the Beatles*, *The Beatles' Second Album*, *Hard Day's Night*, *Something New*, and *Beatles '65*, which actually came out in December of '64. So there's five albums in one year. And then in 1965, I think there were four records. They were actually starting to spend more and more time on their records. Like *Help*, *Rubber Soul*, and *Revolver*, they would spend more time. So in '65, they had four records; in '66 they just had *Yesterday … and Today*, and *Revolver*. Then '67 they got in *Sgt. Pepper's* and *Magical Mystery Tour*, then the White Album, *Yellow Submarine*, *Abbey Road*. I think they grew tremendously by having all that time to create. And any new piece of gear, amplifier, keyboard, microphone, anything that came along ended up at Abbey Road for them to try out. They got their hands on any of the latest stuff, and so they were very experimental in their recording and they were encouraged by George Martin and Geoff Emerick, who became their favorite engineer from *Rubber Soul* on. They were encouraged to really push the envelope, and they did. It shows in the writing, it shows in the recording. You go back and listen to their records from about *Rubber Soul* on, and that's where the real true genius stuff started, that's where it began for me. Although there's a lot of cool stuff earlier, it started to become more and more consistent.

"I've been to Abbey Road 2. Actually Steve and I went there once. They don't do tours at Abbey Road. It's a very, very private place. Tourists are out front drawing graffiti on the wall, but you don't get in Abbey Road. Nobody gets in Abbey Road. But we had a contact, and there's a British band we were talking about making a record with, and if that was gonna happen we wanted to do it at Abbey Road and we wanted to do it at the old Beatles studio, Studio Two, which has never been changed since the last recording they did there. They redesigned the control room, but the recording space is still the same. So we went over there one morning, early, and spent a couple of hours there, got the full tour of the place. And I did get to talk to Geoff Emerick year before last. He's a funny guy. I asked him a lot of questions about Fairchild 660s and 670s and recording techniques and this and that, how they did certain things. We were talking about recording drums—I had conversations with Glyn Johns as well about recording drums. You know, these guys are real minimal as far as how they mike drums. Like John Bonham's drums were always recorded with three mikes. Now people are using like sixteen mikes on drums, top and bottom and multiple layers of room mikes. But some of the best recordings in history were done with two or three mikes. You listen to a lot of the old Motown records, a lot of those were done with two mikes, an overhead and a kick. So Geoff told me that there was one day that everything changed, and it was either *Rubber Soul* or *Revolver*. Ringo was in there just playing around with the drums, and all of a sudden the drums sounded better than he had ever heard 'em. He ran down the stairs—the control room's on the second floor—and went up to Ringo and asked him what he had just done. He said, 'I lit me a fag.' He smoked a cigarette. He looked down on the snare drum and there was a pack of Lark cigarettes. So he carefully marked it with a pencil and counted how many cigarettes were in the pack, and there were eleven cigarettes. From that day on they always recorded with a pack of eleven Lark cigarettes on the snare drum. Religiously. 'You don't have Lark cigarettes? Somebody go out and get a pack of Lark cigarettes. We can't record without 'em.' I don't know if he was putting me on, but I have a feeling that really did happen.

"The thing is, the Beatles, as far as the band, it's a very complex thing to look at. You can look at it as a whole, and you can break it down into all these different elements; you can break it down to the John Lennon influence and the McCartney influence and the Harrison influence, but when you put it all back together again, it's always the sum of the parts that has the big impact. No one else in history has ever been able to achieve what they did in those short eight years, to make that many great records that will probably stand the test of time, and probably no one will ever sell as many records as the Beatles, because they're being rediscovered all the time by new generations.

"Everything was a performance. And this always leads me back to the way to make records—go for the performance. [In the '60s] they couldn't fix vocals, they couldn't fix guitar parts. It was all going down together. Either on a mono or a stereo track, there'd be drums and bass and acoustic or electric guitar and a vocal, and then there'd be a second take which would be some other elements for the track, a third take or whatever. In other words, instead of doing vocals they'd just do another take. There'd be take 5, take 7, take 12, take 18, whatever, and then when they hit that magic one George Martin would make the call, 'Boys, that's your record right there.' Then they would doctor it up a bit, but they had a whole lot of limitations on what they could do.

"The Beatles stuff, you just push the faders up and there it is, you know. It's that good."[6]

El Corazón
E-Squared/Warner Bros., 1997

Produced by the twangtrust
Recorded and mixed by Ray Kennedy
    at Room and Board, Nashville,
    Tennessee
Assistant engineer: Patrick Earle
Except "NYC" recorded by Jon
    Dunleavy at Ironwood Studios,
    Seattle, Washington
Assistant engineer: Patrick Fisher
Mixed by Ray Kennedy
Mastered by Hank Williams at Mastermix, Nashville, Tennessee

Songs and Musicians
1. "Christmas In Washington" (4:59) (Steve Earle) Steve Earle: guitar, mandola, harmonium, vocals; Ray Kennedy: shaker
2. "Taneytown" (5:13) (Steve Earle) Steve Earle: electric guitar, harmonica, vocals; David Steele: electric guitar; Mark Stuart: acoustic guitar; Kelly Looney: bass; Brady Blade: drums, percussion; Ray Kennedy: hand drum; Emmylou Harris: vocals
3. "If You Fall" (4:10) (Steve Earle) Steve Earle: 12-string guitars, vocals; David Steele: electric guitar; Mark Stuart: mandolin; Kelly Looney: bass; Brady Blade: drums, percussion
4. "I Still Carry You Around" (2:45) (Steve Earle) Steve Earle: guitar, vocals with the Del McCoury Band: Del McCoury: guitar, vocals; Ronnie McCoury: mandolin, vocals; Rob McCoury: banjo; Jason Carter: fiddle; Mike Bubb: bass
5. "Telephone Road" (3:43) (Steve Earle) Steve Earle with the Fairfield Four (Isaac Freeman, Robert Hamlett, James Hill, Joseph Rice, and Wilson Waters, Jr.): voc.; Mark Prentice: music direction for the Fairfield Four; Steve Earle: acoustic guitar, vocals; David Steele: electric guitar; Mark Stuart: acoustic guitar; Michael Smotherman: organ; Kelly Looney: bass; Brady Blade: drums, rub board, tambourine; Jim "Here Comes Jim Bob" Hoke: baritone saxophone; Cheri Knight, Elisa Sanders, Kathleen Cotter: hand claps
6. "Somewhere out There" (3:46) (Steve Earle) Steve Earle: 12-string guitars, vocals; David Steele: electric guitar; Mark Stuart: acoustic guitar; Michael Smotherman: organ; Kelly Looney: bass; Brady Blade: drums, percussion; Michael Kelsh, Scott Miller, Mark Stuart: vocals

7. "You Know the Rest" (2:12) (Steve Earle) Steve Earle: guitar, harmonica, vocals; David Steele: guitar; Ronnie McCoury: mandolin, vocals; Roy Huskey, Jr. —bass; Brady Blade: drums
8. "NYC" (3:37) (Steve Earle) with the Supersuckers: Steve Earle: 12-string guitar, vocals; Eddie Spaghetti: bass; Renaldo Allegre: electric guitar; Dan "Raised by Wolves" Bolton: electric guitar; Dancing Eagle: drums
9. "Poison Lovers" (3:38) (Steve Earle) with Siobhan Kennedy: Steve Earle: 12-string guitar, vocals; David Steele: guitar; Mark Stuart: acoustic guitar; Michael Smotherman: organ; Kelly Looney: bass; Brady Blade: drums; Ray Kennedy: tambourine
10. "The Other Side of Town" (4:17) (Steve Earle) Steve Earle: guitar, vocals; David Steele: electric guitar; Jason Carter: fiddle; Tommy Hannum: steel guitar; Roy Huskey, Jr.: bass; Scott Miller: vocals; T. Money: needle drops
11. "Here I Am" (2:39) (Steve Earle) Steve Earle: electric guitar, vocals; Justin Earle: electric guitar; Brad Jones: bass, vocals; Ross Rice: drums, vocals
12. "Ft. Worth Blues" (4:03) (Steve Earle) Steve Earle: guitar, vocals; David Steele: electric guitar; Mark Stuart: mandola; Tommy Hannum: pedal steel guitar; Brady Blade: drums, percussion; Ray Kennedy: harmonium

January 1994: President Bill Clinton, in his State of the Union address, pushes his controversial health care plan, and tells Congress: "If you send me legislation that does not guarantee every American private health insurance that can never be taken away, you will force me to take this pen, veto the legislation, and we'll come right back here and start all over again."

April 1994: Ethnic warfare erupts in Rwanda. Western governments, including the United States, choose not to intervene. In little more than two months, more than 800,000 lives are lost to genocide.

May 1994: Paula Corbin Jones files civil lawsuit against President Bill Clinton accusing him of sexual harassment.

November 1994: Republicans, led by House Speaker Newt Gingrich, who promises an agenda of conservative reform framed in a document titled "Contract with America," gain control of Congress in the midterm elections.

November 1995: In a dispute over specific cuts in the budget, House Speaker Newt Gingich and his Republican allies angle for a confrontation with President Bill Clinton that results in a shutdown of the federal government. Clinton's position is favored overwhelmingly by the public.

July 1996: President Clinton signs a Republican version of welfare reform, despite his disapproval of provisions that deny aid to legal immigrants. He tells an aide: "This is a decent bill wrapped in a sack of shit."

November 1996: President Clinton wins an overwhelming electoral college victory over Republican nominee Robert J. Dole.

May 1997: In an attempt to waylay the Paula Corbin Jones sexual harassment civil case, President Clinton's lawyers argue before the Supreme Court of the United Sates that a sitting president should not have to defend himself against such lawsuits until he is out of office. The court disagrees, allowing the Jones lawsuit to move forward.

August 1997: President Clinton and the Republicans agree on a balanced budget.

Against a backdrop of increasing hostility, silliness, and malevolent gamesmanship in the nation's capitol, Steve opened his new album with "Christmas in Washington," a gently finger-picked, introspective cry for some real heroes to come straighten us out. The Dems were "gearing up for four more years of things not gettin' worse," the Republicans were drinking whiskey and exulting over the president's reign coming to an end. He beckons Woody Guthrie, and admits he feels he's failed, in all his journeys, to find Woody's "trail." The radio blares only good news, but all around is another scene entirely, one of a society gone straight to hell. He appeals to Malcolm X, Joe Hill, Martin Luther King, Jr., and—probably for the first time ever in popular song history—pioneering anarchist-feminist Emma Goldman. Other than Steve's stark, evocative guitar, the only other instruments on the song are Ray Kennedy's discreet shaker, Steve's mandola and, washing in poignantly on the choruses and then receding, harmonium.

"As I get older, surviving what I've survived, things have gotten really simple for me," Steve writes in notes posted on steveearle.net. "Very black and white. I believe that it is unforgivable for people to go hungry in the richest country in the world. I believe that we're supposed to be getting more civilized, not less, and that it doesn't make sense to take a life in payment for another life. This song is about the state of the nation, but it is also about me, too, about some of the things I've lost along the way."[7]

So much for the quiet. "Taneytown" begins with a series of dark, thick electric guitar notes and keeps up a dirge-like trudge through the story of a young black boy who defends himself against some white attackers by cutting one with his Randall knife, which he drops to the ground as he's fleeing the mob. Later he finds out the mob lynched another black boy who had picked up the knife and been caught with it. The song is relentlessly bleak, with two guitars snaking around each other's lines, a shaker hissing like a rattler about to strike, and the band rumbling low and ominously as the song winds down. Emmylou Harris adds her voice to Steve's on the choruses. Taneytown was a community near Gettysburg, Pennsylvania (the song mentions Gettysburg, and Taneytown can be found on maps of the Battle of Gettysburg); today's Taneytown, Maryland, in Carroll County, is an outgrowth of the original village.

A "guy song," according to Steve,[8] "If You Fall" rides along on cascades of riffs from Steve's 12-string and serpentine snarls from David Steele's electric as the rhythm section booms behind them. The tale contains a classic Steve MacGuffin: he's warning another guy about all the bad things that can happen if he falls for a certain girl, only to reveal at the end that he's going after her himself.

Driving bluegrass in the classic style is the order of the day on "I Still Carry You Around," which Steve admits he wrote "specifically to have something to play with the Del McCoury Band … the best bluegrass outfit in the business right now. Del [McCoury] is the best tenor, Ronnie [McCoury] is the best mandolin player, and Rob [McCoury] plays banjo like no one else."[9] All three of the McCourys acquit themselves admirably, but Steve might have added that Jason Carter, who has a dynamic fiddle solo about midway through, and affable standup bass player Mike Bubb, who keeps the pulse steady through some red-hot instrumental byplay between mandolin, banjo, and Steve's guitar, rank with the finest on their instruments as well.

Steve had met the McCoury band at a "No Depression" night at Nashville's Station Inn, where Peter Rowan had once held forth with his weekly Crucial Country gathering. The show's organizers had asked the McCoury band to perform something with Steve; agreeing to do so, they met with him only a couple of hours before they were scheduled to go on, using the opportunity to run down some of the songs from *Train a Comin'*.

"Then of course the night came and we got up and played with him, and oh, man, he was excited," recalls Ronnie McCoury. "He came off stage and he said, 'My next record's gonna be a bluegrass record, and I really want you guys to do it with us.' We figured it would be awhile before we could do this, and I think that's maybe when we came in and did ["I Still Carry You Around"] with him. He must have been recording that record right then. I think we did it that night, so it must have been right then when he was recording it that we took the time to do it. We figured he had just done this record, so it would probably be another year before we would do anything. Everybody was just thinking that. That must have been the fall of that year."[10]

From a whimsical, opening descending runon acoustic guitar, "Telephone Road" opens up into a dense, thumping sound scape in which guitar figures least prominently, one of the few songs in Steve's canon of which that could be said. The story centers on three brothers, two of whom take off for Houston and better jobs, while the younger stays home in Lafayette, Louisiana, working for a Texaco refinery, saving money to join his brothers on Telephone Road, where "everybody's rockin'." Steve describes the real Telephone Road as a "white-trash strip" in Houston that was the center of attraction for an influx of oil field workers in the '70s.[11] The Fairfield Four are back, buoying Steve's gritty, breathy vocal with deep gospel harmonies. The arrangement is mesmerizing, with prominent bleats from a baritone sax (played by Jim "Here Comes Jim Bob" Hoke), hand claps, drummer Brady Blade (from Emmylou's Spyboy band) scrubbing away eagerly on the rub board, and, most notably, organist Michael Smotherman elevating the proceedings with rich chords and, between verses, interjections of brisk solos that rhythmically mirror Steve's vocal attack.

When Tony Brown talked about how Steve's political songs had too often obscured his gift for writing love songs—"he writes great love songs," is Tony's assessment[12]—he had "Somewhere out There" in mind. From the moment Steve kicks off the song on 12-string with a tumbling riff that feels like a variation on a *Rubber Soul* theme, to when the band comes surging in behind him before a slight ritard as he enters vocally in that sandpapery soft voice he uses when he's getting close to something deep, it feels like a singular moment, majestic and moving, beauty and pain intermingling in the same breath. Indeed, he's singing to someone he's lost but still loves, achingly so ("it's tearing me all apart," he sings) and vows to wait for. The band's roiling commentary complements his emotional turmoil, with Steve himself adding an evocative 12-string solo that comes right out of the Roger McGuinn stylebook. It's hard not to hear it as a love letter to Teresa Ensenat, but in his notes Steve reveals nothing of his motives. "The less said the better," he states. "It's a personal issue."[13]

Moses at the burning bush, Columbus seeking directions, Davey Crockett at the Alamo, Robert Johnson at the crossroads—historical figures at pivotal moments—frame the narrative of the fanciful "You Know the Rest." Playing driving rock 'n' roll spiced with a little bluegrass—Ronnie McCoury cuts loose with a spirited solo about midway through, and Roy Huskey, Jr., is keeping the bottom steady with his slapping bass—the song is a lighthearted romp (which fact Steve acknowledges as the end when he sings that the song "ain't got no reason, hell, it barely rhymes"), an occasion for some lively instrumental interplay. It's also a humorous interpretation of history of the sort that rarely surfaced anymore in contemporary music but had long been common in country (of more recent vintage, Carl Perkins's "Let Me Tell You About Love" had been a No. 1 hit for the Judds in 1989) and occasionally in rock 'n' roll via such wacky absurdities as Larry Verne's 1960 chart-topping "Please Mr. Custer."

The forceful acoustic strumming that opens "N.Y.C." gives way after the opening verse to a furious grunge assault and a processed vocal by Steve that makes him sound like he's singing through a megaphone. An outgrowth of Steve's flirtation with grunge via a session at Ironwood Studios in Seattle with the Subpop group Supersuckers, "N.Y.C.," "a midlife crisis set to music," according to Steve,[14] describes a guitar-slinging hitchhiker, going to New York City for no reason other than he "likes the way it sounds" and he's "heard the girls are pretty." He's picked up by a fellow who's been there, done that and found out those pretty girls wouldn't talk to him. So he beat a retreat back to Tennessee,

STEVE EARLE & THE SUPERSUCKERS

where he mulls whether he should warn his young rider of what awaits him. Instead, he passes him a $20 bill and wishes him luck. The Seattle sessions were cut short when Steve returned to Nashville to attend Bill Monroe's funeral, but a five-song EP, *Steve Earle with the Supersuckers*, was released on Subpop that year to lukewarm reviews. Steve did a passable job covering the Supersuckers' "Creepy Jackalope Eye," and the Suckers gave Steve's "Angel Is the Devil" an earnest reading, but the same songs done by the original artists were more persuasive. A cover of a prime-time Keith Richards classic, "Before They Make Me Run," was approached a bit too reverentially to be memorable.

An exquisite heartbreaker, "Poison Lovers" is a wrenching admission of the toxicity between lovers who recognize both their repulsion and attraction to each other. Never at a loss for vibrant female vocalists to accompany him, Steve wrote this song intending to duet with Ray Kennedy's wife Siobhan. Ray and Siobhan, an Irish lass, had met years earlier when Ray was hired to work on a record by a group called Kindred Spirit, which was a project teaming Siobhan with ex-Bangle Debbie Peterson, for Miles Copeland's I.R.S. label, home of the Police. Prior to Kindred Spirit, Siobhan had spent more than a decade in a popular English band called River City People, which was signed to EMI in London. On "Poison Lovers," she adds a light, chirping presence to the track, her airy voice sounding wistful but determined. And appropriately, on a song that stands with early beauties such as "Someday," someone, either Steve or David Steele, adds a familiar, and plaintive, twangy solo from where Richard Bennett lived on Steve's first two albums. "Poison Lovers" was one of three songs Steve wrote in Galway, Ireland. "It's a great spot to write as it turns out," Steve says, "one of those towns like Key West and Santa Fe where tourist money allows a permanent slacker population to exist. I've always been comfortable in places like that."[15]

The sound of a vinyl record crackling introduces a Western swing tearjerker, "The Other Side of Town," with the Del McCoury Band's Jason Carter entering early with a moaning fiddle solo that he sustains throughout the song; Tommy Hannum joins the fray on steel guitar, adding keening fills around Carter's lines, then commanding center stage for a solo break ahead of another spotlight turn for Carter. Somewhere in the midst of all this the ghost of Bob Wills must have been smiling at the sorrowful lyrics made more intensely painful by the virtuoso musicians' sense of the dramatic. The lyric is about a place everyone goes to nurse their broken hearts, a place located in no-man's-land and where, in anonymity, they can drown in their sorrow. Steve likens the narrative to that moment in his life when he indulged his drug habit in the projects in South Nashville "because black people generally don't listen to my music and don't know who I am."[16]

The last 11 seconds of "The Other Side of Town" are nothing but the sound of a needle clicking in a record's end groove. No sooner does it end than do we hear the steady riffing on the top string of an electric guitar and Steve announcing his "manifesto," another song that addresses who he is, where he's been, and where he's at now. He sings of having blood on his hands, scars and broken hearts on the path he's walked to get here. The verse stops and after a "1-2-3-4!" countdown takes off like a Ramones blitzkrieg fueled by a fierce, driving, distorted electric guitar riff fashioned by Steve's son Justin, in his first appearance on record. "It's intentionally arrogant," Steve says of the song, "a State of Me song."[17]

That romp sets up a plaintive sendoff to *El Corazón* in Steve's tribute to Townes Van Zandt. Although the full band comes in on the second verse and establishes an eerie hum throughout, with steel guitarist Tommy Hannum breaking out midway for a lovely, mournful solo of delicate beauty, the album's circle is complete with Ray Kennedy's harmonium lending a music box delicacy, as he did on the opening "Christmas in Washington."

* * *

El Corazón was a typical quick record for Steve, but the sessions were not without their frustrations, at least for Mark Stuart. After his stewardship of Steve through the years of madness, Mark was feeling some bond between them and a sense that Steve was "targeting" him to be in his band proved out when he was asked to join the I Feel Alright tour. He thought he would be playing electric guitar, his main instrument, but instead, Steve used him as a utility man, filling in on mandolin, organ, acoustic piano, and rhythm guitar. On the road Steve started working up, and into the set, some of the new material that wound up on *El Corazón*.

"[Steve] was writing newer material that was gonna be the *El Corazón* stuff, and we would work those songs up at sound check," Mark says. "The New York City song was one of them we worked out; 'Somewhere Out There'; maybe another one. And we would play these at sound check, and by the end of the I Feel Alright tour, we were already starting to play these songs in the set. He would throw 'em in as an encore number."[18]

When the album sessions came around, Mark brought David Steele from his band into the studio lineup, expecting they would divide the guitar duties. But "once again, he bumped me back to where I was playing no guitar; David Steele was doing it all. Steve and Ray Kennedy were putting me on a mandola, acoustic guitar, which was just buried in the mix; it was very much not an issue in the record. I played on about half the record. But it was very frustrating because I wasn't playing much guitar, and Steve, very much aware of that, told me, 'You're gonna do all the harmonies on the whole record. You're gonna do all the singing on it.' In fact, I did no singing on it. So that was sort of like the real turning point when I realized that there's no future in this for me and I need to get back to what I'm doing."

For the first time Steve and Ray Kennedy billed their collaboration as "the Twang Trust" on an album. Anyone who didn't understand the moniker hadn't been paying attention to Steve's music lo these many years. In the studio as coproducers Steve and Ray developed their own chain of command that was, according to Mark Stuart, deceptive to the naked eye.

"Steve has a really, really strong overpowering kind of personality. So you constantly feel like Steve is the one driving the boat. But at the same time Ray had a very pronounced influence on everything you were doing. You kinda got the impression that sometimes, really, Ray was the one silently—as far as production and technical things—making a lot of the wise decisions, but Steve was barking louder. [Steve] certainly is on top of what he wants when it comes to the song and maybe the arrangement of the song; he's writing them, of course. But Ray very much is quite a musical mind and has a pretty big force in it. They were partners, and Ray had a lot of input into what was going on. And Steve knew that deep inside. I know that he knew that. So he treated Ray wonderfully. But if you're not one of those guys who Steve feels like he's getting something out of, you're very likely to be treated badly. It's one of his bad traits, I think."

* * *

The last anyone would hear of Roy Huskey, Jr,. on a Steve Earle record couldn't have been more appropriate, the Western swing weeper, "The Other Side of Town." It spoke musically to Roy's heritage as the son of Junior Huskey, one of the most beloved and most sought-after Nashville session bass players in the '50s and '60s, who had been recruited by John McEuen and the Nitty Gritty Dirt Band to join the elite players on their magnificent 1972 tribute to traditional country music, *Will the Circle Be Unbroken.*

Peter Rowan met Junior Huskey in the '60s, when both were playing the Grand Ole Opry, Rowan as a member of Bill Monroe's Bluegrass Boys, Huskey with any number of artists who wanted to enlist the best bass player in town for their gig.

"[Junior] made the acoustic bass have a recording presence that few others could," Rowan says. "He just pulled those strings in a certain way that there was a tremendous, sharp, definitive bump, like a push from the note. And for whatever you were doing, it made everything easy."[19]

Rowan moved away from Nashville in 1967, and when he returned 17 years later, Junior's son Roy was heralded as the finest bass player around. He became a fixture in Rowan's Crucial Country bluegrass nights at the Station Inn, and a beloved confidant. Roy was only seven when his father passed away. He had inherited all of Junior's instruments, and one day, according to Rowan, "without ever having practiced he picked up the bass and made it his own."

Like his father before him, Roy was "getting a tremendous snap out of them. He had the whole slap thing down. But never having seen Roy practice, I had no idea. It's almost like he was born complete with everything. He'd always surprise you; he'd always have a new little touch. There's a particular actual musical thing that comes out of that old way of playing bass in Nashville, which is because so many country songs go to the V chord before they end, do that little turnaround at the end. But if you're playing bum-bum-bum-bum, the chord goes to that second note. So you don't want to play that second note, the fifth, as part of the pattern before you go into the V chord, because you'll have already given it away. All the bass players in town have a way of syncopating the beat with a little run; how they reach the last phrase of the song is a real classic thing. There's kind of signature runs, and Roy knew them all, had the complete stockpile. Even if the chord changed, he could stay on the chord before and make it sound right. And the thing about Roy is that he saw music in terms of colors and textures. He knew a certain note had a certain color. You know, we talked the same language. I'm big on tone, and one of the things that happens during the recording process is the altering of the tone of things. Many people very quickly settle for what's on tape and go, 'Well, that's it.' Roy was able to pull a tone out of the bass that never lost the vibrancy and kind of 'fat' acoustic thing. It's certainly an art, because there's plenty of bass players that have their own way of doing it, but nobody could quite get that thick, vibrant pulse that Roy could get."

Ronnie McCoury did some session work with Huskey, Jr., and like everyone else came away awestruck at what he witnessed. He remembers Huskey, Jr., as "a real quiet-natured guy who was a musical genius" who had perfect pitch, and "saw music in colors.

"The first things ever written about music were written by monks and it was all in colors," McCoury says "Each chord had a color. Roy didn't know all this; he was pretty much just a country guy. But they say when he was little he would tell his mother, 'Play the red records.' Each chord was in a color."

Roy died in September 1997 after a two-year bout with cancer. McCoury was told that on his deathbed, Roy woke up and said, "I know what chord the universe is tuned in, in Gabriel's horn. It's B-flat, it's real black."

With that, Roy reached up "like he hit a bass note. And that was it."[20]

• • •

On the way to *The Mountain*, Steve's activist bent—specifically his opposition to the death penalty—placed him in a spot that only strengthened his conviction that "if it's wrong to kill, it's wrong to kill."[21]

Jonathan Wayne Nobles, sentenced to die by lethal injection for murdering two young girls, had been corresponding with Steve for nearly 10 years as he appealed his sentence. Once a violent inmate, he had experienced a spiritual transformation while incarcerated, leading to his becoming a Franciscan friar. As Nobles's early October execution date neared, Steve, whom Nobles had asked to witness his execution ("so there would be one person there who didn't hate me," Nobles said), spent nearly two weeks in Huntsville, Texas, visiting with the condemned man every day.

Steve knew the Huntsville prison well. In June 1998 he had joined up with the death penalty abolition group Journey of Hope on its 17-day mission in Texas "against and information about the death penalty around the state of Texas, led by the families of murder victims," Steve wrote in note posted on the steveearle.net Web site. Sister Helen Prejean, author of *Dead Man Walking*, was among the group, and Steve performed at every rally. "Texas is not suiting up and showing up at our events," Steve wrote. "We expected it to be tough down here, but this makes me ashamed to be a Texan."[22]

At home in Ashland City, Tennessee, where they had relocated near the end of 1994, Jack and Barbara Earle were taking it easy when the phone rang on a sunny September day. The caller was Jonathan Wayne Nobles, then only hours from his execution.

"I just wanted to see if you were all right, so I could tell Steve when he gets here," Nobles said to Barbara. He asked how Justin was doing, and before hanging up said, "I just wanted to let you know that Steve's gonna be all right." Steve had told Nobles that his mother was worried about him witnessing the execution.

"I was impressed because he was about to die," Barbara says of Nobles's call. "Steve was really surprised when he heard about that. When they cremated him after he was executed, Steve had made him a promise to get his ashes to Ireland, and it was a time before he could go. So the ashes were delivered to Steve's house. They delivered them and they were on the mantle, and stayed there for some months until Steve could take them to Ireland. I told Steve they were a benign presence, because that man was no longer even close to being the person he was when he committed the crime—that's the thing. You're not executing the same person. He had been a drug addict and killed people, but when he was executed, he was a Franciscan friar. They buried him in his robe."[23]

To the Houston *Press* (in a piece filed by John Lomax III's son John Nova Lomax) Steve recounted Nobles's final moments: "His mother had finally called, and for the first time in the 12 years he was in prison, he was allowed to talk to her. She told him that she used to love the way he sang 'Silent Night' when he was a little boy. So, as his last act, he sang this carol for the mother who'd abused him and who'd allowed his stepfather to abuse him, and then, at a prearranged signal, the IV was switched on.

"Suddenly, in the middle of the word *child*, all the air blew out of his lungs. It was a really loud sound, like 'HUHHH!' and it looked like an invisible cinder block had dropped on his chest. The force was so violent his head pitched forward and his glasses bounced off his chest and fell on the floor. Then his eyes became fixed and he didn't move anymore."[24]

"He didn't have the right to do what he did," Barbara says of Nobles, "but we don't have the right to do what we did to him, either. But I don't know when Texas is ever going to get turned around. I love Texas, but they're pretty bloodthirsty."

For Steve, witnessing Nobles's execution steeled his resolve to speak out against the death penalty whenever and wherever he could. After Sister Helen Prejean, he became America's most visible opponent of capital punishment, with the roots of his dissent deep in the heart of the place he called home, a place he was finding more difficult to recognize as it set the pace in killing convicts.

"Texas is getting harder and harder for me," Earle told Andrew Dasby of *Texas Music* magazine. "It's where I grew up, and it's still home and I still miss it. But a lot of it has to do with the fact that I watched the state of Texas kill somebody two years ago, and that definitely colors the way I feel about it when I get on a plane or bus to go to Texas.

"So many people have been executed that it's created this really ugly dynamic," he opined to Dasby. "People are starting to look twice at the death penalty—if for no other reason than because it's becoming obvious that sometimes people are executed who are innocent. It came close to happening several times that we know of in Illinois, and I know of several cases where I'm absolutely sure that innocent people were executed in Texas and elsewhere. But in Texas, if they stop killing tomorrow, that's tantamount to admitting that they're wrong for killing. There's 460 people on death row in Texas now, there's a lot of blood on their hands. Once they stop killing, they have to admit that they might have been wrong for killing all the people that they killed before that. So Texas has more of a twisted incentive to keep killing than anything else because it means having to atone for all the people that died before. It's going to be harder to change in Texas than anyplace else. It's one of the reasons I fought so hard to keep the first execution from happening in Tennessee."[25]

* * *

The Mountain
E-Squared/Artemis, 1999
Steve Earle and the Del McCoury Band

Produced and mixed by the twangtrust and Ronnie McCoury
Recorded by Ray Kennedy at Room and Board, Nashville, Tennessee; assisted by Patrick Earle
Mastered by Hank Williams at Master-mix, Nashville, Tennessee

Musicians
Steve Earle: guitar, vocal
Del McCoury: guitar, vocal
Ronnie McCoury: mandolin, vocal
Rob McCoury: banjo
Jason Carter: fiddle
Mike Bub: bass

Songs
1. "Texas Eagle" (3:28) (Steve Earle)
2. "Yours Forever Blue" (2:30) (Steve Earle)
3. "Carrie Brown" (4:18) (Steve Earle) Del McCoury: tenor vocal
4. "I'm Still in Love with You" (4:04) (Steve Earle) with Iris DeMent: vocals; Stuart Duncan, Jason Carter: twin fiddles; Gene Wooten: dobro
5. "The Graveyard Shift" (2:36) (Steve Earle) Ronnie McCoury: tenor vocal
6. "Harlan Man" (3:20) (Steve Earle) Steve Earle: mandolin; Ronnie McCoury: guitar and harmony vocal
7. "The Mountain" (4:43) (Steve Earle) Ronnie McCoury: harmony vocal; Jerry Douglas: dobro
8. "Outlaw's Honeymoon" (2:02) (Steve Earle)
9. "Connemara Breakdown" (2:17) (Steve Earle) Steve Earle and Ronnie McCoury: mandolins; Stuart Duncan and Jason Carter: fiddles
10. "Leroy's Dustbowl Blues" (3:04) (Steve Earle) Del McCoury: tenor vocal; Gene Wooten: dobro

11. "Dixieland" (2:56) (Steve Earle) Dan Gillis: tin whistle
12. "Paddy on the Beat" (2:00) (Steve Earle) Steve Earle: mandolin; Ronnie McCoury: bouzouki; Stuart Duncan and Jason Carter: fiddles
13. "Long, Lonesome Highway Blues" (2:58) (Steve Earle) Del McCoury: tenor vocal
14. "Pilgrim" (5:27) (Steve Earle) Sam Bush: mandolin; Ronnie McCoury: bouzouki; Jerry Douglas: dobro; Stuart Duncan: low fiddle; Steve Earle and Rob McCoury: guitars; Steve Earle: high-string guitar

Harmonies (in order of appearance): Emmylou Harris, Sam Bush, Kathy Chiavola, Tim O'Brien, Gillian Welch and Dave Rawlings

Chorus: Lisa Huskey, Taylor Huskey, J. T. Huskey, Steve Earle, John Hartford, Ronnie McCoury, Emmylou Harris, Meghann Ahern, Marty Stuart, Cowboy Jack Clement, Dave Ferguson, Sam Bush, Tim O'Brien, Kathy Chiavola, Gillian Welch, Dave Rawlings, Benny Martin and Peter Rowan

Born in Bakersville, North Carolina, on February 1, 1939, Delano Floyd (Del) McCoury was introduced to bluegrass music by his brother Jerry, by way of Grand Ole Opry radio broadcasts on Saturday nights, and, in 1950, by his first listen to a Flatt and Scruggs recording, namely, "Rolling in My Sweet Baby's Arms." Teaching himself from Flatt and Scruggs recordings, Del became a proficient banjo player. In 1958 he teamed up with another musician, Keith Daniels, to form Keith Daniels and the Blue Ridge Partners. McCoury then went into the service, but was soon discharged for medical reasons. Returning home he joined his brother Jerry in the Franklin County Boys and then in the Virginia Playboys, who were led by Bill Monroe alum Jack Cooke. Monroe attended one of Cooke's shows and was impressed enough to take ask both Cooke and McCoury to go out on the road with him to fill in for some band members who couldn't make the next trip. In February 1963 Monroe invited McCoury to become a full-time Bluegrass Boy, on guitar, and McCoury accepted, staying for nearly a year, into early 1964, when he quit to move to California to work with another group. When that gig didn't pan out to his satisfaction, he relocated to York County, Pennsylvania, where he worked construction at a local nuclear power plant for a bit before taking a job with a logging company. In his off hours he continued to develop his music in the fertile bluegrass scene in the Pennsylvania-Maryland-Virginia axis. In 1967 he formed his own band, Del McCoury and the Dixie Pals, which had a floating membership and was more a hobby than a dogged pursuit.

"Back then I didn't take it as seriously as I do now," Del says. "It was more of fun thing. Musicians would come and go. I played the bluegrass festivals on weekends, sometimes a thousand miles away, just to keep a band together. I did that all through the '70s. I recorded some pretty good albums and had some good bands, especially for being just part-time."[26]

Indeed, Del was becoming a fan favorite in the bluegrass world. Blessed with a keening mountain tenor, he could deliver the high lonesome sound with the best of his generation and had a unique way with phrasing that enhanced the drama of his heartbreakers and brought the party home on the barnburners. This being the bluegrass world, the musicianship in his bands was always impeccable but never sanitized—it was always about performance and feel. And not least of all, Del cut an impressive figure onstage. Always impeccably attired in a nice suit and tie, as were his bandmates, with his full head of hair sprayed tightly into place, he never seemed at a loss for a warm smile or a friendly word. It wasn't about show, his appearance, but about respect for the music, as he had been taught by the master, Bill Monroe.

During his tenure as a Bluegrass Boy, Peter Rowan had questioned Monroe about his attire. "I asked him what was the thing about the white shirt, because that was kind of legendary. He kept bragging, 'Before I came on the Opry everybody wore checkered shirts. I had the first white shirts on the Opry.' I asked him, What was that from? He said he played for country people, farmers who only put on a white shirt to go to church on Sunday; they had one white shirt. He said country people would understand the pride he took in his music if they saw him dressed up like that, with a tie and everything. It was unheard of. You look at pictures of the Grand Ole Opry, there's only one guy in a tie and that's Bill Monroe and his band. To give respect to the music."[27]

In 1981 Del's 13-year-old son Ronnie joined the band part-time on mandolin, the instrument that had possessed him from the time he had been allowed to play Bill Monroe's mandolin backstage after a show at New York's Lincoln Center. In 1987 Del's other son, Robbie, joined up, first on bass, then moving over to banjo, on which he would be recognized as one of the genre's finest players. With so many McCourys around, it seemed only natural that the group should now be billed as the Del McCoury Band. Recording for Rounder (Del's home, off and on, since the early '70s), the band's 1990 album *Don't Stop the Music* featured a powerful Del original, "I Feel the Blues Moving In," that garnered a Song of the Year nomination from the International Bluegrass Music Association (IBMA) and significantly elevated the band's national profile.

In 1992 Del and his family relocated to Nashville, and the band's lineup solidified with the addition of bassist Mike Bub and fiddler extraordinaire Jason Carter. Their 1993 album, *A Deeper Shade of Blue*, introduced this formidable quintet, as well as a new production team in Ronnie McCoury and Jerry Douglas, the latter also being the most gifted dobro player of his time. At that point Del and the boys started rolling, picking up IBMA awards almost as a matter of course, drawing to their shows fans from outside the hardcore bluegrass constituency and generating critical acclaim across the spectrum of music publications and in august journals such as *The New York Times*. Del proved himself open to new ideas suggested by his young charges in the band, and with that his repertoire expanded in fascinating ways, as he found bluegrass footholds in folk-flavored tunes from the likes of the respected Nashville singer-songwriter David Olney ("Queen Anne's Lace," from 1992's *Blue Side of Town*), in Lefty Frizzell's vibrant warhorse, "If You've Got the Money, Honey" (from *A Deeper Shade of Blue*), in an early George Jones–penned waltz, "Don't Stop the Music" (the reconfigured titled tune from the like-titled 1990 album). In more recent years Del's offered up a gleeful rendition of Frank Sinatra's "Learnin' the Blues," giving the 1951 jilted lover's lament an attitude adjustment, and an intense rendering of folk-rocker Richard Thompson's "1952 Vincent Black Lightning," with Ronnie's fleet-fingered mandolin lines underscoring the desperation driving the song's fugitive narrator (both songs appear on 2001's *Del and the Boys* album). And although they never met, Del's path crossed that of Steve Earle in 1992, when Rounder's Ken Irwin suggested Del record an early Earle tune, "If You Need a Fool." After listening to Steve's version, Del agreed to cut it but thought it was too short. Irwin tracked Steve down in California, and shortly afterward, Steve phoned in another verse.

"Steve told me later that was a really down time for him," Del says in the liner notes to *High Lonesome and Blue*, a Rounder anthology of his work for the label. "He was in bad shape." In his liner notes for the McCoury Band's 1996 *Cold Hard Facts* album, Steve wrote that the verse he supplied "turned out to be the only four lines I would write for the next three and a half years."

◦ ◦ ◦

"There's your ghost story, son"

Ronnie's expectation that it would be another year or so from the time they recorded "I Still Carry You Around" to the beginning of sessions for the bluegrass album they agreed to do with Steve turned out to be off, way off. "It was only a few months, and we were in the studio with Ray Kennedy," he says, still amazed at how quickly it all came together. "It was sometime in the fall."

Steve had been showing up on Tuesday nights at the Station Inn, where Ronnie held forth with his band the Sidemen, which included some of his Del McCoury Band mates, sitting in and working up what Ronnie now knows to be songs that he had written for the bluegrass album. And, as Tony Brown had observed of Steve years earlier, the artist was doing his homework. He constantly quizzed Ronnie about "some elements of bluegrass songs," Ronnie says, explaining that "I told him some things he may not have got together. He'd listen to some, but of course I'm born and bred. He kind of knew the foundation of bluegrass—lost love and all that, heartache—I said, 'Of course, there's the gospel element,' and there's this and that, but I had mentioned something about a ghost—I said, 'There's even ghost songs.'"

The Del McCoury Band

The Cold Hard Facts

The next time he came to the Station Inn, Steve performed a slow, haunting ballad about the memories that haunt an old miner after the coal company seals the hole in the mountain where he had worked.

"He got done and he said, 'There's your ghost story, son,'" Ronnie recalls. "It was 'The Mountain.'

"He took everything—he's a sponge," Ronnie adds. "Anything you say he's gonna soak it up.

"I had nothing to do with any of his songwriting. He already had in mind what he was gonna do. It's funny. He recorded the record in the sequence he wanted it, which I had never done before. I thought that was really interesting. That was the way he wanted to do it. So he already had in mind what he wanted to do. He just needed us to help him get it across."

The result of the McCoury-Earle collaboration is a moment of breathtaking musicianship and instrumental interplay, finely honed tunes that seem channeled whole cloth from an earlier time in American song and history. And Steve turns in some vocal performances that, even in their ragged moments, reveal a depth of commitment from somewhere deep in the heart. It can be understood intellectually, it can be parsed for its critical components, but ultimately its impact comes from the indelible mark it traces on the listener's spirit.

Following a curious prelude—Steve intoning, "M-I-C-K-E-Y, M-O—you gotta put your hat on, boy. Awright. You wanna be in the band, you have to put your hat on," he strums his acoustic gently, quickly picking up the pace until the McCoury Band enters, with Jason Carter sawing a sprightly line that evokes a train rumbling down the tracks; sure enough, it's the "Texas Eagle." A tale at least semi-autobiographical, it recounts the narrator's memories of riding the old Texas Eagle railroad with his granddad, all the way to Palestine, and from there hitching back. When he grows up he rides the same train to San Antone. A final verse describes the demise of the line, although the sound of its whistle remains vivid in the narrator's mind. The song is a showcase for Carter's furious fiddle work, but Ronnie McCoury on mandolin engages him periodically in some spirited instrumental give and take.

Bluegrass heartache takes center stage for the next two numbers, a lilting tune of lost love, "Yours Forever Blue," with Robbie giving a banjo clinic with his plaintive solos, and "Carrie Darling," a spirited duet between Steve and Del recounting the murder of the narrator's rival for the affections of Carrie Brown, with Carter injecting striking swirling lines between verses that sound like the bluegrass interpretation of Bernard Hermann's screaming *Psycho* soundtrack violins.

From the vaunted legacy of old flames reuniting, the yearning "I'm Still In Love with You" finds Steve dueting with a mournful Iris DeMent in a wrenching tearjerker, as mandolin and fiddle pour on the sorrow. "That's a great cut," Ronnie says. "After it was finished, Steve said, 'I'm in love again,'" ominous words to be sure.

"Graveyard Shift," a perhaps too jolly story of a ladies' man who delights in stealing women who have been neglected by their significant others, sets up two of the most vivid and moving songs Steve had ever recorded back to back, both addressing the working class that bluegrass had embraced from the pioneering days of Bill Monroe. In "Harlan Man," Steve nasally articulates the determination of a Harlan County, Kentucky, coal miner to stay on the job as long as his luck and lungs hold out. Driving hard to the song's finale, Steve's mandolin pushes the arrangement as Jason Carter steps up with some urgent fiddle lines. All the while down in the mix Robbie McCoury flails away on banjo and Mike Bub maintains a persistent *click-clack* on the standup bass.

Nervous, trilling mandolin lines introduce "The Mountain," just ahead of Jason Carter's wailing fiddle lines and Jerry Douglas's moaning interjections on dobro. Steve proceeds to describe an old miner's sorrow at finding the mine where he worked his whole life now sealed up, its memories and secrets buried deep underground and in the memories of only those who worked way down below. Carter has a beautiful fiddle solo at the midway point, which gives way to another aching, poignant dobro turn from Jerry Douglas. "The Mountain" climbs to an epic plateau on the edge of restraint. Steve, with a deliberate, weary vocal that magnifies the old miner's horror at the scene he sees unfolding, Carter and Douglas on solos that are models of economy and impassioned commentary.

Following the drama of "Harlan Man" and "The Mountain," the light-hearted, finger-picked "Outlaw's Honeymoon" is a welcome breather with a nice ensemble instrumental passage between verses and a wry lyric worthy of John Prine, all the more appropriate since the song is so in the Prine style. The same spirit informs the bustling instrumental "Connemara Breakdown," an energetic workout for Steve and Ronnie on mandolins and especially for the twin fiddles played by Stuart Duncan and Jason Carter.

"Leroy's Dustbowl Blues," for all its high energy and feisty instrumental work—the late Gene Wooten on dobro practically owns the song with his pungent solo lines throughout—tells the tragic tale of an Oklahoma farmer wiped out by the dust storms and trekking west to California for a better deal. No Tom Joad he—before he can even reach the West Coast paradise, state police beat him bloody and toss him on the roadside, where he contemplates his next move knowing his children are hungry and dressed in rags. No moralizing here; rather, it's a tale of bones and dreams shattered, and questions looming that can't be any better answered in the Golden State than they could have been in the Sooner State.

(In January of 2000, in the midst of teaching a seven-week course at the Chicago Folk Institute, Steve told Chicago *Sun-Times* reporter Bobby Reed that "Leroy's Dustbowl Blues" was a "pressure" song written on the spur of the moment when he realized he needed another uptempo tune for *The Mountain*. In one of his classroom lectures, Steve had illustrated for his students how Woody Guthrie had borrowed melodies or lyrics from older songs and then retooled them for use in his own songs. Now he could use himself as an example of such artful appropriation. "I lifted two things," he said of "Leroy's" genesis. "I lifted the subject matter from [Guthrie's] 'Do-Re-Mi,' and I lifted the phrasing from "Tombstone Blues" by Bob Dylan."[28])

One of Steve's most powerful story songs blended fact, fiction, and stirring Irish music, recalling nothing so much as *Copperhead Road*'s "Johnny Come Lately" in its style and narrative. In "Dixieland," Steve sings in the voice of an Irish "fightin' man" named Kilran, who escapes certain hanging by the British by fleeing to America on the vessel *Arrianne*. Once here and being a "fightin' man," he signs up with the 20th Maine infantry unit, one of the most famous in Civil War history. Organized in Portland, Maine, in August 1862, the 20th was mustered into federal service on August 29, its ranks numbering 961 officers and enlisted men. The regiment's original lieutenant colonel was Joshua Lawrence Chamberlain, who was wounded six times during the war and by

1865 had assumed the rank of major general. The 20th fought in some of the war's bloodiest battles, including Antietam, Chancellorsville and Gettysburg, among others. In "Dixieland," Kilran speaks with pride of fighting for Chamberlain, whose courage he extols for standing forthright with his men "when the Johnnies came like a banshee on the wind." Again and again Kilran emphasizes that he's a "fightin' man" and expresses disdain for all who are not. After Gettysburg, when "the air smelled like death," Kilran looks around and sees a tale told in the day's violence: "And we spilled our blood in the battle's heat / Now we're all Americans …"

In advancing Steve's narrative, the McCoury Band's rousing ensemble voice is a thing of beauty, as is a production that allows Ronnie's bustling mandolin lines and Jason Carter's keening fiddle excursions to ascend from the mix between verses and then smoothly recede when Steve enters to continue the story. Wafting over the top, Dan Gillis's tin whistle (like the Pogues' Spyder Stacey's on "Johnny Come Lately") has an eerie but triumphant presence. (Gillis is Steve's road manager-turned-manager, former bus driver and, it appears, occasional guest musician.)

In recognition of its unparalleled contribution to the Union effort, the 20th Maine was chosen to receive the Confederate Army's colors and arms when General Robert E. Lee's Army of Northern Virginia surrendered at Appomattox Court House on April 9, 1865. And Major General Chamberlain would become president of Bowdoin College, the governor of Maine, and a recipient of the Congressional Medal of Honor.[29]

With Ronnie on bouzouki, Steve on mandolin and Carter and Duncan on twin fiddles, another captivating Irish melody ensues, this a sweet-natured instrumental titled "Paddy on the Beat." Sounding every bit like an intentional, healing retort to the brusque entreaties of Kilran in "Dixieland," the tune's lilting, rolling rhythm and those evocative twin fiddles evoke a calm after the storm, a healing. When it ends, there's a pause, after which Steve announces, "White people could dance to that one."

The album ends with Steve and Del teaming up on a rough-and-tumble "Long, Lonesome Highway Blues," a pretty standard upbeat workout, which serves as a setup for the closing hymn, "The Pilgrim," at 5:27 one of the longest cuts in Steve's body of work. In all its solemn grace, Steve, with Emmylou Harris harmonizing, signals the end of the journey that has been *The Mountain*. The pilgrim he sings of, as Sam Bush plucks a resonant solo on mandolin and Stuart Duncan blesses the proceedings with a sturdy, humming solo on low fiddle, is Roy Huskey, Jr., who's seen as merely a visitor to this planet, on his way to a greater reward in heaven. An all-star lineup of musicians who knew Roy, alongside some Huskey family members, join in on the chorus.

But in the context of the journey this album describes from first cut to last, "The Pilgrim" serves a greater purpose, as the final testament of the character

Steve's embodied here. At the song's close, the poignant vision remaining is of a solitary man traveling on a long gone railroad to places where ghosts haunt the memories of old coal miners, old soldiers, old lovers; where those memories are stained by blood; and where hearts, wounded but undeterred, continue their quest for love.

* * *

A Conversation with Ronnie McCoury

"That record is just oozing with feel"

Of *The Mountain* sessions, Ronnie McCoury recalls, "We did it as live as possible, and we did it in one room together. Steve stood facing us as the five of us kind of faced him. He would run down some songs. He asked me to coproduce it with him. He knew that's where I come from. I was really excited about all that. I kind of got to dip into his world, the way they record and everything. And they have some old equipment, from Apple Studios. Steve of course is a Beatles fanatic, and so is Ray, and they really try to break down the records—like *Rubber Soul* had a lot of acoustic guitar stuff in it, and that sound is what they really enjoyed. It's got a lot of compression to it, which is totally different from the way we do things, so that was a learning experience for me. I know that he had a couple of mandolin tunes that he wanted to do; as far as producing goes, I said it'd be good if we had twin fiddles on a couple of cuts. I got Gene Wooten to play dobro. He was an awesome player, but he passed away. On 'Leroy's Dustbowl Blues' he really tore it up and it was exciting for Steve."

You mentioned that they recorded differently than what you were used to. What are the differences in their approach and yours?

A lot more isolation. We're normally in the same room because you get a whole-room sound, you know. But you're baffled more; baffles sitting between you in case of mistakes that you have to redo. Not normally in a booth, but that does happen with a lot of recording sessions. You get into a booth where you're totally isolated. But with Steve, we did it in that one room, standing all together. That gives you that live, spontaneous thing—you gotta do it, there's no fixing it. Which is exciting. That's the way bluegrass was recorded all through the '40s, '50s, '60s, a lot into the '70s, then it got into being isolated a lot more. But that gives you that sound and that's what Steve wanted.

Do you recall any of the cuts as being particularly difficult to get? Did you labor over anything?

You know, I don't recall anything being too difficult or we weren't getting it. As I had a buddy say, "It's warts and all" on the record. Sure, there's some things that may not be perfect, but it's the feel. That record is just oozing with feel.

What did you observe of the relationship between Steve and Ray Kennedy?

Steve would call Ray "the mad scientist." He had no worries about what Ray was doing. That's how I felt. I forgot what number record that was for him, but he had really cranked 'em out. He knew what he was gonna do. He would come in and just sing; if he overdubbed anything, it was just a line or a couple of words. It was very fast. He's not the type of guy who sits there and sings it a thousand times. He let Ray do what he does. He may have a little bit of input, but from what I remember it wasn't much. He just trusted Ray so much.

Did Ray have any interaction with you and the band?

I tell you what, he really had a lot of faith in what we had to say. I helped him mix the record. He definitely wanted me to be there and to help out; he felt more comfortable about me dealing with these acoustic instruments, because Ray's pretty much from the country rock 'n' roll world with electric guitars and drums. Of course, he knows what he's doing there; I know little about that. So I think he appreciated any input I might have. I know that he thanked me at the end for being there and helping out.

From a producer's standpoint, what's the key to recording acoustic instruments effectively?

You know, it's microphone selection, and to me, to get the absolute most natural sound out of the instrument that you can get, with little effect. I think once you do that, then it's the musician. That's it to me.

Do you have a preferred microphone for acoustic instruments?

Each one has the one that matches him the best. And of course everybody's always trying to show you something new and bring you something new. There's a lot of guys that stick to one thing and have for a lot of years. Me coming from the mandolin world, I kind of know what suits the mandolin. There's a Sony C30 that I like to use, and there's a Neumann KM84 that a lot of mandolin players have used through the years. Of course, in the old days the records that I love, they stick these big ol' Neuman 46s in front of the mandolins and they just turn it on. Those records that were done in the '40s and '50s were with, like, two microphones, three microphones. Amazing.

How did Steve fit in the bluegrass world? How do you assess him as a bluegrass player?

I think he really tried hard to do what we do and to dress the part and all that. At the beginning, he went out and got all these suits, and of course he buys the finest. He said, "You know, when I started this gig I didn't even use hair spray. I just stood beside Del waitin' for the fallout. Now I'm up to a bottle a week."

But musically he really tried. You know, he's coming from a whole different background. But he tried and really wanted to do it. I think he really enjoyed it.

• • •

Steve not only recorded with the Del McCoury Band; he toured *The Mountain* with them. And up to a point it was an eye-opener for the McCoury fellows. They were traveling in a style to which they would like to have become accustomed.

"I enjoyed it," Ronnie says of the jaunt with Steve. "I don't know how to say it. We had just never been on the road quite like that with the same thing every day where people take care of you. They did their best to take care of us, these guys did. Had a great sound guy on the road, and Steve's manager was on the road at that time, kind of road managing and taking care of us. All that was really great. And we'd step out there and do it every night, and I knew a lot of his one-liners by the end of tour. Boy, he's got 'em! Girls would yell, 'Copperhead Road'! 'Guitar Town'! And he'd say, 'Somebody put something in her mouth.' They'd be obnoxious. Some of the places were loud bar scenes, rock-club type. And then we'd play theaters where it wasn't as bad. He'd say, 'Hey, man, I think your chick's starting to dig me. You better quiet her down.' And he'd say a few that he was pretty vulgar about.

"Going to Europe was probably most beneficial for us. We'd been over there, but not like that, not hittin' a 30-day run and playing all these places where he's so appreciated—he's definitely more appreciated there than he is here. In Germany we played at the same place the Beatles played all that time they were there, a dance hall. Then we played the Royal Albert Festival Hall— Royal Albert Hall's beside it, it's like 6,000 seats; this one's like 2,500. We sold it out. Some of the places he hadn't been able to sell out, so I think there was a buzz about the show. We played maybe some more theaters than normal. I knew that he's got a rock club scene he hits over there and we did a lot of that."

But the tour disintegrated when it came back to the States, for a variety of reasons that had never been confirmed by the McCourys. It has been reported variously that Del was upset over Steve getting top billing over the McCoury Band at bluegrass festivals, over his band's rate versus Steve's, over having to play a shorter set than normal so that Steve could play his full set.

"I've read everything—money, dad opening," Ronnie says wearily. "My dad's not like that at all, and money was never the issue."

Rather, it was Steve's foul language on stage that bothered Del, a fact Ronnie ascribes simply to a "generation gap" between Del and Steve. "The fans that my dad had for years would come to the shows and bring their families, with kids. And my dad got letters from these people. Steve's language on stage really bothered my dad. I think my dad had had enough of that. The guys in the band were younger and more in tune with [Steve], but my dad's from a different era when it comes to onstage performances. But that's water under the bridge. I never had any problems with him. Dad and he, they've shook hands and everything's fine."

To finish out the tour Steve quickly assembled the Bluegrass Dukes, whose members were exceptional musicians, schooled in bluegrass and all manner of roots musics. They included multi-instrumentalist Tim O'Brien, Darrell Scott on dobro and banjo, Casey Driessen on fiddle, and Dennis Crouch on bass.

* * *

As 1998 bled into 1999, Steve was, as the Supremes once sang, "falling in and out of love again." A live-in romance with MCA A&R rep Kelley Walker began to fade out at the moment in mid-1998 when Steve encountered Sara Sharpe, a Wisconsin-born, Tennessee-raised death penalty abolitionist and aspiring actress who was active in the Journey of Hope. They met in an airport in Texas, where both had come to attend the Journey's Texas mission. Despite her feelings for Steve, and his for her, she kept him at arm's length for the longest time. She was then emerging a single mother of two from a failed marriage that had found her living the past six years a virtual hermit, in a cult, in South Pittsburgh, Tennessee.[30] Steve's courtship of Sara would be interrupted by her brief reconciliation with her husband, during which time he returned to Galway, Ireland, and worked on a group of short stories and wrote at least one new song, titled "Galway Girl," for a new album.[31] Eventually Sara divorced her husband, and she and her two children moved into a log cabin in the woods of Sewanee, Tennessee, about equidistant from Nashville and Chattanooga. Within a few months, their budding romance had flowered to the point where Steve moved into the cabin too, where he lived a sedate, orderly existence marked by a deep immersion in poetry, literature, and reflection. It was a fair distance from the days filled with drugs, guns, jails, desperation, and the roar of his insatiable ego.

* * *

Transcendental Blues
E-Squared/Artemis, 2000

Produced and mixed by the twangtrust
Mixed by Ray Kennedy
Assisted by Patrick Earle
Mastered by Hank Williams at Mastermix, Nashville, Tennessee

Songs and Musicians
 1. "Transcendental Blues" (4:13)
    (Steve Earle)

Recorded by Paul Smith at Frank's Auto, South Philly, Pennsylvania; additional recording by Ray Kennedy at Room & Board, Nashville, Tennessee, assisted by Patrick Earle
Steve Earle: guitars, harmonium, mini-Moog, vocals; Dan Metz: bass; Ron Vance: drums

2. "Everyone's in Love with You" (3:30) (Steve Earle)
Recorded by Ray Kennedy at Room and Board, assisted by Patrick Earle
Steve Earle: electric guitar, vocals; David Steele: electric guitar; Kelley Looney: bass; Will Rigby: drums, percussion; Tom Littlefield: vocals

3. "Another Town" (2:22) (Steve Earle)
Recorded by Ray Kennedy at Room and Board, assisted by Patrick Earle
Steve Earle: acoustic guitar, vocals; David Steele: electric guitars; Kelley Looney: bass; Will Rigby: drums, percussion

4. "I Can Wait" (3:16) (Steve Earle)
Recorded by Ray Kennedy at Room and Board, assisted by Patrick Earle
Steve Earle: 12-string acoustic, vocals; David Steele: electric guitar; Kelley Looney: bass; Will Rigby: drums, percussion; Tom Littlefield: vocals

5. "The Boy Who Never Cried" (3:46) (Steve Earle)
Recorded by Ray Kennedy at Room and Board, assisted by Patrick Earle
Steve Earle: 12-string guitar, harmonium, vocals; David Steele: bouzouki Kelley Looney: bass; Will Rigby: drums, percussion
Strings arranged and conducted by Kristin Wilkinson and performed by the Love Sponge: Kristin Wilkinson: viola; John Catchings: cello; David Angell: violin; David Davidson: violin

6. "Steve's Last Ramble" (3:38) (Steve Earle)
Recorded by Ciaran Byrne at Totally Wired Studios, Dublin, Ireland, assisted by Keith McDonald; additional recording by Ray Kennedy at Room and Board, assisted by Patrick Earle
Steve Earle: acoustic guitar, harmonica, vocals; Sharon Shannon: accordion; Mary Shannon: banjo; Liz Kane: fiddle; Yvonne Kane: fiddle; Jim Murray: gut-string guitar; Bill Wright: bouzouki; David Steele: electric guitar; James Blennerhassett: upright bass; Noel Bridgeman: drums

7. "The Galway Girl" (3:05) (Steve Earle)
Recorded by Ciaran Byrne at Totally Wired Studios, Dublin, Ireland, assisted by Keith McDonald; additional recording by Ray Kennedy at Room and Board, assisted by Patrick Earle
Steve Earle: Mandolin, vocals; Sharon Shannon: accordion; Mary Shannon: banjo; Liz Kane: fiddle; Yvonne Kane: fiddle; Jim Murray: guitar; Bill Wright: bouzouki; Dan Gillis: tin whistle; James Blennerhassett: upright bass; Joyce Redmond: bodhran; Noel Bridgeman: drums

8. "Lonelier Than This" (3:11) (Steve Earle)
   Recorded by Ray Kennedy at Room and Board, assisted by Patrick Earle
   Steve Earle: acoustic guitar, vocals; David Steele: Resonator guitar;
   Kelley Looney: bass; Ray Kennedy: electric guitar; Will Rigby: drums,
   percussion
9. "Wherever I Go" (1:57) (Steve Earle)
   Recorded by Ray Kennedy at Room and Board, assisted by Patrick Earle
   Steve Earle: electric guitar, acoustic guitar, vocals; David Steele: electric
   12-string guitar; Benmont Tench: organ, piano; Kelley Looney: bass;
   Will Rigby: drums
10. "When I Fall" (4:34) (Steve Earle)
    Recorded by Ray Kennedy at Room and Board, assisted by Patrick Earle
    Steve Earle: acoustic guitar, harmonica, vocals; Stacey Earle: vocals;
    Doug Lancio: electric guitars; Ray Kennedy: bass; Patrick Earle: drums,
    percussion
11. "I Don't Wanna Lose You Yet" (3:22) (Steve Earle)
    Recorded by Ray Kennedy at Room and Board, assisted by Patrick Earle
    Steve Earle: acoustic guitar, vocals; David Steele: electric guitars;
    Benmont Tench: organ; Kelley Looney: bass; Will Rigby: drums,
    percussion; Tom Littlefield: vocals
12. "Halo 'round the Moon" (2:13) (Steve Earle)
    Recorded by Ray Kennedy at Room and Board, assisted by Patrick Earle
    Steve Earle: Resonator guitar, harmonium, vocals; David Steele: Res-
    onator guitar; Kelley Looney: bass; Will Rigby: drums, percussion
13. "Until the Day I Die" (3:22) (Steve Earle)
    Recorded by Ray Kennedy at Room and Board, assisted by Patrick Earle
    Steve Earle: guitar, vocals; Tim O'Brien: mandolin, vocals; Darrell Scott:
    banjo, vocals; Casey Driessen: fiddle; Dennis Crouch: Upright bass
14: "All of My Life" (3:27) (Steve Earle)
    Recorded by Ray Kennedy at Room and Board, assisted by Patrick Earle
    Steve Earle: guitar, harmonium, vocals; Ray Kennedy: bass; Patrick
    Earle: drums, percussion
15. "Over Yonder (Jonathan's Song)" (3:21) (Steve Earle)
    Recorded by Ray Kennedy at Room and Board, assisted by Patrick
    Earle
    Steve Earle: acoustic guitar, harmonica, vocals; David Steele: mandola;
    Kelley Looney: bass; Will Rigby: drums, percussion

It opens with a harmonium droning a single, steady chord, and the background gets busy almost at once. Low voices can be heard speaking, with some
degree of urgency, although their words are inaudible; a swoosh of synth cuts
across the sound scape, someone strikes a glissando on the acoustic guitar as the

rhythmic pulse of a tabla emerges, and the voices rise again, more insistent, one of them a male with a vague British accent with a familiar ring—he sounds like the voice speaking the words "Number nine, number nine, number nine" on the Beatles' "Revolution No. 9" from the White Album. The harmonium drones on, the tabla gains momentum, the guitar slowly edges into a sturdy rhythm, drums kick in with a boom, and an electric guitar is playing a wiry, circular figure. Steve enters drawling, purposely straining his voice to its upper limit for effect, slurring his words to the point where it would be difficult to understand all but a few of the lyrics without consulting the lyric sheet. But the phrase "Transcendental blues" comes through loud and clear, and the album is under way. Then it gets more cluttered—with a synth buzzing away like a line with a short in it and the tabla—or what sounds like a tabla—in a spirited rhythmic monologue, until it all meshes into one big wall of sound and then, as suddenly as it began, it stops dead in its tracks, and all is silent. What it all means lyrically is open to interpretation—there's a reference to how nothing's changed on the highway, and how the back roads can't get a person to where he wants to go and leave a body only the "transcendental blues" to show for the effort. It's one of Steve's most inscrutable narratives, and perhaps that's meant to be. In his liner notes he worries—philosophically worries, that is—the whole matter of the definition of transcendence, never finding one to his satisfaction, until he concludes, "… for me, for now, transcendence is about being still long enough to know when it's time to move on. Fuck me."[32]

Which suggests he has no better answers than the befuddled listener, except to say that he's back out on that road again.

"Everyone's in Love with You" follows, and it picks up the drone from "Transcendental Blues" and hardens it into a pile-driving thrust, with guitar lines coiling around each other, percussion thundering, and double-tracked voices adding a rough texture to the title sentiment.

Two songs in and no one would be surprised to find out that during the sessions for *Transcendental Blues*, a copy of the Beatles' *Revolver* was sitting on the recording console. Indeed, to this point, the songs "Transcendental Blues" and "Everyone's in Love with You" sound like the bastard offspring of Lennon-McCartney's "Tomorrow Never Knows"—a point emphasized (or proven) when, following a stop-time measure, the voices return, in reverse, as the song fades out.

But the third song, "Another Town," returns to familiar Steve Earle territory, with a ringing acoustic chord signaling its start before the band comes in at a steady gallop and rocks its high-spirited way through the story of a fellow down on his luck who's bound and determined to head on down the road, to a place where he's sure he can make a brighter future for himself. Steve sings the song triumphantly, certain of the better fate that awaits him at the next stop, and David Steele emphasizes that feeling with a searing, snarling electric guitar solo that is the sound of a man breaking free, unencumbered, from darkness into light.

A similar forceful acoustic guitar riff, hard strummed, announces a touching mid-tempo love song, "I Can Wait," that has the same tension and release of *Copperhead Road*'s "Waiting on You" and a similar lyric about holding true to a feeling about someone, and hanging in until they find common ground, "as long as it takes." Steve's 12-string acoustic rings beautifully throughout the track. David Steele has a trebly, angular solo jumping out near the end, and new drummer Will Rigby, late of the dB's, keeps a steady, low-key beat on the bottom—simple, solid, unassuming drumming that gets the job done. Steve and Ray knew what they had in the heart-tugging choruses, and the production spins on the Beatles-like harmonizing of Steve and Tom Littlefield at those junctures.

With the harmonium droning behind him, Steve introduces the elliptical "The Boy Who Never Cried." The music at first is carried by the harmonium's drone, and the terse, brittle notes of a bouzouki (played by David Steele), until the end of the first verse, when a cello sounds an ominous warning; a few seconds later a string section (arranged by Kristin Wilkerson, returning from *I Feel Alright*'s "Valentine's Day" session) comes screeching in, like it was lifted from an outtake of the Beatles' "Baby, You're a Rich Man," adding to the dark tint. The boy's identity is never revealed, except that there are multiple hints that he could be Jesus—an only child, visited by pilgrims from faraway lands who congregated outside his birthplace. He grows to manhood, feared by the elders, who warn their daughters to beware the boy who never cries. Living alone his entire life, he finally sheds a tear on the day of his death, weeping for that same boy, who might be a vision of his younger, colder self, or someone else entirely.

In the November 30, 2000, issue of *Magnet*, Steve told writer Robert Baird of his finding that *Transcendental Blues* was a puzzlement to many of his fans. "I think there's a perception by some people that these songs aren't as well written as songs I've written in the past, simply because they tend to be more emotion-driven and relationship-driven and less narrative," he said. "But the truth is that the songs on this record were harder for me to write and, I think, harder for anybody to write and write well. My favorite song on *Transcendental Blues*—and it might be the song I'm proudest of as a writer in my entire career—is 'The Boy Who Never Cried.'"[33]

The depth of his commitment to Sara Sharpe is most evident in his own words in the stomping, shambling, Irish-tinged country-rocker "Steve's Last Ramble," a song whose very title is telling. Recorded at Totally Wired Studios in Dublin with the great Irish accordion virtuoso Sharon Shannon, the song is a toe-tapping testimonial to impending domesticity. Steve announces at the outset, in the very first stanza, in fact, that he's "thinkin'" about giving up his rambling ways. Conditional, yes, but it's still as far as he's ever gone in proclaiming his interest in settling down. He goes on to admit to feeling empty on the road without the one he loves in his arms. The second verse reiterates the sentiments of the first and reprises that familiar phrase of his, "highway sound," as he describes the lure of the road in times past; the third verse bids adieu to his road buddies Highway Dave and Southside Sue and muses about them passing a jug around, singing "the lonesome highway blues" in his absence. The track is joyous and celebrating, especially after the first verse, in a brief instrumental interlude when the fiddle, banjo, guitar, harmonica, and percussion break into a triumphant, gleeful bash. After the third verse, in which he sings about finding his way back home to his lover, he quickly shouts, "Here I come!" and the ensemble kicks into overdrive one final time before striking a clanging, closing chord.

Not a hint of sorrow, not a hint of second guessing, no regrets—Steve has never sounded so purely happy on a recording; the easy swing in his rough voice bespeaks a man in his comfort zone, at last, and eating it up. In the journey he's taken since the first notes of *Guitar Town*, here, then, he breaks clear into the light, sure of himself and of where his path leads. Always fearless in his declarations of love, his words are special enough, but the more revealing moment is a vocal one. At the end of the first verse, when he sings of finding his way "back home to you," he draws out the word "you"—it would read more like "yeeewww," intoned deliberately and emphatically, in a way that personalizes this song like no other he's ever sung, even those wrenching odes presumably inspired by Teresa Ensenat. On the track "yeeewww" flies by in about a second, but it packs an emotional wallop in the life Steve breathes into his phrasing.

Steve performing in 2000, on the Transcendental Blues *tour.*

Before a listener can even recover from "Steve's Last Ramble," Steve comes on the track saying, "Knickers. Let's magnetize this motherfucker!" A harmonica sounds a lilting phrase, Steve vamps on the mandolin then settles into a steady, marching rhythm, and begins singing a bright Irish melody, introducing a tale of meeting a lovely lass while out walking, her hair of black, her eyes of blue immediately captivating him. It's a Galway (Ireland) girl, and they take a stroll to an area of Galway city, near the seafront, known as Salthill Prom. It starts raining, she invites him up to her flat, he gives her "a twirl," and awakes alone the next morning, "with a broken heart and a ticket home"—but nonetheless exhilarated. Mary Shannon on banjo, Sharon Shannon on accordion, and Dan Gillis on tin whistle energize the reel with their combination of hard-picked single-note soloing (banjo), jaunty humming (accordion), and in the wind a soaring, jubilant soul taking flight (tin whistle). In the end, even when he finds himself abandoned and brokenhearted, he takes the high road, not pitying himself his loss or for being used, but cherishing an indelible memory of fleeting passion. What's a fella to do?

But who exactly is the Galway girl? Barbara Lindberg asked in the July 1, 2000, issue of the western Ireland magazine *Magpie*. "Though noted as a traveling type all his life," Lindberg writes, "this is one road Steve refuses to go down. 'I'm a gentleman and I'll never tell,' though he's quick to add, 'the women in the West of Ireland are the most beautiful women in the world.' "[34]

All this life-affirming celebration is transitory, as it turns out, because from the high of "Galway Girl" *Transcendental Blues* takes a decidedly unsettling, if not outright dark, turn. The old fears of inadequacy return, the broken love affairs come back to haunt ("Halo 'round the Moon"), and even hope is shadowed by doubt ("When I Fall"). "Lonelier Than This," from its spare, finger-picked preamble, echoes the astringent beauty of Townes Van Zandt's tearjerkers. Detail upon revealing detail accumulates as the verses unfold, a catalog of heartache in sharp, vivid images: "my heart outside my skin," "an empty place where your love should be," "dusty corners that the shadows know," and on and on. Sung in a sandpapery whisper, with Will Rigby's rolling figures on the snare drum lending it the feel of a death march, "Wherever I Go" sounds like what it's not, and that's a celebration of something. With the band roaring into a rock groove from the start, their rich sound supplemented by the vibrant organ and piano work of Heartbreaker Benmont Tench, the song has a bright, joyous feel, doubly so for the swirls of chiming electric 12-string riffs out of the Roger McGuinn repertoire as interpreted by David Steele, whose impeccable solo near the end is an angular, personable wonder. The story tells of an ache that has followed the singer around from his birth and recounts how he escapes his troubles by drinking "corn whiskey" until he's blotto and hitting the highway, even though wherever he goes he's trailed by the blues. At the end his simple wish is to go to where he can't be found, where his troubles might come to end, but for the realization that his is always a bad moon rising.

And there's a mighty streak of fatalism at work here too, with Steve suggesting in two stirring numbers—"I Don't Wanna Lose You Yet" and the piercing "When I Fall"—that the losing of love and the falling in love are matters of when, not if. "I Don't Wanna Lose You Yet"—which happens to feature one of Steve's most sensuous choruses in its earnest entreaties for physical affection—finds Benmont Tench returning to add depth with his plaintive organ fills, as David Steele frames Steve's enervated vocal with electric guitar solos that shift the song's texture by being alternately straightahead strikes of single chords that he lets ring for a couple of bars and fat, twangy multistring runs that curl all around Steve's singing. Once again a supporting voice, Tom Littlefield turns out to be a most affecting companion in harmony,

Preceding "I Don't Wanna Lose You Yet," a different cast of musicians on "When I Fall"—Doug Lancio on electric guitars, Ray Kennedy on bass, and Steve's brother Patrick on drums and percussion—strike a moody, churning atmosphere. Steve responds with a measured vocal that's perfect for driving a story of a man who knows someone's out there for him when he missteps. In the third verse Stacey Earle makes her return in stirring fashion: singing in a nasally, pinched tone, full of palpable, lived-in feeling, she reflects, in a verse that cuts close to the bone, of watching someone "trip and stumble," always fearing the worst, the memory of those wrenching events ever fresh as she recalls the desperate hours. There's a little catch in her voice when she sings the word "cost" in the phrase "considerin' the co-ost," adding an extra syllable, but more to the point, adding feeling like a raw nerve has been struck, a moment riveting in its subtle but devastating impact. Lancio then surfaces with a dramatic solo, fuzzed out and tumbling, echoing both Roger McGuinn and Richard Bennett, before a series of pungent single notes set the stage for Steve's sputtering entrance on harmonica. Then Stacey and Steve mesh their voices in a lovely concluding verse that reiterates both the inevitability of the fall and the promise, in a touching, poetic turn of phrase, that "in my heart there's a place for you to run to."

This was a different Stacey Earle from the eager but unformed artist who burned her way through "Promise You Anything" on *The Hard Way*. In the comedian George Carlin's memorable phrase, she had been "tempered in shit" by being on the front lines during Steve's years of madness at a time when she was trying to find direction in her own life as her first marriage was coming undone, leaving her a single mother with a junior high school education and two children to support. She had worked minimum-wage jobs, sometimes more than one at a time, to make ends meet for her and her children. Inspired by Steve, she taught herself the basics of guitar and started writing. Playing open-mike nights around Nashville, she being Steve Earle's sister naturally attracted the attention of major-label talent scouts. She tried to play the game—"I remember standing in my first showcase in a sparkly bolero jacket and high heels. It was not me. I couldn't even stand on my high heels."[35] But she played only as long as it took to record some demos for inquiring major labels and going her own way instead, because the mainstream route chafed at her sensibility as an artist. Although neither political nor literary like her brother, Stacey she did have one thing in common with him: she wrote what she knew, and that was her life, struggling at the lower rung of society, trying to understand how and why people connect, or disconnect, as well as her own heart. In 1999 she had made her move, assembling a small acoustic ensemble led by Mark Stuart and cutting an album of 13 original tunes that was championed by Brad Hunt at E-Squared, who arranged for its distribution and subsequently wound up managing Stacey and Mark. Titled *Simple Gearle*, its poetry lay in the simple: simple declarative sentences for lyrics, simple instrumentation, and simple, heartfelt, unadorned singing that reached the listener on a fundamental level.

"Her music is a folk-country hybrid, and is just the sort of thing that label executives in Nashville don't want to acknowledge exists in their vicinity," Martin Monkman observed in a perceptive review in the *All-Music Guide*. "Her songs are exclusively about the relationships between women and men. These aren't narratives so much as finely drawn descriptions of emotional responses to situations. The emotions seem real, and drawn from experience, perhaps because they are ambiguous enough to sound like honest attempts to describe the indescribable. The sparse instrumentation aids Earle's knowing vocals in getting the emotions across. … *Simple Gearle* has an immediacy and an honesty that is rare these days; Stacey Earle is a real treasure."[36]

Steve approached Stacey about singing on the track after what had been a tough year for them on a personal level. After inviting Mark to play on *El Corazón*, he had reduced him to a secondary role in the studio band. During a break in recording, Steve and Mark got into a dispute over a referee's call in a Dallas Cowboys football game they were watching in the lounge. A Cowboys fan, Steve thought the ref had blown the call, but after watching the replay, Mark, who is from Tennessee and more into baseball and basketball than football and is most certainly not signed up with America's Team on any level, pointed out that the ref got it right—the tape proved it. Steve's sarcastic response was to inform Mark that he was only in the band because he was married to Stacey; Mark's reasoned response was to quit the band, and with that he was gone.

Hurt by Steve's treatment of her husband, Stacey returned a guitar her brother had given her, and they had barely spoken to each other in the ensuing months. But with time came healing. When Steve asked her to sing on "When I Fall," Stacey was in sessions for her second album (which would be titled

Dancin' with Them That Brung Me and again include all original songs save for a bluegrass-inflected rendition of "Promise You Anything"; Sheryl Crow sat in on vocals on a lovely ballad, "Kiss Her Goodnight"). The invitation came at a family barbecue at Patrick's house. Steve explained to Stacey that he was writing a song for a movie titled *You Can Count on Me* and he wanted her to sing the second part. The song did not wind up on what was a first-rate soundtrack (released on E-Squared) to a well-reviewed small film that launched the career of Laura Linney (and costarred Mark Rufalo as her troubled, drug-loving prodigal brother), but Steve liked it so much that he rolled it out for *Transcendental Blues*.

In the studio at Room and Board, Stacey was isolated in a vocal booth, with Ray Kennedy, who plays bass on the track, off to one side of her. Steve was in another room entirely, cutting his vocal at the same time. They ran through the song, stopped halfway through, then rolled tape for a second go-'round, and nailed the take.

What Steve and Ray didn't see was Stacey "bawling like a baby." Her verse hit her hard, it was so dead-on as to what she experienced through the dark times with her brother.

"I started crying during the first few words and didn't stop," she says. "Maybe a part of me wished it was written for us. Steve says it wasn't, but you know he had maybe the emotions to write it.

"I had never cried like that before in my life. It was like 20-something years just completely rushed out of my body. I wasn't crying so hard that it messed up the take, but I think it was many years and finally this roller coaster stopped. It came to an end."

As she listened to the playback with Steve and Ray, Stacey cringed at the sound of her voice—all she could hear were the tears. "Boy, my voice really sounds, uh … I don't know, guys," she said blithely, politely politicking for another take.

"No, we're keeping it," Steve announced. And so it was.

"I kept asking to do it one more time, because I thought it needed to be prettier," Stacey says.[37]

Returning to *Mountain* territory, Steve assembled the Bluegrass Dukes (Tim O'Brien, Casey Driessen, Darrell Scott, and Dennis Crouch) for a rousing ballad of murder, deception, and betrayal, "Until the Day I Die," its jolly ambiance in stark contrast to it subject. But the Dukes are up to the task, and O'Brien especially stands out with some frisky mandolin work behind and between Steve's vocals. When the track ends, a pause ensues, and then Steve returns, saying, "And always remember, friends: there's no room in vulgarity for bluegrass," inadvertently confirming Ronnie McCoury's account of the McCoury Band's falling out with Steve. Which immediately precedes the sound of tape starting to roll and a grungy rock 'n' roll sound thundering across the track. A tight little trio—Steve on multiple instruments, Ray Kennedy on bass, and Patrick Earle on drums and percussion—burns its way through "All of My Life," a steel-tough, brutal number that would have fit quite well on *The Hard Way*, with Steve spitting out a mean vocal of restrained fury, his subject being the roiling internal monologue of possibly a deranged stalker who is certain some particular someone was meant to be his.

But it's hard not to see "All of My Life" as a setup for the album-closing benediction "Over Yonder (Jonathan's Song)," a soft, acoustic-driven last will and testament written in the voice of Jonathan Wayne Nobles on the eve of his execution. Steve's finger-picked guitar, David Steele's mournful, trilling mandolin, Steve's moaning harmonica, with the rhythm section of Kelley Looney (bass) and Will Rigby (drums) solid on the bottom, strike a contemplative mood, ascending ever so slightly in the chorus and quieting again when returning to the verses.

Steve's character's only agenda, somberly stated, is nothing more than distributing his belongings, making amends by way of his death bringing peace to his victims' survivors, and anticipating his arrival in a place where he won't be haunted by the ghosts that shadow this life. A quiet, dignified farewell, it is sung with restraint and a palpable measure of sorrow, in keeping with the man Nobles had become.

"He wasn't cocky," Steve told the Associated Press's David Bauder of Nobles's final minutes before the toxins flowed into his veins. "He cried, but he wasn't whining. It wasn't about him. He apologized to one survivor of the attack, and he apologized to the mother of one of his victims. It was a heartfelt apology, and then he read a Bible verse.

"He went out like a warrior. I was really proud of him, but I was also sad about the fact that we destroyed something precious."[38]

A Conversation with Steve Earle

by Travis McGee

"I don't believe in suffering for your art, but I do believe that if you're suffering it should be in your art."

The following interview was conducted by Travis McGee for barnesandnoble.com and is reprinted here with permission. Looking back from the vantage point of 2005, it's an interesting take on what Steve thought the immediate future held for him and how far he had traveled to get to this point. In discussing his book, *Doghouse Roses*, his music, and his muse, he sounds like the man he claims to be: "disgustingly happy." That contentment comes through in his words. It was a long time coming.

What was your mind-set was going into the making of Transcendental Blues?

Some of the songs were written by the time I started touring with *The Mountain*, and some more were written over the course of the tour, so I knew where it was going. I knew it was going to be what I consider to be essentially a rock record, but for me being a songwriter that covers a lot of ground. Most bluegrass records don't sound like *The Mountain* does, so I think there's a case for *The Mountain* being a rock record too. I knew that I wanted it to be pretty expansive, because my records generally are, but I really wanted to make a record that was big enough and covered enough ground so that I wouldn't feel like I had to make another record in 12 months. I've done that for five years, and I think I want a little break between this record and the next one. It won't be as long as a lot of artists take, for me, but it won't be 12 months either.

What do you plan on doing during that break?

We will be touring with this for a year, and I've got a play that I'm writing, and I want to workshop that, so that'll take a little time. The tour ends next summer so I'll be occupied with the play for several months after the tour, and then I'll start thinking about another record.

I hear you've got a book of short stories coming out, too.

Yes, that'll be in the spring, I suddenly have a deadline and I didn't before. But that's fine, I've got one more story I'm in the middle of right now and I'll finish it before the tour starts. The tour starts on July 11 in Atlanta.

What type of stories are they?

There are all kinds of stuff. [The book] represents, mainly, the first 11 stories that I've written. I started about five years ago. And it's been written over a period of five years. There are three of them that are sort of related, they weren't really written in sequence but they have the same central character. They'll be arranged chronologically in the book although probably not together. The rest of them are unrelated and are about everything you could possibly imagine.

Back to the new album, there seems to be a lot of duality in the writing. It sounds like you're at peace with yourself, but there is still that sense of urgency and discontent.

That stuff is hard to totally get rid of. I'm the happiest I've ever been. I'm kind of disgustingly happy. But I've got plenty of misery to last a lifetime to draw on if nothing bad ever happens to me again. I think writers draw on memory as much as anything else, and there are no exceptions here.

Do you find it easier to write about past experiences when you've been removed from the experience and you're not as emotionally tied?

I think you write differently when you're removed from it. In some ways it's better and in some ways it's better to write in the moment. The stuff that I write "in the moment" when I look at it years later, I'll say "Mmm … I was in a very weird place when I wrote that."

It sounds like there's a lot of regret but at the same time a lot of hope, too.

Well, yeah, regret I don't do well. I've discovered it's pretty toxic for me, so I wouldn't say that regret is anything that I spend a lot of time on. There's certainly some things that I'm not proud of that I've done, but dwelling on them— which is what regret is—is counterproductive, so I try not to do that. It doesn't mean I'm successful at not doing it all the time, but I try not to.

I think "Another Town" did a good job of summing up the complexities of what you were going through.

"Another Town" is weird because I actually didn't write it for me. I was giving voice to another person, who was a friend of mine at the time and is my girlfriend now. You don't always write from your own standpoint, sometimes you lend your voice to somebody else and that's what I was doing on that particular song.

How important is it as an artist to be constantly in flux?

It's the most important thing to me. I always try to do things I haven't done before. I think my songs have gotten stronger because I do write short fiction, I do write poetry, and I am writing a play. I'm writing a haiku a day now for a year, which I started about four months ago. I just made a commitment to do one a day for a year. I just became interested in haiku and I wanted to do it myself. And teaching, I taught at the Chicago Folk Institute in January and February, and I learned a lot doing that.

How has your other work, your poetry and short stories, affected your approach to writing songs?

I think poetry has, especially if you look at songs like "Transcendental Blues" and "The Boy Who Never Cried," they're much more ambiguous and much more inward than my songs usually are. Most of my stuff is really more related to narrative than it is to poetry, the vast majority of it. The stuff I'm always proudest of, simply because it didn't come as easily, is the stuff that is more emotionally driven and more poetic.

Is that because the more emotions you're feeling the tougher it is to get down on paper?

It's a different discipline. You have to not think too much. Poetry is a really hard-core pure form. No matter how poetic song lyrics may sound, poetry and songwriting aren't the same thing strictly because a poet has one line to turn your brain off and turn your heart on, because that's what you listen for in poetry. And a poet has to do it without the effect on emotions that sheer tonality has. I can play the right chord in the front end of a song, or the right riff, and I've got your ass before I even open my mouth, because I've been doing it for a long time. Poetry is tougher.

How do you feel the response has been to you venturing into different styles over the last five or six years?

Well, I've had two poems published in a little journal in Ireland, and my book of short fiction is coming in the spring. So we'll see I may get my ass kicked, but that probably won't stop me from doing it.

From a musical standpoint, how do you feel people have responded to your changing styles?

I think there are some people that are confused by it, but I think most fans expect that of me. The 100,000 people in the States and the other 150,000 scattered around that always buy my records totally understand that. And if this keeps going the way it's going, the audience is going to be bigger than that. My responsibility is to the core fans because they are the people who have allowed me to make records exactly the way that I want to and make an embarrassing amount of money doing it. It's not necessary to sell millions of records to make a really, really comfortable living, and I've been doing it for a long time and I'm very, very grateful for that.

How have your live shows changed over the past few years?

They haven't changed very much. They tend to be two hours and 15 minutes instead of three hours and 15 minutes. That may be me getting older or just me getting sick of myself after two hours and 15 minutes. I think I hit a groove in the first couple of tours and there's a way I do shows that people expect. Some people think I talk too much during the course of shows but usually not the people who buy all my records, so I'm not really concerned about it. I'm really just trying to make a connection with the audience, and that's the best way I know how to do it, rather than just going out there and blasting through the songs. You can see that on television.

Are your shows on this tour going to be a heavier rock sound?

We're a brutal little four-piece rock band.

How has kicking your drug habit affected your approach to music?

Well, I don't have to wake up in the morning and find $500 worth of dope before I do anything. So I feel like I have a lot more time and a lot more energy, and I think I'm writing better than I ever have.

Does it change your point of view at all because it's made it easier to write?

I don't think I ever bought the idea that dope enhances creativity. I didn't take dope to be more creative; I took dope to stop hurting. The mistake I was making was not realizing that everybody fucking hurts and you're supposed to hurt sometimes. And also it was sort of shortsighted. If you stop hurting altogether, you don't have fucking anything to write about. I made the same generic mistake that all addicts make, and all the bad stuff that happens to addicts eventually happened to me.

How did the experience with the addiction itself affect your approach to songwriting?

I'm a much different person than I was five years ago. I had to change because if I didn't change I'd be dead. So those changes are a lot of what this record is about. Actually, a lot of what the last five records have been about. You know, I don't believe in suffering for your art, but I do believe that if you're suffering it should be in your art.

As far as your campaigning against the death penalty, to what extent do you feel that should carry over into the music?

It's important to me and I think people expect it of me, so nobody in the core audience is put off by it, even though some of them don't agree with me. They've been pretty good about letting me have my say. I don't beat people over the head with it at shows. I do allow any death penalty organizations to table at my shows, and the subject will come up once during the show. But I don't play "Billy Alston" and "Over Yonder" all in the same show; I play one of them. This year it will probably be "Over Yonder" because it's new. When that song comes up in the show they know their going to have to hear it. It's something I believe very strongly in and I work very hard for.

I read a transcript from a speech you gave at SXSW last year. In introducing your stance on the death penalty you said, "If you support the death penalty, that's okay, you don't have to listen to me." I thought that was an admirable stance that most activists don't seem to take.

There's a moratorium in place in Illinois right now and it's the result of people who oppose the death penalty being willing to work with people that fundamentally support the death penalty, but do agree that 13 wrongful convictions is way too many and it needs to stop and be examined. That's what coalition is. I think the U.S. government could be vastly improved by forming a true coalition of diverse political parties, rather than having "brand A" and "brand A and a half," which is what we have with the Republicans and the Democrats right now.

Did your own time in prison affect you point of view on the death penalty at all?

I was always opposed to it, but I do have a connection with guys that I talk to when they tell me "it's time for count" and they've got to get off the phone. I know what they're talking about.

• • •

True to his word, Steve did not release another album until the late summer of 2002. In the interim, Tony Brown organized a reunion concert of the *Guitar Town* musicians to honor the album being certified gold (and the release of its remastered version, with new liner notes by Steve); Steve and Sara Sharpe founded the not-for-profit Broadaxe Theater in Nashville and christened it with a production of Cuban-American playwright Maria Irene Fornes's drama *Mud*; and in June of 2002, Steve's book of short stories, *Doghouse Roses*, was published by Houghton Mifflin. It won wide praise from fellow writers and generally sympathetic reviews, none raves but all respectful of Steve's effort. Writing for barnesandnoble.com, Jonathan Cook praised some of the book's 11 stories, notably those that "channel Earle's political activism," damned several others as "hackneyed stuff," and concluded that "the integrity and empathy of Earle's writing wins you over; *Doghouse Roses* is the latest stage in an impressive and multifaceted career."

At the rehearsal for the *Guitar Town* reunion concert, scheduled for the Ryman Auditorium in Nashville on February 6, 2002, Steve played some songs he was going to record for his new album. There wasn't a "chick song" among them. The world he was returning to had undergone a cataclysmic upheaval since the time of *Transcendental Blues*. When the landscape turned red on September 11, 2001, he set out to bear witness to, and attempt to make sense of, the postapocalyptic madness engulfing America at the end of history.

The Devil's
Right-Hand Man

I. Alpha Male Ascending, v. 7.0

On the morning of September 11, 2001, Jack Earle was one of millions of people around the world watching televised images of the 110-story World Trade Center's north tower spewing flames and billowing smoke after being struck by a hijacked United Airlines jet flown by Arab terrorists on a suicide mission. He had called his son Steve to alert him to the disaster unfolding in New York City when he saw another jet flit across the TV screen and plough into the second of the famous Twin Towers, sending another huge plume of smoke and fire into the sky and launching tons of debris and countless victims off the structure onto the ground below.

Once a pilot, always a pilot, and so it was that Jack, though numbed by the horror of what he was seeing, still found it remarkable that the second plane managed to hit its mark.

"I couldn't believe it. I was sitting there looking at one tower burning and all of a sudden here comes a big jet in a very tight left turn," Jack recalls. "I don't know how, this guy, not being an experienced pilot, how he controlled it through that turn and didn't just lose it out there. I was just amazed that he got that turn in."[1]

On the other end of the line, Steve was seeking answers as to the who, what, when, where, and why of this disaster. It turned out to be an orchestrated, well-planned (over a period of years) attack on America, with 19 terrorists, most of them from Saudi Arabia but trained in Afghanistan in camps operated by the Al-Qaeda terrorist group under the command of Osama bin Laden. Working in teams, they hijacked four jetliners that day; of the two others, one plunged into the Pentagon in Washington, DC, and the other crashed in a field in Pennsylvania, apparently after passengers fought to prevent the plane from reaching its intended target: the White House of George W. Bush. The day after the attack, President Bush stood amid the rubble of Lower Manhattan and vowed that America would respond. Shortly after that, he told reporters that he made the capture of bin-Laden "dead or alive" his first priority.

On October 7, 2001, the president announced Operation Enduring Freedom, a military operation designed to dismantle the repressive (and anti-American) Taliban regime that had seized power in Afghanistan and returned it to an almost prehistoric theocracy while sympathizing with and supporting bin Laden's Al-Qaeda network. In the ensuing battle, the U.S. military managed to oust the Taliban, with help from the anti-Taliban Northern Alliance military, but Osama bin Laden and his top advisers escaped into the mountains and continued to direct Al-Qaeda operations from points unknown.

On October 26, 2001, after scant debate, the U.S. Congress passed the 342-page Public Law 107-56, "Uniting and Strengthening America by Providing Appropriate Tools Required to Intercept and Obstruct Terrorism (USA Patriot Act) Act of 2001." The American Civil Liberties Union immediately issued a bulletin denouncing the Patriot Act as a threat to civil liberties, claiming it threatened rights granted Americans under the first, fourth, fifth, sixth, eighth, and fourteenth amendments. For "intelligence purposes," government agencies were now allowed to monitor communications between government detainees and their lawyers; to spy on religious and political organizations and individuals without evidence of criminal wrongdoing; to hold suspected terrorists indefinitely in military custody without granting them access to legal counsel or charging them with any specific crime(s); to bar the public and the press from immigration court hearings of those detained after 9/11; and to prohibit the court from even announcing such hearings and … so on, in a document so profoundly surreal, oppressive, and repressive that it might have stunned George Orwell.

Unable even to get a good look at bin Laden, except in videotapes sent to the Arab TV network Aljazeera showing him socializing with friends and chortling over the success of the World Trade Center operation, the Bush administration got the boogeyman it needed on November 25, 2001, when Northern Alliance forces captured an expatriate American, 20-year-old John Walker Lindh, who was fighting with opposition forces. In an uprising at the makeshift prison where Lindh was being held, CIA agent Mike Spann, who first interrogated Lindh, was killed and Lindh was shot in his right thigh. Lindh took refuge with some other jihad fighters in a basement bunker, only to be flushed out on December 2 when the Northern Alliance diverted an irrigation stream and flooded the bunker. Initially, Lindh identified himself as Abdul Hamid, but when interviewed by CNN's Robert Young Pelton, he revealed his true identity, and admitted he had trained at bin Laden's camp and belonged to a bin Laden-supported jihadist army called Al Ansar. Requesting, but denied, an attorney, Lindh signed a confession, leading to his indictment and return to the United States for trial. A federal grand jury then indicted him on 10 charges—among those, conspiring to support terrorist organizations and conspiring to murder Americans—which carried a penalty of three life terms and 90 additional years in prison. On February 13, 2002, Lindh pleaded not guilty to all 10 charges.

Then the government ran into problems in its prosecution of the hapless Lindh. As summarized at wikipedia.org, the case unfolded thusly:

"Photos emerged from Lindh's captivity of him being held naked and trussed up like a trophy deer wearing an obscenity-covered blindfold. When details of the conditions of his captivity began to emerge, it was discovered that he had initially been wounded and hid for a week with limited food, water, and minimal sleep in conditions of freezing water before being captured. After being captured and taken to a room with the only window blocked off, Lindh had his clothes cut off him and was duct-taped to a stretcher and placed in a metal shipping container for transportation. When interrogated, he was denied a lawyer despite several requests, and was threatened with denial of medical aid if he didn't cooperate.

"The court scheduled an evidence-suppression hearing, at which Walker would be able to testify about the details of the torture to which he was subjected. The government faced the problem that a key piece of evidence—Walker's confession—might be excluded from evidence as having been forced under duress. Furthermore, the hearing would turn a spotlight on the way that U.S. soldiers had conducted the interrogation.

"To forestall this possibility, Michael Chertoff, the head of the criminal division of the Justice Department, directed the prosecutors to offer Walker a plea bargain: he would plead guilty to two charges—serving in the Taliban army and carrying weapons. He would also have to consent to a gag order that would prevent him from making any public statements on the matter for the duration of his 20-year sentence, and he would have to drop claims that he had been mistreated or tortured by U.S. military personnel in Afghanistan and aboard two military ships during December 2001 and January 2002. In return, all the other charges would be dropped.

"Walker accepted this offer. On July 15, 2002, he entered his plea of guilty to the two remaining charges. The judge asked Walker to say, in his own words, what he was admitting to. 'I plead guilty,' he said. 'I provided my services as a soldier to the Taliban last year from about August to December. In the course of doing so, I carried a rifle and two grenades. I did so knowingly and willingly knowing that it was illegal.' On October 4, 2002, Judge T.S. Ellis formally imposed the sentence: 20 years without parole."[2]

On Lindh the American mainstream press was in complete accord: if he wasn't the Antichrist, he would do until a better one came along. But in fact, John Walker Lindh was nothing more than a sensitive young man seeking a better, more spiritually enriching world than the one being fed to him in the American popular culture of his time.

Born in Maryland and raised in Northern California, in Marin County, across the bay from San Francisco, Lindh was described by a family friend as "very sweet, unassuming, very spiritual young man—rather frail, not an all-American football player or anything like that, certainly not a fighter."[3]

His interest in Islam began when he was 12, after seeing Spike Lee's film biography of Malcolm X. At age 16 he converted to Islam and began attending a mosque in Mill Valley, where he was known as Suleyman al-Lindh and Suleyman al-Faris. In 1998 he went to Yemen and studied Islam for nine months, returned to California, then went back to Yemen in early 2000 to continue his studies. In October he moved to Pakistan, where he enrolled in a madrasah, an Islamic fundamentalist school with a pronounced anti-Western bias. His first experience with jihad came as a member of Harakat-ul Mujahedeen-Al Almi, or HUM, which, among other dubious achievements, was blamed for an assassination attack on Pakistani president Pervez Musharaff. He fell out with HUM and joined the Taliban, and spent seven weeks in training at an Al-Qaeda camp, where he claimed to have had a fleeting encounter, along with other recruits, with bin Laden himself.

During his interrogation by the U.S. military, Lindh, according to an FBI report, showed "remorse and signs of regret" over the 9/11 terrorist attacks and revealed that one of his instructors had said those attacks were the first in three waves planned against U.S. interests.[4]

In the end, it seemed John Walker Lindh had been abandoned by all but his parents and his attorney, James Brosnahan.

"My love for him is unconditional and absolute, and I am grateful to God that he has been brought home to his family," said his mother, Marilyn Walker.

"He was a soldier in the Taliban. He did it for religious reasons. He did it as a Muslim, and history overcame him," said Brosnahan.

"John loves America. And we love America. God bless America," said his father, Frank Lindh.

At his sentencing hearing on October 14, Americans heard the only other words John Walker Lindh has spoken in public since the CNN interview. "Had I realized then what I know now, I would never have joined [the Taliban]," he said, adding that he "never understood jihad to mean anti-Americanism or terrorism.

"I understand why so many Americans were angry when I was first discovered in Afghanistan," he said. "I realize many still are, but I hope in time that feeling will change."[5]

Hewing to the Bush administration line, the press continued to vilify Lindh, even to the point of some right-wing pundits demanding his execution as a traitor. The public consensus on Lindh was not going to change any time soon in this heated climate in which due process was subjugated to mob will, but back in middle Tennessee, Steve Earle was seeing a different perspective. His son Justin was the same age as Lindh and had made his own misjudgments growing up, as had his father before him.

"I don't condone what [Lindh] did," Steve said at the time. "Still, he's a 20-year-old kid. My son Justin is almost exactly Walker's age. Would I be upset if he suddenly turned up fighting for the Islamic Jihad? Sure, absolutely. Fundamentalism, as practiced by the Taliban, is the enemy of real thought, and religion too. But there are circumstances … He didn't just sit on the couch and watch the box, get depressed, and complain. He was a smart kid, he graduated from high school early, the culture here didn't impress him, so he went out looking for something to believe in."[6]

The attacks of 9/11, the aftermath, and the Lindh episode spurred Steve on to a songwriting binge. And an urgency about the state of the body politic caused him to rethink his plan to put more space between his albums as he explored other avenues of artistic expression. Releasing a new album "in a timely fashion," he told *MIX* magazine reporter Gaby Alter, "started becoming important to me. In other words, the material seemed perishable. So we just bumped up the timeline to my next record."[7]

Among the new numbers he had played for his bandmates at the *Guitar Town* reunion rehearsal was one he quipped would "get me kicked out of the country."[8] It was a slow, churning blues, the lyrics coming from John Walker Lindh's perspective, trying to explain himself and his actions. It was called "John Walker's Blues."

After hearing the song, Tony Brown, wary of the country's mood at the moment, thought to himself, This may be the time to pull back a little bit, Steve. He kept the thought to himself. Shadrach, Meshach, Abednego, and Steve Earle— these guys knew how to walk into fire and not be consumed by it.

* * *

The music was his dance in the auditorium of enemies.

—Coming through Slaughter

Jerusalem
E- Squared/Artemis, 2002

Produced by the twangtrust
Engineered by Ray Kennedy

Assistant engineer: Patrick Earle

Recorded and mixed at Room and Board, Hermitage, Tennessee, except "Amerika v. 6.0 (The Best We Can Do)" recorded by Tim Hatfield and assisted by David Chernis at Cowboy Technical Services Rig, Williamsburg, Brooklyn, New York, with additional recording at Room and Board

Musicians

Steve Earle: guitar, bass, mandolin, banjo, harmonica, harmonium, mini-Moog, organ and vocals
Eric "Roscoe" Ambel: guitar and vocals
Kelley Looney: bass
Will Rigby: drums and percussion
Patrick Earle: percussion
Siobhan Maher-Kennedy: vocals on "Conspiracy Theory"
Dane Clark: drum loop on "Conspiracy Theory"
Emmylou Harris: vocals on "I Remember You"
Ken Coomer: drums on "I Remember You"
John Jarvis: electric piano on "Go Amanda"
Mike Bubb: bass on "The Truth"
Kenny Malone: drums and percussion on "The Truth"

Songs

 1. "Ashes to Ashes" (4:02) (Steve Earle)
 2. "Amerika v. 6.0 (The Best We Can Do)" (4:19) (Steve Earle)
 3. "Conspiracy Theory" (4:14) (Steve Earle)
 4. "John Walker's Blues" (3:41) (Steve Earle)
 5. "The Kind" (2:04) (Steve Earle)
 6. "What's a Simple Man to Do?" (2:29) (Steve Earle)
 7. "The Truth" (2:21) (Steve Earle)
 8. "Go Amanda" (3:34) (Steve Earle)
 9. "I Remember You" (2:52) (Steve Earle)
10. "Shadowland" (2:52) (Steve Earle)
11. "Jerusalem" (3:56) (Steve Earle)

The statement that is *Jerusalem* begins with Tony Fitzpatrick's cover art. Born in 1958 and based in Chicago, well traveled and well read, Fitzpatrick works in drawings-collages. He had been doing Steve's album covers since *I Feel Alright*. Each one of them sprang from discussions he had with Steve about the content of the particular album and was meant to reflect something of the dialog contained therein. He will not discuss his work with Steve, as he considers it the outgrowth of their private, intimate conversations relating to the music and viewpoint unique to each new collection of songs. People who have spent their adult lives scrutinizing Bob Dylan's lyrics for hidden meanings and obscure cultural references could have a field day with Fitzpatrick's artwork as it relates to Steve Earle's music.

On *Jerusalem*, the cover art looks like a scene of the earth from an airplane window, except that the main road is the body of a spotted, multicolored snake with no head. A green and red snake was also the dominant feature of the *I Feel Alright* cover, slinking up the middle of a collage, its head a beautiful blooming flower surrounded by honeysuckle vines, orchids, with what are either planets, moons, or Christmas tree balls suspended in the air around the snake's body. It's a dainty, if typically inscrutable, Fitzpatrick cover.

But on *Jerusalem*, the colors are washed-out browns and dark greens. There appear to be two minor roads under the main road (the snake's body), that lead to nowhere. Clouds hang overhead, a tornado funnel spins out of one, the sun is shining in the right hand corner of the frame, and each end of the snake's tail has twisting lines drawn around it, as if it's twirling furiously.

Fitzpatrick's covers have typically featured flowers as a binding concept, which he frames with vintage images (he's had an exhibition of collages made from images collected from old matchbook covers, and those same matchbooks may be a source of the images seen on Steve's albums) of birds, astrological symbols, naked young ladies, dice, Asian text, skull and crossbones, constellations and galaxies far, far away. *The Mountain*, for example, features a pronounced astronomy theme in its collage, with a flower, on the cover and on the CD itself, surrounded in the interior of the collage by Ursa Major, Hydra, Lynx, Perseus (one of the largest constellations in the Northern Hemisphere; Fitzpatrick does not show the figure of Perseus, which holds the head of Medusa in his hand, with the star beta Per representing Medusa's evil eye), and the galaxy M81, easily observed from Earth even though it is 12 million light-years away. *El Corazón* is the most literal of Fitzpatrick's album covers, its dominant image being a blood-red heart (which from a certain perspective looks like a clenched fist) with an arrow through it, over a green background of faded text, framed by collage images, including a skull and crossbones, a quarter moon, a scorpion, a seeing eye, the constellation Hydra (which would be reprised on *The Mountain*), a bright red bird with a yellow breast, and a disembodied, radiating hand holding in its palm some kind of coin. *El Corazón* also features, at the top of its cover illustration, dead center below Steve's name, three stars, the middle one larger than the two adjacent to it; on *Transcendental Blues*, above Steve's name, and on the back above his photo, are three gold king's crowns, the middle one larger than the two adjacent to it. Why three of each, and why stars are transformed into king's crowns is open for debate.

At the Web site for the Sue and Eugene Mercy, Jr., Gallery (mercygallery .org), Fitzpatrick is described as "a very large man with tattoos and an unusual history, which includes some time in prison for car theft. He is also an actor (*Philadelphia*), a poet with several books of poetry to his credit, a radio talk-show host and a remarkable artist with a gift for imagery and detailed drawing in both small and large formats. He lives and works in Chicago, and he makes frequent forays to mount exhibitions all over the country."

In a February 2005 interview with Simon Sandall for readersvoice.com, Fitzpatrick was asked whether his appropriation of what might otherwise be lost images was akin to "bringing them back to life again." He responded, "I hope so. You know, I hope I'm giving them a second definition and creating like a benchmark of history for them. These are all kind of blighted objects that most people throw away, and I see a certain historical value in them. I see them as part of how I tell a story or tell a history."[9]

Although he is not asked at all about Steve Earle in the interview, it's easy to spot the common ground between the two artists, up to a point anyway. He says he comes from "a big Irish family" in which the oral tradition was paramount. "There was a real tradition of storytelling, from my uncles and my grandparents, and it all kind of got passed down. So the sense of an oral history has been very prominent in my life."[10]

Among his favorite books he cites *Doghouse Roses* by Steve Earle (the only mention of Steve in the entire interview), and Michael Ondaatje's *Coming Through Slaughter* ("It's the story of Buddy Bolden and the invention of jazz and the combination of genius and madness it took to bring that forward at the turn of the last century"[11]), which Steve cites as one of his favorites as well.

The most succinct summation of Fitzpatrick's work, which would seem to apply to his Steve Earle album covers as well, came from *New York Times* reporter Roberta Smith, reviewing a Fitzpatrick exhibit at the Pierogi Gallery in Williamsburg, Brooklyn, New York, in the January 21, 2005, edition. "Vivid in every detail," Smith observed, "these works bring to mind all sorts of pieced-together mediums beyond collage: quilts, altarpieces, scrapbooks, marquetry. Compressing several forms of expression within their limited borders, they remind us that when the world created is complete enough, originality is beside the point."[12]

* * *

Notorious well before its release, *Jerusalem* arrived with a sensible explanation of John Walker Lindh's unsettling odyssey and a pervasive sense of history in four other powerful songs addressing the events of 9/11 and their aftermath. By this point Steve was well into being excoriated by neocon ideologues for "John Walker's Blues," but this somber, deliberate testimony is most persuasive in its depiction of a young man whose estrangement from the MTV culture inspired a spiritual quest that led him first to Allah and then to the wrong place at the wrong time, culminating in his arrival back on native soil "with my head in a sack." To some the character Steve adopts is no more sympathetic than the condemned killer in "Over Yonder," but he's every bit as spiritually developed and is doing the work of the God he believes in. Part of what makes the song so compelling is Steve's reserve—he never breaks out of character to moralize or to pamphleteer but remains true to a confused John Walker puzzling over how his spiritual journey went so horribly awry, a state of mind that's evoked by the tangled mesh of distorted, processed guitar lines following the last verse, which is then followed by a 30-second snippet of Quranic prayer as the song fades out. In a bit of synchronicity that was overlooked in all the brouhaha over the song, its opening line—"I'm just an American boy"—linked it to "Johnny Come Lately" on *Copperhead Road*, suggesting that "John Walker's Blues" is the next chapter in an epic about three generations of fighting men, this latest returning home neither hero nor nonentity, but reviled.

Elsewhere the gritty, anxious rock guiding "Ashes to Ashes," "Amerika v. 6.0 (The Best We Can Do)," and "Conspiracy Theory" and Earle's restrained growl of a voice offer vivid lessons in historical inevitability, as does the title number in closing the album by referencing Biblical prophecy concerning Judgment Day. "Amerika v. 6.0 (The Best We Can Do)" is a snarling, sarcastic kiss-off to a society that has ceded its humanity to the hubris and greed of them that have, leaving the have-nots to fend for themselves. "Conspiracy Theory" lives up to its title with a foreboding ambiance: Steve's breathy, conspiratorial vocal over a steadily pounding snare drum and thumping bass line is joined by a whining, extended synth line and cooing female voices advising "cover your head and close your eyes." The atmosphere grows angrier as the song unfolds, Steve musing on what might have happened if the assassinations in Dallas and in Memphis had been averted ("We wouldn't be livin' in a dream that died"). The message is, though, that all the nightmares are real. These are all strong, thought-provoking epistles guaranteed to spark heated debate. But the strength of *Jerusalem* is also in the songs that aren't shaped by the events of 9/11, because these happen to be among Earle's finest. "The Kind" is one of his most winsome heartbreakers. The jaunty Tex-Mex air of "What's a Simple Man to Do" frames a compelling tale of a fellow who compromised his values in the name of survival. And the languid "I Remember You" is a stirring interior monologue of a man haunted by the memory of a woman he shouldn't have let slip away. When Emmylou Harris enters, echoing the lyrics Earle is singing about his broken heart, a communion of parted lovers elevates to a mystical plateau. It's *Jerusalem*, a place where every answer suggests another question, and the truth lies somewhere in the shadows.

• • •

In a rare and revealing interview in *MIX* magazine, Ray Kennedy opened up about the process of making the painstaking journey from concept to reality in the studio. It's not dramatically different from the way Steve worked with Tony Brown and Joe Hardy, but it does embrace more of a mix of digital and analog gear to achieve the desired ambiance.

"We go for the live performance," Ray says. "Why go in with the attitude of, 'This is just a scratch guitar track,' or 'This is just a scratch vocal'? I don't believe in that. I believe in, 'Let's just really go for it!' When people are encouraged to do that, they end up performing better than they think they can."

Steve's acoustic guitar sound, always so robust on his recordings, was captured on *Jerusalem* with vintage late-'50s and early-'60s nickel-capsule Neumann KM56 microphones. "The way acoustic guitars are recorded [in other studios], they're mostly clean," Kennedy told reporter Gaby Alter. "We push them a little harder. I'll slam tape pretty hard and try to get the guitar to really respond so that you cannot just hear it, but feel it."

Jerusalem is the least Beatles-influenced of Steve's albums to this point, but that's not to discount the Fab Four's impact on the twangtrust's approach to sound here. For instance, the drums, always booming, were captured using Universal Audio 1176 compressors, which produced a sound akin to that of Fairchild limiters, Beatles producer George Martin's preferred tool. The technique, according to Kennedy, was to take "a lot of components of the mix and chain them off to a pair of 1176s or an 1178, and then bring that up into the mix so that the drums have this kind of continuous roar about them."

For vocals, Ray's and Steve's preferred mikes were a Fred Camron custom-modified Neumann U67 microphone, a Telefunken V-76 M Series preamp and, Ray adds, an 1176 compressor to "pull the sound out of [Steve's] throat, his chest. [The 1176] makes the microphone more sensitive, and makes it really dig in and reach out for the character of the vocal." And Joe Hardy may wince when he listens again to *The Hard Way* because of all the reverb he put on it, but Ray Kennedy never has to worry about that: "There isn't any reverb used on any of Steve's records, at least since I've been involved with him. It's all natural acoustics."

Ray also doesn't deny Richard Dodd's fear that his influence on the twangtrust may have come in showing them how to overdo the compression during the sessions he produced for *I Feel Alright*. Compression, at Room and Board studio, is heartily embraced. "Everything on the tape is a big, bold stroke," Ray asserts. "If it's not, it shouldn't be there. There's nothing subtle about Steve Earle records."

Almost immediately after completing *Jerusalem*, Steve and Ray went to work again, this time on the soundtrack for the documentary *Just an American Boy*. Directed by No-Wave cinema pioneer Amos Poe (whose 1975 documentary on the New York punk scene, *Blank Generation*, a collaboration with Patti Smith

Group guitarist Ivan Kral, remains the most fascinating look at the heady early days of the American punk movement's birth), the film followed Steve around on the road, at home, and in radio interviews. The music was uniformly stirring—a typical set touched on almost all of his albums; the Dukes—now solidified with former Del Lord (and original member of Joan Jett's Blackhearts) Eric "Roscoe" Ambel on guitar, Will Rigby on drums, and Kelly Looney on bass—proved itself worthy of Steve's description of it as a "brutal little four-piece rock band." But given Steve's colorful history, even lately with the release of and controversy over *Jerusalem*, *Just an American Boy* was tepid in its offstage footage. His family was largely missing from the film; there was too little interaction with the band members for any of them to make much of an impression; and there was precious little insight into his music making or the philosophy driving his artistic impulse these days.

The soundtrack, though, tested the twangtrust. Lacking a budget for a sound truck, the producers called upon digital technology to get the job done. A laptop, a copy of Digital Performer, and a few Firewire drives were the tools of the trade, and a signal was sent directly out of the house console onto the Performer's eight tracks. Kennedy then had to do something he hates to do, and that's to employ Pro Tools, cross-fading the tunes to follow the song sequence as it was in the film. "It was the best way to mix songs from different shows," Kennedy said. "My biggest job on that record was to make it not sound like Pro Tools."

Indeed, the performances, and the sound of the performances, are the best part of the documentary. Kennedy's got the formula down: "If you have great guitar sounds, great drum sounds, great vocal sounds, everything sounds really great, and you get the performance on top of that, then you've got a great-sounding record. You have a record that's gonna have appeal, because it's gonna have an emotional quality to it because of the performance basis. It's not that thought-out, it's not programmed, it's not intellectualized; it's just people playing together."[13]

II. "It's easy to vilify, because it doesn't require compassion"

The national furor over "John Walker's Blues" began July 21 with an item in the New York *Post* (owned by right-wing British media baron Rupert Murdoch) headlined "Twisted Ballad Honors Tali-Rat." Writer Aly Sujo claimed, erroneously, that the song "glorified" Walker Lindh and called him "Jesus-like." With that, the floodgates opened, as the *Wall Street Journal*, Fox News, CNN, and all the conservative radio commentators quickly fit the battle. Not a one of them paused from their heated rhetoric to consider what Ian Bruce of the World Socialist Web site (wsws.com) called "a legal and human rights travesty from the outset."[14]

What Steve was up against was most dramatically illustrated by several exchanges on the July 23, 2002, edition of CNN's "Talkback Live," hosted by Kathleen Kennedy and featuring as its guests Nashville radio host Steve Gill from station WTN and *No Depression* magazine publisher Grant Alden. After listening to a snippet of the song, Kennedy asked her guests what they thought of it.

Gill: "I think it's outrageous, and particularly when we're still within one year of the September 11 attacks on America. This is a sympathetic, glorifying approach to John 'Taliban' Walker. The guy is a traitor to his country and I think, frankly, Steve Earle was trying to push the edge of the envelope, but it's time for the American people to push back."

Alden: "I think that's making a lot out of not very much. It doesn't glorify him. The song is a blues, not a ballad. And what it argues is that John Walker is a slightly more complicated character than we know at this point. I don't think that's a radical statement, but apparently it is now."

Gill countered with a statement so outlandish it would be comical if it weren't so repugnant and misguided. Hitler, he said, may have been a more complicated man than anyone knew, but what American would have tolerated a sympathetic view of der Führer during World War Two? Or of a Japanese Zero fighter pilot?

"That's one of the really silly things that's come up in this discussion. He's not drawing the comparison," Alden countered, adding sensibly: "If my very limited understanding of Islam is correct, the Muslims believe that Jesus Christ was a prophet and a martyr. And the link being made in that song is that, like Christ, if John Walker Lindh dies in his jihad, he will rise to heaven as a martyr. That's all it says."

At that point an audience member chimed in, noting that if Steve had written and recorded the song "in a Muslim country that practiced Islamic law and referred to that country as the land of the infidel, he would have his tongue cut out or his hand chopped off. You know, he can come and write it here, and we just kind of say, oh well."

Alden, again striving for the higher ground, responded rhetorically: "Isn't that one of the things that makes us, actually, a good place to live—that we invite different opinions as part of our public discourse? Isn't that kind of the whole idea?"

In his retort, Gill took the typical right-wing gambit and responded not to the issue at hand but raised instead another issue that was tangential at best and had nothing to do with Steve Earle's obligations, whatever those might be, as an artist.

"It certainly sounds like the guy that's being glorified by Steve Earle was certainly a guy that Steve Earle found sympathy with," Gill said. "My sympathy is on the other side, or with Mike Spann, who was killed by the allies of John Walker. And if John Walker had told the U.S. troops that had him in custody that some of his fellow Taliban-ites had weapons and were planning an uprising in that prison revolt, then perhaps Mike Spann wouldn't be dead and his family wouldn't have fatherless children and a widow trying to make do in Alabama."

"All of which is utterly irrelevant to the discussion as to whether Steve Earle should have recorded this song or not," Alden countered.

Indefatigable, Gill shot back, tossing in the requisite right-wing T-bomb to boot: "Maybe Steve could have done a song from the perspective of Mike Spann and shown sympathy for him, instead of this traitor to America."[15]

Saying "John Walker's Blues" "pissed off all the people I was trying to piss off," Steve had the last laugh. *Jerusalem* topped *Billboard*'s Top Independent Albums chart, peaked at No. 7 on *Billboard*'s Top Country Albums chart, peaked at No. 12 on *Billboard*'s Top Internet Albums chart, and at No. 59 was his highest-charting album on *Billboard*'s Top 200 since *Copperhead Road*.

At the height of the controversy over "John Walker's Blues," Steve was on vacation in Europe. Upon his return he began responding to his critics, few of whom seemed to grasp the difference between trying to understand a situation from another person's point of view and aiding and abetting the enemy. He even bearded the lion in his den when he accepted an invitation to be a guest on the November 6, 2003, edition of Fox News's top-rated "The O'Reilly Factor," hosted by modern-day Joe Pyne wannabe Bill O'Reilly. Dimly remembered

Just an American boy: Steve performs at Shepherds Bush Empire in London on April 1, 2003. His feelings about America's invasion of Iraq are spelled out on his t-shirt.

today, Pyne, during his heyday in Los Angeles of the '60s, was a pioneering right-wing TV talk show zealot and bully. He routinely dismissed guests with whom he disagreed by suggesting they "go gargle with razor blades." What novelist-screenwriter-media gadfly Harlan Ellison wrote of Pyne in his November 28,1968, column in the *Los Angeles Free Press* serves as an uncannily insightful appraisal of O'Reilly and his audience today. Describing Pyne's viewers as "snake pit freaks" and "sadomasochists of the purest stripe," Ellison observed: "They watch Pyne only because the Roman Arena was shut down, and they have nowhere else to go where they can turn thumbs down and see some poor slob get a trident through his chest. The redneck schlepps who dig Pyne's brand of hypocrisy and brutishness are the ones who can be convinced only by demagogues and rabble-rousers."[16] Like Pyne, O'Reilly posed as being above the fray, a seeker of only the Truth in what he called his "no-spin zone," in which he of course spun like a top. In true Pyne fashion, O'Reilly's thrust-and-parry style seemed to unnerve Steve as he stumbled through answers to questions about where he stands politically and fell back on his stock lines. ("I'm—I'm a socialist in the respect of—that I think that it's—it embarrasses me that people go hungry in the richest country in the world. But, you know, I'm—I have no problem with capitalism, but I only have—unless it's, you know, a—I have a problem with the capitalism as an ideology or a religion but not as an economic system.") Steve was, however, more persuasive when asked to explain the philosophical underpinnings of his Tell Us the Truth tour. "Tell Us the Truth is about media consolidation and other factors around media in this country and how they affect the quality of our—you know, in terms of the music business, what I do for a living and the quality of information that we receive." But when Steve seemed to suggest that he could live with the government controlling the media, because he had seen it work well in some countries he had visited, O'Reilly smelled blood and attacked.

O'Reilly: Yes? All right. So you want the government to run—

Steve: So I don't have a problem with that.

O'Reilly: —all the social programs. You want the government to run the media. I mean, you know, hey, you really trust the government that much? I mean you don't like President Bush. I mean, why do you want to give him all that authority?

Steve: Well, in this particular case, I think that the media directly affects, you know, the outcome of our elections. I think—

O'Reilly: Yeah, but you don't think that politicians are going to have anything to do with that, Mr. Earle, if they control the media?

Steve: Oh, I—

O'Reilly: Come on!

Steve: I absolutely believe that they have something to say about that, but I think that people have—look, I'm not one of these people that think, you know—I'm, I'm on one end of the spectrum, you're on another end. I don't have—

O'Reilly: Yes, but I'm trying to find out how you arrived at your conclusions, sir, and you're a little evasive. I mean, you don't know what to give Lindh. You don't know—you say you want the government to run the media. Then I point out that, if the government runs the media, they're certainly going to have an impact on free elections here because, right now, you have the left media, the right media. The government's going to run it any way they want to run it. And, you know, it doesn't look like you've thought these things through. Am I wrong?

Steve: No, I think about these things all the time.

At which point Steve regained his footing and offered his most lucid commentary of the segment:

Steve: Government running the media I don't think is necessarily a solution, and it may not be the solution in this country, but I do believe that there was a time when at least the news media was kept completely—the decisions made around what we saw on news media was kept completely separate from other programming on television. I don't believe that's completely true now.

But when you—when it gets to the point where we have a media climate that participates in accusing people that speak out against these policies of being unpatriotic and un-American, I think that's dangerous.

O'Reilly: Well, I agree with you. I think anybody who's sincere should be able to speak out and should be heard and—which is why we are happy you came on "The Factor" tonight, Mr. Earle. Good luck with your concert tour.

Earle: All right. Thank you very much.[17]

O'Reilly seemed to have prevailed, as his guest's halting responses made him easy prey for the cocksure host, whose closing "good luck" could not have been a more dismissive sendoff. Speaking several months later, though, Steve offered at least a partial explanation of the reality, or unreality, of confronting O'Reilly on national TV.

"Anything that has anything to do with Rupert Murdoch, as political discussion is like thinking pro wrestling's real. It's just not," Steve says. "I did 'The O'Reilly Factor.' Well, in 'the no-spin zone' I was edited. I zinged Bill O'Reilly and they edited out that part of the interview. He said, 'You wrote a song about John Walker Lindh, who was tried for treason—' I said, 'No, he wasn't.' He goes, 'Well, what was he tried for?' I said, 'Giving aid and comfort to an enemy of the United States.' He goes, 'Well, you're right, but he's a traitor.' I did my interview on tape, and they edited that part of it out when they aired it. People need to know that about Fox News, that that happens."[18]

"All the shit he took for that ballad," Rosanne Cash says. "When [husband, producer] John [Leventhal] and I heard that song, we said, 'Man, Steve is the only one with any balls in this entire business.' It's true. He really doesn't care.

He puts it out there, his own truths, doesn't matter about the flack he gets. I love him for that."[19]

"It's easy to vilify because it doesn't require compassion, it doesn't require self-examination, and it doesn't require sophistication," says Rodney Crowell. "Innocence is to be cultivated and to be protected, but ignorance is not far over across the line from it. Ignorance is a sin to me. 'John Walker's Blues' was compassionately written, I thought. I thought the presentation of it was very compassionate from the point of view of that young man. That's like shooting the messenger, how Steve was treated. When I heard that song I thought, This is a real eloquent piece of writing, and a sophistication to put yourself into that place and to get that chorus to work like it did. But you know what? When people are afraid and taking their cue from television, that kind of thing happens. It's unfortunate, it's sad."[20]

III. The Seeker

March 19, 2003: President Bush launched Operation Iraqi Freedom to end the regime of Iraqi dictator Saddam Hussein and its support of terrorism.

May 1, 2003: Outfitted in a fighter pilot's flight suit and swaggering aboard the USS *Abraham Lincoln* for his "Top Gun" moment, President Bush declared an end to major combat operations in Iraq, saying, "Mission accomplished!"

The news from the Middle East was never good, usually frightening, often bizarre, and sometimes insulting to Americans' intelligence. Vice President Dick Cheney's former employer, Halliburton, Inc., was awarded a multimillion-dollar contract to put out oil well fires in Iraq, and the veep disavowed any influence in the administration's decision. Halliburton sent civilian contractors into Iraq to work with Iraqis and the military, and as of March 2005, reported 34 of those personnel "lost … while performing services under our contracts in the Kuwait-Iraq region."[21]

In March 2005, April Johnson, daughter of Tony Johnson, a truck driver who was killed in Iraq the previous year, sued Halliburton and its subsidiary KBR, claiming that her father was not properly shielded from harm in his work. Tony Johnson was killed in an ambush on April 9, 2004, when insurgents attacked a truck convoy delivering fuel to Baghdad International Airport. Six other drivers were killed, and another, Thomas Hamill, was taken hostage (and later escaped).

A statement from April Johnson's attorneys (Lopez, Hodes Restaino, Milman & Skikos) contends that "Halliburton/KBR deployed its civilian truck drivers into a hostile active war zone despite knowledge from intelligence sources that there existed a substantial certainty the civilian drivers, moving in U.S. military vehicles, would be ambushed by Iraqi insurgents and killed or seriously injured." The lawsuit charged further that Halliburton "intentionally sent the convoy as an enemy 'decoy' in the U.S. military camouflage vehicles, to ensure the safe arrival and delivery of a second H-KBR fuel convoy.

"The civil action against Halliburton and KBR alleges, and will seek to demonstrate, that Halliburton fraudulently misrepresented the employees' working conditions in Iraq and that in fact, Halliburton's civilian employee deaths in Iraq were far greater than reported."[22]

In a report from October 20, 2004, Christian Coalition founder Pat Robertson, a staunch Bush supporter, appeared on CNN's "Paula Zahn Now" and told the host that prior to the invasion of Iraq, he had urged President Bush to prepare Americans for the likelihood of casualties in the coming war, and Bush had replied, "Oh, no, we're not going to have any casualties." Marveled Robertson: "He's the most self-assured man I've ever seen."[23]

With the 2004 election approaching, Steve was mobilizing to be part of the national debate in the best way he knew how—through his music. The American military's abuse of prisoners at Abu Ghraib prison in Iraq was all over the news and not going away; the 9/11 Commission's findings had blown holes in both the Clinton and Bush administrations' accounts of their responses to terrorist threats, perhaps the most shocking being future Secretary of State Condoleeza Rice's dismissal of a report that Osama bin-Laden planned attacks within the borders of the United States as being "historical information based on old reporting."

"Back home in Tennessee," Steve noted in his liner notes for his next album, *The Revolution Starts … Now*, "me and my boys had a deadline to meet.

"The most important presidential election of our lifetime was less than seven months away and we desperately wanted to weigh in, both as artists and as citizens of a democracy. All but two of these songs were recorded within 24 hours of the first line hitting the paper. We worked 12- and 14-hour days and in between takes and over meals we talked about the war, the election, baseball, and women, in precisely that order."[24]

Q: Your liner notes indicate there was a special urgency to get this record out.

Steve Earle: Yeah. I wrote "The Revolution Starts Now" and "Rich Man's War," and once I got those two songs, I really wanted it out before the election. And enough before the election so that it would get heard before the election. I called [Artemis Records president] Danny [Goldberg] and asked him what the deadlines would be for that, and he said, "If you want to get it out in September, you need to deliver it by the middle of July." I said, "When in July?" And he said, "Well, early in July is earlier in September." We ended up beating it. Once we delivered it, Danny managed to shuffle things around and Danny got it out, you know, two weeks ahead of that deadline.

"We were all on the same page as far as what was important to us, especially our drummer, Will Rigby. He and I sat up on the bus on election night last time around. We were playing New Orleans on that Wednesday, so it was the beginning of like the third leg of the tour, the *Transcendental* tour. We were watching the election returns, and we were the only two that stayed up and stayed up and stayed up. We played the gig with no sleep the next night, 'cause nothing was decided. We got into New Orleans in the wee hours of Wednesday morning. Will's the most politically informed and involved of anybody in the band; I mean, everybody is, but Will is the person I talk to more than anybody else. Everybody really pulled together and it was working. They had some time to sit around while I was writing, because basically the way we did it was, after the first two songs were recorded it was wake up in the morning with a blank piece of paper, and I'd go to the studio around one or two to finish a song, and we'd record and leave at one or two the next morning with a finished track, then get up the next day and do it again. We did it that way for two and a half weeks."[25]

The Revolution Starts ... Now
Artemis/E-Squared (2004)

Produced by Steve Earle and Ray
    Kennedy for the twangtrust
Recorded and mixed by Ray Kennedy
    at Room & Board, Hermitage,
    Tennessee
Assisted by Patrick Earle
Production coordinator: Elisa Sanders
Guitar technicalities: Greg "Chief" Frahn
Masteredy by Jim DeMain at Yes Master
    Studios, Nashville, Tennessee

Musicians
Steve Earle: guitars, mandola, organ, harmonica, harmonium,
    vocals
The Dukes
Eric "Roscoe" Ambel: guitars, vocals
Kelley Looney: bass, vocals
Will Rigby: drums, percussion, vocals
Patrick Earle: percussion
Emmylou Harris: vocals on "Comin' Around"
String quartet on "The Gringo's Tale" arranged and conducted by Chris
    Carmichael: Chris Carmichael: viola; David Angell: viola; David
    Henry: cello; Edward Henry: violin
Claps and shouts: Dukes, Chief, David Kissner, Dave Nokken, Bruce
    Kronenberg

Songs
1. "The Revolution Starts ..." (3:10) (Steve Earle)
2. "Home to Houston" (2:41) (Steve Earle)
3. "Rich Man's War" (3:25) (Steve Earle)
4. "Warrior" (4:11) (Steve Earle)
5. "The Gringo's Tale" (4:32) (Steve Earle)
6. "Condi, Condi" (3:08) (Steve Earle)
7. "F the CC" (3:10) (Steve Earle)
8. "Comin' Around" (3:41) (Steve Earle)
9. "I Thought You Should Know" (3:40) (Steve Earle)
10. "The Seeker" (3:10) (Steve Earle)
11. "The Revolution Starts Now" (4:23) (Steve Earle)

It's not, cut-for-cut, a towering work in a league with *Guitar Town*, *Copperhead Road*, *The Mountain*, or *Train a Comin'*. But *The Revolution Starts ... Now* is Steve's most provocative state of the union/state of the heart message yet. Storming the Bastille like never before, using ideas as his maps, Steve's new songs examined the lives of common folk charged with preserving and protecting our country's security, and cast a wary eye on the profiteers whose misguided morality enmeshes them in horrors unforeseen. He references late-Beatles rock ("The Revolution Starts Now"), stomping rockabilly ("Home to Houston"), country ballads both topical ("Rich Man's War") and lovestruck ("Comin' Around," with Emmylou Harris). "The Warrior" is a fierce spoken-word final testament of a fighting man who might be the modern-day counterpart of Kilran, the main character in Steve's potent Civil War mini-epic, "Dixieland," from *The Mountain*. Unlike Kilran, however, this warrior finds there are "no honorable frays to join." There's a finger-picked, bluegrass-inflected family epic ("The Gringo's Tale") with a surprising Beatles-esque string quartet rumbling evocatively and forebodingly starting about midway through, calypso rhythms (how better to send a surprising musical love letter to then–National Security Advisor Condoleeza Rice?), and merciless, driving rock 'n' roll (the grunge-laden "F the CC," the classically styled rocker "The Seeker"). The plight of the common folk and the greed of the profiteers comes together most persuasively in "Home to Houston," its buoyant rockabilly bounce in stark contrast to a gut-wrenching tale of a civilian contractor who goes to Iraq hoping to make a buck, unaware of the quotidian terror awaiting him, and now scrambling to get home in one piece, "then I won't drive a truck anymore." Earle's bemused attitude seems to mock the trucker, whose mercenary's roll of the dice didn't pay off. "The Gringo's Tale" is another family epic, this one centered on a mercenary (he references fighting in Grenada and Nicaragua) following in his forebears' footsteps only to find himself on the run, with a price on his head for his subversive activities. Conversely, "Rich Man's War," a mid-tempo, lilting tale, sympathizes with exploited underclass youths "sent off to fight a rich man's war," whether the subjects be Americans who enlist hoping to find a direction in life only to find that life unwind or young Arabs who choose the martyrdom of suicide bombing over life. In the context of these desperate, tragic scenarios, singing songs to Condoleeza Rice seems a waste of time, however humorously intentioned, and the message in the profane "F the CC" is undercut by an obscenity-laced chorus from a poet who has a far surer grasp of language as a weapon of dissent than he demonstrates here. In a poignant, folk-styled moment of self-assessment, "Comin' Around," with Emmylou Harris adding a spiritually resonant second verse, Steve's steady humming harmonium heightens the drama of a man and a woman trying to overcome some formidable self-imposed obstacles to get to a place of healing and redemption. As lovely as it is bittersweet, "I Thought You Should Know" is the quintessential Steve dialectic of love. Even as he admits to all sorts of internal tumult stemming from having fallen in love again, he kisses off the object of his affection with the warning that if she has any designs on hurting him, she might as well hit the road—"just pick up your little black dress and go," he sneers in the churning chorus—but at the end he fashions a beautiful proposition in promising "two arms to hold you tight" and a vow to give of himself completely "and keep your secrets for as long as I live." Pounding and driving, guitars all Byrds-jangly, "The Seeker" brings Steve's granddad back again as he reflects on the lessons he learned at the old man's knee, mainly, "Whatever you do, be a seeker." As a statement of purpose, it's a promise fulfilled on Steve's part; as a song, it has the triumphant feel of a man who has found himself and his purpose.

A Conversation with Steve Earle

"It's important to remember that being able to sit around and talk about the state of the world in any kind of detail is almost a luxury; working people don't get to do it." *(This interview was conducted in New York City by the author on August 25, 2004, shortly before the start of the Republican National Convention.)*

Was this a quick record for you? Were any of the songs problematic in the recording?

Not a lot of takes on very many of them. There's a couple of first takes—"The Seeker" was a first take. There was another first take. After an adjustment was made, I changed keys on "I Thought You Should Know," and after we changed keys I got it on the first take.

Altogether how long were you in the studio?

We worked a week, then we took a week off and I wrote, but I still only finished a couple of things. I had [a play] *The Exonerated* up in Nashville, my theater company did during the first week. Actually we took about five days off, started again and worked for one more week and basically everything was cut. All we had to do was mix; another week and a half to mix it.

What's Ray's role in the process?

He's the engineer. It's a little different on my records than it is when we're producing someone else's records, and Ray produces records on his own too. I'm usually the arranger and Ray becomes more of an engineer on my records. When we produce other records, I do a lot of arrangements, but we do more of them together. When he produces younger bands on his own he's actually kind of a song doctor and really works on structure and arrangements. But I've been doing this a long time, so I don't need that kind of help usually. He's the producer in the sense that he's the monitor of my performance, because you know I can hear what everybody else is doing a little easier than I can hear what I'm doing. So he's the vocal coach, he's the one that decides, listens for pitch and all that kind of stuff.

In terms of the stories you tell, one thing I've always liked about your songs is that you look at how policies and practices affect the rank and file instead of generalizing about how everything sucks.

I think that's important. I am an unapologetic leftist. But, you know, I only got through the eighth grade. I could've gone further. I'm relatively privileged and have been all my life. I'm lucky that I'm pretty acutely aware that when you start trying to decide what's good for working people when you're not one, there's a disconnect that happens there. It's important to remember that being able to sit around and talk about the state of the world in any kind of detail is almost a luxury; working people don't get to do it. I just think you're more effective when you try to stay aware of how it affects everybody. Even writing "John Walker's Blues," I connected to that through my son, who's exactly the same age as John Walker Lindh. For some reason when I saw him on TV, I related it to my son. That skinny and that age, exactly. I thought, He's got parents and they must be sick. So I think it's really important to go out of your way to make sure you at least try to come to some sort of understanding of how the issues you're talking about affect ordinary people.

I'm not sure, on "Home to Houston" and "Gringo's Song," if you're really sympathetic to these people, though. In "Home to Houston" the main character is essentially a mercenary; he's a truck driver who's gone over to Iraq to profit off the war.

Yeah, he's a mercenary, but he's also a working guy who took a job that was better than what he had here. The way it happened was, that guy that was driving for Halliburton and came back to Mississippi and had just gone on the news and talked about it, he made a lot of patriotic statements and said he was going back. I don't think he's gone back yet. I didn't buy it. So the song's not about him. It is about an imaginary guy and it's about a risk. I think there's got to be a lot more guys who went over and said, "I'm never fucking doing that again!" Several have been taken hostage; there's been a few killed. And they're targets in a guerrilla war, and all targets are targets of convenience—you take out the targets you can take. It is a guerrilla war, it's still going on and it's going to be a really, really ugly guerrilla war.

So what's the reaction been to "Condi, Condi"? She doesn't strike me as someone who would have a sense of humor about the song.

You know, I think she's kinda hot. There's no accounting for taste. She has the usual fashion challenges Republicans have to deal with; she needs to do something about her hair, because, damn! But I'm single and she's getting ready to be unemployed. Never can tell. She fascinates me, actually, her very existence. She's exactly my age. A black woman exactly my age with a really, really good education, ending up where she is, is really fascinating to me. The only reaction to the song has been in the New York *Daily News*, because they ran it as a cute little column piece; the very first thing written about this record was about that song. I thought, Here we go again. It hasn't really worked out that way. In fact, I got a four-star review in the New York *Post*, which bummed me out! One of my proudest accomplishments was a one-star review in the New York *Post*. It's the only review I've ever framed; I've got it in my office. I'm really thrilled with the reaction to this record so far. The reviews have been consistently good. The radio airplay is really good. We've struggled the last few records. It makes me optimistic about the election. I think people are starting to wake up; I think they're starting to get it. I don't blame the state the country's in on "them"—there's always a "them." I blame it on us; I think we quit participating in large enough numbers to be significant and surrendered the field to them.

It does seem as if there is a deep well of disdain for Bush and it's getting deeper. But at the same time, I well remember the most reviled politician of another era, Richard Nixon, and all the sentiment that seemed lined up against him. And he won landslide victories.

Yeah, I know. It's because of fear. You know, the reason the Republican Convention's in New York is because of that hole in the ground downtown. That's the only platform they have. No matter what they say about Kerry's record, and conservatives—they're not conservatives. I understand conservatives. I don't agree with them. I think government is supposed to do something for its citizens. That's a fundamental disagreement. But you know what? I'm okay with real conservatives. But neocons aren't real conservatives. And Bush isn't even a neocon. I fear what he's become is a fundamentalist Christian. I think he really thinks he has God on his side. If that's true, then we've got a fundamentalist squaring off against fundamentalism, and he's not smart enough to realize he cannot win that war. The other guys around him, they can't control him. He is President of the United States. Condoleeza did manage—this is another reason I'm really impressed with her—she did teach him to walk on his hind legs. That's an accomplishment, no doubt about it. This is a hundred times scarier than Nikita Khrushchev saying "We will bury you," which he didn't really say anyway. When I was a small child I really believed if I ever encountered Nikita Khrushchev he would eat me. I was lucky I was rescued from that fear at a relatively early age. I don't know why, but that's when I started playing music in coffeehouses, which was just an accident, because I was fairly precocious, and I started playing and wanting to play out before I was old enough to get in bars. They were coffeehouses and it was during the Vietnam War, and the three or four that were in San Antonio were pretty politically oriented, and they were very much anti-war-oriented, being a military town.

Do you see this record as an optimistic one?

Yeah, I do. I think "The Revolution Starts Now" is very optimistic. It's not about something that's going to happen in the future; it's not about something that's happened in the past. It's going on right now; it's never stopped; we may have gone to sleep, but they're up there, people are up there fighting every minute of every day. I mean, I remember being really impressed with Danny Goldberg and Robert Greenwalk and a bunch of us that were in *It's a Free Country*, a compilation of essays. We were reading that book at Midnight Special in Santa Monica. It's gone now from that location, old pinko bookstore, been in Santa Monica forever. We were reading there and the very first big march had just happened in L.A. in the windup to the war. People came in straight from the march, and a lot of the people that were there, and the people who had organized the march, had never stopped being active—they didn't open waterbed stores and have children named Dylan and Chelsea. But you know, there's a lot of things that happen when you have kids. The Beach Boys are an amazing phenomenon too. I don't know how you get from Transcendental Meditation to being a Republican. But people do. But there are people who have been involved all along. It's about being accountable. I believe if we are accountable and are vigilant, then democracy works through our Constitution. I don't get all that excited about the flag, because I've lived through times where it represented enough things that I find reprehensible that I just don't get as excited about it. But I do get excited about the Constitution. But Alan Bushman here at the Culture Project—a theater company— was looking for … in his marketing process, he had someone call GSA and get copies of the Constitution. To order a bunch of the books. I think he was going to sell them as merchandise in the theater lobby. But it's out of print. U.S. government is not printing the U.S. Constitution at the moment. They haven't printed it, it's out of print, and they have no plans to print it again. You can't get a copy of the U.S. Constitution from the U.S. government. That's as of last week. It's a mind-blowing thing.

I don't even know what to say.

I know. Everybody reacts the same way.

What I like about The Revolution Starts … Now *and the penultimate song, "The Seeker," are the appeals to listeners to stay on their toes. It's about the revolution that starts inside each of us, not necessarily in the streets.*

Right. Democracy requires vigilance, and there's never a time when that's not going to be true. If Kerry's elected, the work starts the day after the election. And that's really, really true. We're not in the game until we get rid of Bush. As long as Bush is president, he will continue to do whatever he wants to do, regardless of what we think. There was a lot of opposition to the war, and it was completely and totally ignored. He bullied—well, he didn't even have to bully, but he did. Everybody was ready to defer to him, and he realized it and seized the moment. We had the whole world on our side after September 11, and we managed to squander that in nine months. We alienated the entire world. I'm voting for John Kerry because I believe with all my heart that one thing will happen, is that the day after the election I think John Kerry will start reaching out to the other countries in the world. Because he has to. He's gonna be stuck with having to get us out of Iraq. I think he wants to get us out of Iraq. I don't think he's going to say that overtly as an unconditional antiwar statement, and I understand why. But I do believe we get back in the game come January 21.

I bought an anti-Bush T-shirt last night from some activist kids who were smart enough to get into Manhattan before it gets shut down. They're gonna stop letting pinkos on this island in a couple of days. That's why I'm here. I always planned, even before we knew the record was gonna come out right now, to get in here several days before the convention started, because I saw what happened in Miami. What they did there was to basically shut down downtown Miami, which is much easier to get into than Manhattan. They'll limit the number of marchers by separating them from each other and trying to thwart their efforts to do what they did in Seattle, which was communicate with each other. In Seattle they didn't realize that trade unionists and environmental activists were communicating with each other on the Internet. It's a whole new game now.

On that notion of the album being optimistic, "Comin' Around" certainly fits that description.

I wrote that for a film. It's the only thing that didn't have anything to do with the rest of the song cycle when I started it. But it was written in the cycle. I wrote it for a film called *An Unfinished Life*, which is coming out in December. It's Robert Redford, Morgan Freeman, and Jennifer Lopez. And it's a really good movie, real human story; nothing blows up in it. I wrote it for that film; it was commissioned. The part I'm singing is based on the Robert Redford character and the part Emmylou is singing is based on the Jennifer Lopez character. The movie's about forgiveness, it's about lettin' go of stuff that's not helping you anyway and taking up too much of your energy and too much of your life. I wrote it about that, but all that stuff, once I got finished with it, I figured was more about me than it was about the movie. That's one of the things that's good about my job.

There's a strain in your songs of family showing up, and your grandfather shows up in the opening lyric of "The Seeker." It's not the first time he's made an appearance.

Yeah, he pops up all the time. That first line of the song is absolutely true—I was exactly eight when my grandfather died. It's sort of a metaphor and it's sort of not. My grandfather used to take me for walks, show me deer tracks, show me raccoon tracks, and that's where the line comes from. My dad moved to Tennessee 10 years ago, and one of the main motivations for him was his grandkids being there, because both Stacey and I are there, and Patrick's there, my brother, who's my tour manager. Most of his grandkids are in Tennessee, and he knows which back roads to drive. You know, that's what he does; that's his thing. That's why I bought him a Cadillac. It's about that deal of when we stop paying attention to our surroundings and stop asking questions, then it's kinda over. And in a democracy it's really over. I have no problem with, and in fact think we're much better off when there's not a disconnect between spirituality and politics. I'm not talking about religion—you have to disconnect religion, because religion is political. Spirituality is a totally different thing. A lot of people come to 12-step programs having had a real bad experience with religion. You have to believe in a power greater than yourself to get clean; I really do believe that. I've never known anybody able to do it otherwise. People need to learn that there's a difference between religion and spirituality. Religion is a group of peoples' agreement about what God is and a relationship with God—that's political, because it requires a consensus. Spirituality is one person's intimate, one-on-one relationship with God. That's above and beyond politics. I don't care, Jesus Christ can be your personal savior all you want, but as soon as you start telling everybody else that they've got to get to God that way, you're in trouble, it becomes political.

Emmylou has become the female vocalist of choice on your albums. You've had some terrific female vocalists accompany you over the years, including your sister Stacey.

Emmy's done a lot of background things, and I finally wrote a duet for us on the last record, and I did it again on this record. She was gettin' pissed. I had specifically written duets for several other singers and had her come in and do background vocals, which she likes to do. But this is two in a row now. We live in the same town; we usually see each other elsewhere, more out of town than at home. But it'll probably happen again.

You don't have to justify using Emmylou Harris.

She's Emmylou Harris. You know?

• • •

George W. Bush was reelected without the aid of a U.S. Supreme Court ruling in his favor. From the time the president declared "mission accomplished" aboard the USS *Abraham Lincoln* on May 1, 2003, to this writing in August 2005, the American death toll in Iraq stood at 1,726, with 1,372 of those deaths coming in combat. The body count for the entire war was at 1,863 (1,480 in combat). The government's official count of the wounded was 13,877; other sources estimated the number of Americans wounded in Iraq as being anywhere from 15,000 to 42,500. Mid-August polling found 51 percent of Americans believing the war with Iraq is wrong, the first instance of an antiwar majority the pollsters had found since the U.S. commenced military action. Bush's steadily declining job approval rating was down to 45 percent.[26]

The Revolution Starts ... Now was nominated for Grammy Awards in the categories of Best Contemporary Folk Album and Solo Rock Vocal Performance, and won the former. It was his first Grammy win as a solo artist after 10 nominations. (He and Ray Kennedy, the twangtrust, had won in 1999 as producers for Lucinda Williams's million-selling *Car Wheels on a Gravel Road*.)

Winning friends and influencing people all over, Steve's scheduled July 30, 2005, headlining appearance at the Southeast Alaska State Fair in Juneau ignited a flurry of protest from locals who regarded him as anti-American. Writing in the June 19, 2005, edition of the *Juneau Empire State News*, reporters Korry Keeker and Brandon Loomis revealed that the fair's executive director Herb VanCleve (who said he knew very little about Steve's music when he booked him, but "in throwing around his name, everyone was like, 'Hell yeah!'") began receiving letters of protest in early May, among the first coming from a retired Haines resident named Al Kelly, who objected to what he regarded as profane lyrics.

"What happened is that I'm a country music fan and a bluegrass fan, and when I saw that Steve Earle was coming to the fair and Laura Love and that other fellow [Elvin Bishop], I thought I'd go on the Internet to find out a little about them," Kelly said. "I saw there was a lot of vulgarity and that [Earle's] concerts are very much political. And I didn't think the fair was a place for that, the fair being a family-type of gathering.

"The state fair, they've got the animals, the kids, and there are so many beautiful things about it," he added. "To bring this in and dump it in the middle is insulting."

Another Haines resident, miner-prospector Merrill Palmer, researched Steve online and was disturbed by his findings.

"He says what he is," Palmer said of Earle. "He says he's a borderline Marxist. He does not believe in the capitalist system. He has a red star on his T-shirt and he calls his album *The Revolution Starts Now*." Palmer added that Steve "runs around with these communist hammer-and-sickle symbols as he goes all over the world, and I'm just saying, this is outrageous. This is not something that Haines should support."

Palmer even bought two pages of paid commentary in two different issues of the *Chilkat Valley News* to protest Steve's appearance. "Here's the bottom line: Would we in Haines, Alaska, in the Southeast Alaska State Fair, would we support Nazis?" Palmer wrote. "To me, the communist symbols that this guy runs all over the world with are 30 times worse than the Nazis, if you want to go by how many people died."

Steve, by all accounts, was lukewarm to the idea of playing Alaska until VanCleve told him of the Juneau area's abundant fishing streams. "I pointed out that we had the best fishing in the known universe. That got their interest."

Apparently the general populace didn't share the naysayers' low opinions of Steve. Advance sales for the show were the strongest they had ever been in the fair's history.[27]

IV. Alpha Male Ascending, v 8.0

"May God forgive us our insanity, and we'll keep pressing on"

In 2001 Rodney Crowell broke out of a mini-slump commercially with an intensely personal album, *The Houston Kid*, released on the independent Sugar Hill label (where Dolly Parton had reclaimed her art and artistry a year earlier with her bluegrass gem *The Grass Is Blue*). Crowell had found himself in a rut as the '90s wound down, and his muse was aching. A project with a band he called the Cicadas was the turning point. "My intention with that record was to get me out of this mind-set that I oughta make music for a record company because I owe them something—that being hits to get on radio. I was of the opinion awhile back that that was stifling me from being able to do what I would like to do to get my own self-respect. That's been a mantra I've had about this."[28]

Recording in his own home studio, paying production costs out of his own pocket, he raised the stakes again with an unflinchingly diary-like song cycle that was a journey through life lived on his native Houston's rough side of town, where violence is a constant, lives take horrifying twists in the blink of an eye, and love is understood on a deep, metaphysical level because it is so elusive, so hardwon. *The Houston Kid* represented the finest sustained writing of Crowell's recent history; and true to his influences, it felt more folk than country, and the country touches had a pop flavoring. It was, in short, Crowell's *Rubber Soul*, in production, in content, and in mood. It also happened to be a grand return to an incisive, insightful style of songwriting that has made Crowell songs among the most distinctive for the past quarter century.

He topped himself and *The Houston Kid* in 2003 with *Fate's Right Hand*, which returned him to the major label, Columbia, where he had scored his biggest triumphs as a solo artist. *Fate's Right Hand* accomplished the seemingly impossible by being every bit as personal as *The Houston Kid*, but rather than the ghosts of a rough childhood, it examined a man at midlife, full of self-doubt, needing affirmation of his very being, questing spiritually, yet finding pockets of optimism that drive him on to a new day—even to the point of giving him enough courage to assure his young child of a bright future in spite of this ol' world's mean-spiritedness (the closing country rocker, "This Too Will Pass"). Unsurprisingly, the music matched the lyrics' thrust, from Béla Fleck's galloping banjo lines that infuse "Earthbound" with an antigravity ambiance to Tony Harrell's "Runaway"-style organ lines in the infectious, Beatles-ish "Come On Funny Feeling," to Bill Livsey's eerie electric harmonium punctuation that rises up from the mist in "Ridin' out the Storm." Sometimes, though, Crowell needed nothing more than his voice and his acoustic guitar to cut to and through the bone: the somber, eloquent "Adam's Song," a prayer for friends who lost a child, could not be more comprehending of or sensitive to the aching void that will never be filled in those parents' lives. And when Crowell quietly caressed the key lyric—"we're just learning how to live with a lifelong broken heart"—it brought a listener into the confidence of an absolutely masterful writer who has

The Devil's right hand man: Steve at the Wychwood Music Festival, Cheltenham Racecourse, June 4, 2005.

a lot more to tell you about yourself than you could ever imagine. *Fate's Right Hand*, pure and simple, is a work of art.

In early 2005, Crowell was asked how he viewed the political slant Steve's songwriting had taken in recent years. Had he seen it coming?

"No. No," he said emphatically. "I would say that's a byproduct of maturity. I go back to those early days, when you're 19, 20, 24, 25 years old, it's just instinctive. There's very little actual intellectual consideration of the politics or the craft or any of that stuff. You learn it instinctually and you act it out. The political position comes as a result of living in this world and growing and maturing. It didn't come from me until later. This new record that I have is probably the most political I've ever gotten, and it's because you live in this world, your awareness overtakes you and it's like, oh, man."[29]

That "oh, man" resulted in a humanistic masterpiece, 2005's *The Outsider*. Topically *The Outsider* was preceded by Joe Ely's searing 2003 gem, *Streets of Sin*, which limned an America in which no one was safe, no one was secure, most were on the run from something they couldn't even define, and even the Earth, ravaged by floods and droughts, was rebelling. Two years later the scene had deteriorated further, and that's where Crowell came in. *The Outsider* was the moment when one of the great songwriters of his time took the world's pulse and found it racing to the Apocalypse. Ely pleads, "Don't talk to me right now / I've got survival on my mind"; Crowell prays, "My God forgive us our insanity and we'll keep pressing on." Ely spits, "The ones who set the policy / Don't give a damn about our needs"; Crowell howls, "The slick politicians, man, you've got to admit / Seem crazy as bedbugs and they don't give a whit / About the man on the street with his back to the wall." In the pounding "The Obscenity Prayer (Give It to Me)," Crowell torches conspicuous consumption, hypocrisy ("The Dixie Chicks can kiss my ass / but don't forget my backstage pass") and unbridled greed. Against a furious rock 'n' roll assault of booming drums and snarling guitars in "Don't Get Me Started," Crowell chronicles the madness born of "scamming for oil"—in the Middle East inferno; in the corporate rape of "working-class suckers"; in the rampaging national debt. Still and all, Crowell finds hope arising in a stirring, hymnlike appeal to the better angels, "Ignorance Is the Enemy," with Emmylou Harris and John Prine taking turns narrating lyrics as the voice of God; in the folk-country strains he applies to Dylan's benevolent "Shelter from the Storm" (again, with Emmylou); and in the rousing album-closing call to arms, "We Can't Turn Back," the rock 'n' roll brew is spiced with a pronounced Irish twist, complete with an evocative tin whistle flight courtesy John Mock. Mature, outspoken, tender, literate and uncompromising, *The Outsider* found Rodney Crowell at the peak of his artistry, casting his eye on the America of Steve's v. 6.0 and finding cancers on society's cultural and political bodies. Nevertheless, Crowell's journey through some bleak landscapes inspired in him not cynicism but rather a bouyant hope for the future.

"At the end, the line in 'We Can't Turn Back,' 'may God forgive us our insanity and we'll keep pressing on / we can't turn back now,' I took that to be a very positive statement and purposely ended the record with it. And that is another self-examination. You know what, man? I live the examined life. Sometimes I wish I could give it up."[30]

Out there in America, Steve was watching as the body count mounted in Iraq, and come late summer, as a 48-year-old mother endeavored to confront the president of the United States in an effort to ascertain what exactly her 19-year-old son had died for when he was killed on the streets of Sadr City, Iraq, on April 4, 2004.

And he was in love again.

Epilogue

*As if everything in the world
is the history of ice...*

—*Coming Through Slaughter*

Nine-thirty A.M. on a December morning, 2004. Tony Brown was at home when the phone rang. His wife Anastasia beckoned him from the other room.

"Tony!" she said. "It's Steve Earle and he's calling from Germany."

The next voice Tony heard was Steve's.

"Hey, man," he called out, "me and Allison are about to go onstage in Germany and we're in the dressing room and thought we'd give you a call and say hello and give you a heads-up before you heard it on the street. I came in to talk to her about producing her next album, and she kissed me on the mouth and we fell in love and she's divorcing Butch."

Allison was Allison Moorer, younger sister of Shelby Lynne and a highly regarded singer-songwriter in her own right who had yet to break through. Tony had been instrumental in getting her started too, signing her to MCA, where she cut three albums that left the label about $2 million in the hole, in Tony's estimate. Her songwriting partner was her husband, a muscular, tattooed fellow named Butch Primm ("He's got Allison's name tattooed all over his body," Tony says), and their songs tended to be rather dark, not the best strategy for getting radio's attention, although it did wonders for her critical standing. Typically she would sell 50,000 to 60,000 CDs right out of the box and then hit a wall. "She became so despondent that we couldn't get past that," Tony

Tony Brown today, in his office at Universal South Records, which he co-founded. Among his important signings: the young superstar Joe Nichols, and Waylon Jennings' son Shooter, whose debut album, "Put the O Back In Country," marks him as one of the top new artists of 2005.

says. She left MCA and signed with Sugar Hill, released another excellent album (*The Duel*, in 2004), and sold even less than she had been selling on MCA. Tony knew she was on tour overseas with Steve, because she had e-mailed him with a message to that effect, adding: "Even when we leave the fold we still work together."

To Steve, Tony said: "Is this a dream? Am I dreaming this or am I talking to you really?"

Steve: "Well, talk to her. Let her tell you."

Allison came on the line and confirmed Steve's news.

"Congratulations," Tony said. "If it makes you happy, it makes me happy."

"It makes me happy," Allison told him.

And Tony sat there nonplussed, thinking to himself, Boy, if I were y'all, I wouldn't get off the plane. Butch Primm is a big guy and he's as intense as his songs. There goes his Christmas. No fun this year for Butch.

But the musician-producer-executive saw another angle too: "[Allison's] getting sort of a chip on her shoulder because people like Tift Merritt get a Grammy nomination, and Mindy Smith has scanned like 200,000 records. And I think she's getting to feel people are out to get her. And that's too bad because she's a great singer and she's a good writer. She just needs a little bit different angle, and maybe Steve will give her that."[1]

. . .

At home in Ashland City, Jack and Barbara Earle took the news of Steve's impending seventh marriage in stride. The summer before, at a family celebration honoring their parents' fiftieth wedding anniversary, Steve's siblings had prevailed upon him to toast their mom and dad. He demurred, saying, "I don't know why they're having me do this with my track record." But he stepped up to the task and moved his parents with remarks about what a good example they had set in their commitment to each other, and how they were reason enough for him to keep trying to get it right.

Jack chuckles at the mention of six, now seven marriages. "Well, it's not necessarily my thing," he says, laughing, "but two or three of his marriages never should have been anyhow, then there were two or three good ones. Of course, one of them was a repeat"—he laughs again—"but I guess I'm not one to let something like that bother me too much, other than it wouldn't be my thing. And I hated to see it happen. I just thought and thought and thought of him, and the kids, just floatin' loose and their situation kept changing real fast. You hate to see that with the two boys."[2]

. . .

On January 17, 2005, friends and family organized a surprise fiftieth birthday party for Steve at a Nashville club. The guest of honor arrived with his new fiancée in tow and was startled when everyone shouted "Surprise!" as he entered. "Steve didn't know what was going on," says Ronnie McCoury, who came by to offer his congratulations. McCoury didn't recognize the young lady on Steve's arm. "I think her hair was different, pulled back, and in the dark club I just thought, Wow, that's a pretty girl."

Steve made the rounds, thanking everyone for attending and of course talking a blue streak. "Did you see Allison?" he asked Ronnie offhandedly as they were chatting.

"Is that Allison Moorer?" Ronnie queried in return.

"Yeah," Steve said. "I'm gonna marry that girl."

"Really?"

"Yeah, we went over to Europe together, and the next thing you know…"

"You know what?" Steve added. "I been married six times and I even married one of 'em twice. But I didn't even get married in my forties."

"I tell you," Ronnie says, "he's a quick-witted guy and he's funny. He's quite a character."[3]

. . .

Writing on Thursday, December 2, 2004, to his fans on steveearle.net, Steve, who hadn't been heard from since the reelection of George W. Bush in November, began a note with words in all capital letters—"NO, I HAVEN'T DEFECTED …" and continued: "…I'm just in love. If I wasn't in love, and I wasn't in Europe, I would probably have slit my wrists on November 3rd."

Steve's marriage to Allison Moorer took place on August 11, 2005, at the Hermitage Hotel in Nashville. Ever vigilant, the newlyweds rolled into Crawford, Texas, on August 20 to play a concert in support of Cindy Sheehan, the 48-year-old mother of Casey Sheehan, an American soldier killed in Iraq a year earlier. On August 6 Sheehan had set up camp outside President Bush's ranch, demanding a meeting with the commander in chief and the immediate withdrawal of troops from Iraq. "All of those reports prove my son died needlessly," she said. "This proved that every reason George Bush gave us for going to war was wrong."[4] Her protest inspired countless candlelight vigils and antiwar rallies across the country, and a predictable counterresponse as well from Bush supporters. (Crawford alone was expecting attendance of up to 3,000 at a pro-war rally to be held at its high school football stadium on August 27.)

Following a set by James McMurtry (son of the great Texas novelist Larry McMurtry), Steve opened his 10-song set with an eloquent statement of purpose, explaining that despite his opposition to it, the Vietnam War had ended only "because my dad opposed it." The growing support for Cindy Sheehan's protest, he predicted, was the start of a mainstream uprising that would ultimately bring the troops home. His acoustic set included a beautiful version of "Comin' Around" with Allison sitting in, and gained powerful momentum with the trifecta of "Warrior," "Christmas in Washington," and "Rich Man's War" preceding an urgent reading of the closing number, "The Revolution Starts Now."

At steveearle.net, fans were howling about Steve selling "The Revolution" to Chevy for use in a truck commercial. In Crawford, Texas, on August 20, 2005, that song sounded like the truth.

* * *

We give each other a performance, the wound of ice. We imagine audiences and the audiences are each other again and again in the future. "We'll go crazy without each other you know." The one lonely sentence, her voice against my hand as if to stop her saying it. We follow each other into the future, as if now, at the last moment we try to memorize the face a movement we will never want to forget. As if everything in the world is the history of ice.

—*Coming Through Slaughter*

Anthologies, Compilations, and Miscellaneous Recordings

(Domestic Releases Only)

Essential Steve Earle (MCA, 1993)

These 13 tracks compiled by Tony Brown tilt heavily to *Guitar Town* and *Exit 0*, the albums Brown was most involved in as a producer. Only two tracks—"The Devil's Right Hand" and "Copperhead Road"—are from *Copperhead Road*; two others are from the soundtrack of the John Candy–Steve Martin film *Planes, Trains & Automobiles*, namely, the Dave Dudley trucker's classic "Six Days on the Road" and a reworking of the *Pink & Black* EP's "Continental Trailways Blues." All good stuff, some of it great, but no reason not to own the original albums, especially *Copperhead Road*.

Fearless Heart (MCA Special Products, 1995)

Slight at 10 tracks, this long player also leans heavily on the first two studio albums, save for the inclusion of "The Devil's Right Hand" and "Six Days on the Road." What were they thinking? Both *Essential* and *Millennium Collection* titles are more sensible buys than this, for about the same price, but ultimately *Ain't Ever Satisfied* is the anthology of choice.

Johnny Too Bad/Steve Earle & the V-Roys (E-Squared, 1997)

An EP featuring Steve fronting the V-Roys on two versions of the Slickers' "Johnny Too Bad," the first being an upbeat "Sunshine Mix," the second a grinding "Hillbilly Mix" that would have fit nicely on *Guitar Town*. The V-Roys offer up a driving original, "Straight Highway," that features some hot-shit guitar, and the EP winds up with Steve and the Fairfield Four on an alternate take of the moving "Ellis Unit One." Hardly monumental, but interesting nonetheless, in the way that attention must be paid whenever Steve lends his voice to a project.

Early Tracks (Epic, 1997; Koch, import, 1998)

The Epic issued collection of recordings Steve made for LSI and then for Epic, which was rushed out after *Guitar Town* became an unexpected smash. (See more details about these sessions in Chapter 7, "Phases and Stages.") Note: the Koch import has liner notes penned by John Lomax III, who reflects on his business/professional relationship with Steve.

Ain't Ever Satisfied—The Steve Earle Collection (Hip-O, 1996)

Now this is more like it: two CDs, 30 songs, spanning the studio work from *Guitar Town* through *The Hard Way*, plus covers of Springsteen's "State Trooper," the Stones' "Dead Flowers," the Sir Douglas Quintet's "She's About a Mover," and the *Planes, Trains & Automobiles* songs. Great sampling of Steve's many sides, from the rockin' ("Guitar Town," "Copperhead Road," "Johnny Come Lately"—curiously, one of his fiercest song, *The Hard Way*'s "Promise You Anything," is not included), to the hard country ("Hillbilly Highway"), to the lyrical Outlaw folk poet ("My Old Friend the Blues," "Nothing but a Child"). Those seeking an overview of the key tracks of an important career would be well advised to start here.

Steve Earle & The Supersuckers (SubPop, 1999)

(See review in Chapter 17, "A Clear Field.")

Sidetracks (E-Squared, 2002)

It may have served as a between-albums stopgap, but *Sidetracks* deserved a spot on 2002 year-end best-of lists. The man is simply a craftsman par excellence, a fact underscored by these literate, beautifully realized songs (many of them from film soundtracks). It includes "Some Dreams" from *The Rookie*, "Me and the Eagle" from *The Horse Whisperer*, "Open Your Window" from *Pay It Forward*, and an alternate take of "Ellis Unit One" from *Dead Man Walking*, featuring the Fairfield Four. From the *Transcendental Blues* sessions comes the previously unreleased gem "Dominick St.," an infectious jig with Sharon Shannon on accordion. Among the cover songs he offers are the Slickers' "Johnny Too Bad," recorded with the V-Roys and released on a 1997 EP (see above). Elsewhere, he delivers a torrid take on Nirvana's "Breed" and an aggressive rendering of the Chambers Brothers' '60s classic "Time Has Come Today," which features a searing vocal from a gravel-voiced Sheryl Crow, along with snippets from Abbie Hoffman's anti-establishment rants. Best of all is his version of Dylan's "My Back Pages." Apparently, Earle's strained, urgent vocal was intended as a "scratch," or guide, vocal for a duet by Joan Osborne and Jackson Browne to be used in a film that never materialized. Fortunately, the tape was saved, and it lends this soulful collection a resonant, vibrant finale.

20th Century Masters—The Millennium Collection: The Best of Steve Earle (MCA, 2003)

One cut shorter than but otherwise hewing to the same concept as *Essential Steve Earle*, right down to the inclusion of the two songs from *Planes, Trains & Automobiles* and the curious second-class citizen status of *Copperhead Road*—*Essential*'s two *Copperhead* songs are here reduced to only one, the title track. Barnesandnoble.com's William Ruhlman nailed it when he described the album as a "bare-bones primer on Earl's most commercially successful music of the 1980s."

Live from Austin, TX (New West, 2004)

An absolutely terrific live recording of Steve and an early Dukes lineup flush with the unexpected smash success of *Guitar Town*. Steve's forceful acoustic strumming kicks off the set on a fierce note, as he scorches "Sweet Little '66" even before the band comes blowing in. By the time the set is three songs old—with "Goodbye's All We Got Left" and a powerful version of "Guitar Town" nipping at "Sweet Little '66"'s heels—a couple of facts are evident: For one, Steve's performance, even on disc, is so forceful and energized that he could have carried the show without any help. His acoustic playing here is an object lesson in why so many people marveled over and raved about it; for another, if he wasn't going to play solo acoustic, he had the support of a doubly formidable Dukes lineup, especially Harry Stinson on drums and Mike McAdam on a sizzling lead guitar, playing the Richard Bennett licks like he owns them and adding some vibrant personality of his own to boot. Also note evidence of Steve's prolific pen—six of the songs here wound up on *Exit 0*, the concert (originally broadcast on "Austin City Limits" on September 12, 1986) serving as a trial run for the new material, which didn't change dramatically on record from the versions offered here. (Note too a revitalized version of "The Devil's Right Hand" that has now taken the form it would assume on *Copperhead Road*, having evolved from the rather milquetoast treatment on the *Pink & Black* EP.) Throughout the proceedings Steve is a confident, affable front man, already a seasoned performer comfortable with an audience and savvy with regard to the construction of his set list for maximum emotional impact in its balance of ballads and barnburners. Check out the lilting, lyrical rockabilly–honky tonk fusion on "Think It Over," with affecting instrumental contributions from Bucky Baxter on pedal steel, Ken Moore on the 88s, and McAdam on lead electric guitar—a stirring ensemble performance and a captivating, sweet vocal from Steve mark it as timeless. This is the sound of an artist seizing his moment with a vengeance. It's a wonder to behold.

The Original
Unofficial Covers

Songs written or cowritten by Steve Earle and recorded by other artists, as compiled by and reported with permission of steveearle.net. Additional research by Kieran McGee.

"Angel Is the Devil" (Steve Earle)
Supersuckers (with Steve Earle): *Steve Earle & the Supersuckers* (CD single: Sub Pop SP 388, July 6, 1999).
Bap Kennedy: *Domestic Blues* (E-Squared 51058, May 19, 1998; produced by the twangtrust).

"Arianne" (Scott Miller, Steve Earle)
V-Roys: *All About Town* (E-Squared, Oct. 6, 1998; produced by the twangtrust).

"As Long as Love's Been Around" (Steve Earle, John Scott Sherrill)
Steve Wariner: *One Good Night Deserves Another* (MCA, 1989).

"Bible and a Gun, A" (Steve Earle, Jason Ringenberg)
Jason and the Scorchers: *Thunder and Fire* (A&M, Dec. 7, 1989).

"Christmas in Washington" (Steve Earle)

Joan Baez: *Dark Chords on a Big Guitar* (CD: Koch Records, Sep. 9, 2003).
Joan Baez: KGSR, Live version (CD: KGSR 2003).
Steve Arvey: *Soul of a Man* (CD: Mad, Sep. 24, 2002).
Eve Selis: *Long Road Home* (CD: Stunt Records STCD 1013, May 1, 2000).
Linda Wolfgram: *Just Me* (1999); contact LWolf54572@aol.com for
    ordering info.

"Copperhead Road" (Steve Earle)

Farmboy: *Farmboy* (CD: Sep. 23, 2003, Binky).
Grass Cats: *By Request* (CD: New Time Records NT 1005, 2000).
Todd Thibaud: *Favorite Waste of Time* (album: Doolittle 358019, Jan. 20, 1998)
    (hidden track #13).
Billy Burnette: *Steel Cowboys: Bikers Choice, Vol. 1* (CD: Platinum
    15095-9352-2, 1999).
The Bullfrogs: *From Time to Time* (CD: 1999, U.K.) (also includes "Johnny
    Come Lately").
Wil Gravatt: *Ready to Cross That Line* (CD: Dart, 1998).
Jerry Adams: *Outlaw Love* (CD: Macola 1185, July 18,1995).
Lee Kernaghan: *Three Chain Road* (CD: ABC Australia, 1994).

"Cry Night after Night" (Stacey Earle, Mark Stuart, Steve Earle)

Stacey Earle and Mark Stuart: *Never Gonna Let You Go* (CD Special Edition:
    Evolver, June 3, 2003).

"Darlin' Commit Me" (Stephen Earle)

Slim Pickens: *Slim Pickens* (album: Blue Canyon BCS 506, 1977).

"Devil's Right Hand" (Steve Earle)

Webb Wilder: *It Came from Nashville* (album: Landslide, 1986; remastered
    and reissued, Sep. 3, 2004).
Johnny Cash: *Cash Unearthed* (album: Lost Highway 000167902, Nov. 25, 2003).
Lance Larson: *To Make a Long Story Short* (album: 2001).
Highwaymen: *The Road Goes On Forever* (album: Capitol 28091, Apr. 4, 1995).
Highwaymen: (7-inch single: 1995, NO PS).
Barrence Whitfied: *Cowboy Mambo* (CD: East Side Digital, Feb. 21, 1994).
"The Klansmen" (the musicians are the band Demented Are Go and the
    singer is Skrewdriver singer Ian Stuart): *Rock 'n' Roll Patriots* (CD: 1992,
    West Germany) (You can draw your own conclusions about the intent
    of the album from the pseudo band name.)
Waylon Jennings: *Betrayed* (movie: 1988).

CCCP (Claudia Scott, Carlene Carter, Casino Steel, and John Payne):
  Let's Spend the Night Together (album: Plateselskapet AS (GHP20),
  1986, Norway).
Waylon Jennings: *Will the Wolf Survive* (album: MCA 5688, Mar. 1986).
  "To Make a Long Story Short" (Garry Tallent on bass).
Scooter and the Streethearts: *Stories to Tell* (album: 1996, Germany).
Susan Shore: *Old 218* (album: 1995).
Lowbudget Blues Band (headed by Mats Ronander): *Lowbudget Blues Band*
  (album: 1990, Scandinavia).

"Dixieland" (Steve Earle)
Whistlepig: *Down on the Farm* (Aquamarine Music album: 2003).

"Down on My Luck" (Steve Earle, Tom Benjamin)
The Bill Lyerly Band: *Requiem Mess* (CD: Broadcast Records 20013, 2001).
The Bill Lyerly Band: *Cobalt Blues* (CD: Riviere International Records RIVI
  CD 98, 1999, original release).
The Bill Lyerly Band: *Prodigal Son* (LP: LSI Records LSI 8206-1, 1982).

"Down the Road" (Steve Earle)
Trigger Gospel: *Oh the Stories We Hold* (CD: Undertow Music, Nov. 18, 2003).

"Du Står Stadig Der" (Steve Earle)
(see "You're Still Standing There")

"Far Cry from You, A" (Steve Earle)
Rhonda Vincent: *A Dream Come True* (album, Rebel Records 1682,
  Aug. 25, 1994).
Marsha Thornton: *Maybe the Moon Will Shine* (album: 1991, MCA,
  Feb. 19, 1991).
Connie Smith (promo 7-inch single: 1985, PS, Epic Records).

"Farväl" (Steve Earle): see "Goodbye"

"Fearless Heart" (Steve Earle)
Siobhan Maher-Kennedy: *Immigrant Flower* (album: 2001, U.K.,
  BMG/Gravity, Mar. 18, 2002).
Gregg Cagno: *Present Moment Days* (CD: Black Potatoe 6326, June 27, 2000).
Heidi Noelle Lenhard: *Fame L.A.* (Soundtrack) (Polygram 555612
  Mar. 31, 1998).

Shawn Colvin [live]: *Cover Girl ... Extra!* (CD5: Columbia CSK 6549, 1994, PROMO).

Shawn Colvin [live]: *Every Little Thing (He) Does Is Magic* (CD5: Columbia 01-660600-17, 1994).

Soulmates: *Fall Down Laughin'* (Hazel Wood Music, 1992).

Henning Staerk: *Hard to Handle* (album: 1991, Denmark).

"Feel Alright" (Steve Earle)
Roger Clyne and the Peacemakers: *Honky Tonk Union/Real to Reel* (Double CD, www.azpeacemakers.com, Emma Java, Apr. 4, 2000).

"Ft. Worth Blues" (Steve Earle)
Guy Clark: *Cold Dog Soup* (CD: Sugar Hill 1063, Oct. 26, 1999).

Melody Guy: *Ready for Sunshine* (CD, 1999).

"Gajoverden Gajovaerd" (Steve Earle)—see "I Ain't Ever Satisfied"

"Good Ol' Boy (Gettin' Tough)" (Steve Earle, Richard Bennett)
Confederate Railroad: *Keep on Rockin'* (album: Atlantic 83024, Oct. 20, 1998) [Steve on rhythm guitar and vocals]

Sawyer Brown: *The Boys Are Back* (album: Curb, Sep. 12, 1989).

"Goodbye" (Steve Earle)
The Pretenders: *G.I. Jane* movie soundtrack (album: Hollywood Records 162109, Aug. 12, 1997).

The Pretenders: "Goodbye" [including the "G.I. Jane" Radio Edit, "G.I. Jane," Chrissie's, a cappella "G.I. Jane," and Instrumental "G.I. Jane" versions of "Goodbye"] (promo CD5: Hollywood Records PRCD-10713-2, 1997).

Emmylou Harris: *Wrecking Ball* (album: Asylum 61854, Sep. 26, 1995).

Emmylou Harris: "Goodbye" [including single remix of "Goodbye"] (promo CD: 1995).

Christina Lindberg, Andra Tider, and Andra Vägar [*Other Times & Other Roads*] (in Swedish, song title translated as "Farväl") (CD: Frituna 0327-2, Sweden).

Christina Lindberg: Ännu En Dans (in Swedish, song title translated as "Farväl") (CD5: Frituna 15041, Sweden).

Totta Näslund: *Duetterna* [in English, *Duets* (sung by Totta Näslund and Sara Isaksson)] (in Swedish, song title translated as "Farväl") (CD: EMI 2001-03-26, Sweden).

"Guitar Town" (Steve Earle)
Roger Creager: *Texas Outlaws* (CD Compilation, Compadre, Apr. 8 2003).
Willie Heath Neal: *Willie Heath Neal* (CD, Headhunter Records, Aug. 14, 2001).
Emmylou Harris: *At the Ryman* (album: Reprise/WEA 26664, Jan. 14, 1992).
Roger Clyne and the Peacmakers (album).

"Heatin' Up" (Steve Earle)
Ozark Mountain Daredevils: *Modern History* (album: Conifer Records, 1989,
    Produced by: Wendy Waldman).
Ozark Mountain Daredevils: *Heart of the Country* (album: 1987).

"Henk Is Enne Lollige Vent" (Steve Earle):
    see "I'm Just a Regular Guy"

"Hillbilly Highway" (Steve Earle)
Ricky Skaggs: *Life Is a Journey* (album: Atlantic/WEA 83030, July 29, 1997).

"Hole in My Heart" (Steve Earle, Richard J. Dobson)
Kelly Willis: *Well Traveled Love* (CD, MCA MCAD 6390, May 25, 1990).

"Hometown Blues" (Steve Earle)
Curtis Stigers: *Secret Heart* (CD, Concord Records, Apr. 23, 2002).

"I Ain't Ever Satisfied" (Steve Earle)
Todd Thibaud: *Dead Flowers* (CD5: Blue Rose 1999BLUCD0094, 1999).
Gretchen Peters (promo CD5 single: Imprint, 1996, PI).
Gretchen Peters: *The Secret of Life* (album: Imprint 1000, June 4, 1996).
Brother Phelps: *Anyway the Wind Blows* (album: Elektra/WEA 61724,
    Mar. 7, 1995).
Angelo Palladino (with the Honky Tonk Cowboys): *The Honky Tonk Cowboys
    Are on a Mission … Impossible* (soundtrack to the movie *Wild West*) [CD:
    Cooking Vinyl Cook CD 056, 1993, U.K.]; also includes Steve's versions
    of "Nowhere Road" and "Fearless Heart"; also includes the cover of
    "No. 29" by Angelo Palladino (with the Honky Tonk Cowboys).
Allan Olsen: Gajo (in Danish, song title translated as "Gajoverden Gajovaerd")
    (album: 1990).
Trash Mavericks: *Off the Tracks* (CD: Lizard Skin Records LS700).

"I Thought I Was Dreaming" (Greg Trooper, Steve Earle)
Lawnie Wallace: *I Thought I Was Dreaming* (album: 1996).
Greg Trooper: *Everywhere* (album: Ripe & Ready Records 2205 Oct. 4, 1994).

"If You Need a Fool" (Steve Earle)
Del McCoury Band: *Blue Side of Town* (CD: Rounder CD 0292, Feb. 14, 1992).

"I'm Just a Regular Guy" (**"Henk Is Enne Lollige Vent"**) (Steve Earle)
Rowwen Heze: *Boem* (CD: Hans Kusters Music, the Netherlands, 1991).

"I'm Not Getting Any Better at Goodbye" (Steve Earle)
Buddy Miller: *Cruel Moon* (CD: Hightone 8111, Oct. 19, 1999, U.S.).
Mark Chesnutt: *Longnecks and Short Stories* (album: MCA 10530, Mar. 31, 1992, U.S.).
Mark Chesnutt: *I'm Not Getting Any Better at Goodbye* (7-inch single: 1992, NO PS, U.S.).

"I've Never Really Been in Love Before" (Steve Earle)
Jim Mundy (promo 7-inch single: Dot DOA-17678, 1976, NO PS).

"Jerusalem" (Steve Earle)
Joan Baez (CD: 2005 *Bowery Songs*, Koch Records).

"Johnny Come Lately" (Steve Earle)
The Bullfrogs: *From Time to Time* (CD: 1999, U.K.) (also includes "Copperhead Road").
Matchbox: *Comin' Home* (Matchbox Records, 1998).
Buffalo Power: *Live I Lundgrens Garage* (*Live at Lundgren's Garage*) (album: 1991, Sweden).
Billy Ray Cyrus: *Achy Breaky Heart* (compilation album, U.K.).

"Little Bit in Love, A" (Steve Earle)
Patty Loveless: *If My Heart Had Windows* (album: MCA 42092, Oct. 25, 1990).
Patty Loveless: "A Little Bit in Love" (45: Epic, 1988).
Patty Loveless: *16 Top Country Hits, Vol. 4* (various artists, CD: MCA MCAD-10078, U.S.).
Patty Loveless: *Contemporary Country* (various artists, CD: Time-Life, U.S.).

"Live Wire" (Steve Earle)
Zella Lehr: *Zella's Greatest Hits* (CD).

"Love's to Blame" (Steve Earle, Mary Cutrufello)
Mary Cutrufello: *Who to Love & When to Leave* (CD: 1996).

"Lucy Dee" (Steve Earle)

Vince Gill: *The Best of Vince Gill* (album: RCA 9814, Sep. 25, 1989).

"Mercenary Song, The" (Steve Earle)

The Cory Morrow Band: *The Cory Morrow Band* (album: SKU CM007, Feb. 27, 2001).

"More Than I Can Do" (Steve Earle)

The Villas: *Set for Life* (CD: ThinkTank Records, July 8, 2003) [www.villasongs.com].

Michael Banahan: *Tecumseh Valley* (CD: ANEW Records NEWD 410, Ireland, 1997).

Brian Setzer: (recorded but not released).

"Mustang Wine" (Stephen Earle)

Carl Perkins: "Mustang Wine" (U.K. 7-inch single: Jet Records S JET 117, 1978).

Carl Perkins: *Presenting Carl Perkins* (album).

"My Baby Worships Me" (Steve Earle)

Reckless Kelly: *Acoustic, Live At Stubb's BBQ* (album: Valley #15116, June 6, 2000).

Tom Principato: *Hot Stuff!* (album: Ichiban Old Indie #4106, May 29, 1991).

Tom Principato: *Smokin'* (album: Powerhouse, Oct. 1985).

"My Old Friend the Blues" (Steve Earle)

Patty Loveless: *Dreamin' My Dreams* (CD, Sony Nashville, Sept. 13, 2005).

T. Graham Brown: *The Next Right Thing* (CD, Compendia, May 20, 2003).

Dave Kelly: *Resting My Bones* (CD: Hypertension 1209 HYP, 2002).

Beth and Apr. Stevens: *Sisters* (album: Rounder Select #396, Oct. 1, 1996).

Susan Shore: *Old 218* (album: Self-Released, 1995).

Eddi Reader and the Patron Saints of Imperfection: *Storytellers* (various artists, album: 1994), also includes Steve's version of "Copperhead Road"

Eddi Reader: *Storytellers* (various artists, CD: Nectar NTRCD012, 1994, U.K.). (also includes Steve's version of "Copperhead Road").

Angelo Palladino (with the Honky Tonk Cowboys): *The Honky Tonk Cowboys Are on a Mission.... Impossible* (soundtrack to the movie *Wild West*) [CD: Cooking Vinyl Cook CD 056, 1993, U.K.]; also includes Steve versions of "Nowhere Road" and "Fearless Heart"; also includes the cover of "I Ain't Ever Satisfied" by Angelo Palladino (with the Honky Tonk Cowboys).

Pahinui Brothers: *The Pahinui Brothers* (album: Private Music #82098, Aug. 25, 1992).
Eddi Reader and the Patron Saints of Imperfection: *Mirmama* (album: 1992).
Janie Frickie: *Labor of Love* (album: Sony, June 19, 1989).
The Proclaimers: *Sunshine on Leith* (album, Capitol #21668, Oct. 25, 1988).
Arranmore: *Another Chapter* (album, CS Records).

"The Note" (Stacey Earle, Mark Stuart, Steve Earle)
Stacey Earle and Mark Stuart: *Never Gonna Let You Go* (CD: Evolver, June 3, 2003).

"Nothin' but You" (Steve Earle)
Robin Lee: *Heart on a Chain* (album: Atlantic/WEA, June 25, 1991).
Robin Lee (7-inch single: 1991, NO PS).
The Nighthawks: *Live in Europe* (album: Varrick, July 13, 1987).

"Nothing but A Child" (Steve Earle)
Donnie Munro: *On the West Side* (CD: Hyper Records, 2000).
Kathy Mattea: Saving Grace (v/a CD: Polygram Chronicles 555885, 1998).
Lee Ann Womack: *A Country Superstar Christmas 2* (various artists, CD: Hip-O HIPD-40124, 1998).
Tom Sheehan: *Where You Are* (CD: Orchard Records, 1998).
Robin and Linda Williams: *Child's Celebration of Christmas* (various artists, CD: Rhino 72878, 1997).
Kathy Mattea: *The Way in a Manger: Country Christmas* (various artists, CD: Warner 46750, 1997).
Gina Jeffries: *The Flame* (album: 1995, Australia).
Robin and Linda Williams: *A Prairie Home Christmas* (various artists, CD: High Bridge HBP 42704, 1995).
James Blundell: *Spirit of Christmas* (album: 1993, Australia) [Polygram, released as a fundraiser for the Salvation Army]
Kathy Mattea: *Good News* (album: 1993).
Phon Roll: *Sunset Boulevard* (album: 1993, Switzerland).
Pete and Maura Kennedy: *A Holiday Feast, Vol. II (Hungry for Music)* (various artists, CD) *A Holiday Feast, Vol. II* is the second in a series benefiting children's programs in the Washington, DC, area. You can order *A Holiday Feast, Vol. II* by calling (in the U.S.) 1.888.843.0933.
Nicolette Larson: *Have Yourself a Merry Christmas* (album).
Robin and Linda Williams: *Sugar Plums: Holiday Treats from Sugar Hill* (various artists, CD).

"Nowhere Road" (Steve Earle)

Willie Nelson and Waylon Jennings: *Switchback* (soundtrack) (CD: BMG, 1997, U.S.) [same version as on *Wanted! The Outlaws*, song coproduced by Steve]; also includes Steve's version of "Feel Alright."

The Outlaws: *Wanted! The Outlaws* (1976-1996 20th Anniversary) (CD: RCA #66841, Apr. 30, 1996) [song coproduced by Steve].

"No. 29" (Steve Earle)

Angelo Palladino (with the Honky Tonk Cowboys): *The Honky Tonk Cowboys Are on a Mission … Impossible* (soundtrack to the movie *Wild West*) [CD: Cooking Vinyl Cook CD 056, 1993, U.K.]; also includes Steve's versions of "Nowhere Road" and "Fearless Heart"; also includes the cover of "I Ain't Ever Satisfied" by Angelo Palladino (with the Honky Tonk Cowboys).

Trace Adkins (recorded but not released).

"Other Kind, The" (Steve Earle)

Mark Linskey: *Stay Hard, Stay Hungry, Stay Alive—Songs of Freedom* (album: Roachenders Records, 2003).

Brother Phelps: *Anyway the Wind Blows* (album: Asylum, 1995).

"Paddy on the Beat" (Steve Earle).

Cochon Bleu: *Relooké* (Big Deal records CD: c. 2000).

"Poor Boy" (Steve Earle)

McKennard: *McKennard* (four-track CD: c.1996, Sweden).

"Promise You Anything" (Steve Earle, Maria McKee, Patrick Suggs).

Siobhan Maher-Kennedy: *Immigrant Flower* (album: BMG/Gravity, Mar. 18, 2001, U.K.).

Stacey Earle: *Dancin' with Them That Brung Me* (album: Evolver #312803, May 9, 2000, U.S.).

Lowbudget Blues Band (headed by Mats Ronander): *Country File* (album: 1994, Scandinavia).

"Rain Came Down, The" (Steve Earle, Michael Woody)

The Woodys: *The Woodys* (album: Rounder #613149, Jan. 13, 1998).

Allan Olsen: *En Gros* (in Danish, song title translated as "Regn På Vej") (CDs: 1999).

Montana Rose: *There's a Dream* (CD: The Orchard #3388, Mar. 18, 2000).

The Thompson Brothers Band: *Cows on Main Street* (album).

"Regn På Vej" (Steve Earle, Michael Woody):
see "The Rain Came Down"

"Regular Guy" (Steve Earle)
Pierre Le Rue—"Fiddle Gumbo" (CD, WEA, Nov. 27, 1995).

"Sincerely (Too Late to Turn Back Now)" (Steve Earle,
Robert Earl Keen, Jr.)
Kelly Willis: *Bang Bang* (album: MCA MCAD 10141, Apr. 16, 1991).

"Slippin' Away" (Steve Earle, Chris Gates, David Roach)
Junkyard: *Sixes, Sevens & Nines* (album: Geffen, May 28, 1991).
"Some Blue Moons Ago" (Steve Earle, Richard Bennett).
Patty Loveless: *Patty Loveless* (album: MCA #5915, Oct. 25, 1990).

"Someday" (Steve Earle)
Joel R.L. Phelps and the Downer Trio: *Inland Empires* (album: 2000,
Moneyshot).
Shawn Colvin: *Cover Girl* (album: Sony #57875, Aug. 23, 1994).
Shawn Colvin: *One Cool Remove* (U.K. CD single: 1994, Columbia 661134 5).
Tim Mahoney: *Tommy Alverson and Boot Hill Live at Ozona's* (album).

"Sometimes She Forgets" (Steve Earle)
Kasey Chambers and the Dead Ringer Band: *Hopeville* (album: Massive/
Warner Bros., 1998).
Stacy Dean Campbell: *Hurt City* (album: Sony, July 25, 1995).
Travis Tritt: *Sometimes She Forgets* (7-inch single: 1995).
Travis Tritt: *Greatest Hits—From the Beginning* (album: Warner/WEA #46001,
Sep. 12, 1995).
Martin DelRay: *What Kind of Man* (album: Atlantic/WEA, Nov. 10, 1992).

"Somewhere Out There" (Steve Earle)
Lucy Kaplansky: *Ten Year Night* (album: Red House Records #126,
Mar. 23, 1999).

"South Nashville Blues" (Steve Earle)
Corey Harris and Henry Butler perform the (rewritten) song over the opening and closing credits of the HBO show *The Corner* (1999 or 2000).

"Sorry Sue" (Scott Miller, Steve Earle)
V-Roys: *All About Town* (album: E-Squared, Oct. 6, 1998; Produced by the
twangtrust).

"Taneytown" (Steve Earle)
The United 32's: *Snipers in Derelict Houses* (various artists, CD: Triage, 1999).

"The Usual Time" (Steve Earle)
Eric "Roscoe" Ambel: *Knucklehead* (CD: 2003, Lakeside Lounge).

"Tom Ames' Prayer" (Steve Earle)
Bluecats: *Goin' Straight* (CD: Gypsy Sun Records, 1998, U.S.).
Robert Earl Keen: *Gringo Honeymoon* (album: Sugarhill #1044, July 26, 1994).

"Valentine's Day" (Steve Earle)
Michael Banahan: *Tecumseh Valley* (CD: ANEW Records NEWD 410,
    Ireland, 1997).

"When You Fall in Love" (John Scott Sherrill, Steve Earle)
Johnny Lee: *Greatest Hits* (album: 1983).
Johnny Lee: *Bet Your Heart on Me* (album: 1981).
Johnny Lee: (7-inch single: 1981, NO PS).

"While You Sleep" (Charlie Sexton, Steve Earle)
Charlie Sexton: *Charlie Sexton* (album: MCA #6280, Oct. 25, 1989).
Charlie Sexton (7-inch single: 1989).
"Window Song, The" (Mic Harrison, Scott Miller, Steve Earle).
V-Roys: *All About Town* (album: E-Squared, Oct. 6, 1998; Produced by the
    twangtrust).

"You're Still Standing There" (Steve Earle)
Lucy Kaplansky: *Every Single Day* (album: Red House, Sep. 11, 2001).
Badlees: *50:45* (CD, 2000).
McKennard: *McKennard* (four-track CD: c.1996, Sweden).

"You're Still Standing There" (**"Du Ståar Stadig Der"**)
(Steve Earle)
Nikolaj Christensen: *Vi Er Paa Vej Til Et Sted, Hvor Blomsterne Faar Lov Til At
    Blive Nede I Jorden Og Droemme* (album: Kick Music KICKCD 63, 1996,
    Denmark).

Prologue

1. Author interview with Jack and Barbara Earle, June 20, 2005.

1. The Hard Way: A Template

1. Author interview with Jack and Barbara Earle, June 20, 2005.
2. www.wwits.net/cities/jville.phtml
3. Lauren St. John, *Hardcore Troubadour* (New York: St. Martin's Press, 2003), 5 (hereafter cited as *Hardcore Troubadour*).
4. *Ibid.*, 6.
5. Author interview with Jack and Barbara Earle, June 20, 2005.
6. *Ibid.*
7. *Ibid.*
8. *Hardcore Troubadour*, 4.
9. Author interview with Jack and Barbara Earle, June 20, 2005.
10. *Ibid.*
11. *Ibid.*
12. *Ibid.*
13. *Ibid.*
14. *Ibid.*
15. *Ibid.*
16. *Ibid.*
17. *Ibid.*

2. "Fighting It All the Way"

1. Author interview with Jack and Barbara Earle, June 20, 2005.
2. *Ibid.*
3. Author interview with Stacey Earle, Feb. 7, 2005.
4. Author interview with Jack and Barbara Earle, June 20, 2005.

5. *Ibid.*
6. *Ibid.*
7. *Ibid.*
8. *Ibid.*
9. *Hardcore Troubadour*, 24.
10. Author interview with Jack Watson, July 3, 2005.
11. Check *Just an American Boy* CD for this quote.
12. Author interview with Jack and Barbara Earle, June 20, 2005.
13. *Ibid.*
14. *Hardcore Troubadour*, 16.

3. Outcast Ascending

1. Author interview with Jack and Barbara Earle, June 20, 2005.
2. *Ibid.*
3. Andrew O'Hehir, "The Salon Interview: Steve Earle," Salon.com, Nov. 13, 2002 (hereinafter cited as "The Salon Interview: Steve Earle").
4. Author interview with Jack and Barbara Earle, June 20, 2005.
5. *Hardcore Troubadour*, 26.
6. *Tracks*, Feb. 2004.
7. *Ibid.*
8. *Ibid.*
9. *Ibid.*
10. *Hardcore Troubadour*, 26.
11. Author interview with Jack and Barbara Earle, June 20, 2005.
12. Jay Cocks, "The Color of Country," *Time*, Sep. 8, 1988.
13. *Hardcore Troubadour*, 26.
14. Marty Racine, "Musical Labels Won't Work with Steve Earle," *Houston Chronicle*, Mar. 20, 1989.
15. "The Salon Interview: Steve Earle."
16. *Hardcore Troubadour*, 19.

4. The Other Kind

1. *Hardcore Troubadour*, 32.
2. Author interview with Jack and Barbara Earle, June 20, 2005.
3. *Ibid.*
4. *Hardcore Troubadour*, 31.
5. Author interview with Jack and Barbara Earle, June 20, 2005.
6. "The Salon Interview: Steve Earle."
7. *Ibid.*, 37.
8. Author interview with Jack and Barbara Earle, June 20, 2005.
9. Author interview with Jack Watson, July 3, 2005.
10. *Hardcore Troubadour*, 37.
11. Author interview with Jack and Barbara Earle, June 20, 2005.
12. *Hardcore Troubadour*, 36
13. Author interview with Jack and Barbara Earle, June 20, 2005
14. *Ibid.*
15. *Ibid.*
16. *Ibid.*
17. *Ibid.*
18. *Hardcore Troubadour*, 43.
19. *Ibid.*, 44.

5. Lone Star State of Mind, 1970–74

1. John Lomax III, *Nashville: Music City USA* (New York: Harry N. Abrams Incorporated, 1985), 99 (hereafter cited as *Nashville: Music City USA*).
2. www.michaelmartinmurphey.com.
3. *Ibid.*
4. Liner notes by Earl Willis, *Live at the Old Quarter, Houston Texas* (Tomato Records).
5. www.townesvanzandt.com.
6. *Ibid.*
7. *Ibid.*
8. *Ibid.*
9. *Ibid.*
10. *Ibid.*
11. Guyclark.com/biography.
12. www.townesvanzandt.com.
13. *Ibid.*
14. Peter Blackstock, "Can't Keep a Good Man Down," *No Depression*, spring 1996.

15. Joanne Serraris, *Steve Earle in Quotes* (self-published, 2004).
16. *Hardcore Troubadour*, 65.
17. *Ibid.*, 65
18. Author interview with Rodney Crowell, Apr. 6, 2005.
19. *Hardcore Troubadour*, 45.
20. Details about Steve's marriage to Sandy Henderson are published in *Hardcore Troubadour* (pp. 51–71) and corroborated by the author's interview with Jack and Barbara Earle, June 20, 2005.
21. *Hardcore Troubadour*, 51.
22. *Hardcore Troubadour*, 54.
23. Author interview with Jack and Barbara Earle, June 20, 2005.
24. All quotes in this section from author interview with Jack Watson, July 3, 2005.

6. Waylon and Willie and the Boys

1. www.cmt.com/artists/az/walker_jerry_jeff/bio.jhtml.
2. *Nashville: Music City USA*, 39.
3. Waylon Jennings, with Lenny Kaye, *Waylon: An Autobiography* (New York: Warner Books, 1996), 211 (hereafter cited as *Waylon: An Autobiography*).
4. Bill C. Malone, *Country Music USA* (Austin, TX: University of Texas Press, third paperback printing, 1993), 375.
5. *Ibid.*, 375.
6. Chet Flippo, liner notes for the 2000 reissue of *The Red Headed Stranger* (Columbia/Legacy, OK63589).
7. *Ibid.*
8. www.countrymusichallofhame .com/inductees/waylon_jennings.
9. *Waylon: An Autobiography*, 209.
10. *Ibid.*, 201.
11. *Ibid.*, 202.
12. *Ibid.*, 199–200.
13. Rich Kienzle, liner notes, *Honky Tonk Heroes* reissue (1999, BMG/Buddah 7446599619 2).
14. *Waylon: An Autobiography*, 209.
15. *Ibid.*, 242.
16. *Ibid.*, 243.
17. *Ibid.*, 236, 244.

7. Phases and Stages

1. *Hardcore Troubadour*, 61.
2. *Nashville: Music City USA*, 107.
3. *Ibid.*, 107.
4. Author interview with Rodney Crowell, Apr. 6, 2005.
5. *Ibid.*
6. Earle, Steve, liner notes, *Train a Comin'* (Winter Harvest, 1995).
7. *Hardcore Troubadour*, 69.
8. Author interview with Tony Brown, Mar. 8, 2005.
9. *Hardcore Troubadour*, 80.
10. *Ibid.*, 84.
11. Author interview with Rodney Crowell, Apr. 6, 2005.
12. *Hardcore Troubadour*, 89.
13. *Ibid.*, 91–92, 95.
14. *Ibid.*, 95
15. Michael Ondaatje, *Coming through Slaughter* (New York: W.W. Norton & Company, Inc., 1977), 63.
16. *Nashville: Music City USA*, 116–117.
17. Chart positions from Joel Whitburn, *The Billboard Book of Top 40 Hits* (New York: Billboard Books, 2000).
18. *Hardcore Troubadour*, 83.
19. *Ibid.*, 97–98.
20. *Ibid.*, 100.
21. *Ibid.*, 101.
22. Author interview with Richard Bennett, Feb. 17, 2005.
23. *Ibid.*
24. *Ibid.*
25. *Ibid.*
26. *Ibid.*
27. *Ibid.*
28. *Hardcore Troubadour*, 103.
29. *Ibid.*, 111.
30. *Ibid.*, 107.
31. *Ibid.*, 109.

8. Me, Tarzan

1. All quotes from Tony Brown in this section from author interviews, Dec. 2, 2004, Dec. 7, 2004, Dec. 14, 2004, Mar. 8, 2005.
2. Bill Bentley, "Local Yoakam," *L.A. Weekly*, Nov. 26, 1984.

9. "Are You Ready for Me?"

1. Unless otherwise indicated, all quotes from Tony Brown in this section are from author interviews with Tony Brown, Dec. 2, 2004, Dec. 7, 2004, Dec. 14, 2004, Mar. 8, 2005.
2. Author interview with Richard Bennett, Feb. 17, 2005; all quotes from Richard Bennett in this section are from this interview, unless noted otherwise., and the account of Richard and Steve's Los Angeles meetings is drawn from this interview as well.
3. Author interview with Harry Stinson, Feb. 21, 2005; all quotes from Stinson in this section are from this interview.
4. Alannah Nash, *Behind Closed Doors: Talking to the Legends of Country Music* (New York: Alfred A. Knopf, 1988), 133–139.
5. Associated Press, "Selma Says Speed Trap Reputation Undeserved," Jacksonville (Texas) *Daily Progress*, June 7, 1989.

10. Odyssey 1985–86

1. Nash, op cit., 138.
2. From e-mail correspondence between author and John Lomax III, July 14, 2005.
3. *Hardcore Troubadour*, 125.
4. From e-mail correspondence between author and John Lomax III, July 14, 2005.
5. Earle, Steve, liner notes, *Guitar Town* (MCA Nashville reissue, 088 170 265-2, 2002).
6. Author interview with Richard Bennett, Feb. 17, 2005; all quotes from Richard Bennett in this section are from this interview, unless indicated otherwise.
7. *Ibid.*
8. Author interview with Tony Brown, Dec. 7, 2004.
9. Author interview with Harry Stinson, Feb. 21, 2005.
10. Author interview with Tony Brown, Dec. 2, 2004.

11. Author interview with Rosanne Cash, May 17, 2005.
12. All quotes, unless otherwise indicated, from author interview with Pam Lewis, Feb. 2, 2005.
13. Marty Racine, "Between Two Worlds," *Houston Chronicle*, Aug. 5, 1986.
14. Author interview with Pam Lewis, Feb. 2, 2005.
15. Racine, Marty, op cit.
16. Merrill, Jane; Stromberg, Gary, *The Harder They Fall: Celebrities Tell Their Real-Life Stories of Addiction and Recovery* (Center City, MN: Hazelden Publishing & Educational Services, 2005), 240 (hereinafter cited as *The Harder They Fall*).
17. Author interview with Ray Kennedy, Mar. 6, 2005.

11. Alpha Males (Gettin' Tough)

1. Author interview with Tony Brown, Dec. 7, 2004; all Tony Brown quotes in this section from author interviews, Dec. 2, 2004, Dec. 7, 2004, Dec. 14, 2004.
2. Author interview with Richard Bennett, Feb. 17, 2005; all quotes from Richard Bennett in this section are from this interview, unless indicated otherwise.
3. Author interview with Harry Stinson, Feb. 21, 2005; all quotes from Harry Stinson in this section are from this interview, unless indicated otherwise.
4. Author interview with Tony Brown, Dec. 7, 2004.
5. *Hardcore Troubadour*, 171.
6. *Ibid.*, 176.
7. Harold DeMuir, "The Hillbilly Boss, "*Pulse!*", Aug. 1990.
8. *The Harder They Fall*, 240.
9. Author interview with Tony Brown, Dec. 7, 2004.
10. *Ibid.*
11. *Ibid.*
12. *Hardcore Troubadour*, 183.
13. Author interview with Jack and Barbara Earle, June 20, 2005.

14. Author interview with Harry Stinson, Feb. 21, 2005.
15. Author interview with Tony Brown, Dec. 2, 2004.
16. Author interview with Harry Stinson, Feb. 21, 2005.
17. *Hardcore Troubadour*, pp. 193–194.
18. Author interview with Tony Brown, Dec. 7, 2004.
19. Author interview with Pam Lewis, Feb. 2, 2005; all quotes from Pam Lewis in this section are from this interview, unless indicated otherwise.

12. Copperhead Road

1. Author interview with Tony Brown, Dec. 2, 2004.
2. Author interview with Richard Bennett, Feb. 17, 2005.
3. *Ibid.*
4. Author interview with Tony Brown, Dec. 14, 2004
5. *Ibid.*
6. Author interview with Joe Hardy, Jan. 21, 2005.
7. Author interview with Tony Brown, Dec. 14, 2004.
8. *Ibid.*
9. *Ibid.*
10. *Ibid.*
11. Author interview with Joe Hardy, Jan. 21, 2005.
12. *Ibid.*
13. "The London Blitz, 1940," Eyewitness to History, www.eyewitnesstohistory.com (2001).
14. http://news.bbc.co.uk/1/hi/world/asia-pacific/716609.stm.
15. www.camdentown.co.uk/camden7.htm.
16. Author interview with Tony Brown, Dec. 14, 2004.
17. Author interview with Philip Chevron, Apr. 7, 2005
18. Author interview with Tony Brown, Dec. 14, 2004.
19. Author interview with Philip Chevron, Apr. 7, 2005.
20. Author interview with Jack and Barbara Earle June 20, 2005.

21. Author interview with Tony Brown, Dec. 14, 2004.
22. Author interview with Joe Hardy, Jan. 21, 2005.
23. Author interview with Tony Brown, Dec. 2, 2004.
24. *Ibid.*
25. *Ibid.*
26. *Ibid.*
27. Author Interview with Tony Brown, Dec. 14, 2004.
28. Holly Gleason, "Steve Earle: A Bad Boy Settles Down," *Rolling Stone*, Jan. 26, 1989.
29. Crowell, Rodney, liner notes for 2001 reissue of *Diamonds & Dirt*, (Columbia/Legacy, 2001).

13. The Hard Way: A Reality

1. *Hardcore Troubadour*, 81.
2. Author interview with Stacey Earle, Feb. 7, 2005.
3. *Ibid.*
4. Author interview with Jack and Barbara Earle, June 20, 2005.
5. *Ibid.*
6. *The Harder They Fall*, 242.
7. Author interview with Stacey Earle, Feb. 7, 2005.
8. Author interview with Joe Hardy, Jan. 21, 2005; all quotes from Joe Hardy in this section are from the Jan. 21, 2005 interview unless indicated otherwise.
9. Author interview with Tony Brown, Dec. 14, 2004.
10. Author interview with Tony Brown, Dec. 7, 2004.
11. Author interview with Joe Hardy, Jan. 21, 2005; all quotes from Joe Hardy in this section are from this interview unless indicated otherwise.
12. Author interview with Stacey Earle, Feb. 7, 2005; all quotes from Stacey Earle in this section are from this interview unless indicated otherwise.
13. Author interview with Stacey Earle, Feb. 7, 2005; all quotes in this section are from this interview, unless indicated otherwise.

14. Author interview with Joe Hardy, Jan. 21, 2005; all quotes from Joe Hardy in this section are from this interview, unless indicated otherwise.

14. Lost & Found

1. Author interview with Tony Brown, Dec. 7, 2004.
2. Author interview with Jack Watson, July 3, 2005.
3. Author interview with Rosanne Cash, May 17, 2005.
4. Author interview with Pam Lewis, Feb. 2, 2005.
5. *The Harder They Fall*, 242.
6. Author interview with Mark Stuart, Feb. 7, 2005; all quotes from Mark Stuart are from this interview unless indicated otherwise.
7. Author interview with Stacey Earle, Feb. 7, 2005; all quotes in this section are from this interview, unless indicated otherwise.
8. Author interview with Pam Lewis, Feb. 2, 2005.
9. Author interview with Jack and Barbara Earle, June 20, 2005.
10. *Hardcore Troubadour*, 278.
11. *The Harder They Fall*, 245.
12. Author interview with Joe Hardy, Jan. 21, 2005.
13. *Ibid.*
14. posting on steveearle.net, 25 May 1999, by Steve Earle
15. Earle, Steve, liner notes for *I Feel Alright* (E-Squared/Warner Bros., 1996).

15. Resurrection

1. Author interview with Norman Blake, Mar. 16, 2005; all quotes from Norman Blake in this section are from this interview unless otherwise indicated.
2. Author interview with Peter Rowan, Mar. 4, 2005; all quotes from Peter Rowan in this section are from this interview unless otherwise indicated.
3. *Hardcore Troubadour*, 325–326.

4. From a copyrighted story by Beverly Keel in *The Nashville Scene*, May 28, 1998.
5. Author interview with Pam Lewis, Feb. 2, 2005.
6. Chris Morris, "Rehab Complete, Earle Offers New Album,"*Billboard*, Mar. 18, 1995; all quotes in this passage are from this interview.
7. www.lasjunction.com/people/mccullob.htm.
8. Author interview with Ray Kennedy, Mar. 6, 2005.

16. Tough Love

1. *Hardcore Troubadour*, 318.
2. *Ibid.*, 309–310.
3. Author interview with Peter Rowan, Mar. 4, 2005.
4. Author interview with Brad Hunt, Feb. 11, 2005.
5. steveearle.net.
6. *Hardcore Troubadour*, 327.
7. Author interview with Brad Hunt, Feb. 11, 2005.
8. *Ibid.*
9. *Ibid.*
10. Author interview with Richard Bennett, Feb. 17, 2005.
11. Author interview with Richard Dodd, Feb. 22, 2005; all quotes from Richard Dodd in this section are from this interview, unless indicated otherwise.
12. Author interview with Richard Bennett, Feb. 17, 2005.
13. Author interview with Ray Kennedy, Mar. 6, 2005; all quotes from Ray Kennedy are from this interview, unless indicated otherwise.

17. A Clear Field

1. Author interview with Peter Rowan, Mar. 4, 2005.
2. *Steve Earle in Quotes*, 164.
3. *Hardcore Troubadour*, 341.
4. *Ibid*, 336
5. *Ibid*, 341
6. Author interview with Ray Kennedy, Mar. 6, 2005.

7. From Steve's song-by-song description posted on steveearle.net/discography.
8. *Ibid.*
9. *Ibid.*
10. Author interview with Ronnie McCoury, July 14, 2005; all quotes from Ronnie McCoury in this chapter are from this interview, unless indicated otherwise.
11. From Steve's song-by-song description posted on steveearle.net/discography.
12. Author interview with Tony Brown, Dec. 14, 2004.
13. From Steve's song-by-song description posted on steveearle.net/discography.
14. *Ibid.*
15. *Ibid.*
16. *Ibid.*
17. *Ibid.*
18. Author interview with Mark Stuart, Feb. 7, 2005; all quotes from Mark Stuart are from this interview unless indicated otherwise.
19. Author interview with Peter Rowan, Mar. 4, 2005; all quotes from Peter Rowan are from this interview unless indicated otherwise.
20. Author interview with Ronnie McCoury, July 14, 2005.
21. Author interview with Jack and Barbara Earle, June 20, 2005.
22. Posted at steveearle.net titled "Journey of Hope, 7, 11 June '98."
23. Author interview with Jack and Barbara Earle, June 20, 2005.
24. John Nova Lomax, "Born Again," *Houston Press*, Nov. 9, 2000.
25. Andrew Dansby, "Steve Earle's Journey from Heroin Addict to Activism, Incarceration to Creative Freedom and Texas to Tennessee," *Texas Music*, Oct. 1, 2002
26. Del McCoury quotes from bio found on delmccouryband.com.
27. Author interview with Peter Rowan, Mar. 4, 2005.
28. Bobby Reed, "The Professor of Folk Rock," Chicago *Sun-Times*, Jan. 25, 2000.

29. Ray Bisio, "20th Maine Volunteer Infantry: Unit History," 20thmaine.com.
30. *Hardcore Troubadour*, 354–356.
31. From a posting on steveearle.net, dated mid-Dec. '98.
32. Earle, Steve, liner notes for *Transcendental Blues*.
33. Robert Baird, "Runnin' Down a Dream," *Magnet*, Nov. 30, 2000.
34. Barbara Lindberg, "Transcendental Meditations," *Magpie*, July 1, 2000.
35. Author interview with Stacey Earle, Feb. 7, 2005.
36. Martin Monkman, *All Music Guide* review by posted on barnesand noble.com.
37. Account of "When I Fall" session from author interview with Stacey Earle, June 23, 2005.
38. Associated Press story by David Bauder, June 29, 2000.

18. The Devil's Right-Hand Man

1. Author interview with Jack and Barbara Earle, June 20, 2005.
2. "John Walker Lindh," wikipedia.org.
3. "The Case of the Taliban American," cnn.com, 2001.
4. *Ibid.*
5. All quotes from cnn.com story cited above.
6. Steve Earle quoted in press materials accompanying advance copies of his album *Jerusalem*, 2002.
7. Gaby Alter,"Steve Earle," *Mix*, Feb. 1, 2004.
8. *Hardcore Troubadour*, 381.
9. Simon Sandall, "Tony Fitzpatrick," readersvoice.com, Feb. 2005.
10. *Ibid.*
11. *Ibid.*
12. Roberta Smith,"Art in Review: Tony Fitzpatrick," *New York Times*, Jan. 21, 2005.
13. All quotes from Ray Kennedy are from Alter, "Steve Earle."
14. Ian Bruce, "U.S. Country Singer Steve Earle Subjected to Witch-Hunt," World Socialist Web site, Sep. 20, 2002, www.wsws.com.
15. "Talk Back Live" transcript, July 23, 2002, cnn.com.
16. Harlan Ellison, untitled article, collected in *The Glass Teat* (New York: Ace Books, 1973), 54; originally appeared in *Los Angeles Free Press*, Nov. 28, 1968.
17. "The O'Reilly Factor," transcript, Nov. 6, 2003.
18. Author interview with Steve Earle, Aug. 25, 2004.
19. Author interview with Rosanne Cash, May 17, 2005.
20. Author interview with Rodney Crowell, July 29, 2005.
21. money.cnn.com, Mar. 23, 2005.
22. *Ibid.*
23. www.poe-news.com, 10-20-04.
24. Steve Earle, liner notes for *The Revolution Starts … Now.*
25. Author interview with Steve Earle, Aug. 25, 2004.
26. anti-war.com, Aug. 20, 2005; poll numbers corroborated by a CNN-Gallup poll posted the same day on npr.com.
27. Korry Keeker and Brandon Loomis, "Fair Singer's Politics Riles Some in Haines," *Juneau Empire State News*, June 19, 2005.
28. Author interview with Rodney Crowell, Jan. 25, 2001.
29. Author interview with Rodney Crowell, Apr. 6, 2005.
30. Author interview with Rodney Crowell, July 23, 2005.

Epilogue

1. Author interview with Tony Brown, Dec. 14, 2004.
2. Author interview with Jack and Barbara Earle, June 20, 2005.
3. Author interview with Ronnie McCoury, July 14, 2005.
4. U.K. Guardian, "Mom of Deceased GI Seeks Meeting with Bush," indybay.org, Aug. 7, 2005.

Books

Ellison, Harlan. *The Glass Teat.* New York, Ace Books, 1973.

Jennings, Waylon with Lenny Kaye. *Waylon: An Autobiography.* New York: Warner Books, 1996.

Lomax III, John. *Nashville: Music City USA.* New York: Harry N. Abrams Incorporated, 1985.

Malone, Bill C., *Country Music USA.* Austin, TX: University of Texas Press, third paperback printing, 1993.

Merrill, Jane and Gary Stromberg. *The Harder They Fall: Celebrities Tell Their Real-Life Stories of Addiction and Recovery.* Center City, MN: Hazelden Publishing & Educational Services, 2005.

Nash, Alannah. *Behind Closed Doors: Talking to the Legends of Country Music* New York: Alfred A. Knopf, 1988.

Serraris, Joanne. *Steve Earle in Quotes.* Self-published, 2004.

St. John, Lauren. *Hardcore Troubadour.* New York: St. Martin's Press, 2003,

Articles

Alter, Gaby. "Steve Earle." *Mix*, Feb. 1, 2004.

Associated Press. "Selma Says Speed Trap Reputation Undeserved." Jacksonville (Texas) *Daily Progress*, June 7, 1989.

Baird, Robert. "Runnin' Down a Dream." *Magnet*, Nov. 30, 2000.

Bentley, Bill. "Local Yoakam." *L.A. Weekly*, Nov. 26, 1984.

Bisio, Ray. "20th Maine Volunteer Infantry: Unit History." 20thmaine.com.

Blackstock, Peter. "Can't Keep a Good Man Down." *No Depression*, spring 1996.

Bruce, Ian. "U.S. Country Singer Steve Earle Subjected to Witch-Hunt." World Socialist Web site, www.wsws.com, Sep. 20, 2002.

Cocks, Jay. "The Color of Country." *Time*, Sep. 8, 1988.

Dansby, Andrew. "Steve Earle's Journey from Heroin Addict to Activism, Incarceration to Creative Freedom and Texas to Tennessee." *Texas Music*, Oct. 1, 2002.

DeMuir, Harold. "The Hillbilly Boss." *Pulse!*, Aug. 1990.

Gleason, Holly. "Steve Earle: A Bad Boy Settles Down." *Rolling Stone*, Jan. 26, 1989.

Graff, Gary. "Steve Earle Delivers Keynote to SXSW Attendees." GO.com, Mar. 16, 2000.

Keeker, Korry, and Brandon Loomis. "Fair Singer's Politics Riles Some in Haines." *Juneau Empire State News*, June 19, 2005.

Lindberg, Barbara. "Transcendental Meditations." *Magpie*, July 1, 2000.

Lomax, John Nova. "Born Again." Houston *Press*, Nov. 9, 2000.

Morris, Chris. "Rehab Complete, Earle Offers New Album." *Billboard*, Mar. 18, 1995.

O'Hehir, Andrew. "The Salon Interview: Steve Earle." Salon.com, Nov. 13, 2002.

Racine, Marty, "Between Two Worlds," Houston *Chronicle*, Aug. 5, 1986.

Racine, Marty. "Musical Labels Won't Work with Steve Earle." Houston *Chronicle*, Mar. 20, 1989.

Reed, Bobby. "The Professor of Folk Rock." Chicago *Sun-Times*, Jan. 25, 2000.

Sandall, Simon. "Tony Fitzpatrick." readersvoice.com, Feb. 2005.

"Talkback Live" transcript, July 23, 2002, cnn.com.

"The Case of the Taliban American," cnn.com, 2001.

UK Guardian. "Mom of Deceased GI Seeks Meeting with Bush." Aug. 07, 2005, posted at *indybay.org*.

The oft-asked question about this project has been "So, is Steve cooperating with you?" Depending upon the time of year the question was posed, the interlocutor would have been given one of three answers. The first, had the question been asked anytime in the fall or early winter of 2004–2005, would have been yes. The second, had the question been asked in the early spring of 2005, would have been no. The third, had the question been asked at the end of spring/start of summer 2005, would have been "Sorta."

The "yes" answer applied following my August 25, 2004, interview with Steve for barnesandnoble.com. After we completed our interview, which took place in a conference room at Artemis Records's New York office, I gave Steve a copy of my Carl Perkins biography, *Go, Cat, Go! The Life and Times of Carl Perkins, The King of Rockabilly*, as well as a new CD from our mutual friend James Talley ("I just saw him at a political meeting in Nashville," Steve said). I then explained the concept of this book, how it focused on the inside accounts of the album sessions and so forth, and even before I had completed my pitch, he said, "You have to call Tony Brown." I told Steve that Tony and I are old friends, he had been the first person I had called, and he had agreed to discuss his history with Steve. Next I asked if I had his blessing to contact his partner and coproducer Ray Kennedy and he gave a quick, one-word answer: "Absolutely." To the next question, as to whether he himself would be available to discuss any of his other records, he responded in the affirmative and said I should write his manager, Dan Gillis, in Nashville and request he set up interviews around Steve's touring schedule. I sent said letter via Federal Express in early November 2004; as this is written in mid-September 2005, Dan Gillis has yet to grant me the courtesy of a response (the letter has since been e-mailed to him, at the request of Steve's sister Stacey).

Other interviews—Tony Brown, Richard Bennett, Harry Stinson, Peter Rowan, Norman Blake, Richard Dodd, Joe Hardy—proceeded without complication. But as Ray Kennedy and I were trying to get started in the midst of his hectic production schedule, word came through Lisa Kemper, who along with Clint Harris does a wonderful job running the steveearle.net Web site (they're the type of knowledgeable, dedicated fans every artist needs) that in a recent communication with Steve, he had disavowed any knowledge of me or this book project. To his credit but to my detriment, Ray Kennedy then cut off our interviews almost before we had even started. I have an hour and a half of him on tape discussing his personal background, his musical and sonic influences, and some of his philosophy of production, almost all of which has made it into this book, so rich were his thoughts and insights. His is the sort of loyalty every artist needs. At that point I was left without access to Steve, his band, and most critically to this book, to Ray.

Come late spring Stacey Earle intervened on my behalf as best she could, and Steve apparently had enough change of heart to tell his parents that they could talk to me if they wanted to. They did, more than once, and were a fount of valuable information and always available for follow-up questions. Moreover, they took time, as did Stacey, to pack up a huge box of family archives in the form of photos and clips from newspapers and magazines dating back to the start of Steve's career, saving me hours, days, weeks of time burrowing in libraries and on the Internet for these rare items. Jack and Barbara Earle are the salt of the earth. They've raised five children through some frighteningly lean times and managed to do it with a sense of humor and solid values. Plus, Jack, on tape, sounds exactly like one of my favorite actors, Ben Johnson, in his incarnation as Sam the Lion in *The Last Picture Show*. How could you not love the guy? I am as greatly in their debt as I am admiring of the courage and strength they've shown in their own lives and in keeping the Earles a close-knit family, above all else.

So in the end, the "sorta" answer yielded a bountiful harvest, although the book is not better off for Ray being mostly absent and Steve's current band members being totally unrepresented in their own words.

This is not intended to be, nor was it approached as, a definitive biography. Yes, it touches on some personal details that belong in a serious biography, but in keeping with the Lives in Music series concept, it keeps a tight focus on the music making—although in Steve's case, his private life informs his music making, so it would be impossible for and irresponsible of an author to ignore it. So what the reader gets here is an overview rather than an intimate portrait, in hopes this will at least provide a context for each new recording project and its aftermath. Somewhere down the line someone will fill in the gaps, and there will be the definitive, sourced biography that does not yet exist. There is much more to tell about the particulars of the promotion of Steve's singles while at MCA and the conflicts that arose between him and the promotion/marketing departments; the particulars of his various management deals and why and how they fell apart; the particulars of his marriages, and why and how they fell apart; and many more particulars of his years as a drug addict, and why and how he fell apart. The stories are legion, often colorful and frequently, as in the case of the marriages and the drugs, heart-wrenching. Also, there are almost as many of these stories that are pure apocrypha.

This then is the story about a life and how it bled into the music, or how the music bled into the life. Both, really. For helping bring it all into focus I owe heartfelt gratitude to those aforementioned sources, all of whom took time out from important projects of their own to make a contribution to this story. Tony Brown, a longtime trusted friend, devoted four hours to this endeavor and was generous in sharing his own story as well as that of his work with Steve. (Thank you too to Tony's assistant Amy Russell, who had to find a place for me in her boss's crowded calendar and was always prompt in responding to my calls to Tony.) Richard Bennett was hustling to prepare for a worldwide tour with Mark Knopfler, but he too had time to recount his memories of the *Guitar Town* and *Exit 0* sessions, what went on in and out of the studio and in between albums, and also promptly answered follow-up questions sent via e-mail. I have a record on which Harry Stinson is identified as "Gentleman" Harry Stinson; these days, touring with Marty Stuart as a Fabulous Superlative, he is introduced nightly as "Handsome" Harry Stinson. Well, he's both, and I believe he cares a lot more about being a gentleman than about being handsome. A first-rate drummer and incredibly soulful singer, he does exactly what one critic once observed of Chris Hillman, and that is to make every record he appears on better for his presence. I know a lot of musicians in Nashville who believe that to be true of Stinson, which perhaps explains why they're all trying to get him to play on their sessions. Another gentleman, this one of British extraction, is Richard Dodd, who produced some of the key tracks on *I Feel Alright* that signaled Steve Earle's return to the living in a major way, among those being the exquisitely beautiful "Valentine's Day," a song that belongs in heavy rotation throughout the year. With family matters pending, Richard sat patiently and reconstructed that moment when his path crossed Steve's, held back nothing, and altogether displayed a quick wit, a discerning intellect, and a craftsman's pride in the art of production. Joe Hardy was lounging amongst his banana trees in Houston when I tracked him down through the auspices of one of the great men of the recording industry, Ardent Studios's founder and owner John Fry. Joe's reflections on the *Copperhead Road* sessions (which he engineered) and those for *The Hard Way* (which produced) are prime time stuff, thus allowing for the first deep-focus portrait of those two important projects. And because he saw such distinct differences between the Memphis way of recording and the Nashville approach, a more complex account of the process that produced those albums became possible.

Both Norman Blake and Peter Rowan opened up a whole new world of insight into the making of *Train a Comin'*. After reading the transcripts of our interviews, I felt honored that these two towering musicians trusted me to tell their stories of those sessions in full for the first time. Although Peter is judicious in his playing, he was expansive in his reminiscences of Steve, the sessions, and especially of his friendships with Roy Huskey, Jr., and Townes Van Zandt, both gone too soon. The rarely interviewed Norman, as the reader will see, speaks as he plays—no note or word is wasted, and you best be prepared for him to articulate his sense of the moment in a way you could never have predicted or articulated beforehand yourself. Thank you, gentlemen. I am a better man for having crossed your paths.

Not the least of the contributions here—indeed, in some ways the most important of all—came from Rosanne Cash, Rodney Crowell, the Pogues' Philip Chevron, and from Steve's sister and brother-in-law, Stacey Earle and Mark Stuart. Rosanne's insights are so sharp, an interlocutor doesn't even need to ask many questions in order to get to the heart of the matter. She seemed a little surprised that our interview ended so quickly (actually, Rose, I was so enjoying that French toast pastry I couldn't concentrate anymore; and I'm still waiting for you to buy me that fruit tart so you can watch me eat it), but, as the reader will find herein, what she said was simply perfect in all dimensions. All I can say is, Rose, your Boswell awaits you. Rodney, as the reader will discover, articulated a major subtheme of the book when he went off into the ether about the Texas alpha male and the peculiar nature of Texans as liars. That was all very amusing and it was interesting to see, as I hadn't before this, the subtle competition that has existed between Rodney and Steve (and, by the Rodney construct, all East Texas singer-songwriters) through the years, right up to the present day, when Rodney has released a politically charged album, *The Outsider*, that stands with the best of his illustrious career. Besides that, Crowell is one of America's great songwriters, and to have the benefit of his insights into the process as it relates to him and Steve is an unqualified blessing. My friend, you're on your way to being venerable. Philip Chevron was in the midst of a whirlwind trip to New York when I tracked him down, and the hour that we had together in a hotel lobby was one of the highlights of my career. A true Renaissance man with a serious interest in theater as well as music, Chevron was captivating in his reconstruction of the Pogues' session with Steve for the monumental "Johnny Come Lately," as he shares with me the same opinion of this song as being a towering work of history and music all at once. Best of all, for an author in search of history, he sees every event, or every tale, in Panoramic detail: what came before it, what happened while it was taking place, and its aftermath. That the past informs the present and the future is hardly a revelation, but I have encountered few artists who feel and can express their sense of the moving hand of time with Chevron's fervor and intelligence. And he happens to be hilariously funny while he's also being provocative.

Stacey Earle and Mark Stuart were behind this book from the start. Our interviews were strictly no holds barred, and they asked that nothing unflattering about Steve be excised but only that it be given its proper context. Stacey and Steve's relationship appears complex and problematic, and it is at times, but it's also one of great love and respect, which has not always come through in print. I didn't go into some of the more sordid tales of Steve's drug addiction that were found in Lauren St. John's *Hardcore Troubadour*, for instance, because I felt Stacey's and Mark's accounts were so harrowing that not much more need be said in order to make the point about the needle and the damage done. I thank them for their honesty, and for being on my side all the way. It was Stacey who arranged the interviews with her parents, it was Mark who brought Jack and Barbara Earle a copy of my Carl Perkins biography and championed it to them as the calling card of someone they could trust. They were special to me long before I met them, because the music they make together is so affecting, and my respect for them multiplied as this journey unfolded. To a great couple, thank you, over and over. A special tip of the hat, too, to Stacey's and Mark's manager, Brad Hunt, not only for arranging our original interview, but also for sharing his personal experiences as a key member of the E-Squared infrastructure and as a close personal friend of the label's late cofounder, Jack Emerson.

A special thank you to Ronnie McCoury of the Del McCoury Band, whose warmth, civility, and honesty make him such a pleasure to interview. Another true gentleman in the Harry Stinson mold (or maybe I should say, in the Del McCoury mold), Ronnie actually took time out from his family—and on a Sunday, no less— to sit for an interview that had had a number of false starts owing to the McCoury

Band's tour preparations, for which he offered several unnecessary apologies. As with Peter Rowan and Norman Blake, the untold story of a great album's making is finally revealed, thanks to Ronnie, as is the reason for the McCoury Band's falling-out with Steve on *The Mountain* tour. I look forward to the next go-'round with him, because I always learn something about music making in the studio that had otherwise escaped me. American music could use a few more good men like Ronnie McCoury, not to mention some instrumental virtuosos of his caliber as well. For arranging the interview and keeping it on the front burner until Ronnie was available, I offer warm thanks to Ronnie's manager, Chris Harris, who really went the extra mile on behalf of an author he didn't know to make sure this interview happened. And for leading me to Chris, warmest regards go out to one of the all-time great publicists, Kay Clary, who set an imposing standard in her profession with her company Commotion PR before she closed up shop to take a high-level job with BMI. To say that her counsel and help is missed is to be guilty of understatement.

I knew I would get some smart, unvarnished insights from Pam Lewis, and she certainly didn't disappoint. She was a remarkable woman even before she survived Garth Brooks, but even more so now in her own personal quest for a more meaningful life within and without the music business. Plus, back in 1989, when I was preparing to move to Nashville, she recommended a place to live because she thought its wide open spaces would be ideal for my young sons. She could not have been more on the mark, as the McGee boys (father and sons) had four good years in a green, bucolic environment. I won't forget that, or you, Pam.

As always, I have the best support possible in my agent Sarah Lazin and my indefatigable copy editor Patty Romanowski, and I certainly know how lucky I am to have these two amazing women believing in me. In the matter of believing in an author, I have had tremendous enthusiasm for my efforts from my editor Richard Johnston, and from the astute Backbeat marketing team of Nina Lesowitz, Kevin Becketti, and Steve Moore. There were many long days in the writing of this book, and to have the Backbeat folks' support at the end of this journey is extremely gratifying. Thanks to you all. And once again, Laura Fissinger performed like a champ for pitiful compensation in searching the Internet and libraries for Steve Earle stories.

And what would I be without my Tulsa crew? To Larry Gibson, Gary Hamilton, Mike Rowley, and honorary Tulsan Jonathon Skiba, your friendship is invaluable and irreplaceable. Even apart we are always together. That's a rare and true love indeed.

For my sons Travis and Kieran, this one's for you. All those hours on the road, a good number of them spent blasting the *Copperhead Road* tape from Nashville to Wounded Knee to Missoula to Death Valley, all came back to me as I wrote this story. How those songs seemed to shape so many of those trips, and left enduring, vivid memories of all those summers when we sought refuge in aluminum and steel. I love you guys, always and forever. And to you, my beloved Mary Lenore, here's an everlasting love. In my heart there's a place you can run to.

New York City–based author and music historian David McGee penned the previous Lives in Music entry, *B.B. King: There Is Always One More Time,* and is also the author of the Ralph J. Gleason Awards finalist, *Go, Cat, Go! The Life and Times of Carl Perkins, The King of Rockabilly*. He began his career with *Record World* magazine in 1974, started writing for *Rolling Stone* in 1975, and was the editor of *Rolling Stone's* now-defunct all-music monthly, *Record Magazine,* from 1981 to 1985. He has contributed to all four editions of the *Rolling Stone Album Guide,* to the *Rolling Stone Jazz & Blues Guide,* written the concluding chapter of *American Roots Music* (the companion volume to the PBS series), and penned liner notes for albums by B.B. King, Dr. John, and The Chieftains. Currently he is the editor of trade show publications at CMP Media; country music contributing editor at barnesandnoble.com; and also writes for *Acoustic Guitar, The Absolute Sound,* and *Rolling Stone*. He has also served as an assistant curator at the Rock and Roll Hall of Fame and Museum.